TRANSACTIONS

IN

INDIA,

FROM

THE COMMENCEMENT OF THE FRENCH WAR
IN SEVENTEEN HUNDRED AND FIFTY-SIX

TRANSACTIONS

IN

INDIA,

FROM

THE COMMENCEMENT OF THE FRENCH WAR
IN SEVENTEEN HUNDRED AND FIFTY-SIX

GYAN

Published by

GYAN

Gyan Publishing House
5, Ansari Road
Daryaganj, New Delhi-110002
Phone: 011-47034999, 9811692060
E-mail: books@gyanbooks.com

Distribution Network
gyanbooks.com
India, USA, Canada, UK, Australia

ISBN: 978-93-7133-884-4 (PB)

First Published, 1786

2nd Impression 2025

Printed at: Gyan Press, Delhi.

TRANSACTIONS IN INDIA, FROM THE COMMENCEMENT OF THE FRENCH WAR IN SEVENTEEN HUNDRED AND FIFTY-SIX

TRANSACTIONS

IN

INDIA,

FROM

THE COMMENCEMENT OF THE FRENCH WAR

IN SEVENTEEN HUNDRED AND FIFTY-SIX,

TO

THE CONCLUSION OF THE LATE PEACE,

IN SEVENTEEN HUNDRED AND EIGHTY-THREE.

CONTAINING

A HISTORY

OF THE

BRITISH INTERESTS IN INDOSTAN,

DURING A PERIOD OF NEAR THIRTY YEARS;

DISTINGUISHED BY TWO WARS WITH FRANCE, SEVERAL REVOLUTIONS AND TREATIES OF ALLIANCE, THE ACQUISITION OF AN EXTENSIVE TERRITORY, AND THE ADMINISTRATION OF GOVERNOR HASTINGS.

LONDON.

PRINTED FOR J. DEBRETT, OPPOSITE BURLINGTON-HOUSE, IN PICCADILLY.

MDCCLXXXVI.

CONTENTS.

CHAPTER I.

CHAPTER II.

CHAP.

CONTENTS.

CHAPTER III.

CHAPTER IV.

CHAPTER V.

CHAP.

CONTENTS.

CHAPTER VI.

CHAPTER VII.

CHAPTER VIII.

CHAPTER IX.

CHAPTER X.

CONTENTS.

CHAPTER XI.

CHAPTER XII.

CHAP.

TRANSACTIONS

IN

INDIA.

CHAPTER I.

Introduction—The ambitious projects of Dupleix—His acquisitions—Lawrence and Clive oppose him with success—The decline of the French interest—Mahomed Ally gets possession of the Carnatic—Expedition to Gheriah—Dupleix recalled—A suspension of hostilities—A new war—The French and their allies defeated—Pondicherry captured and erazed.

EMULATION is one of the most forcible and operative principles in states or individuals. Man in his social and solitary capacity is the artificer of man. But it is still one of the most important desiderata in morals or politics, whether this master-spring in his nature be ultimately beneficial to the species, or whether, on the whole, its best are not greatly overbalanced by its worst consequences?

The

The hiſtory of the two rival nations, which eminently exemplifies, at the ſame time that it approaches neareſt to a decifion of this point, is that of France and England. The inceſſant interference of their commerce and ambition, has created ſuch a ſpirit of envy, occaſioned ſuch a ſeries of depredations, rivetted ſuch implacable prejudices, and, for a long ſucceſſion of ages, produced ſuch a carnage among the ſpecies, as are but little alleviated by all the advantages derived to either, from their ſettled antipathies or reciprocal hoſtilities!

This ancient and prevailing characteriſtic in the genius of each, has oftener than once portended the deſtruction of both. A political contention, however, has thus eſtabliſhed itſelf between them, which more or leſs affects their minuteſt and moſt important operations. It is ſtrengthened and pampered by that luxury which rages in the centre, and extends its baleful influence to the extremities of all their dependencies.

Such are thoſe radical enmities which have not only deluged the whole continent of Europe repeatedly in blood, but which in every quarter of the globe, and among all the nations on earth, exhibit to the eye of ſpeculative humanity, groupes of objects which render them equally ſhocking and immortal.

Theſe were but too ſeriouſly and openly avowed, by the firſt European government that ever interfered in the politics of Indoſtan. It was to defend themſelves againſt the deep deſigns and daring intrigues,

intrigues of a Dupleix, that the Engliſh in that part of the world originally took up arms. And all thoſe ſplendid achievements which have hitherto marked their fortunes in India, bear a ſtriking reſemblance to the genius and meaſures of that conſummate ſtateſman.

Paris and London are not greater rivals in Europe, than Pondicherry and Madraſs were formerly in Aſia. Their religious prepoſſeſſions and peculiarities, their natural averſions, and their intereſted jealouſies, were unhappily corroborated and extended by their vicinity, in being ſituated in the ſame province, their commerce, in trading in the ſame articles, and their aim, in accumulating and graſping at the ſame advantages.

Dupleix, who added to a wary, ſubtle, and penetrating underſtanding, the moſt romantic and indefatigable ſpirit of enterpriſe, inſpired his fellow-adventurers with all the inveterate and hereditary animoſity of his native country againſt the Engliſh. His envy was peculiarly heightened and aggravated by our ſuperior proſperity. We had ſecured ſeveral valuable eſtabliſhments in various parts of Indoſtan, many years before the French. Our countrymen, much to their honour, had happily and wiſely conciliated the good opinion of the natives. Their traffic was fair, and their manners irreproachable. Circumſpect in their intercourſe with the Indians, punctual in their payments, and faithful to their engagements, they commanded reſpect, and were treated with confidence. The goods they imported were of the beſt quality; and the quantities of Aſiatic manufacture, and various other commodities, which they ſent to Europe, were prodigious. Theſe circumſtances were contemplated by the French with envy, in proportion as they intereſted the neighbouring princes in our ſucceſs.

The genius of Dupleix was ill calculated to brook ſuch a manifeſt inferiority. His ambition was rouzed, and he determined on a ſeries of meaſures which, he flattered himſelf, could not but terminate in eſtabliſhing the French on the ruin of the Engliſh intereſt. Notwithſtanding the formidable obſtacles which he had to ſurmount, from the advantageous ſettlements we poſſeſſed, the prejudices of the natives in our favours, and the regular and permanent form our commerce had aſſumed, his abilities were equal to the taſk. And at a time when the government of the Mogul ſtruck Europeans as irreſiſtible; when to them the magnitude of an Indian army was an object of aſtoniſhment and terror; when their ſettlements were yet in their infancy, and commerce on a very narrow ſcale, ſecluded every idea of conqueſt; when their diſtance from the parent ſtate, the paucity of their number, the deſpotiſm of the laws by which they were protected, and the barbarous forms of juſtice to which they were daily witneſſes, rendered them affable, aſſimulating, induſtrious and inoffenſive: this ſagacious politician diſcovered the two leading principles by which the preſent ſyſtem of rapacity, oppreſſion, and peculation, has been matured, and is ſtill ſupported.

A ſecure

A ſecure and unremitting attention to the trade of India effectually convinced him, that it never of itſelf, and as it then ſtood, could be any conſiderable object to the French nation. The infinite reſtrictions and diſadvantages under which it laboured, were by no means compenſated either to the public or individuals, by the profits it produced. Every article in which they dealt was ſubjected to ſuch a variety of duties, and obnoxious to ſuch a numerous train of great and petty officers, through whoſe juriſdiction it paſſed, that it was impoſſible to bring it to the market with almoſt any certain proſpect of gain. It was alſo cuſtomary for the Nabobs to extort with rigour and exactneſs a certain ſum annually from all Europeans who preſumed to trade in their dominions. They were, at the ſame time, obliged to keep garriſons in their ſeveral factories, and ſupport ſuch a force as they deemed neceſſary for the protection of their perſons and properties in the event of a war among the country powers. All this occaſioned ſuch an immenſe expenditure, as the emoluments of a commerce, thus contracted, impeded, and precarious, was by no means calculated to defray.

The perfect conviction of a fact ſo mortifying to the pride of adventure, by which the French, eſpecially under the conduct of a Dupleix, were animated, muſt have impelled them to have finally abandoned India, but that his ſagacity and diſcernment ſuggeſted a competent reſource in the defect of martial genius, which he could perceive,

 even

even then, to be a predominating feature in the character of the natives. No European troops, before his time, had once took the field against the Prince in whose dominion they resided, or acted as principals in the political altercations of the country. The plains of Indostan were, notwithstanding, perpetually covered with armies. A general peace was unknown, and from the spirit of dissention that prevailed, seemed impracticable in the empire. The whole continent of India was a theatre of discord, in which a violent struggle for supremacy, treasure, or territory, was constantly carrying on by some of its Rajahs or Nabobs.

Thus, the want of adhesion in the political system; the want of discipline in the armies; and the want, perhaps, of the true military spirit in the natives of Indostan, tempted Dupleix to conceive, that by taking such a part in the competition as a prudent use of circumstances might direct, there was a much greater certainty of accumulating wealth, and acquiring glory from fighting, than from commerce. He consequently resolved, without hesitation, to profit by these discoveries, and to render his observations at once subservient to the interest of his employers, and the honour of his nation. A more than ordinary attention was henceforth paid to the affairs of the military. The state of the army was inspected with accuracy, the discipline of the troops was enforced with additional circumspection, and every possible expedient was adopted to complete their numbers, to rouze their ardour, and to render them formidable.

The

The execution was not less masterly than the conception of his plans. He attached himself to the interest of Chundasaheb, whose powerful connections on the one hand, and desperate fortunes on the other, rendered him no improper tool of French policy. This man had given several specimens of an enterprizing mind, but all his projects had hitherto failed. His parts, his address, and his magnanimous temper, endeared him to his friends, and even procured him respect from his enemies. Though at this time a prisoner in Satarah, where he had been closely confined for eight years, the power of the Carnatic, on the bloody usurpation of Anwarodean, deemed him the fittest person to contest the nabobship with that hated tyrant. Dupleix guaranteed the ransoms for which the Marratoes consented to release him. And after a great variety of military adventures and vicissitudes, in which the celebrity of his talents, as a soldier, was established and extended, he was received with open arms by Murzafajing, grandson of Nizimmuluch, who then disputed the vice-royalty of the Deccan with his uncle, Nazirjing.

This prince soon perceived the ascendancy of his new ally, and treated him with a confidence and distinction not inferior to the opinion he had formed of his abilities and integrity. Chundasaheb readily acknowledged his authority, and easily prevailed on him to renew and authenticate his claim on the nabobship of Arcot, by issuing letters patent for that purpose. A resolution was consequently formed, of ſubjugating Anwerodean, as a preliminary ſtep to a ſucceſsful conteſt with Nazirjing. The French intereſt was ſolicited; Dupleix approved of a ſcheme probably formed at his inſtance. The Nabob of Arcot was defeated, and fell at the battle of Amboor; but his death proved to Dupleix, and his allies, only cutting off the head of a hydra. The cauſe of Mohommedally, ſecond ſon of Anwarodean, was eſpouſed by a ſtrong party of the neighbouring armies, who dreaded the ambition of Chundaſaheb. At their deſire, Nazirjing marched into the Carnatic with a ſtrong army. His nephew, Murzafajing, who oppoſed his claim to the ſubaſhip, was now induced to accept of the offers made by his uncle.

This ſudden agreement deranged for a moment the affairs of the allies. But Dupleix, ever fertile in reſources, found means of creating diſſenſion in the court of the ſuba [1750]. A conſpiracy immediately took place; and while Nazirjing, relying on the faith of the French, with whom a formal treaty had juſt been concluded, and the loyalty of the tributary Pitans, who were with him in the field, abandoned himſelf to effeminacy, the former made an attack on thoſe unſuſpecting troops who were moſt in his intereſt; and the latter raiſed the banners of rebellion, and murdered their prince in the midſt of his guards and the view of his army.

By this unexpected revolution, Murzafajing, the ſteady friend of the French, was inſtantly proclaimed Subah of the Deccan. A large territory in the vicinity of Pondicherry, a diſtrict ſtill more valuable

valuable, near Karical, in the kingdom of Tanjore, with the city of Massulipatnam, and all its dependencies, which produced, in all, an annual revenue of about thirty-eight thousand pounds, were instantly ceded to the French.

The treasures of Nazirjing were valued at two millions five hundred thousand pounds. Dupleix shared of this immense booty two hundred thousand pounds, besides jewels. In the gorgeous dress of a native prince, he was the first that did homage to the new subah. He was then declared governor for the Mogul, of all the countries south of the river Kirstna, a territory nearly equal in extent to the whole dominions of France in Europe. He was invested with the power and title of Munsub, or commander of seven hundred horse. He was even permitted to bear, among his ensigns, that of the *fish*, an honour never conferred but on natives of the highest distinction. All money, current in the Carnatic, was also to be coined at Pondicherry; and all the Mogul's revenues in the countries of which Dupleix was appointed vicegerent, were in the first instance to be deposited with him. Chundasahab was appointed nabob of Arcot, under his authority.

By the death of Murzafajing, [Jan. 4, 1751] who, like his uncle, fell a victim, soon after him, to the rapacity of the Pitans, this torrent of good fortune received a temporary check. The genius of Dupleix, however, prevailed over every misfortune. Chundasaheb for a while supported his authority in the Carnatic, under the auspices and support of the French interest,

intereſt, with proſperity. Mahommedally, aſſiſted by the Engliſh, and all the adherents of his family, retreat before his victorious army. He followed them to Utatoor, to Siringham, and to Trichinopoly. The deſtinies of this great warrior overtook him at laſt. Reduced by the ſuperior conduct of his enemies to capitulate, he put himſelf in the power of Monahjee, the Myſorean general, who immediately ordered his head to be cut off [1752]. Thus was this formidable army, in the ſpace of little more than two months, reduced to the neceſſity of throwing down their arms, and ſurrendering at diſcretion.

Even this diſaſter was in ſome degree compenſated, by the ſucceſs of the French arms, in ſupporting the claims of Salabatjing, to the ſubahſhip in the northern provinces of the Decan. This campaign was conducted by Buſſy, a ſoldier of experience and capacity. He marched to Canaul, the capital of the Pitan nabob, who had ſlain the former ſubah, and determined that the city ſhould ſuffer for the treachery of its lord.

Having put all the garriſon to the ſword, and impriſoned the wife of the late nabob, with her two ſons, after treating with the general of the Marrattoes, the army entered Golconda, where Salabetjing publickly aſcended the throne or muſned, as ſubah of the Deccan. He then received letters from an ambaſſador, who pretended to come from the court of Dehli, for the purpoſe of thus inveſting him with all the enſigns of goverment. This he deemed neceſſary to ſecure a welcome reception

in

in Aurengabed. Balgerou, the Marrattoe general, found new causes of breaking with him, but he forthwith invaded their country, and the difference for the present was adjusted. He was opposed by a formidable conspiracy of combatants, in his march to Golconda, but had the good fortune to defeat them in a pitched battle. His rival and elder brother, Ghaziodin Khan, was dispatched at Aurengazeb by his mother, who poisoned him. The important services of Dupleix were rewarded by a solemn appointment to the nabobship of Arcot.

In this manner did Dupleix proceed in aggrandizing his nation, accumulating advantages to the Company, increasing his own fortune, and establishing his reputation. He raised up Rajahsaheb, the son of Chundasaheb, to counteract or defeat the interest of Mohommed Ally in the Carnatic; and with exquisite address, by his ascendancy over the native princes, by the liberality of his presents, and by the sagacity of his intrigues, as well as by the terror of the French arms, he finally realized the claims of Salabetjing. His views, however, were not sufficiently seconded by those officers, to whom the various expeditions he planned were entrusted. He did not receive those reinforcements and that assistance from home, which the exigencies of his situation required, which his projects supposed, and which he had been taught to expect. But, the greatest impediments to his success arose from the British Triumvirate, Lawrence, Clive, and Sanders, who, at that time, had the charge of our affairs in India.

During

During the brilliant career of Dupleix, the English, restrained by the Company at home, had hitherto remained most unaccountably inactive.—The daring assassination of Nazerjing, which overwhelmed them with horror and astonishment; the variety of white flags, which, as trophies of conquest, ensigns of sovereignty, or signals of defiance, surrounded the English presidency of Fort St. David, are the two memorable circumstances which co-operated with national enmity, to rouze their lethargy, and excite their emulation. The death of the subah, by the treacherous Pitans, struck them as the black contrivance of Dupleix, that his politics of interest and conquest might be no longer thwarted, by managing the opposite interests of two such powerful rivals. And they considered the triumphant flags which streamed in the vicinity of Fort St. David, as an insult to the British character, since it was impossible to open their eyes, without contemplating the mortifying signatures of their own insignificance and disgrace.

The presidency was then under the direction of Mr. Sanders, who arrived in India but a short time before the death of Nazirjing. Convinced by that event, of the vast ambition and extensive object to which Dupleix aspired, he resolved to frustrate his projects as much as possible. His sagacity, his perseverance, and his resolution, enabled him, on many occasions, to command a success, under circumstances peculiarly inauspicious. But the military departments were filled by officers of genius and enterprize. Major Lawrence was the first

first who introduced a regular discipline among the British forces in India, and trained the natives who joined them, to fight in the European manner. It was under this hardy veteran that Clive imbibed the rudiments of war. By the joint efforts of these two great men, occasionally assisted by able Admirals, and subordinate officers of considerable merit, the bold designs of Dupleix, and the Court of Versailles, were disappointed, of establishing an universal monarchy in the empire of Indostan, to the utter exclusion of every other European.

The nature of this work, however, prevents our going, with any degree of minuteness, into the detail of the several campaigns which distinguished these early periods of the Indian war. It is necessary only to recapitulate such a series of general facts as may preserve our narrative entire, and introduce us to a more distinct and circumstantial acquaintance with the later and more interesting part of the history of our commercial establishments and territorial acquisitions in that quarter of the globe.

The first favourable circumstance which revived the courage of the English, and impressed the natives with a conviction of their bravery, was an expedition against the province of Arcot, under the command of Clive. With an handful of undisciplined men, he surprised the capital of this rich district, and sustained it against a regular siege of three months, by a numerous army, whom, notwithstanding a furious assault in three different places, he repulsed with great slaughter [1754].

He

He was then reinforced by a party from the army at Trichinopoly, and a confederate body of Mahrratoes, which encouraged him to march in ſearch of the enemy. The forts of Timrey, Aranic, and Conjeveram, fell before him, and in a general engagement at Caveripauke, he routed at leaſt three times his number of troops, and took a large party of French priſoners. The fort immediately ſurrendered.

Marching acroſs the country he came to the ſpot where Nazir-jing had been treacherouſly ſlain. There a town was rearing with great alacrity, to commemorate that execrable tranſaction. Its name was Dupleix-Fateabat, or the town of Dupleix's victory. Coins were ſtruck with ſymbolical repreſentations of the fact. A ſtately pillar was at the ſame time preparing, inſcribed with ſeveral elaborate deſcriptions in the French, Malabar, Perſian, and Indoſtan languages, to be erected as a monument of French proweſs and good fortune. Clive ordered the whole to be erazed, which the army accompliſhed with expedition and dexterity. It probably inſpired them with an auſpicious preſage of their ſucceſs over the declining fortunes of the enemy.

From this place the troops proceeded to Fort St. David; nor did they meet or ſee a ſingle ſquadron or party of the French, or their allies, during the whole march. Their late defeat ſucceeding to former diſgrace, had totally broken their ſpirits, deranged their operations, and diſperſed their numbers. Their cavalry attached themſelves to the governors of ſuch diſtricts as were

yet

yet in their intereſt, the Europeans and Sepoys were recalled to Pondicherry, and Dupleix was ſo incenſed againſt Rajahſaheb, the ſon of his former friend and ally, with whom, on that account, he had intruſted the command, that it was ſome time before he would allow him to appear in his preſence.

Thus the Engliſh ſucceſſes, under the auſpices of Major Lawrence and Captain Clive, recovered in the ſpace of a few months, in favour of Mahommedally, the tried friend of the Company, an extent of country in the Carnatic, thirty miles in breadth, and ſixty in length, the annual revenue of which, including that of the famous pagoda of Tripetti, amounted to upwards of one hundred and ſixty thouſand pounds.

It was at this time [1752] Major Lawrence returned from England, and aſſumed the command of the army. He poſſeſſed the ſingular magnanimity of regarding with admiration, the certain preſages of ſuperior genius in young Clive, whom, notwithſtanding his youth and inexperience, he conſulted on all occaſions. By the advice of this officer, the army was directed. Major Lawrence remained with the main body, on the ſouth of the Caveri, while Clive was ſent with a ſtrong detachment to make a diverſion on the north of the Caleroon.

Clive ſucceeded even beyond the Major's moſt ſanguine expectations. The troops ſeemed inſpired with the ardour of their leader. Notwithſtanding the ſuperior force of the enemy, they poſſeſſed themſelves of Pithandah and Otatoor. D'Auteuil, who commanded the French, was known to aim at

a junca junction with the confederate army, who encamped at Seringham, and for whom he had a reinforcement both of men and money. It was of consequence to intercept this succour. The forces under Captain Dalton were consequently ordered to join those of Clive; and this generous officer, though senior in command, that no disputes might impede the service, had the gallantry to accompany the expedition as a volunteer. This party coming up with the enemy at Valconda, a smart engagement took place. The French were so completely vanquished, that the whole, with their commander at their head, were made prisoners by the English.

Nor had the Major less success. He perceived and availed himself of the dissensions which prevailed in the enemy's camp. He followed them into the island, and by every military manœuvre which the most consummate skill in the profession, zeal in the service, and a perfect acquaintance with the characters of the Indian chiefs, enabled him to perform, cut off all communication with the country, and rendered their situation a complete blockade. In consequence of these operations, the various powers of which the confederacy consisted began to shift for themselves, and to make what terms they could with the English. Many of them joined the opposite interest; some having obtained leave to pass the river, returned to their respective homes; and the French, shut up in the pagoda of Jambakistria, were soon obliged to capitulate.

This whole war, in which a profusion of blood and treasure was expended, was almost confined to Trichi-

Trinchinopoly and its dependencies. A variety of inferior forts, in the adjacent territories, were constantly changing masters. No considerable advantage was gained on either side, though many skirmishes took place, and several bloody battles were fought. It was a scene in which the genius of the natives was exhibited to advantage. The Europeans contemplated with astonishment the profound duplicity which reigned in their camps, and the consummate address by which they incessantly endeavoured to over-reach one another. To their want of accuracy and manliness in the discrimination of character and conduct, they added a manifest defect of resolution and foresight. Their wars were carried on with the same inattention to system, as fierce, as cowardly, and as merciless, as those of tygers. Their politics degenerated into intrigue, or consisted only in the piddling manoeuvres of sharpers, who have no other object than circumvention. Their alliances invariably originated in avarice or revenge. Their confederacies were without unanimity or spirit, and their attachments equally destitute of friendship and principle.

Nor were the Europeans an object of less novelty to such of the natives as were capable of observation. The decision of the field generally depended on the conduct of the French or English. No spectacle could be more curious and interesting to a person placed in the pagoda of Trinchinopoly, than one of those battles which were fought in its vicinity. The action for the moſt part was left entirely to thoſe rival troops, who, though ſeldom more than a thouſand in number, were often hotly engaged, while their reſpective allies, in prodigious ſwarms, hovered at a diſtance, ſpectators of the fray, and anxious for the iſſue.

A war thus tedious and abortive, diſpoſed the preſidencies of the two companies to think of compromiſing their differences by treaty. This produced the famous congreſs at Sadraſs, which, after much diſcuſſion and altercation among the commiſſioners, produced nothing but a complete proof that the titles of Dupleix were a forgery. Mr. Sanders, who ſuperintended this conference with his uſual fidelity and accuracy, perceiving his candour and moderation oppoſed only by preſumption and evaſion, after proteſting, in the moſt ſolemn manner, againſt whatever had been aſſumed on the fictitious claims of Dupleix, diſmiſſed the deputies, and put an end to the buſineſs.

This detection, for the preſent, baulked the expectations which the proſpect of peace had raiſed in both preſidencies. Hoſtilities were therefore continued, and had probably been protracted to great length, as well as agitated with freſh ardour and animoſity on both ſides, but that Dupleix was recalled from the government of Pondicherry, and his ſucceſſor ordered to make peace on any terms.

No news could be more acceptable to all who were diſpoſed to promote the commercial intereſts of the two companies. Gadeheu, the new governor, announced his propoſitions to the preſidency

of

of Madrafs without delay. A fufpenfion of arms, for three months, was inftantly declared, and it was agreed, provided the two companies, who referved to themfelves the right of altering or annulling whatever in the treaty they might think proper, acquiefced in the opinion of their fervants; to renounce for ever all Moorifh government and dignity; never henceforth to interfere in any differences which might take place among the princes of the country, and to deliver up to the government of the empire, all places captured by either during the war, excepting fuch as fhould be ftipulated to remain in the poffeffion of each company.

The revenues arifing from this war to the refpective companies, at the ceffation of hoftilities, which were prodigioufly in favour of the French, demonftrate how different the motives were on which it was carried on, and how fuperior, perhaps, the meafures of Dupleix had always been to thofe of his rivals. The exchange of the prifoners alfo proved, that however inferior we might be in the cabinet, we beat them in the field. For though their reinforcements from time to time, as well as their allies, were much more numerous than ours, nine hundred French prifoners were now in our cuftody, for two hundred and fifty Englifh which were in theirs.

Notwithftanding thefe appearances of tranquillity, a variety of circumftances occurred to render a general peace impracticable. The finances of Mahommedally were almoft totally exhaufted.— The tributary Polygars, with great profeffions of attachment, were united only in the backwardneſs of their payments. The collection of the Arcot revenues were indiſpenſible. A party of troops were therefore diſpatched, under the command of Colonel Heron, to recover what arrears were due to the nabob, in the ſouthern diſtricts. This unfortunate expedition, without effectually ſerving the nabob, ſtimulated the preſidency of Pondicherry to new hoſtilities; which, however, by prudence and arrangement on our part, were for the preſent happily quaſhed.

The eſtabliſhment of Mahommedally in Arcot, the capital of his dominions, was alſo attended with a variety of petty diſputes, which could only be ſettled by a military force. The principal ſcene of theſe tranſactions was the Northern Circars. The detachment which went on this ſervice was commanded by Major Kilpatrick. But, after exhauſting every reſource of evaſion which cunning, chicanery, and even treachery could ſuggeſt, without effect, moſt of the Polygars made good their contributions, and acknowledged their dependance.

It was about this time that Admiral Watſon and Captain Clive undertook an expedition againſt the piratical confederacy on the Malabar coaſt. The numerous rivers which interſect this part of the country, ſwarmed with fleets of armed veſſels, which ſubſiſted only by plunder. Every ſpecies of trade carried on in thoſe ſeas, was conſequently harraſſed and obnoxious to perpetual outrage, by the banditti who frequented and infeſted them.

One

One Angria was at the head of this formidable combination. He derived from his predeceſſors a powerful fleet and conſiderable territory. His depredations on the ſhips of all nations, who did not purchaſe his protection at a great price, daily increaſed his conſequence. The Company were at the annual expence of fifty thouſand pounds, in order to exempt their commerce from his rapacity.

Admiral Watſon, in conjunction with ſeveral tranſports commanded by Clive, directed his • ourſe for Gheriah, the capital of this naval robber. Though ſtrong by nature, and conſiderably fortified by art, it could not withſtand the danger to which theſe preparations expoſed it. Angria retreated to the Marattos, whom he hoped to appeaſe by preſents, or amuſe by ſtipulations. The garriſon, without a commander in whom they could confide, the aſſiſtance of engineers, or indeed any ſolid proſpect of ſucceſs, did not even attempt a regular defence. The fort ſurrendered, after a ſmart cannonade, and there were found in it a large quantity of military ſtores, and a hundred and twenty thouſand pounds in money, which, without any reſerve either for the nation or the Company, was ſhared among the captors on the ſpot. And happy had it been for the Britiſh character, for the natives of Indoſtan, and for the intereſt of the Company, if their civil or military ſervants had never indulged a ſpecies of more criminal peculation.

No event ſince the late treaty bore a more favourable aſpect to the Engliſh intereſt than the diſmiſſion of the French troops under the command of

De Buſſy, from the ſervice of the ſubah. It happened at Savanore, which lies two hundred miles ſouthweſt of Galconda. This formidable connection had been long an eye-ſore to the Company, who knew it to be a ſource of certain aggrandiſement and opulence to their rivals. The miniſtry of Salabatjing were alſo diſguſted by an ally, whoſe conduct was no leſs aſſuming and lofty than his demands were exorbitant and inſatiable. The Engliſh had conſequently the leſs difficulty of undermining De Buſſy and the French intereſt in the viceroy's favour. Their agents, though it is alledged without any authority from them, ſtipulated in their name that the ſubah ſhould have the ſame aſſiſtance from the preſidency of Madraſs, which he had formerly received from Pondicherry, and without any of thoſe mortifying conditions which the French had thus ungenerouſly extorted from him, under the preſſure of the moſt critical circumſtances.

The party againſt the French, among the various intrigues going forward in the vizir's court, was every day acquiring additional influence from the well known principle of eſpouſing the cauſe of the ſtrongeſt; and Salabatjing, notwithſtanding his regard for Buſſy, had not ſufficient reſolution to oppoſe ſo powerful a combination againſt him. He was, in truth, like moſt other great men, without a will of his own, and the more arbitrary a tyrant, from being ſo much a ſlave. Buſſy, the moment the refractory nabobs had made their ſubmiſſion, was therefore, at the inſtigation of his enemies, ordered

to

to leave the ſubah's camp, and march without delay for Pondicherry.

This able officer received, and immediately prepared to obey, the unexpected mandate, with that indignant pride which it is ſo natural for the noble and brave to feel, when their beſt ſervices are only thus rewarded with the blackeſt ingratitude.

In this manner had the conteſts of the Europeans long raged in the Deccan like a hurricane. By the attention of the Preſidency to the Company's intereſt at the mouth of the Ganges, the ſtorm for a moment ſubſided. Buſſy, in the mean time, effected a reconciliation with the ſubah, and during this ſhort interval of repoſe, the affairs of his government were interrupted only by the petty intrigues of rival omrahs.

Nothing of material conſequence, indeed, to either party, was at preſent agitated in the Carnatic. The chiefs, as uſual, carried on the trade of plunder, treachery, and aſſaſſination, in the frontiers, while the heart of the country enjoyed a momentary ceſſation of hoſtilities. It was, however, but the tranſient ſlumber of the wretched, who ſuddenly awake to new and more aggravated miſeries.

The war which France and England ſoon afterwards commenced, involved, more or leſs, all their intereſts and dependencies in India. Many of the principal provinces of the Deccan, and eſpecially the ſouthern and northern vicinities of the Carnatic, were univerſally embroiled by freſh diſturbances.

The two Companies regarded the motions and connections of each other with jealouſy and rancour.

cour. The policy of the natives in all its darkneſs and obliquity became the favourite ſtudy of both, and both made wonderful proficiency in this pernicious and diſgraceful ſcience.

A new competitor put in his claims for the ſubahſhip of the Deccan, ſupported by all the weight of legal authority, and a powerful combination of the moſt warlike princes in the empire; a ſtrong reinforcement of troops landed from Europe, and the ſovereignty of the Indian ſeas was diſputed on the Coromandel coaſt by the Engliſh and French fleets, with the utmoſt inveteracy and valour. Every part of this vaſt peninſula, where either of theſe nations had any intereſt or alliance, ſuffered all the ravages of war for a ſeries of years. The two preſidencies, and the principal of their reſpective factories, were alternately beſieged and relieved by their reſpective forces and allies. Many of them, even in the courſe of a few months, repeatedly changed their maſters, their inhabitants, and their garriſons. Here the Britiſh arms evidently partook of the general good fortune which at that period every where attended them. They baffled every confederacy that threatened to check their ſucceſs. They defended Madraſs; they took Pondicherry; they recovered Calcutta, with infinite advantages; and they acquired the revenues of a rich and extenſive territory, amounting, it was ſaid, to upwards of three millions a-year.

The romantic campaigns of Lally are freſh in every man's remembrance, who recollects the glorious and triumphant concluſion of that memorable

war.

war. He loſt Maſulipatam, and the northern provinces, by recalling De Buſſy from Salabatjing, and appointing an officer of inferior abilities to ſucceed him in that critical ſituation. He waſted much time, much treaſure, and many lives, without effect, in an inveſtment of Madraſs, which might have been occupied in co-operating with the allies of the French Company, and extending their intereſt. He crippled his army by the large detachments which he ſent to Seringham, and enabled the Engliſh, in conſequence of their taking poſſeſſion of Vandevaſh and Corangoly, to extend their barrier ſouth of the Palier.

Theſe, however, were not the cauſes which ruined the French in India. There is no country in the world in which war is ſo expenſive as this. The loſs of the French, and our advantage, by the capture of Chandernagore, and our other important acquiſitions in the rich province of Bengal, drove them from India. The Britiſh conqueſts on the Coromandel and the Malabar coaſts were atchieved by Clive on the banks of the Ganges.

Lally might be deficient in the local knowledge of the country. Perhaps he conceived too contemptibly of the native princes to make the beſt uſe of their aſſiſtance. But he was obliged to act on the ſea coaſt without a ſquadron, and when he penetrated into the interior parts of the country, his allies were refractory, and his troops mutinied for want of pay. Notwithſtanding theſe impediments, out of ten battles he had only loſt one, and might well be allowed, after gaining nine battles, and

and taking ten places with the ſame troops, to retreat before ſuperior numbers.

But Lally, like many other great men, owed his fall to the rectitude of his feelings, the contumely of his wit, and the ſeverity of his diſcipline. From the moment he landed at Pondicherry, he expreſſed the moſt determined averſion to the venality which every where ſurrounded him. Superior to the mean practices connected with pecuniary purſuits, he regarded thoſe who had no other object, with unequivocal contempt. He was ordered to inveſtigate thoſe enormities which had impoveriſhed the Company, and to puniſh the delinquents. The evils he was deſtined to redreſs, were peculation, diſobedience, treachery, plunder, cowardice, and mutiny.

The office was unpopular, and Lally erred, in thinking himſelf entitled to a cordial reception from thoſe who deteſted, and thought their ſafety endangered by his buſineſs. He was ſoon convinced what he may expect who would wreſt from the wicked the ſpoils of iniquity. A league was inſtantly formed to defeat the end of his appointment; and thoſe who ought to have co-operated with him in the ſervice, were ſtudious only to harraſs him with difficulties, as their own ruin could be avoided no other way than by accompliſhing his.

Whatever conjectures may be formed of the many ſplendid events which give a luſtre to this period of the Britiſh ſtory in the Deccan, and throughout the whole Indian peninſula, as in every other part of the world, our arms were ultimately

ultimately victorious. This ſeems not to have been the ſcene in which the French were deſtined to reap their laurels. Their troops, perhaps, had never any where behaved ſo uniformly ill.— They fled at *Caveripauke*, they fled at *Bahoor*, they fled twice in *Tanjore*, they laid down their arms at *Volconda*, they ſurrendered at diſcretion in *Seringham*, they failed twice before *Cudalore*, twice before *Arcot*, twice before *Trinchinopoly*, and at the ſiege of which one half of them were made priſoners.

They were now finally worſted. Peace was once more reſtored to the Carnatic, and the enemy every where diſlodged from their faſtneſſes. Pondicherry was captured and eraſed. Vellore was alſo taken, after a vigorous reſiſtance. The grants of the northern circars to France were at the ſame time diſannulled, and their ſovereignty perpetually inveſted in the Engliſh. And, by the peace of Paris, *Mahommedally Cawn* was acknowledged nabob of the Carnatic, and Salabatjing lawful ſubah of the Deccan.

CHAP.

CHAPTER II.

Revolutions in Bengal—Surajah Dowlah—Meer Jaffier—Cossim Ally Cawn—The Company's accession to the Dewannee—Sujah ul Dowlah—Treaties—Lord Clive goes out to India—Select Committe—Altercation with the Members of the Board.

OUR military transactions on the coast of Coromandel were suddenly suspended, by intelligence which the presidency of Madrass received from Bengal. Surajah Dowlah, a young prince without parts, experience, or humanity, had almost annihilated our interest in that division of the empire.

In June, 1756, Fort William, after a brave defence, under circumstances peculiarly distressing, surrendered to an immense army, headed by the nabob in person. The town was burnt and pillaged, the treasury of the Company plundered, the publick works demolished, and a hundred and fifty of the garrison, who survived the capture, thrust into a strong dungeon, not more than eighteen feet long, and fourteen feet wide, with only two holes barricaded by iron bars, where they remained all night in such a state of suffocation, from want of fresh air, the heat of the season, and their own perspiration, that most of them perished in a violent delirium. On the morning twenty-two were found merely alive,

alive, and exhibited ſuch a picture of diſtreſs, as human nature has ſeldom ſuffered or ſurvived.

This dreadful information was received by our countrymen on the coaſt with infinite horror and indignation. It was a misfortune the more ſerious and alarming, that it had not been foreſeen, and which required all the ſtrength of the Company to ſurmount. After a mature, and, on ſuch an emergency, perhaps a tedious deliberation in the council of Madraſs, Clive was ordered for Bengal, at the head of nine hundred Europeans, and a thouſand five hundred ſepoys. Watſon and Pococke were at the ſame time deſtined to ſecond his operations by ſea, with a fleet of two ſhips of the line and three large frigates.

The armament which had thus left Madraſs in October, after encountering various diſaſters from croſs winds and adverſe currents, appeared in a very ſhattered condition before Mayapore, in the latter end of December. And notwithſtanding many of our forces were not arrived, the fort of Buzbuzia, ten miles up the river, was attacked next day and carried, though not without conſiderable difficulty.

The army, eager to regain Calcutta, and to revenge the ſhocking cataſtrophe of their countrymen, preſſed forward to that place; which, however, was abandoned by the garriſon on exchanging a few ſhot with the ſhips which anchored in the road. The general devaſtation which a barbarous and infuriate enemy had committed on a ſpot ſo endeared to the Engliſh by long reſidence, the con-

convenience of its harbour and ſituation for commerce, and the ſplendour of its public edifices, was a ſpectacle which many of its late inhabitants on their return, and thoſe who knew it in its better days, contemplated with the ſtrongeſt expreſſions of horror and anxiety.

There was, however, no time to waſte in unavailing regret. Clive entrenched his troops within four miles of the factory. In a few days the exaſperated ſubah made his appearance at the head of a prodigious army, approached within a few miles of the Engliſh, and pitched his own tent in a garden at the back of the town. An attempt was made to amuſe our people with offers to form the baſis of a negotiation. But ſuſpecting treachery in theſe overtures, a plan was formed for attacking the head-quarters next morning. For this purpoſe between four and five hundred ſailors landed from the fleet at one o'clock. About two the troops were under arms, and marched by four to the attack of the nabob's camp. Clive's intention was to have ſeized his cannon, and ſtormed his tent; and his plan had probably been executed; but when day-light appeared the army was involved in ſuch an impenetrable fog, that they could not ſee three yards before them. This circumſtance equally affecting our troops and the enemy, the greateſt confuſion enſued, and continued till the Engliſh had marched through the whole Indian camp.—So briſk a fire was however kept up, that we loſt near a hundred men; the enemy twenty-two officers

cers of diſtinction, ſix hundred ſoldiers, and about the ſame number of their moſt uſeful animals.

The ſucceſs of this unexpected attack ſo effectually damped the ſubah's ſpirits, as well as the courage of his omrahs and the great men near his perſon, that he was now as anxious to conclude a ſerious reconcilement with the Company, as he had formerly been to harraſs or amuſe them. It was therefore agreed, that he ſhould reſtore the Company's factories, with ſuch of the plundered effects and monies as had been regularly brought to account in the books of his government. He allowed the fortifications of Calcutta to proceed; gave leave to coin money in a mint of our own; exempted all merchandiſe under the Company's paſſports from tax, fee, or impoſition; permitted them to take poſſeſſion of the thirty-eight villages aſſigned them by the emperor Furrukſhir, and reinſtated them in all their former privileges.

Political treaties in Indoſtan, as in Europe, are binding only while it continues the intereſt of neither party to infringe them. The Engliſh did not enjoy their advantages with moderation, nor the nabob regard his engagements with fidelity. They captured the French ſettlements at Chandernagore without his conſent, and he afforded their enemies aſſiſtance without conſulting either their intereſt or his own honour. A freſh rupture was the conſequence, and both prepared for new hoſtilities.

A committee for directing the military operations in Bengal, had been appointed on the commencement of the war. It conſiſted of Drake,

Watſon,

Watſon, Clive, and Kilpatrick. Clive ſuggeſted the indiſpenſible neceſſity of an immediate revolution in the government of the ſubahſhip, without which, in his opinion, there could be no permanent eſtabliſhment of the Engliſh intereſt. His idea was implicitly adopted, and the completion of the meaſure left to his management, in concert with Mr. Watts, the Company's reſident at the court of the nabob.

It was a curious and ſtriking occurrence in the viciſſitudes of human ſociety, for the agents of a mercantile aſſociation, at ſuch an immenſe diſtance from their native country, to meditate the downfal of a government by whoſe indulgence they enjoyed a multitude of privileges, and which, for extent of territory, for population, for revenue, and for commerce, had ſcarcely an equal in the world.— Nor was it the leaſt extraordinary circumſtance attending a conſpiracy thus ſingularly daring and attrocious, that the execution of it was entirely conſigned to the petty commander of a few battalions, a mere pecuniary factor, and one or two inferior agents, of deſperate fortunes and equivocal principles.

It was the ruin of Surujah Dowlah, that, to the ſtrongeſt habits of obſtinacy and avarice, he added ignorance, temerity, and cruelty in the extreme. Intoxicated with ideas of his own conſequence, the high prerogatives of his ſituation in the empire, the inſignificance of his ſubjects, and the impotence of his enemies, he not only acted without foreſight and without ſyſtem, but there was not a ſingle om-

rah

rah in whom he could place the ſmalleſt confidence, or who could afford the leaſt advice. All of them conſulting his humour, rather than the difficulties under which he laboured, encouraged him in the abſurd and fatal policy of making war on the Engliſh, whoſe power and reſources muſt have appeared fully to him, who has been heard to ſay that he did not believe there was ten thouſand men in all Europe, altogether incapable of ſeriouſly affecting his intereſt. Indeed he had only affected from the firſt to be offended with their ſcrupulous attention to their own ſafety, as implying a diſtruſt of his ability or inclination to protect them, or from an idea of their immenſe opulence, was deſirous, under the pretext of aſſerting his authority, to poſſeſs himſelf of their treaſure. This unworthy object was, however, proſecuted with an ardour and ſteadineſs which would have done credit to a better cauſe. Little ſuſpecting, while thus inveſted with all the enſignia of ſovereignty, ſurrounded with multitudes of ſlaves, and controuling the finances of the empire, that his throne was ſhortly to be uſurped, his fate pronounced, and his riches divided by a handful of traders.

Even among his own friends and dependents, his choleric and avaritious diſpoſition, his treacherous and daſtardly paſſions, were ſources of eternal apprehenſion and miſtruſt. The diſſatisfactions of the court ſoon pervaded the camp, and the principal officers in the army, from motives of ſelf-preſervation as well as of reſentment, agreed with Clive and Watts to annihilate the power of the

D tyrant.

tyrant. So deſperate and determined are the greateſt ſlaves in nations the moſt effeminate and puſillanimous ſometimes rendered, by the rigid exerciſe of deſpotiſm; and ſuch is the dangerous pre-eminence of occupying a throne eſtabliſhed in blood.

The choice of a ſucceſſor fell on Meer Jaffier, on account of his riches, his high rank, and the great influence he poſſeſſed both in the army and the councils of his ſovereign. The treaſonable negotiation was carried on by the intrigues of Omichund, a black merchant, who, anxious to profit by ſo important a tranſaction, put a moſt enormous price on his treachery. The principals, on fixing the eſtimate of the whole, deeming his demands arbitrary and impracticable, reſolved on diſappointing his venality, without endangering their ſcheme, by trifling with his reſentment.

To accompliſh this manœuvre with the greater certainty, two treaties were prepared and authenticated by the ſignatures of the reſpective parties; one in which the terms of Omichund were expreſſed; another intended only to be obſerved, in which no mention was made of his name. No arguments could induce Admiral Watſon to ſign ſo infamous an inſtrument, but he connived at the ſtratagem, by ſuffering another, at Clive's ſuggeſtion, to affix his name.

The treaſures of Surajah Dowlah were calculated exceedingly beyond their value. Clive dictated the negotiation; and ſpecified the diſtribution of the booty. Dazzled by the dignity to which he

aſpired,

aſpired, Meer Jaffier implicitly acquieſced in whatever was propoſed. He engaged to give the Company one million two hundred thouſand pounds; the European ſufferers ſix hundred thouſand; the ſame ſum to the navy and army; two hundred and fifty thouſand to the natives of the country, and a hundred thouſand to the Armenians.

It was alſo ſtipulated, that theſe treaſonable arrangements ſhould only take place when Meer Jaffier ſhould have foully betrayed his maſter in the field. This memorable inſtance of perfidy was acted in the Grove of Plaſſey, [June 26, 1757] where the ſtandard of rebellion was hoiſted, and where a few hundreds of Britiſh ſoldiers are ſaid to have acquired immortal honour, by facilitating the ſanguinary machinations of traitors againſt the dominion and life of their lawful ſovereign, by taking advantage of an enemy thrown into confuſion, and convulſed by the death or deſertion of its officers, and by deluging the plains with the blood of an unwieldy multitude, without arms, union, confidence, or diſcipline, and equally incapable of reſiſtance or retreat. Meer Muſdan, the moſt faithful and accompliſhed of Surajah Dowlah's generals, being mortally wounded by a cannon ball, the command devolved on the confederate of the Engliſh. This accident probably decided the conteſt, as it removed the only individual who, by his prudence and ability, might have checked the conſpiracy. Clive, who had gone to reſt while the tragedy was acting, only awoke to witneſs the concluding ſcene. After reprimanding his officers for daring to fight without his orders, while he was asleep, he marched with his usual coolness and intrepidity at the head of a party, and drove the enemy from an advanced post, where a few pieces of artillery had done considerable execution. The troops of Meer Jaffier, at that instant, drew off from the field of battle. This movement, connected with the profound neutrality which Clive had observed in that division of the army, soon convinced him who they were. This spectacle was not more pleasing to him than the news of it proved alarming to the nabob.—Plunged as he was in despair, from the conviction that his confidence had been placed in a traitor, and no longer able to discriminate his friends from his foes, he hurried from the fatal spot, and snatched an interval of miserable respite from the destinies that surrounded him, by hurrying himself a moment, for the last time, among his women and his wealth. His defeat was complete. Most of the troops preferred the fortunes of Meer Jaffier. And Surajah Dowlah, as a dreadful lesson to tyrants, was reduced, from wielding the rod of oppression, to consult his own safety under the disguise of a vagabond. His retreats were soon discovered, and those who had deprived him of his throne, thought themselves also entitled to put an end to his life.

In this manner was fought the celebrated battle of Plassey. Truth will ascribe the achievement to treachery, when the lustre of the actors ceases to give brilliancy to the fact. It was no new mode

of

of difplaying military heroifm, and Clive was but a fervile imitator in making the experiment, firft to bribe the general, and then to maffacre the troops.

No fooner was Meer Jaffier feated in the mufnud, [June 30th] than he found the treafures of his predeceffor utterly inadequate to the full and immediate difcharge of all his pecuniary engagements. His debts, by the ordinary expences of government, accumulated of courfe; his allies were diffatisfied; his officers in difguft neglected the difcipline of the army, and a total relaxation prevailed through all the gradations of authority.—Eight hundred thoufand pounds in fpecie was at one time remitted to Calcutta. The tardinefs of the fubfequent difburfements, the jealoufies of the court, the encroachments and infolence of our countrymen, the nabob's fufpicions, and the intrigues of his confidential fervants, produced fuch a complicated feries of altercation, as terminated in an inveterate diflike on both fides.

The Company, on receiving the difpatches which announced the fuccefs of their troops at Plaffey, had appointed Clive governor of Calcutta. It was then that the French were making their laft efforts, under Lally, on the coaft of Coromandel. Clive projected the fcheme of driving them from the Northern Circars, which yielded a revenue of four hundred thoufand pounds a-year. This expedition was commanded by Colonel Ford, whofe fuccefs was as brilliant and complete as, from the infinite difficulties he had to encounter, it certainly was unexpected.

In the month of August, 1759, the Dutch made their appearance in Hughly river, in a hostile manner. Notwithstanding we were then at peace with that nation, the governor determined to oppose them. The nabob was called upon to fulfil his engagements, to order them forthwith to leave the river, and in case they did not comply with his orders, the English resolved, under his sanction, to attack them. Seven ships full of men came within a mile of Calcutta, and landed fifteen hundred. Colonel Ford, who had just returned from the conquest of the Circars, was ordered to intercept them in their march to their factory Chinsura.— This he did, with about a force of a thousand men, so effectually, that of seven hundred Europeans not above fourteen reached the place of their destination. The ships commissioned by the Dutch for this clandestine expedition were at the same time all taken. A treaty however took place, in which the Dutch East-India Company agreed to defray the expences of the war, and that they should never introduce forces into the nabob's country without his consent, or keep at all their settlements together more than a hundred and twenty-five soldiers. The English also returned the captures they had made, which were valued at half a million sterling.

This unaccountable event was roundly attributed to the connivance of the nabob, who was now become odious for his cruelty, and despicable for his insig-

insignificance. The English immediately conceived the plan of a new revolution; but had the address to disguise their intentions, under the appearance of cordiality with the subah. While affairs were in this tranquil posture, and Meer Jaffier deemed himself secure in his government, he was suddenly divested of sovereignty [1760], in favour of his son-in-law, Cossim Ally Cawn.

Excuses were easily fabricated for the repetition of this violent measure. The defects of his government were resolved into his want both of capacity and principle. He was charged with ingratitude to his benefactors, because the Company's servants were not uniformly preferred to his own countrymen. His private conduct was exposed and blackened by libels of the grossest enormity. But the truth seems to have been, that Meer Jaffier had adopted a policy which might not eventually coincide with the ambition and venality of his new masters. Intoxicated by their late extraordinary success, and overwhelmed by the vast torrent of wealth which incessantly flowed in upon them, the speculations, the projects, and the desires of fresh acquisitions, which agitated the minds of these men, knew no bounds. And the natural inclination which the nabob unavoidably discovered for recovering that independence which he had lost, and which he had deemed essential to the utility of his high situation, only stimulated them to hold the domination they had grasped with a tighter hand.

Cossim Ally Cawn was not more patient under the controul of the Company, though he felt the neceſſity of an implicit ſubmiſſion. An eſtabliſhment founded on their protection ſtruck him, as not leſs mortifying than precarious. It was attended with circumſtances which diveſted his character of its proper influence. He thought himſelf entitled to the command of troops who were occupied in his ſervice, and whom he was bound to pay. But every European in his army affected an independence, incompatible with the diſcipline of the whole. The officer who headed theſe detachments took a pleaſure in diſputing his moſt trivial orders, and expoſing the imbecility of his government to the deriſion of his ſubjects. From the hour of his acceſſion to power, ſcarce a day paſſed in which occaſion was not taken, from the moſt trivial occurences, of leſſening his dignity, inſulting his impotence, and rendering his dependence on the patronage of the Company irkſome and inſupportable.

It is impoſſible that two governments of equal authority in any country can uniformly coincide or long ſubſiſt, without claſhing in matters of importance. The abuſes in moſt of the ſubordinate factories were become groſs and enormous. They aſſumed the privilege of deciding in every diſpute where their own intereſts were concerned; ſoldiers and ſepoys attended their orders, and even officers in conſiderable ſtations in the country government, were ignominiouſly beat at their deſire. They forcibly ſeized the property of others, dealt indiſcriminately in all merchandize, fixed their own prices, extorted payment, hoiſted Engliſh colours, forged ſorged paſſes, and treated every idea of juſtice with ridicule and defiance. The conſequence was, that ſhops were ſhut up, and villages abandoned; and the whole province was in an uproar, with outcries againſt the tyranny of the Engliſh, and the encroachments of the nabob. But every ſtruggle made by the peaſantry, and others, to prevent and repel theſe extortions, was conſtantly conſtrued into an attack on the rights of the Company. When the nabob ſtated theſe grievances, they were not redreſſed, and when he attempted to compromiſe them, he was charged with partiality.

Theſe inſtances of diſreſpect were ill calculated to conciliate the attachments of a prince, formed on maxims of the moſt barbarous deſpotiſm. But he had ſtrength of mind to render his feelings ſubſervient to his duty and his intereſt, and to make the experiment whether he could not obtain by policy, what he had ſo little hope of remedying by complaint. His firſt care was to reform the various abuſes which had crept into all the departments of ſtate. He diſcharged the Company's debt, and the heavy arrears of the army, retrenched the expences of his court, which had ſo frequently impoveriſhed his predeceſſors, eſtabliſhed his own authority over the country, by leſſening that of the Zimindars, increaſed the number of his troops, and diſciplined them in the European manner; and by a conſtant attention to the operations of commerce, conſiderably improved the reſources of the revenues.

The Mogul princes, who underſtood the true intereſts of the empire, had, for the encouragement

ment of commerce, exempted the English East India Company from many duties to which the natives were subjected. They were possessed of a passport, which procured their exemption at all the custom-houses and toll-bars in the country. But the servants of the Company, aware of their recent ascendancy over the government of the province, prostituted this privilege, to the obvious detriment of the customs. Cossim Ally Cawn regarded this imperious commerce with indignation. He saw subjects excluded as aliens from their own trade, and the finances involved in the ruin of the country. He adopted the magnanimous resolution of declaring a free trade through all his dominions. This wise expedient was met with the confidence of avowed and determined injustice. The presidency openly denied him the power of protecting his subjects, by the remission of his own duties.

He was therefore reduced to the necessity of either tamely acquiescing in their decision, or coming to an immediate rupture. The first was a meanness repugnant to his temper and principles, the second a measure which involved the most imminent difficulty and danger. He resolved, however, to enter on the task prescribed to him by these untoward circumstances, with caution and firmness. To avoid the inspection of the factory at Calcutta, he removed his court from Morshedabad to Monghir, two hundred miles higher up the Ganges. He fortified his situation with art and expedition, and enlisted all the Persians, Tartars, Armenians, and other soldiers of fortune, whose military

military abilities and experience might be of service to his own. Every vagabond European, and all the ſepoys who had been diſmiſſed or deſerted from the Engliſh, he collected and incorporated with his troops. He changed the Indian muſquets from matchlocks to firelocks, and had the ingenuity to provide his army with an excellent train of artillery. And that his movements might not be reported or rendered abortive, through treachery or diſſenſion, he purged his court of ſtrangers, and ſecretly cut off or threw into priſon every conſiderable perſon in his dominions, who had ſhewn any attachment to the Engliſh.

Theſe preparations ſufficiently indicated his intentions. The knowledge of them threw the preſidency at Calcutta into a flame. The ſtate of his army and finances had lulled them into ſecurity; but they wiſely dreaded the intelligence, the enterpriſe, and the fortitude of his character. Inured to the hardſhips of the field, he united the gallantry of the ſoldier with the ſagacity of the ſtateſman; and his mind, both from experience and information, was fertile in all the reſources of the country, and all the expedients of military adventure.

It was by his obſervations on the character and foreſight of this politic ſubah, that Mr. Haſtings, who reſided for ſome time at his court, laid the foundation of that celebrity which has ſince diſtinguiſhed him in India and England. His opinion that Coſſim Ally Cawn was driven to extremity by the temerity of the Company's ſervants, eſpecially in the ſubordinate factories, has been confirmed by every authentic document tranſmitted from the ſcene of action. Vanſittart, preſident of the council, uniformly avowed the ſame conviction, and manfully oppoſed every outrage which, in the whole of that fatal policy, ſo inevitably tended to plunge the Company and the country into a freſh ſeries of bloody and expenſive hoſtilities. Nor did he remit his endeavours to accommodate the difference thus unhappily ſubſiſting, till the breach, by the obſtinacy of the one party, and the cruelty of the other, became abſolutely irreparable.

His pacific intentions, however, were unfortunately controuled by a majority in the council, who fomented the enmities, indulged and avowed by the chief of the factory at Patna, againſt the nabob. Mr. Ellis, who acted in that capacity, had, in many recent inſtances, treated the country government with contumely and defiance. The letters of Coſſim to the preſidency are full of invectives againſt the inſolence and affectation of authority which diſtinguiſhed his conduct. And Mr. Ellis, in his correſpondence with the board, has treated the ſubah with a virulence and contempt which could originate only in the moſt inveterate prejudice.

Mr. Ellis was, unhappily, ſupported in all his violence by the government in Calcutta. He commanded a force for the protection of the factory, nearly three thouſand ſtrong. With this army he ſurprized Patna, a large city of conſiderable trade, ſituated on the Ganges, about three hundred miles

above

above Fort William. The aſſault was carried almoſt without reſiſtance. But the captors were too eager after plunder, to render their ſucceſs of any ſolid advantage to themſelves or the Company. The Indian governor returned to Patna, within four hours after he had left it, re-took the place with as much eaſe as it had been loſt, and the Engliſh troops were every where either cut to pieces, made priſoners, or driven to take refuge in the fort.

This event happened the very night in which Amyatt was diſmiſſed from the nabob, at whoſe court he had been reſident for ſome time, and where he had endeavoured, without effect, to bring Coſſim to an acquieſcence with the meaſures of the council. The conduct of this man, from a variety of circumſtances, bore at beſt a ſuſpicious appearance; and in his way to Calcutta, [June 24, 1763] with ſeveral other gentlemen of his party, he was treacherouſly aſſaſſinated by ſome of the nabob's people, as they paſſed the city of Morſhedabad.

The council of Fort William immediately conſidered themſelves as impelled to unanimity, in their own defence. The murder of their ambaſſador inſtigated revenge. Firſt aggreſſors, as they were in their attack on Patna, where ſhoals of the innocent and induſtrious inhabitants fell a ſacrifice to the ferocious rapacity of our troops, they allow nothing for the reſentment of the natives, on account of that atrocious action, but deemed every ſubſequent barbarity juſtified by the death of Amyatt. This is made the oſtenſible reaſon of declaring

claring war againſt a people of whom multitudes were maſſacred before that event was known, or could take place. Such an outrage to humanity and reaſon is the arrogance of little minds in the exerciſe of deſpotiſm.

Major Adams was therefore ordered to take the field, at the head of the Company's forces, and to direct his march to the capital of Bengal. Twice did the enemy diſpute his approach to Morſhedabad, with a fierceneſs and reſolution ſuperior to every exertion before obſerved in an Indian army. [Auguſt 2d].

This important capture might diſcourage, but did not diſperſe the enemy, Coſſim did not ſtake his all on a ſingle battle, but defended his dominions paſs by paſs. Nor did he hazard his own perſon in any engagement, where his officers might have made a merit of their treachery in betraying him. Theſe errors, which had ruined ſo many of the Indian princes, he carefully avoided. His army, however, was ſtill unequal to meet that of the Company, diſciplined after the beſt manner, fluſhed with victory, and animated in this rich and populous country with the conſtant proſpect of immenſe booty.

Soon after the two armies met on the plains of Garceah, in which the Indians appeared divided in regular brigades, with a train of fine artillery, well ſerved; the ſame arms, the ſame accoutrements, and the ſame clothing as the Engliſh. Nor did they commence the cannonade till our troops began the attack. They maintained their ground

in

in an obſtinate diſpute of four hours conſtant firing. In that time they broke a part of the Engliſh army, and captured two pieces of cannon. But though twenty thouſand horſe, and eight thouſand foot ſtrong, they were obliged at laſt to quit and abandon all their cannon to the Company's forces, who did not amount to more than three thouſand.

The victorious Engliſh thus left maſters of the field, purſued the enemy to the gates of Monghir. This place was ſtrongly fortified. It was the nabob's reſidence, and the center of all his military arrangements. It did not, however, much protract the progreſs of the conquerors, but ſurrendered after only nine days open trenches.

Coſſim placed his laſt hope on Patna, which he had omitted no care or expence to ſtrengthen and ſecure. He enforced the garriſon with ten thouſand men, and harraſſed the extremities of the beſiegers with large bodies of cavalry, which every where hovered round them.

It was about this time that the cruelties of Coſſim's nature, impelled by the circumſtances to which he was reduced, were chiefly diſcovered, by his maſſacre of the Engliſh priſoners in his cuſtody. This barbarous ſervice could only be performed by one Somers, a German of mean extraction and flagitious principles. The Indian ſoldiers revolted at the ſhocking command, and with a heroiſm that does them honour, deſired that arms might be given to the hapleſs men they were ordered to murder. They were, however, compelled to the odious ſervice. The priſoners made a brave defence,

fence, with no other weapons than their plates and their bottles, but were at last all ſlaughtered.

This ſavage manœuvre was of no advantage to Coſſim. The beſiegers redoubled their exertions. Patna, notwithſtanding its fortifications and the repeated ſkirmiſhes which the enemy had with our troops, did not reſiſt the attack above eight days. This reduced the nabob to abandon the province, [November 6th]. He had loſt all his poſts, and moſt of his troops. Sujah Dowlah, ſubah of a neighbouring province, received him with open arms, but would not permit his troops to enter his dominions. He wiſhed to provide the unfortunate prince with an aſylum, but was unwilling to bring the Engliſh into his country.

Thus ended a campaign conducted throughout with ability and expedition. Major Adams compleated, in leſs than four months, the entire conqueſt of Bengal. He fought in that time four capital actions, forced the ſtrongeſt entrenchments, took two conſiderable forts and near five hundred pieces of cannon, and totally defeated one of the moſt reſpectable and reſolute enemies we ever had in India.

The remains of the Indian army, though prohibited to follow their leader, were ſo far from being idle, that in a ſhort time Coſſim preſented his new ally with the heads of ſome Engliſhmen whom his troops had cut off and preſerved, as a dreadful proof of their activity and zeal in the ſervice. The great Mogul was now with Sujah Dowlah. This barbarous trophy probably tempted them to

eſpouſe

espouſe the cauſe of Coſſim. The council at Calcutta were, however, ſoon informed that theſe powers were reſolved to reinſtate him in the government of Bengal.

The preſident and council immediately wrote to Sujah Dowlah on the ſubject. They could not credit a report ſo derogatory to his honour, that while he profeſſed alliance he was capable of acting with hoſtility. But they were ſolicitous to acquaint him, that in caſe he ſhould take their enemies into his friendſhip, they were determined to protect Bengal from moleſtation of every kind, and that rather than involve their provinces in any freſh calamities, they would carry the war into his own country.

The Company's ſervants were ſoon ſatisfied that what they had heard was but too well founded. The confederacy they dreaded had actually taken place. The Mogul and Sujah Dowlah were in the field, at the head of an immenſe body of troops. Major Adams had reſigned the command, and was ſince dead. Major Carnac was appointed to ſucceed him. The council, therefore, in their diſpatches to him, urge, with great earneſtneſs, that the war ſhould, from that moment, be carried on offenſively. The enemy left not the alternative to the Engliſh, but preſented themſelves in order of battle where the Major was encamped near Patna. This battle was ably fought. Carnac's little army was furiouſly attacked in front and rear, but proved invincible to all the ſwarms of freſh troops that were ſucceſſively brought againſt them. The enemy was completely routed. Our troops were, however, too much fatigued to pursue. Their loss was considerable; but from a long, close, rapid, and well aimed fire, that of the confederates must have been immense.

An expedition was immediately carried into Sujah Dowlah's own country, in order to remove the ravages of war from the Ganges to the Soane. Letters were at the same time received from the king and Sujah Dowlah, with assurances that Cossim should be arrested and punished. They were answered, that nothing would reconcile the English, but the actual delivery of Cossim, Somers, and the deserters.

The moment hostilities commenced in Gazypour, Sujah Dowlah hastened with his army to repel the invasion. The most decisive action in the war was soon after fought at Buxar, on the banks of the Caramnassa. Major Hector Monro commanded the English army, which he had found in so mutinous a condition, that he deemed it expedient to punish the ringleaders as an example. Twenty-four were sentenced to be blown away from the mouth of cannon. Four of these brave but unfortunate men, who were grenadiers, insisted, as they had always the post of honour, they might also have it now, and suffer first. There have been few commanders of reputation at least, with whom such a sentiment would not have saved them. But the Major was satisfied with literally indulging their request.

He

He found the enemy ſtrongly poſted [October 22, 1764]. Before them lay a maſs ſo judiciouſly lined with cannon, that it was impoſſible to approach them without being galled. The Major, however, encamped ſo judiciouſly, and with ſo much precaution, that the allies began the attack. The cannonade commenced at nine o'clock in the morning, and in half an hour the action became general. Before twelve, the Indians were put to flight. They left ſix thouſand men on the ſpot, a hundred and thirty pieces of cannon, a proportionable quantity of military ſtores, and all their tents ready pitched.

The day after the battle, the Mogul, who had been a ſtate priſoner in the enemy's camp, wrote a congratulatory epiſtle to the Engliſh commander, complimenting him on the victory. He had left Sujah Dowlah the night preceding the engagement, and now very earneſtly requeſted to be taken under the protection of the Engliſh. The council of Calcutta conſented, and his majeſty ſoon joined our army.

The Engliſh had no ſooner arrived at Benares, than the miniſter of Sujah Dowlah preſented himſelf before the commander, with overtures of peace. Monro would liſten to none which did not put Coſſim and Somers in his power. This was the ſingle condition, without which he would not treat. Several expedients were ſuggeſted, but he rejected them all as diſhonourable. Pecuniary offers to an enormous amount, it is ſaid, were alſo made, though with no better ſucceſs. Few ſuch inſtances of of disinterestedness shed a lustre on the military profession in that part of the world. What a pity these were not more frequent, and that such as do happen are not better authenticated.

Thus critically were the English situated, when the general being recalled, the command of the army devolved on Sir Robert Fletcher, a major in the Company's troops. Emulous to distinguish himself, before the officer named by the governor and council should arrive to preclude him, he ventured to break up his camp, under the walls of Benares, at midnight [January 14, 1765], and went in quest of the enemy, who drew up twice to receive him, and as often retreated in good order. But on his preparing for a third attack, they fled with precipitation.

On his assuming the command, the army were in a very confined situation, surrounded on all sides by the enemy, straitened for forage and provisions of all sorts. It was in direct opposition to the opinion of most of the officers serving under him, that he then put the army in motion. The measure was, however, justified by its effects. He drove Sujah ul Dowlah from all his posts, took all his fortresses, with several hundred pieces of cannon, and conquered the whole of his dominions in the space of a month.

During these transactions, Meer Jaffier died, on the fourteenth of January, seventeen hundred and sixty-five, at Murshedabad. Though a traitor to Surajah Dowlah, it was a crime to which he had been impelled by the great law of self-preservation.

The

The temptation was at once too ſplendid and preſſing for one of his parts, his principles, or his ſituation. He endeavoured to atone for his perfidy to the nabob, by his fidelity to the Company. The murders with which he was charged, to facilitate his ruin, were afterwards found to be the mere fabrications of malignity. He ſeems to have been weak in council, and irreſolute in action; but his preferences, whether well or ill ſelected, were permanent and inflexible. He ſent for his ſecond ſon, the eldeſt having been dead ſome years, and while the agonies of death were yet upon him, put into his hand a paper of advice. He very naturally recommended the Rajah Nundcomar, his favourite, to continue prime miniſter, that his ſucceſſor might enjoy the benefit of his experience. All the reſident Engliſh were ſent for, with all the great officers of ſtate. In their preſence he deſired that orders might be given that all people throughout the ſubahſhip, ſhould tender the ſame loyalty to his ſon, Najim ul Dowlah, as they had done to him.

The ſervants of the Company paid as little deference to the will of the deceaſed as they had done to his orders while living. The ſucceſſor he nominated was adopted only from a certainty that they could not have made a better, as it would have been dangerous to riſk another choice. Indeed the acceſſion of Najim ul Dowlah to the muſnud, ſeems to have been chiefly improved for the purpoſe of intrigue and extortion.

Early in the beginning of the ſame year Lord Clive arrived in India, in conſequence of being

 requeſted

requested by the proprietors, on account of the abuses prevailing in their new acquisitions, to take upon him the station of president, and command of the Company's military force in Bengal. In order the more effectually to answer the purpose of this extraordinary delegation, a select committe of five gentlemen was also appointed. By this institution, whatever reformation appeared necessary was to be adopted; and the board of council only occasionally consulted. And it was not long till his lordship discovered a strong inclination to extend the Company's authority over the whole Mogul empire, and to retain that immense acquisition by an invincible force.

Sujah Dowlah was still in the field. Abandoned by the Mogul, and without confidence in his army, which had fled so frequently before the English, divested of the dignity and authority of vizier, and wasted by frequent and bloody defeats, he was not, however, without resources, in his own activity and resolution. He gathered his scattered forces with great assiduity, and procured a formidable reinforcement from the Marratto states. With this army he determined once more to face the Company's forces.

General Carnae, who had succeeded Colonel Monro in the command, assembled his troops, and marched immediately to the attack. The engagement happened at Calpy [May 20, 1765]. The enemy were routed with a great slaughter, and obliged, with precipitation, to re-cross the Jumna, and take refuge in their own country.

Sujah

Sujah Dowlah, driven to the laſt extremity, embraced the bold reſolution of throwing himſelf, without heſitation, on the mercy of the Engliſh. Having, with a fidelity unuſual in that country, permitted Coſſim and Somers to eſcape, he ſurrendered himſelf, in three days after this deciſive action, to General Carnac, without any other ſtipulation in his favour than to wait the determination of Lord Clive and the ſelect committee.

Thus were two of the moſt powerful princes of Indoſtan reduced to the melancholy neceſſity, the one of wandering as a fugitive, deprived by his own cruelty of every proſpect of mercy from the conquerors; the other, after the loſs of his country, of making the moſt abject ſubmiſſion to thoſe who had uſurped his rights, ſurrendering himſelf a priſoner at diſcretion, and feeling the mortification of owing his life to the authors of all his misfortunes.

The camp of Alexander the Great was not more ſplendid, while the family of Darius were his captives, than that of Carnac on this occaſion. The firſt and ſecond perſonages of the greateſt empire in the world were both in his cuſtody, and at the diſpoſal of his maſters, the ſervants of a company of Britiſh merchants.

It had been formerly reſolved to put the Mogul in poſſeſſion of Sujah Dowlah's dominions. But Clive, who went to the Engliſh camp at Allahabad, to ſettle that important treaty, was ſatisfied of its impropriety. Beſides driving Sujah Dowlah to deſpair, and combining the powers of the empire in his defence, the Mogul did not appear sufficiently qualified for that critical and hazardous situation. Sujah Dowlah was beloved by his people. His character was every where resolute, enterprising and popular. While his friendship for the English continued, he would prove an insuperable barrier, and effectually protect the Company's territories against all depredations from that quarter. It was on this policy that he was restored to all his hereditary dominions [August 3, 1765]. The surrender of Cossim and Somers was no longer in his power. The one had found an asylum among the Rohillas, and the other among the Jauts. He offered, however, to pay fifty lacks of rupees, to indemnify the Company for the expences incurred by the war.

The negociation with the king was also concluded in a few days. His majesty granted the Company the dewannee of Bengal, Bahar, and Orissa, the provinces of Burdwan, Midnapore, and Chittigong, and the twenty-four Pergunnahs of Calcutta, ceded to them by three successive nabobs, the five Northern Circars of Cicacole, and new confirmations of all their former privileges. For these immense favours the Company engaged to pay the king, from the revenues of Bengal, three hundred and twenty-five thousand pounds annually, and the nabob Najim ul Dowlah, in lieu of the aggregate produce of his government, assigned to them by his imperial majesty, the sum of six hundred twenty-three thousand two hundred and twenty-six pounds.

Lord

Lord Clive enumerates the advantages of these transactions, in his dispatches to the Directors [Sept. 30, 1765], in the following terms:—" Your revenues, by means of this new acquisition, will, as " near as I can judge, not fall far short, for the " ensuing year, of two hundred and fifty lacks. " Hereafter, they will, at least, amount to twenty " or thirty lacks more. The nabob's allowances are " reduced to forty-two lacks, and the tribute to the " king is fixed at twenty-six, and your civil and " military expences, in time of peace, can never " exceed sixty lacks. So that there will be remaining a clear gain to the Company of a hundred and twenty-two lacks, or one million six " hundred and fifty thousand nine hundred pounds " sterling a-year."

The business of this committee, at the head of which his lordship presided, consisted chiefly of accomplishing the treaties now mentioned. The Directors heartily approve of the bargain which Clive has made for them, and only wish to render these acquisitions as permanent as human wisdom can make them.

The luxury, however, which had taken possession of all the Company's servants was also an object of consideration, and the committee state it as bearing a threatening aspect to the prosperity of the Company's affairs. The Directors frankly admit the truth of this observation, and acknowledge, that they owe it entirely to the committee, that the Company are at last considered as principals in the advantages as well as dangers.

The

The committee having assigned the revenues to the Company, were afraid that their servants, unless provided with some other mode of enriching themselves, might do it at the expence of their employers. For this reason they established a society of trade, with an exclusive right to supply the natives with salt, beetle-nut, and tobacco. On these articles they laid a duty, calculated to produce a hundred thousand pounds a-year to the revenue. The profits of this trade they divided among the members of the society, consisting of the Company's civil and military servants.

This regulation did not prove quite so acceptable to the Board of Directors. Not that they wished to see abolished those ancient duties which constituted part of the public resources. The adjustment of these was referred to the discretion of the committee. But they deprecated the consequences arising from innovations in the inland traffic. Nor were they disposed to admit the continuance of them on any condition whatever. And they cautioned the committee against permitting the natives to be oppressed by any such severe exactions.

This is a summary but substantial account of the correspondence which took place between the Court of Directors and the select committee. Thus the Company's servants in India saw their masters in Europe receive the news of their successful rebellion against the government of the empire with approbation, thankfully accept of a gift of the revenues, and make no scruple to a continuance of the duties on salt and other articles. They had, therefore,

fore, this double motive to persist in their extortion, the example of their superiors, and the custom of the country.

On Lord Clive's return to England [July, 1767], the conduct of the committee, in which he presided, was severely arraigned, especially by the friends of the gentlemen who composed the council in Bengal. The recrimination which ensued was mutual, tedious, and uninteresting. One party asserted, that when Lord Clive originally appeared in Calcutta, the Company were merely an association of merchants struggling for existence. One of their factories was in ruins, their agents were assassinated, and an army of fifty thousand men, to which they had nothing to oppose, threatened the immediate destruction of their principal settlement. His lordship left India about ten years afterwards, and in that time his masters in Leadenhall-street, chiefly by his measures and exertions, had become powerful princes, possessed of vast revenues, and ruling over fifteen millions of people.

On the other hand, it ought to be recollected, that the war of India, in which his victories were then conspicuous, was a scene where many other distinguished characters appeared, and acted their parts. The formidable combination which espoused the interests of Cossim Ally Cawn, were utterly dispersed, their territories conquered, and their chiefs reduced to a dependence on the English army, without his lordship's assistance. The select committee only ratified the treaties which resulted from these campaigns, though his lordship, with a characteristic

racteristic modesty, arrogated the merit of the whole to his own endeavours.

Not to mention how he availed himself of his official situation, while in India, in favour of his pecuniary transactions in England, Sir Robert Fletcher, in a letter which appeared in one of the daily papers [October 26, 1773], roundly asserts, "That the noble lord's civil regulations consisted "chiefly of such as were best calculated speedily to "enrich himself and every creature round him. A "monopoly in salt, beetle-nut, and tobacco, and a "gold currency, seventeen or twenty per cent. were "established, and enforced by severe penalties, ri-"gorously carried into execution, to the destruction "of the trade and the ruin of the constitution."

The source of this keen altercation arose from the charges of peculation which his lordship brought against several eminent members of the council. His jaghire being litigated by the Court of Directors, covenants were framed at home, prohibiting the reception of presents from the natives of India, except on the Company's account. All their servants in their various settlements, were forthwith required to acquiesce in this restriction, by signing these covenants. Several gentlemen of the council in Fort William, who had been chiefly concerned in the two late revolutions, and particularly in raising the present nabob to the nizamut, received considerable sums on that occasion. Lord Clive, who had set the example, in his transactions with Meer Jaffier, and whose conduct determined the Company to check the practice, yet criminates it it in them, with all the harshness and acrimony of an immaculate reformer. They deny not that the nabob had distributed money on his accession. They justify their receiving it from precedent and custom. They complain of the covenants as imposing a hardship, from which their predecessors had all been exempted. They are aware, at the same time, that the remedy is inadequate to the disease, as the greatest presents might be broken down into such a number of parts, as totally to elude the prohibition. They state, that these pecuniary gifts were obtained before the covenants were executed on their part. They impute his lordship's zeal in prosecuting this officious inquisition, to other motives than either their guilt or his fidelity. They give a colouring to the whole proceedings of that famous committee, which leaves an obloquy on the character of all its members.

Indeed, to all the rhodomantade with which the noble lord, and his creatures, trumpeted forth the efficacy of his measures, and the profound sagacity with which he explored the evils that existed, and the most probable means of restoring tranquillity and order, it was replied by various queries, to which, in these heroic times, no solution was deigned. The public, however, hesitated, whether the merit of composing the disturbances in Bengal belonged to Lord Clive, and his select committee, or to the gentlemen who expelled Cossim Ally Cawn, and conquered Sujah Dowlah? Or, whether the praises of making peace with Sujah Dowlah were due to those who conquered his dominions,

dominions, and made himſelf a priſoner; or to the perſon by whom thoſe dominions, which are nearly as large as England, were reſtored for ſix hundred thouſand pounds, at the ſame time yielding up Gauzypour and Benares, which brought into the Company's treaſury two hundred and thirty thouſand pounds a-year? Or, whether cenſure might not rather be incurred for raiſing civil and military mutinies, by the aſſumption of illegal power, than thanks for quelling them? Or, whether it could be ſuppoſed that an army which defeated Coſſim Ally Cawn, and Sujah Dowlah, was entirely devoid of diſcipline and ſubordinatton? Or, whether the boaſted re-eſtabliſhment of order and obedience might not, after all, be deemed a uſeleſs parade of generals and colonels? Or, what real honour can be claimed for obtaining the dewannee of Bengal, Bahar, and Oriſſa, under a violation of the moſt ſacred engagements, merely by the ſignature of a prince who muſt equally have ſigned his own death-warrant, if it had been preſented to him?

What are we left to conclude from theſe implacable diſſenſions, but that great and flagrant enormities ſubſiſted at that time among the Company's ſervants; that we owe the diſcovery of many important and intereſting details of frauds and abuſe of truſt, to the petulance and animoſity occaſioned by the diſtribution of the plunder; that the Direction never acted from ſounder policy than in thus empowering one of the firſt and moſt enterpriſing in this iniquitous combination or conſpiracy,

ſpiracy, to detect the profligacy of the whole, and give evidence againſt them; that moſt of the Company's difficulties have originated in rendering the political ſubſervient to the mercantile ſyſtem; that their ſervants being without intereſt in the effects of their own meaſures, renders them obnoxious to irreſiſtible temptation; that moſt of the enormous delinquencies for which they have been blamed, are the natural, perhaps unavoidable conſequences of their ſituation; and that many of thoſe who have been moſt violent and boiſterous in their criminations, would probably, thus circumſtanced, not have acted a better part.

CHAP.

CHAPTER III.

The Company's affairs an object of public enquiry—Their bargain with Government—Debates on their situation in Parliament—Their Dividend restrained—Consequences—A Reflection—Amount of their Debts and Revenues at this period.

THE vast extent of territory, and the prodigious mass of wealth acquired by the Company's arms, on the banks of the Ganges, became a source of contention, as well at home as abroad. The proprietors, who saw their servants accumulating princely fortunes, in the exercise of powers delegated from them, eagerly panted for a participation in the distribution of the prize. They could not reconcile their low dividend with the accounts incessantly transmitted from India, of immense revenues, and a flourishing trade.

The Court of Directors were of a different opinion. Two violent factions were consequently and immediately formed. One of these was for increasing the dividend, the other insisted on keeping it at six per cent. The proprietors considered only the success, the directors saw nothing but the debts of the Company. The former were determined to bring the matter to issue by a general vote at the Midsummer court, but were disappointed by the manœuvres of the latter.

This

This vigorous altercation between the members of the direction and their constituents, afforded much public speculation and discussion. It was strenuously argued by one party, that though the advantages of the Company were numerous and splendid, their measures both civil and military, the multiplicity of their arrangements, and the contingencies incident to their various establishments, occasioned the most enormous expenditure; that their profits were comparatively remote and precarious, while their debts were urgent and inevitable, and that in the first instance, at least, their surplus, whatever it might be, should be sacredly appropriated to liquidate and discharge their incumbrances.

The other party were far from being satisfied by this reasoning. No trading company, they alledged, could ever hope to be without debt, which must always be supposed to increase in a certain proportion to the magnitude of the capital, and the extent of the system in which it was employed. The creditors of the Company who were most interested had no objections to its security. This fact was evinced by the present state of exchange. The Company's bonds bore a premium, and sold for more than their value. Those who had risked their property during the war, while the whole was at stake, might be obliged to sell out, and new purchasers would reap all that benefit to which the former were so justly entitled. In this manner the possessors of India stock were excluded from enjoying the emoluments arising from its natural and neceſſary produce, as operating in their peculiar ſyſtem of commerce.

Theſe intereſting topics were liberally and frequently agitated, not only in private or ſelect companies, and among friends, but in all the periodical miſcellanies of the times, and in multitudes of other temporary publications. The diſpute was of peculiar importance, more eſpecially to the mercantile part of the community. The anxieties, the induſtry, and the heat of both parties, increaſed as the next quarterly meeting approached. It was at the ſame time whiſpered by great confidence, that government intended to interfere.—And a few days before the Michaelmas General Court of 1766, the miniſter actually ſent a meſſage to the Directors. It was then read from the chair to the proprietors at large. The meſſage was from the firſt lord of the treaſury, in theſe words:—"As the affairs of the Eaſt-India Company had "been mentioned in Parliament laſt ſeſſion, it "was very probable they might be taken into "conſideration again; therefore, from the regard "he had for the welfare of the Company, and that "they might have time to prepare their papers for "that occaſion, he informed them, that the par-"liament would meet ſome time in November."

Letters were at the ſame time read, from Lord Clive, and the ſecret committee at Bengal, which greatly exceeded all former accounts of the Company's opulence, the proſperity of its trade, and the permanent baſis on which its intereſts were eſtabliſhed. The Directors, notwithſtanding, oppoſed

ſed an increaſe in the dividend. It was urged with accumulated force by the proprietors. A ballot was demanded, and a diviſion for a day or two evaded. But another general court being called, the queſtion was put, and the dividend to take place from the enſuing Chriſtmas increaſed, by a prodigious majority, from ſix to ten per cent.

On the meeting of Parliament [Nov. 25, 1766] the menaces of the miniſter were realized. The affairs of the Company were ſubjected to the cognizance of a committee appointed by the Houſe. It was ordered in a few days, and after a very intereſting debate, that copies of the Company's charters, their grants from the native princes, their treaties, their letters and correſpondence to and from their ſervants in India, the ſtate of their revenues in Bengal, Bahar and Oriſſa, and other places, ſhould all be laid on the table, with an account of all expences incurred by government on the Company's account, whether in the naval, military, or whatever other departments. This order was followed with another, that theſe papers be printed for the uſe of the members. *

The Court of Directors immediately preſented a petition to parliament, in oppoſition to a meaſure which they ſhewed would be attended with irreparable miſchief to the Company. A motion was conſequently made to diſcharge the former order. A debate enſued, but it was at laſt agreed, that the private correſpondence ſhould not be printed.

* Debret's Parliamentary Regiſter for 1766.

On

On this occaſion, the intereſting point of territorial right, in conſequence of the Company's charter, was warmly and ably debated. The arguments on both ſides appeared ſeparately ſo unanſwerable, and the queſtion involved ſo many points of the greateſt conſtitutional importance, that the Houſe ſeemed averſe to a deciſion. The general opinion was againſt a trial of ſuch a right, in ſuch a place; and that an amicable agreement with the Company was the more eligible meaſure.

Adminiſtration was at this time in too much diſtraction to inveſtigate or ſettle a ſubject of ſuch magnitude. By their declining to take any part in the negociation out of Parliament, a petition, containing two propoſals, was preſented [May 20].

It was propoſed that government ſhould grant the Company ſome advantages from the inland duties on teas; a drawback on the export of them to Ireland and the colonies; and others on raw ſilk, calicoes, muſlins, the recruiting ſervice, and military ſtores. After deducting 400,000l. a year in lieu of their former profits, the Company were to divide equally with government all the net produce of the remaining revenues and trade, provided charges were not included, and the Company's property, in the new acquiſitions, continued for three years. Or it was propoſed, that the Company, on the ſame terms, ſhould continue the ſpecific ſum of 400,000 l. a year, for three years, by half-yearly payments, and indemnify the public for any loſs the revenue might ſuffer, by granting the advantages required in the tea-trade, if the conſumption

tion of it, taken on an average of five years, did not answer that end.

These last proposals were accepted by the House with only this difference, that the agreement was limited to two, instead of three years. A bill was therefore brought in [June 12, 1767], and adopted by the legislature, for carrying the measure into immediate effect *.

Another message from the minister had been read at the general court, restricting the increase of the dividend, and recommending to the Company to admit no farther augmentation till their affairs were more fully investigated. This measure not producing the intended alteration, two bills were framed and brought forward, one for regulating the qualifications for voters in trading companies, and one for further regulating the dividends of the East-India Company.

The last of these actually rescinded the act of the Company, and tied them down from raising their dividends above ten per cent. till next meeting of Parliament. This met with great opposition. All the former arguments were renewed and urged with peculiar ardour and obstinacy. The Company petitioned against it without effect, and even offered, though to no better purpose, that, to defeat a bill thus hostile to their privileges, they would voluntarily bind themselves from any additional increase of their dividend during the whole term of their agreement.

* Debret's Parliamentary Register for 1767.

The abettors of the bill rested its defence for the most part on their anxiety to prevent a fluctuation of stock, and to preserve the credit of the Company inviolate. The public funds might be affected and kept down, and by that means the national debt would be increased, rather than diminished. This measure would at the same time defeat that spirit of speculation and gambling which might otherwise be expected. It would also guard the revenue of the Company's territorial acquisitions against encroachments so effectually, that the claim of the public might not be injured, till the right of these acquisitions should be finally settled.

The bill was charged by opposition with injustice and violence. They denied that any fluctuation could take place, or that the credit of the Company could be injured by the proprietors apportioning their dividends to the situation of their affairs. The proposal made by the Company answered all the purposes for which the bill was intended. It was absurd, that the owners of the capital should not be able to divide 80,000 l. among themselves, on a trade which afforded government 400,000 l. It was altogether without example in the annals of a free country, that the legislature should interpose a controul over the dividend of a trading Company, legally voted, and declared by those to whom the power of doing it was entrusted, and to whom there was no ground to impute an abuse of that power. They had lent their money to the public upon the express condition of using their discretion in their dividends, provided their effects undivided continued equal to their debts.—

It

It was a precedent that might be attended with the most fatal consequences to national credit, as it tended to lessen that security and independence of the power of the state, which had induced all Europe to deposit their money in the funds.

No reasoning, however, is of much use against a majority in the House of Commons. Men warped by the prepossessions of party, are on neither side open to conviction. The bill passed by a great majority [June 26th]. It met with still more opposition in the House of Lords, but was carried, though a protest was entered against it, signed by nineteen lords.

In the course of these proceedings, a variety of facts were produced, which strongly excited the curiosity and attention of the public mind. The richness of the country was exaggerated, and deemed inexhaustible. The natives were described, notwithstanding, as the most abject wretches on earth. Oppressions and enormities of the most odious and shocking nature were imputed to the servants of the Company. The opulence and luxury which they displayed on their return to Europe, were naturally construed into a proof of the grossest peculation and extortion. The despotism exercised with so much severity in all our settlements, and their respective dependencies, was not only abhorent to the feelings of a free people, but considered as an indelible stain on the British character. And though the splendour and magnitude of the whole complex system formed an object peculiarly interesting and attractive, especially while the

 nation

nation was yet in a ſtate of intoxication from the brilliant ſucceſs of the late war, the rapacity of individuals, the expence of a military and civil arrangement, the debts and dividends of the Company, the contingencies of commerce, and the intrigues of government, gave no very ſanguine hopes of an immediate and adequate advantage to the community at large.

The moſt unpopular part of the buſineſs was what the oppoſition, all over the kingdom, branded as an unconſtitutional interference of miniſtry. The clamour of the public kept pace with the graſp of government. The proſperity of the Company, their patronage and emoluments, excited the envy, and tempted the ambition and avarice of prerogative. The revenues ſeemed adequate to all the purpoſes of corruption, and the employments once entruſted to the diſpoſal of the crown, would ſtrengthen and extend the influence of its ſervants, by an increaſe of their dependence.

Various meaſures were adopted for invading and ſubverting the rights of the Company. The emiſſaries of miniſtry were inſtructed to propagate a report that the monopoly ſhould be deſtroyed, and the trade laid open. Several trading towns were even inſtigated to petition parliament for that purpoſe. The ſophiſtry by which the patience of the public was reconciled to theſe outrages was, that the Company owed moſt of its ſucceſs to the exertions of government; that the dominion of the ſea was preſerved by the king's ſhips, and the battles on land fought by his armies. From this it was

con-

concluded, that the prodigious expence of the public in extending the property, ought to be compensated by an adequate share in the profits of the Company. But the nation was aware, at the same time, that there were not more able commanders, nor braver troops, nor in any respect a better appointed, disciplined, or directed army in the world, than those who reared the Company's standard in the fields of Indostan.

The whole expence incurred by the treasury, on the Company's account, according to official statement, amounted to about a million and a half. Their commerce was calculated, on an average, to contribute to the revenue about one million four hundred pounds a-year, besides four hundred thousand pounds, in consequence of the late bargain. Thus, while the public was burdened with four millions and a half by the Company, the Company discharged the public of the interest of about fifty millions. By this calculation the balance in favour of the public, and against the Company, exceeded the interest of forty-seven millions. The Company, in fact, paid at that moment more than a third of the interest of the whole national debt.

Symptoms of an approaching diminution in the source of this extraordinary opulence, were already appearing. It was only while the minds of the people were fired with the marvellous relation of travellers, while report operated on these remote occurrences, as a telescope does on objects beyond the reach of the natural eye, and while individuals, disguised by the sudden and unaccountable posses-

sion

ſion of exceſſive riches, excited univerſal attention and ſurpriſe, that even this fund was deemed inexhauſtible. But when general admiration began to ſubſide and give way to accurate calculation and a ſimple ſtatement of facts, it became a very ſerious and intereſting conſideration, that notwithſtanding all our recent acquiſitions in India, and the vaſt influx of wealth which it occaſioned in the Britiſh empire, the burthens under which the nation groaned received no ſenſible alleviation. Adventurers whoſe neceſſities, avarice, ambition, or inſignificance, had driven them from their native country, roſe not only to independence in a ſhort time, but in equipage rivalled, on their return, the greateſt families in the kingdom; at the ſame time that their manners exhibited a ſtrange contraſt between plebeian habits and Aſiatic luxury. Four hundred thouſand pounds, beſides the immenſe ſums accruing from cuſtom on the various articles of Eaſt-India trade, was an yearly acceſſion to the treaſury, peculiarly ſeaſonable and important. Theſe advantages were, however, reſtricted to a few individuals; but the preſſure of the taxes was general, and, to many orders of the community, almoſt inſupportable. The public had conſequently the mortification to perceive, the moment they came to their ſenſes, that all their ſanguine expectations of relief from the oppreſſions ariſing from the expenditure occaſioned by the late war, from ſuch a ſplendid appendage to the Britiſh empire, had vaniſhed like a South-Sea bubble; and that it was, on the whole, an object which would ulti-

ultimately prove rather pernicious than beneficial, by the venality of the Company's servants on the one hand, and the rapacity of government on the other. The booty was immenſe, and more than adequate to public exigence; but its paſſage lay between the gulph of Charybdis and the ſhore of the Cyclops.

The object which the miniſtry pretended to have, and which the Company at this time certainly had moſt at heart, the liquidation of their accumulating debt, ſeemed alſo exceedingly remote, perhaps altogether impracticable, without a radical change of ſyſtem. Their debt was then nearly ſeven millions ſterling. The groſs annual revenue of their trade, their farms, their cuſtoms, and their territories, amounted to two millions, eighty-ſeven thouſand, ſeven hundred and forty-ſeven pounds. A ſum thus enormous, and ſuſceptible of improvement, might indeed have afforded a ſinking-fund ſufficient to have ſpeedily reſcued the Company from every embarraſſment, but not without putting an immediate end to every ſpecies of embezzlement in the management of their finances.

CHAP.

CHAPTER IV.

Hyder Ally's lineage and power—He quarrels with the Company—A comparative ſtatement of the Diſputants—Battle of Trinomaly—Hyder ravages the Carnatic—Appears at the gates of Madraſs—Peace concluded—An eſtimate of the war—Superviſors appointed—A new bargain with Government.

HYDER ALLY CAWN was the ſon of Nadim Saib, general of ten thouſand horſe in the army of the empire. He was employed to head the Myſoreans when they took the field againſt the Marrattos. He fought that warlike people, and routed them in a pitched battle. The king of Myſore gave him the country and fortreſs of Banguelor, as a reward of his bravery. This enabled him to appear in the Myſorean army, at the head of his own troops.

Hyder was then about twenty-one years old, and his father gave him the command of the forces with which, as a tributary, he was obliged to follow the camp of the ſubah, when [in the year 1750] he made a deſcent on the coaſt of Coromandel. It conſiſted only of fifty horſemen, and two hundred infantry, armed with matchlocks. He was at the battle where Nazirjing was ſlain, and then conceived the idea of training his battalion in the European diſcipline.

The

The first occasion on which he merited distinction was in his contest with Canero, the prime-minister and favourite of the Mysorean sovereign. He was then, by the death of his brother, in possession of an important fortress, a fertile territory, and a body of troops, which amounted to fifteen thousand men, including three hundred Europeans, and three thousand excellent cavalry. The king had also appointed him generalissimo of all his troops.

His generosity, his address, his high spirit, and a love of glory, rendered him obnoxious to the hatred and jealousy of Canero. This man became odious, in proportion to the popularity of Hyder, whom he ardently wished to ruin. Instead, however, of being able to realize his intentions, the genius of Hyder surmounted every snare that was laid by the dark intrigues of his implacable adversary, tore him at last from the bosom of his master, and shut him up in an iron cage, in the middle of the most public place of Banguelore, where it is still seen with the bones of this unhappy man, who lived two years as a spectacle of barbarous triumph, thus constantly exposed to the insults of the populace in the interest of Hyder.

The course of his victories, from this success, was rapid and extraordinary. The terror of his arms rendered his alliance an object of attention and solicitude to most of the princes in the peninsula of India. Like all great men in that country, he was at once a soldier and a politician, and accummulated his acquisitions as much by the wisdom

dom of his treaties, as by the ardour and vigour of his military exertions.

His connections in the Carnatic alarmed the presidency of Madrass. They did not think the Company's settlements perfectly secure, while an armament, thus formidable, encamped in their neighbourhood. They wished to sound his intentions, and for that purpose apprised him in the most respectful terms, that they had appointed an embassy to wait upon him, and confer with his Highness on several particulars between them, which the interest of both required to be more explicitly understood. But, suspicious of their design, he declined the honour they intended him. Aware, at the same time, of their intrigues with the subah, he artfully detached him from their interest, and even prevailed on him to appoint his son nabob of Arcot, in opposition to Mahommed Ally, the steady friend and ally of the English.

Having accomplished this object, he transmitted a memorial to his resident at Madrass, to be presented by him to the governor. He strongly protested that his inclinations were pacific. He enumerated the instances of respect which he had uniformly shewn the Company, and complained that his good offices were returned in a manner that indicated no desire in the presidency to cultivate or preserve his friendship. He attributed it to the intrigues of Mahommed Ally, that their force had united with that of the nizam, to disappoint his projects, and curb his rapacity. He warned the Company against continuing their alliance with a man whose ambi-

tion

tion had so often embroiled the country, or involving themselves in the defence of his usurpations. He urged them to withdraw their forces from such strong holds as were connected with the Arcot provinces. He even offered to indemnify them for what arrears might be due to them from their ally, and in lieu of which they were in possession of so many forts and districts.

In consequence of Hyder's union with the nezam, the Company was rendered a principal in the quarrel. The depredations which he imputed to them, they shifted from their own shoulders to those of the nizam, under whom they acted as allies, and for whose measures they did not acknowledge themselves responsible. They apprised Hyder of the nizam's perfidy, and referred to his breach of treaty with them, as a proof how dangerous it was to confide in him. They disclaimed all intentions of hostility against the Mysore country, of which he was governor. They avowed themselves solicitous to protect the Carnatic from molestation, and thought such places on its frontiers as were necessary to render it secure, should be continued in their possession. They invited him to a correspondence on these particulars, that their mutual good understanding might be solidly established. But they did not fail, at the same time, to make him sensible that they were adequate to their own defence, and equally prepared to fight or negociate.

It was indeed obvious, that Hyder only wished to wound the Company through their ally, and by one masterly exertion to crush their growing influence

fluence, which had now become an object of jealousy and terror to all the powers in the empire. Their late conquest of Bengal, their reduction of Sujah ul Dowlah to an abject vassalage, the chains they had forged for the imperial family, the many dishonourable obligations which Mahommed Ally owed to their interference, and especially the very lofty tone in which they continued to assert their claims of violence and outrage, were considerations peculiarly alarming to all the various states and dependencies in the Deccan, and on the coast of Corromandel.

These Hyder pressed by letters and ambassadors in the several courts of the nabobs and polygars, all over that division of the empire. And there wanted not the most substantial arguments to warrant the confederacy which he wished to establish. The English were intruders on their rights. The part they acted was equally daring and insidious. The advantages which they owed to indulgence were converted to the purposes of fraud, oppression, and even sedition. The country, which embraced and cherished them as traders, had found them to be usurpers. Under the semblance of harmless mercantile pursuits, they concealed the dreadful implements of murder and devastation. They came to deal with the natives for the produce of the climate and the soil, their manufactures and superfluities, and had stript their country of its wealth, inhabitants, fertility and honour. In exchange for the treasures they transmitted to Europe, they had deluged the infatuated kingdoms of Indostan with all their own hereditary vices,

vices, diseases and miseries! The princes whom credulity or misfortune had put in their power, had been treated merely as an article of merchandize, and worth no more than they yielded to the general stock of their aggregate interest. Their treacheries were in proportion to their protestations and forms of fidelity. They valued no ties, any farther than they administered to their rapacity, which, notwithstanding all their professions, was evidently the sole governing principle of their politics.

Facts thus notorious and interesting, united under the banners of Hyder the most discordant powers, whom nothing but a sense of their common danger could have restrained from reciprocal insult. His army was therefore composed of all that variety of tribes, foreigners and fugitives, which are to be found in such diversity among the Indians. The possessions of Hyder were at this time numerous and extensive. They consisted of Mysore and Banguelore, with all those mountaneous countries which fill up that vast track of the Peninsula, which reaches from Amboor to Madura, Travancore, and the coast of Malabar. The kingdoms of Ballapour, Bisnagar, and Canaree, together with the sovereignty of the Malabar coast and Maldive islands. These dominions were connected together, and defended on the part of the English, by a variety of high grounds and narrow passes, and are said to contain nearly one thousand fortified places. The camp of this celebrated warrior, whom fame hailed as the saviour of India, was inſtantly crowded with prodigious ſwarms from theſe immenſe and populous territories. His forces were conſequently eſtimated at two hundred thouſand men, of which twenty-five thouſand were cavalry, and ſeven hundred and fifty good European troops. The ſubah of the Deccan brought likewiſe into the field at leaſt one hundred thouſand, though of theſe there were no more than forty thouſand fighting men, thirty thouſand cavalry, and ten thouſand infantry. Every chief, however, in this great army, was proprietor and abſolute maſter of his own troops. Following Nizam merely as vaſſals of the empire, they were little diſpoſed to riſque their lives, or that of their cattle, on any occaſion, except when inſtigated by the deſire of revenge, or the hope of plunder.

The united army, comprehending ſuch multitudes were, according to the cuſtom of the country, followed by ſhoals of merchants, tradeſmen, mechanics, women, ſuttlers and ſervants. This occaſioned the camp to be vaſtly extended, which, but for the vigilance and experience of Hyder, might have been eaſily ſurpriſed by the Engliſh. The forces of Nizam added to his reputation, and might have procured him many allies, but he was ſuſpicious both of the ſubah and his general. The chiefs in this diviſion of the army were in eternal want of money, and Hyder was too œconomical to gratify their pecuniary demands, at an expence which, by draining his treaſury, might have enfeebled his operations.

A very

A very conſiderable train of artillery, conſiſting at leaſt of one hundred and ten pieces of large cannon, was an object which increaſed the ſtrength of this formidable armament. That of Hyder was more numerous, better provided with ammunition, better mounted, and better ſerved; but, out of ſixty pieces of ordnance, thirty were iron. The artillery of Nizam, on the contrary, were all fine European braſs cannon. Thirty of theſe were caſt in France, and had been wrecked with a French ſquadron, by a hurricane, in the road of Maſulipatam, and by that means came into the Nizam's poſſeſſion, as his predeceſſors were then proprietors of the port. This beautiful artillery, however, was rendered almoſt uſeleſs, for want of ammunition, carriages and gunners.

The Engliſh power in India was now in its meridian. They poſſeſſed Bengal, the richeſt, moſt fertile, and populous of all the provinces in the empire; the coaſts of Oriſſa and Corromandel, having no other limits inland than the gates or mountains, the large towns of Cambay and Surat, the iſland of Bombay and the country of Salſette, on the Marratto frontier, beſides ſeveral inferior forts on the coaſt of Malabar, with a number of ſubordinate factories on the iſland of Sumatra, too remote to be of any advantage in the preſent war. Their forces on all theſe various eſtabliſhments were then reckoned not leſs than ninety thouſand ſtrong. General Smith, who had the command of the army, after leaving the neceſſary garriſons properly enforced, had at his diſpoſal five thouſand Europeans,

peans, two thousand five hundred sipoys, two thousand five hundred horse, including two hundred Europeans, twelve hundred Indians, taught the English exercise, and commanded by European officers. He was also joined by the cavalry of Mahommed Ally, a troop not only inferior to that of Hyder, in point of number, but every way unfit to force them, by their utter want of discipline, and the bad condition of the horse. The other troops of the English allies were altogether in conjunction with those under the nabob of Arcot, about twenty thousand men.

General Smith was at the head of an army, for the most part better disciplined, and more practised in their evolutions than the enemy. He had a numerous corps of Europeans, who were such veterans in the service as to be deemed invincible. His artillery was in every respect perfect in proportion to its size. The army was served with a variety of able officers and engineers, and he was himself much superior to Hyder in military science and experience. But the inferiority of his cavalry obliged him to fix the scene of his operations to the mountaneous part of the country. It was not in his power to prevent the enemy's horse from ravaging the valleys, and cutting off his convoys. Nor could he always procure a sufficient number of oxen for the conveyance of his artillery, ammunition and baggage. The chief obstruction to his success, however, arose from his subordination to the council in Madrass, whose dictates often clashed with his plans; whose selfish manœuvres reduced the

the army to dependance on contractors for subsistence, and whose supplies were as uncertain and dilatory as their orders were contradictory and impracticable.

While Hyder was employed in amusing the Company with terms of negociation, his preparations were carried on with the utmost vigour and dispatch. The circumstances, however indispensible to the march of an Indian army, have always given the European forces great advantages on the commencement of hostilities. General Smith was in the field, and had reduced several forts of the enemy before the main body of the troops made their appearance. Tripatoor, Vaniambady, and Singueman, held out each a few days, but were severally captured without much difficulty. Caveripatnam, a place of some consequence, from its situation, was also invested. Its fortress was commanded by an able officer, and did not yield till seventeen days after the trenches were opened, and then only from seeing no prospect or possibility of relief. Without losing a moment, the army set down before Kistnagerri. This is a fort of no inconsiderable strength. It stands on the brow of a steep mountain, and is rendered almost impregnable by nature, without any material assistance from art. The garrison was commanded by a European, and made a brave defence. The British troops assaulted it twice, in the last of which twenty-four grenadiers and several soldiers were killed.

The diſtance of this place from Banguelore is about twenty-two leagues; and General Smith, learning by his ſcouts, that the two ſubahs had begun their march from that part of the country, thought it improper to waſte more time in an acquiſition of ſo little conſequence, eſpecially as it was connected with ſo much danger. He therefore raiſed the ſiege, and poſted himſelf to defend the paſs of Velore. It was of the laſt importance to render this enterance to the Arcot diſtricts as difficult as poſſible. There were two others, but this which opens about four leagues from Caveripatnam, was the only one through which artillery could be conveniently conveyed. And being in the center with Caveripatnam, a conſiderable town and fortreſs ſituated on the Palier, in their rear, our army could either diſpute the paſs with the ſubahs, or retire in ſafety.

It was however determined in a council of war, which Hyder conſulted on the occaſion, to avoid this paſſage, and to attempt that of Ventigerri. No ſooner were the movements of the enemy announced to General Smith, than he broke up his camp, and haſtened to prevent them. Hyder, perceiving his aim, turned ſuddenly to the right, and by the adroitneſs of the evolution, and an expeditious march, cleared the entrance, which, though even ground, is long, narrow, and winding, without oppoſition or annoyance.

The Engliſh, diſappointed by ſuch an unexpected manœuvre, repaired as quickly as poſſibie to Caveripatnam, where they did not think it expedient

pedient to ſtay, but reinforcing the garriſon with twelve hundred ſepoys, a few topaſſes belonging to the artillery, and thirty European cannoniers, poſted themſelves in a ſituation more convenient for receiving convoys from Madraſs, as well as a junction with the troops under the command of Colonel Wood, who then beſieged the fort of Ahtoore.

Hyder having paſſed the ſtraits, encamped about a league and an half from Caveripatnam, which was immediately inveſted by his cavalry. The town is ſurrounded by an antique wall and a rampart, with ſtrong ſtone towers. The Palier waſhes part of its walls; but this river, which is very broad, was not then above a foot deep. The inhabitants, terrified by the hoſtile appearance on the plains, immediately evacuated and ſet fire to the town. The Indian army, breaking looſe from all reſtraint, ruſhed to the plunder. The cannon from the fort made prodigious ſlaughter among the pillagers. Next morning the enemy opened a battery of twenty pieces, with a view to ſilence the garriſon, and which did much execution. But the Engliſh poured an inceſſrnt ſtorm of cannon and muſquetry from the baſtions, which killed an immenſe number of men, and would eertainly have diſlodged the battery, had they not been ſo much galled by multitudes of markſmen, who hid themſelves behind ſome ruins, that it was impoſſible to ſtand on the rampart. This deſtructive fire obliged the garriſon to hoiſt their flag. Hyder refuſed nothing that was demanded. The troops

 marched

marched out with the honours of war, and were permitted to direct their route for Madrass, without molestation.

The united army, shortly after this, encamping on the banks of the Palier, obliged General Smith to change his position. He moved towards a rising ground, that the enemy's cavalry might not have it in their power to harrass him with the same advantage. Hyder instantly ordered an attack. It was bravely sustained on both sides. The English army were but a handful to the infinite swarm of assailants who surrounded and invested them from all sides of the hill which they occupied. The enemy's infantry were supported by all Hyder's artillery, while ours, by the difficulty of pointing downwards, were less capable of a sure aim. The superior excellence of the British gunners sufficiently compensated for this disadvantage. The Europeans in the service of the enemy broke some of Mahommed Ally's troops, and took two pieces of artillery, but were suddenly repulsed by a few English, who recovered the cannon. Night only parted the combatants.

Hyder lost vast numbers in this battle. Nine hundred grenadiers, who were his best troops, were left in the field. The loss of the English was comparatively trivial, though they judged it expedient to decamp in the night. The enemy were afraid to pursue, notwithstanding the spirits they derived from this semblance of a retreat. They continued, however, to hover at a distance, nor once lost sight of the English army, which soon

reached

reached its destination in good order, till they had advanced and encamped within a league and an half of Trinomaly.

The two objects to which General Smith obviously directed all his manœuvres, were a junction with the army under Colonel Wood, which he expected every day; and a general engagement with the enemy, in such a situation as should in a great measure defeat the utility of their cavalry. Hyder either did not perceive the necessity of intercepting Wood, overlooked, or could not accomplish it. Both our armies, however, were soon united, and forthwith marched to take possession of a post, not more than two leagues from Trinomaly, still better adapted for tempting the enemy to attack them, and where their cavalry was not likely to be of more service. After several artful dispositions of his troops, General Smith brought on an engagement. The Nizam's army was thrown into disorder on the first onset, and fled with precipitation on all sides. Hyder led on his infantry with great firmness and order. His cannonade on our left was served with much regularity and dispatch. His battery was covered by a morass in front. The English, however, soon turned his left, by the advantage of some rising grounds, which brought them to a close engagement. The Indians supported their fire for some time with steadiness and alacrity, but the vigour, impetuosity and ardour of the English were not to be resisted by numbers. Hyder's personal bravery served him in little stead amidst a huge multitude in whom

whom terror and confusion only prevailed. He had now the mortification to perceive, notwithstanding all his attention to the discipline of his troops, that the superiority of the Company's continued still undiminished. A total defeat ensued. Some of the Nizam's artillery fell into the hands of the English, who also took a few prisoners.

During these operations, which happened about the end of September [1767] a detachment of Mysorean cavalry, under the command of Hyder's son, advanced with so much speed and secresy towards Madrass, that the governor, Mahommed Ally, his son, and Colonel Call, several other members of the council, being at breakfast in the country house at the Company's gardens, narrowly escaped falling into the enemy's hands. A domestic of a friend in Hyder's camp appeared but just time enough to announce the approach of Tippoo Saib. Their return to Madrass was cut off. The nabob of Arcot was obliged for his safety to the swiftness of his horse. The rest found refuge in a small vessel, which, fortunately for them, lay by accident opposite to the garden. This unexpected sally flung the whole place into immediate consternation and uproar. The black town, which contains upwards of four hundred thousand inhabitants, alarmed by the fugitives from the country, abandoned their houses and effects, and issued into the fort by multitudes. In an instant the streets, the ditches, and even the glacis, were covered with people. The governor, on his arrival, could with much difficulty force a passage to his house.

The

The place was at laſt ſaved by the exertions of Call the engineer. He armed all the Europeans who could be collected. He diſpatched a battalion of ſepoys to defend the entrance to the black town. The pillagers were conſequently deterred from their plunder, and an interval for deliberation was obtained. The conſultation was hardly finiſhed, when news arrived from General Smith, of the victory he had gained over the army of the ſubahs, at Trinomaly. This was announced to the people and the neighbourhood, from the fort, by one hundred and four guns. Tippoo Saib and his troops, alarmed for the ſafety of Hyder, having ravaged the environs of Madraſs, immediately returned to the army, where he was expected, not without anxiety for his ſituation, and where the exploits of this expedition were regarded as the certain preſages of the greateſt celebrity in future enterpriſe.

Partly to avoid the rainy ſeaſon which had already begun to ſet in, and which is always attended with the moſt fatal conſequences to Europeans, partly to recruit his men, who had ſuffered incredible fatigue, from the various hardſhips to which this campaign had reduced them, and partly to wait the approach of a reinforcement expected from Bengal, General Smith ſent his army into quarters. Having firſt ſtrongly garriſoned Trinomaly, Vaniambady, Ambour, and other advanced places, he diſtributed the remainder of his troops in Velore, Arcot, and ſome other ſtrong contiguous towns.

It

It was while Hyder encamped in a plain five leagues distant from Caveripatnam, that the subahs agreed that the two armies should separate, and that, while Hyder carried on the war against Mahommed Ally, the Nizam should attack the English on the side of Masulipatam, in order to divide their forces. These terms were adopted with apparent cordiality by men who regarded each other with the strongest antipathy. They were at the same time extremely lavish in their professions of mutual esteem, and the treachery which lurked in the hearts of both was laboriously concealed by an excess of luxury and splendour which they alternately displayed, as marks of reciprocal affection and respect.

Vaniambady was without loss of time surrounded by the Indian army. The place was soon found susceptible of being approached by favour of the water, hedges, and trees, without the necessity of opening trenches. The garrison consisted of near a thousand sepoys, and about twenty Europeans. Fourteen iron cannon, which were dismounted by those of the besiegers, composed all the artillery. The place, though well provided with ammunition and stores, though no breach had been yet effected, and though in that case there wanted not workmen to repair the carriages, was taken without much resistence. The only terms insisted upon by the enemy were, that the commander and the other European officers should not, for one year, serve against Hyder.

Hyder

Hyder went from this place ſtraight to Ambour. Here the Company had amaſſed vaſt quantities of ammunition and ſtores. At the foot of the citadel, which is ſituated on the ſummit of a ſteep inacceſſible mountain, is a fort ſtrengthened by the addition of a paliſaded covered way, and a glacis. The fort is at the ſame time incloſed by a town of conſiderable magnitude, defended by a brick wall, with round baſtions and a dry ditch. Half the place was covered by a large pond, at the end of which there was a redoubt, which cloſed the road between the pond and the river, and commanded that on the other ſide.

The town was in one quarter thought capable of being taken by ſtorm, without any breach. Orders were conſequently iſſued for carrying this point. The attack ſucceeded almoſt without reſiſtence. The garriſon had in fact placed their only dependance on the fort and citadel. The town, abandoned of its inhabitants, they foreſaw, by inviting the enemy to plunder, would expoſe them to the fire of as much cannon as they could bear againſt them. The manœuvre was judicious, and ſucceeded to ſuch a degree, that the number killed on the ſtreets and buried among the ruins was prodigious.

The enemy's attempt againſt the citadel and fort was not ſo fortunate. His batteries were no ſooner raiſed than demoliſhed. A great number of his braveſt men were daily ſacrificed to the temerity of this abortive ſiege. He planted cannon on a rock which overlooked the garriſon, who in two days erected ſuch a bulwark as rendered them perfectly

fectly uſeleſs. So that, after ſeventeen days ſevere exertion, the loſs of many Europeans, and the expenditure of much ammnnition, the work was ſtill no more advanced than at firſt. In this ſtate of affairs, news arrived that the Engliſh army was aſſembled at Velore, and marching to raiſe the ſiege. Hyder, without a moment's heſitation, embraced the reſolution of anticipating them, and retreated.

It was about this time that the Nizam had not only parted from Hyder, but renewed his agreement with the preſidency of Madraſs; that Colonel Wood was ſent, at the head of a conſiderable detachment, to reduce ſeveral of Hyder's forts in the vallies, and that it was reſolved General Smith ſhould carry the war into Hyder's dominions, and lay ſiege to Banguelore. The execution of this plan commenced as ſoon as the army were provided with neceſſaries.

A ſmall ſquadron ſailed at the ſame time from Bombay to attack Mangalore, one of Hyder's principal ſea-ports, ſituated in the center of Canaree, on the Malabar coaſt. In this road all his navy for the moſt part lay at anchor. The expedition ſucceeded [Feb. 25, 1768]. All the forts were taken with very little loſs, and the beſt of his ſhips captured. A garriſon was left to defend the town. Tippoo Saib, at the head of the beſt troops in Hyder's army, flew to the relief of the Canarines, who, conſidering him as their deliverer, flocked to his ſtandard, and putting themſelves under his command, retook the town, and made the garriſon priſoners. This, like all the other petty

petty exploits of this young warrior, was, by the parasites in his father's court, immediately magnified, and extoled as an instance of the greatest heroism.

Colonel Wood also took a great number of places. His operations were sometimes checked, but on the whole successful. In an action which was fought [October 4, 1768], he beat an army twenty-six thousand strong, with less than three thousand men, four hundred of which only were Europeans. Indeed the field was alternately lost and won several times, and the engagement which began at eleven o'clock in the forenoon, lasted till five in the afternoon. The enemy were at last obliged to retreat, leaving the field covered with their dead. Three elephants, nine camels, and seven hundred horses were killed on this occasion. We had some brave officers slain, several wounded, and a few taken prisoners, and we lost between two and three hundred men.

The glory of this day was soon and shockingly eclipsed, by the dreadful cruelty which attended our capture of Darampuri. All the garrison, the commander, his son, and every officer, were put to the sword, except twelve Europeans, who were saved by the English grenadiers. This bloody assault is even said to have been made while the white flag was on the breach. It was an outrage which the enemy were not backward to retaliate. For Moctum, Hyder's brother-in-law, shortly after, in cold blood, massacred a considerable body of our sepoys in the plains of Ovilore.

The

The forces under Colonel Wood having rejoined the army, General Smith, in his march to Banguelore, took ſeveral of the enemy's ſtrong holds. He conſtituted Ooſcotta his military magazine, which he fortified with great care. In a hoſtile country, full of faſtneſſes and narrow paſſes, and at the ſame time neceſſarily expoſed to the depredations of an active, intrepid and vigorous enemy, he ſoon found himſelf ſtraitened for proviſions. While he opened the trenches before Ballpour, Hyder inveſted the place where all his ſtores were depoſited. The General, to reſcue his magazine, abandoned the enterpriſe; and thus, without ſaving Ooſcotta, loſt the certain proſpect of an important acquiſition. For it was at this place he received orders to return with the army. Hyder, aware of the defenceleſs ſtate of our ſettlements, availed himſelf of the celerity which his cavalry were capable of exerting on particular emergencies, and in conſequence of ſeveral maſterly motions, got between our troops and the Carnatic, which he entered and ravaged at pleaſure. The Engliſh army inſtantly relinquiſhed all the footing they had obtained in his territories, and haſtened, by forced and fatiguing marches, to the defence of their own and their allies. Hyder, by this manœuvre, recovered without a blow all he had loſt. He was no longer a fugitive flying before his enemies, unable to ſuccour his own; but a vindictive and haughty victor pouring deſtruction on our dominions. His army, drooping and diminiſhing under the hardſhips of a defenſive war, which wants

the

the proper ſtimulus for ſuch troops as are only rouzed into courage and activity by their hopes of plunder, were now entered on a ſeries of operations perfectly adapted to their genius and habits. Under theſe fortunate circumſtances, his forces and allies naturally augmented with his reputation. Thus ſpreading ruin and devaſtation through the territories of Mahommed Ally, he not only gratified his perſonal reſentment to that prince, whom he deteſted for his inſidious connection with the Engliſh, but alſo flung all our inland ſettlements into confuſion and terror, adminiſtered to the malice with which our ſucceſs was regarded by thoſe whom our politics had oppreſſed, and cut off one of our principal reſources for carrying on the war.

His method of fighting was not leſs judicious than the route he had taken. The ſtrength of his army conſiſting of cavalry, he avoided, as much as poſſible, facing our troops, wherever his could not act with freedom. He declined, for this reaſon, with the ſame ſolicitude that General Smith urged a general engagement. His chief object was to attack our detached parties, and intercept our convoys. And in the ſame proportion that theſe ſallies weakened our forces, they neceſſarily ſtrengthened his, by additional numbers and ſpirits. Indeed, all that rendered him formidable was the ſagacity which diſtinguiſhed his operations, as we were never without an army greatly ſuperior to his in the field. And whatever injury he might do the revenues of the Company, he was incapable of otherwise endangering its security.

Hyder having advanced within seven leagues of Madras, the English army were prepared to dispute the passage of the river St. Thomas, when he suddenly disappeared, and while no intelligence could be obtained of his route, shewed himself at the gates on the other side of the town, and dispatched a flag of truce to know what proposition they had to make. The presidency had recently received the orders of the Company to make peace at any terms. It was currently believed that Hyder was entering into an alliance with the Marratos. For these reasons they thought it prudent to decline the contest. The enemy, notwithstanding their advantages, were equally inclined to peace. It was therefore, on the third of April, [1769,] mutually agreed, that both parties should defray their own expences, and the forts or places taken on either side be restored; that the respective prisoners should be released, and a free commercial intercourse allowed, both in the Carnatic and Hyder Ally's dominions; that Mahommed Ally should pay a tribute of six lacks of rupees, or seventy-five thousand pounds, of which the first year's revenue should be laid down; and that there should be a perpetual league, offensive and defensive, between the negociating powers, and a specific number of troops, in cases of emergency, provided by each.

Thus

Thus ended a war commenced without any ſolid principle of policy or diſcretion, conducted throughout by illiberal meaſures, and involving, both in its progreſs and termination, conſequences peculiarly inauſpicious to the general intereſts of the Company.

It appears that the preſidency, in adopting the reſolution of provoking Hyder Ally to hoſtilities, paid but little attention either to the ſtate of their own finances, their military ſtrength, the reſources of the enemy, the dangerous ſituation of their ally's dominions, or the advantages of their employers. They knew that the treaſury of Madras was abſolutely inadequate to the vaſt expenditure which theſe operations would neceſſarily occaſion, and that even the revenues of Bengal, after paying the intereſt of the Company's debt, and its own civil and military eſtabliſhment, could ſpare but little to aſſiſt or relieve them. It was obvious their own territories would be expoſed to depredation, while their troops were occupied on a diſtant ſervice, and that the nabob would be leſs able to ſupport them, as he ſuffered from the enemy. The country, in which Hyder could always ſecure a retreat, notwithſtanding our ſuperiority, was not ſuſceptible of an eaſy reduction. So that from every impartial view of their conduct, it ſeems to have originated chiefly in an empty deſire of aggrandiſement at beſt, or more probably in the apprehenſion that thoſe princes whoſe dominions were moſt expoſed to the depredatory excurſions of the army, might increaſe their private fortunes, by ſecretly purchasing an exemption from the members of the council.

To whatever causes the war may be attributed, the mode of carrying it on admits of no apology. The army was in perpetual want of necessaries, and such as they obtained were not always of the best kind. Their movements were constantly retarded for want of oxen to transport their artillery, which alone could protect them from the sudden attacks of the enemy's cavalry. The general was at the same time deprived of all discretionary power, by the presence of a special delegation, whom the presidency appointed to attend the army, and superintend the campaign. The only man of sound abilities in this committee was Colonel Call, whose opinion, in emergencies of the greatest delicacy and consequence, was habitually over-ruled by the ignorance, timidity, and avarice of his colleagues. This office, unknown in the English service, and pernicious wherever it has been adopted, seems created, on the present occasion, merely for the emolument of those employed, who, deeply concerned in the contracts for supplying the troops, regulated their motions in such a manner as best suited their own convenience and interest. The army felt the bad effects of such an ill-advised measure in all its departments. Brave and experienced officers were disgusted. Some of them quitted the service; others, whose circumstances in such a situation, and at so great a distance from home, did not permit them to act so decisive a part, found the duty irksome, and relaxed their exertions.

And

And not a few, without either character, recommendation, or interest, were employed, advanced, and entrusted. The war was consequently marked with a stigma which had never before disgraced the military honour of the nation; British officers deserting the cause of their country for the service of an inveterate enemy, and forts given up in such a manner as to have an appearance rather of treachery than cowardice.

It was not easy to foresee or demonstrate any possible advantage that could result to the Company from this war. But those only who urged the measure, that the property of their masters might be absorbed in lucrative jobs to them or their friends, could remain blind to its consequences. The council of Madras seem to have been dazzled with the chimerical expectations of realizing, like their fellow-servants in Bengal, an immense territorial revenue. Their general dispatches to the Court of Directors about this period, exhibited these delusive prospects in colours peculiarly brilliant and interesting. They promised no less than to invest their masters with the sovereignty of all the Corromandel coast, and that of Malabar, from Cape Rama to Cape Comorin. This profound and prosperous policy was immediately rendered subservient to pecuniary intrigue. The nation, accustomed to the marvellous adventures of the East, easily became the dupe of its own credulity, and eagerly anticipated more prosperity than it was reasonable to expect. This temporary delirium was not without its effect. India stock rose with rapidity, from the general desire that prevailed to share in the success of the present measures. The report of our victory at Trinomaly corroborated these flattering hopes, by promising to facilitate their accomplishment. In this moment of intemperate joy, from the presumption of a felicity barely possible, the capture of Madras by the son of Hyder Ally, a youth of eighteen, was announced. The revolution in the public mind, from extacy to despair, was instant and universal. The news, because disliked by all, was doubted by many, and anxiously disputed by more. The great body of the people, however, were so much alarmed and chagrined by their disappointment, that India stock was reduced, fell above sixty per cent. in a few days, and was soon expected to fall still lower. Not all the efforts of the Directors could give but a momentary check to this general torrent of despondency. In vain they produced their official dispatches, or asserted that the Company, instead of being in danger, was never in a more flourishing condition. That only which was most dreaded received the greatest credit. A suspicion of the worst was now the epidemical disorder, which time and patience alone could remove. The more the subject was understood, the livelier were people's resentments excited against those who had thus wantonly deceived them. The conduct of the Company's servants, especially in Madrass, was canvassed with freedom, and arraigned with severity. Facts were investigated and proved, which, it was said, exposed them not only to censure, but

to

to punifhment. And the failure of the war was roundly imputed to their iniquitous contracts, monopolies, and extra-appointments. It was found that large remittances had been made from Bengal, to fupply the deficiency of revenue in Madras. Thefe were of a bafe kind of gold coin, by which the Company were fuppofed to have fuftained, in mere exchange, the lofs of forty thoufand pounds. The inveftments ufually made from Madras to China, were confequently fufpended, no filver circulating in the country, and all the various manufactures at a ftand, from the fear of the enemy. The bufinefs of the fubordinate factories was equally obnoxious to injury and interruption from the fame caufe. The tributary polygars, efpecially of Mahommed Ally, were dilatory in their payments, and refolved their backwardnefs into that want of protection which left their property a prey to robbery and devaftation. Thus every pecuniary refource of the Company was affected by this expenfive and pernicious war. Their martial reputation, from the prudence and gallantry of their officers, had fuffered nothing in the eyes of Hyder, who had feen and felt their fuperiority in fo many inftances. But our troops were no longer confidered as invincible by the country at large. It was on this account adopted as a common opinion, that number, unanimity, bravery, difcipline, and conduct, had nearly the fame effect on Europeans and Indians. This war did more. It inculcated in the princes of Indoftan, the neceffity, the importance, and the practicability of a general confederacy, and oppoſed to thoſe hereditary feuds, which in all affairs of commerce and government had given ſuch an aſcendancy to foreigners, this ſoundeſt of all political maxims, that among no people on earth can there be any confidence without fidelity, or any ſafety without union.

The affairs of the Company, as well from their own magnitude as from their inſeparable connection with the proſperity of the whole empire, were now an object of conſtant and general conſideration. The national credit and intereſt were deeply involved with theirs. Some effectual meaſures were therefore deemed requiſite, to put a ſtop to ſuch abuſes and miſmanagement as had ſo foully diſgraced the Britiſh name, both in India and Europe, and which had been attended with effects injurious at once to the Company and community.

With this view a plan was brought forward for inveſting three perſons of competent experience in the conſtitution and buſineſs of the Company, as well as in the nature of Indian politics and connections; with extraordinary powers, and who ſhould be ſent to that country, under full authority, to examine and rectify the concerns of every department. Mr. Vanſittart, Mr. Scrafton, and Colonel Ford, all of whom had formerly ſerved with reputation, the two former in a civil, and the latter in a military capacity, were accordingly appointed to this ſervice, with an abſolute controul over all the Company's ſervants in that part of the world.

This

This appointment, as might be expected, occasioned much warm altercation, and the most exquisite intrigue, especially on their side whose friends accepted ostensible situations in India.—They opposed the measure as nugatory, reprobated the principles of the institution as insidious and fallacious, and branded the powers thus created, as originating in a mean suspicion of their fidelity, in whom, by the constitution of the Company, their confidence was placed. Others, startled at the magnitude of the trust, and the delicacy of the commission. Every inch of the ground was disputed, new objections were constantly raised, and notwithstanding several general courts had assembled and canvassed the merits of the measure, no decision could take place without a ballot.—This was no sooner obtained, and the commission for giving effect to the resolution, than a new delay was occasioned by a requisition from the minister, that the Company should give to a servant of the crown a principal share in the direction of their affairs.

The Directors, during these debates, had applied for two ships of the line and some frigates, as their appearance in the Indian seas tended to facilitate the intercourse of their servants with the native princes. Government gave them no answer, but it was known that a squadron, under the command of Sir John Lindsay, was destined to sail for that part of the world. In order, however, to be certain of a matter thus important to the interest of the Company, the sanction of a general court, it

was

was presumed, would render a similar application so respectable, that ministry would be under the necessity of making some reply. At a meeting, therefore, of the proprietors [July 27], a motion to this purpose was unanimously adopted, and another court appointed to receive the message of government.

At this court, which was held about a fortnight after, a letter was received from Lord Weymouth, one of his Majesty's secretaries of state, signifying that the measure adopted by the Company, had, in the opinion of ministry, been deemed illegal; that he was sorry to find, by their answer, that they had not acceded to the appointment of a naval officer, with full powers to adjust all maritime affairs in India. He now begged they would reconsider the commission in general, and that the particular article of granting unlimited powers to a naval officer might be laid before the proprietary at large.

This extraordinary demand produced an elaborate correspondence between the ministry and Directors. A subject altogether new, and involving questions of the greatest commercial and constitutional importance, was laid before the proprietors. It there appeared, that the authority required by this ministerial mandate, went in fact to superintend the supervisors, as well as all the Company's concerns. The Direction owned a readiness to allow the naval officer a certain participation of influence in their councils abroad, but declined acquiescing in the request at large, both because they thought the trust too great for one person, and because it would

would afford government a perpetual pretext for interfering in the management of the Company's affairs. They ſtated at the ſame time, that the commiſſion had undergone the reviſion of council, and its legality was confirmed by the opinion of the moſt reputable lawyers in the kingdom.

At another court, held by adjournment to a ſhort day, a ſecond letter, which had been received that morning, was alſo read from the ſame miniſter. He ſtated, that by their anſwer the Directors had not properly underſtood him. He meant not to inveſt a naval officer with plenipotentiary powers at large, but only wiſhed him to poſſeſs ſuch a ſhare in the buſineſs of adminiſtration as would at once promote the intereſt of the Company and the honour of government. He begged the proprietary to conſider both the commiſſion and that degree of authority which the ſervant of the crown ought to poſſeſs. He declined giving any opinion on the firſt of theſe; but as government, at the requeſt of the Company, in the eleventh article of the laſt definitive treaty of peace with France, made conditions with ſeveral Indian princes, it highly concerned their honour that an officer of their appointment ſhould be principal agent in all matters offenſive and defenſive.

The deſign of the miniſter was now obvious, and a conſiderable time was occupied in giving due conſideration to the ſubject. It occaſioned at the next general court [Auguſt 30.] a very tedious and warm debate. But, after much argumentation on both ſides, and not a little violence, the matter was

was at length refted on this general queftion, which was to be decided by ballot:—That this court will give the officer of the crown, commanding fhips of the line, a fhare in the deliberations and refolutions of the Company, merely with regard to the two objects of making peace and declaring war, where his Majefty's forces are employed? It was rejected accordingly by a great majority.

The commiffion for the naval commander in chief was in the mean time made out; but as the requifition of extraordinary power had not been granted, his operations were limited to the Gulph of Perfia, where the Company's affairs had for fome time been greatly incommoded by the troubles which embroiled the natives. A fort of compromife thus took place. The power of making peace and war was allowed by the Directors to the naval commander only in the Gulph of Perfia, and the demand for fhips of the line to the Bay of Bengal was fufpended. Two frigates, however, were ordered for that fervice, and at the fame time appointed to convey the fupervifors, whofe powers were at length finally adjufted, and an end put to their tedious conteft.

The Company's agreement with government, and the reftraining bill, being nearly expired, it was deemed expedient to lay before miniftry fuch propofals as were likely to become the bafis of a new bargain. The object of the Directors was to obtain, if poffible, more equitable terms, and a permanent fettlement of the Company's affairs. They were folicitous to realize fome return

turn or compenſation for the great ſum of money which they annually paid to government. A prolongation of their charter for five years was required, and conſidered as a moderate equivalent.— This, however, was abſolutely refuſed. Extorting money from the Company was clearly a part of the miniſterial ſyſtem. Their interference in reſtricting their dividend, demonſtrated that the Company were in the hands of a power which they could not reſiſt. It was too late to inſiſt on conditions. The controul was eſtabliſhed, and might be expected to operate. Even the ſmalleſt relaxation in the reſtrictive power began to be conſidered as a favour, rather than acknowledged as a compenſation.

Thus circumſtanced, after a long train of negociation and conſultation with ſeveral general courts, an agreement was concluded, and a bill brought into parliament grounded on the following principles. That the Company ſhould pay to the public, for five years to come, the annual ſum of four hundred thouſand pounds: That, in that time, they might increaſe their dividends to twelve and a half per cent. the increaſe not to exceed one per cent. in any one year: That if the Company, from any cauſe or emergency, during that term, were under the neceſſity of reducing their dividends, an equal ſum ſhould be deducted from the annual payment made to government; but in caſe their dividends were reduced to ſix per cent. the payment to the public was to be diſcontinued:

That,

That, during these five years, the Company should export British goods equal in value, upon an average, with those exported for an equal number of years past; and that, if any surplus of the Company's cash remained in England, after payment of certain specified debts, it should be lent to the public at an interest of two per cent.

CHAP.

CHAPTER V.

Effects of the various Revolutions which took place in the Provinces of Bengal—Oppressions of Mahommed Reza Cawn—A dreadful famine—Mr. Hastings—His Regulations—His Intrigues with the Country Princes—Sujah ul Dowlah—Shaw Allum, or the Great Mogul—The Rohilla War.

AN entire change in the arrangement of the political establishment was the necessary and immediate consequence of our accession to the Dewannee of Bengal. It produced a revolution which convulsed the state to its extremities, and which, under a series of singular occurrences, gave existence to such a variety of new circumstances, as mark our subsequent transactions in that unfortunate country with a novelty and infamy, which are without a parallel in the history of the species.

From that moment the government assumed a new shape. All the branches of the executive power were transferred from natives to the conquerors. Every official department, every situation of dignity and emolument, every post of confidence, exertion and responsability was seized and occupied by the English. The influence of the subah was substantially annihilated. He was virtually restrained by his new situation from exercising a single act of independent sovereignty. He could

could neither make war nor peace, appoint his own miniſters, controul his own troops, manage his own revenues, or ſuperintend the adminiſtration of juſtice over his own ſubjects. The ſemblance of authority which he poſſeſſed was literally a purchaſe from the Company. They uſurped the very ſettlement of his houſehold; they reſtricted his expenditure to certain limitations; they rendered him a captive in his own palace; they crouded his court with their creatures; they bribed his very domeſtics to betray him; and they conſtituted every wretch in his train a ſpy on his private as well as his public conduct.

To the Dutch, the Danes, and other Europeans, who applied to the preſidency of Calcutta as the ruling power, for the grant of indulgence, or the redreſs of grievances, they conſtantly aſſumed the prerogative, while they artfully eluded the direct avowal of that high character, by yielding or refuſing protection under the name of influence. Equally careful to avoid diſclaiming their own ſupremacy, or roundly aſſerting that of another, their ſovereignty was daily and palpably ſubſtantiated by every part of their conduct. Nor could all the ſubtlety of political ſophiſtry conceal the reality and exertions of an authority which operated openly, univerſally, and irreſiſtibly. Their policy under theſe circumſtances, was a ſilent acquieſcence in the opinion of ſuch as treated the Company as principals, but to ſuffer that conviction to acquire maturity and vigour among the natives, rather from the general tenor of their actions, than from

from any ſtrenuous and poſitive aſſertion of their right.

The principles, the meaſures, the objects, and alliances of government, were conſequently no longer the ſame. While the native omrahs were in authority, notwithſtanding their general depravity of manners, it was but a few of the worſt who dared to introduce any innovations in tyranny. The deſpotiſm which then prevailed throughout the empire, was one eſtabliſhed, invariable, well-known ſyſtem, founded in maxims originating in the habits of the people, ſanctioned by a religion adapted to the circumſtances of the country, and tranſmitted, without any material alteration, through a long ſucceſſion of ages. The higher ranks only were obnoxious, from their wealth or their influence, to the jealouſy or oppreſſion of ſuperiors. The laborious peaſants, mechanics, or manufacturers, were in general exempted from the intrigues, the altercations, and the quarrels of their reſpective maſters, and often followed their humble occupations without moleſtation, while the chieftains around them were deeply engaged in the deadlieſt feuds. And it was no uncommon ſpectacle, in theſe periods of oriental ſimplicity, to ſee the farmer ploughing in one field, while the battle raged in another. The value of political inſtitutions can be eſtimated only by that degree of general proſperity, and internal peace, which they are calculated to confer, eſtabliſh, or protect. To theſe primary and eſſential objects of all good government, the numerous innovations which diſcriminated the British power in Bengal, had no reference. The miserable natives were defended against foreign invasion or depredation, merely for the purpose of securing to the servants of the Company a monopoly in the trade of domestic cruelty and oppression. Intoxicated by the elevated situation to which they were raised, the violent measures they pursued, like diseases which prey on the vitals, were at first attended with symptoms of approaching dissolution. By obtruding on their new dominions various disorders, under the pretext of necessary reform, they violated the venerable forms of antiquity, and superseded establishments and usages which, from time immemorial, the Hindoos had been accustomed to treat with respect. And thus a government took place, calculated in the first instance to promote extortion and rapacity, and in the object and operation of which, the character and happiness of the people at large had no share.

Of this extraordinary system no other account can be given, than that it originated in the mere contingency of mercantile enterprise. Nothing similar, at least, can be found in the inventions or speculations of ancient or modern times, among Gothic or civilized nations. It was a species of absolute delegation, in which the constituent body reserved no authority which could operate as a check on the usurpation or abuses of their representatives. It was radically and essentially defective, as without a faculty of legislation, and without interest in the consequences, it not only possessed, but united the

toms levied on almoſt every article of life, and ſubject to infinite variation, from farms of excluſive privileges, or which have annexed to them certain monopolies; and from fines or forfeitures impoſed on the natives for every ſpecies of miſdemeanor, and by every Banyan in the employ of the Engliſh. The aggregate ſum accumulated by the united produce of theſe reſources muſt be immenſe. Under a government abſolutely military, among a people whoſe chief characteriſtics are ſimplicity, timidity, and ſuperſtition, and where there was no law to guard the helpleſs, or awe the tyrannical, it is eaſy to conceive what dreadful implements of oppreſſion theſe ſeveral branches of finance would become. It was the intereſt of thoſe who hired the ground of the Company only for a year, to reduce the price of labour as much as poſſible, and without regarding futurity, command the greateſt produce in their power. The inevitable conſequence was imperceptible; ruin to the ſoil, the ryot, the zimindar, and the revenue. The demands of thoſe who collected the duties were in every diſtrict and village enforced by parties of armed men. Indeed, whoever had any ſhare in that great chain of dependence and ſubordination, which the Company had inſtituted in this new empire, conſidered himſelf as entitled to the privilege of mal-treating the wretched inhabitants, in proportion to his ſituation in the ſervice. Of the infinite contributions raiſed in theſe devoted provinces, the ſhare brought to the Company's account was, however, but trivial; though in the general tenor of their orders, they have usually shewn more anxiety to swell their revenues than to benefit the public. These are the emphatic words of one of their servants to another *.—" By the " established mode of collection, the agreement is " never observed between the collector and the " tenant. At the end of the year, whenever the " former knows that the latter has made any gain, " he surely seizes it, notwithstanding the agree- " ment being justly paid. By these means all in- " dustry is checked, and all confidence destroyed; " and neither labourer, farmer, collector, and so " upwards to the foujedare, having any trust in " each other, it has made the whole a chain of " rogues and plunderers."

Mahommed Reza, the ostensible minister of finance, studied the character of his masters. He knew the influence of money. Possessed of talents for business, an accurate discernment of men in active life, and a genius for all the refinement and obliquities of the deepest intrigue, his situation gave him the command of treasures, and he applied them with dexterity, in accomplishing at once his interest and ambition. His address in conciliating friendships was irresistible. In pensions and presents among his dependents and abettors, his annual disbursements amounted to nearly half a million sterling. The place of the Company's resident at the court of the subah, was equal, at least,

* Mr. G. G. Ducarell to Richard Beacher, Esq. August, 1769.

to

to one hundred and fifty thousand pounds a-year. The extortions which these immense levies occasioned, subjected the miserable inhabitants to a series of the most wanton cruelties. The emissaries of tyranny and exaction, assisted by select parties of military, suddenly overspread and ravaged the country far and near. In vain did the weaver, the tiller of ground, the handicraft, and the petty trader, accuse their oppressors, or demand a redress of their wrongs, whilst the intimate friends of the aggressors, or the aggressors themselves, presided in every court to which they could apply. They appealed to British justice, but were instantly remanded back to the tribunals of the natives, where the judge was not only a party in the cause, but highly incensed against them, for daring to betray a suspicion of his integrity, by lodging their complaints before his superiors. The men who presided in these prostituted courts, were the summary executioners of the partial and arbitrary mandates of a monster, whose unbounded avarice, not only steeled his heart against every accession of humanity, but at once tempted and enabled him to bribe the indulgence and connivance of his employers, that he might thus riot in the catastrophe of his country. History, averse to record the barbarities which marked his depredations on the cottages of the poor, could wish, for the honour of the species, to consign them, with their author, to oblivion. The whole executive power being entrusted with him, for substantiating the pecuniary expectations of the Company, plunder became the principal object of his attention. The farmers had no interest in their farms above a year. That period comprehended all their cultivation and exertion. The rents were unavoidably raised to anticipate the eager demands of avarice. The wretched inhabitants submitted with unconquerable patience to every species of indignity and outrage, rather than relinquish their household gods, or the cots which their ancestors occupied. Every year they became the property of new masters. Their oppressions only were not changed, because they could not be increased. These petty tyrants were, in their turn, reduced to participate in the sufferings of their laws, and felt, themselves, an excess of that rigour which they had so often inflicted. Many were daily and openly tied and scourged like felons, at a stake. The streets and squares of Moorshedabad resounded with their clamours. Not a few expired in agonies under the lash. Others, driven to despair, abandoned the country, in quest of that lenity abroad which they could no longer enjoy at home. Those who survived the rod of oppression and remained, were deprived of their all, and vast tracts of the most fertile land in the world instantly became waste. It was at the same time strenuously urged, that the revenues of the Company ought to suffer no diminution, notwithstanding the increasing poverty and depopulation of the country.

The system of commerce and regulation established by the select committee, under the government of Lord Clive, united the Company's servants,

vants, and all their various creatures in the country districts, in one black, bloody, and indissoluble association against the inhabitants. Their agents for managing the inland trade repaired without delay to their respective situations. The deputies of merchants, who were soldiers and conquerors at the same time, seized, at one stroke, on all the necessaries of life. This daring and mischievous monopoly, gave them an immediate and full command of the natives, who were without remedy or appeal, as the same set of men who formed the plan, and carried it into execution, were sovereigns of the country. Salt, beetle-nut, and tobacco, were dealt out for money in the first instance, afterwards for goods, and then for almost every species of property which could be realized. The cruelties exerted in extorting the investments from the manufacturers, were so exquisite and intolerable, especially among those in the silk business, that individuals have been known to cut off their thumbs, and otherwise mangle and mutilate themselves, that they might not be compelled to a species of labour which exposed them to so much inconvenience and distress.

The government of Bengal had now to furnish a tribute to the king, a salary to the nabob, and a revenue to the company. The taxes of every kind were, therefore, demanded by the agents of the treasury with more than usual eagerness. The nabob, unable to yield protection to his hapless subjects, was, notwithstanding, importuned from morning till night with their numerous complaints.

Those

Thoſe only who poſſeſſed the power to reſtrain, connived at oppreſſion. The projectors of theſe violent meaſures were ſatisfied that the evil did not exiſt among them, and winked at the crimes of petty offenders, that their reſentment might fall the heavier on more elevated and exemplary delinquents. And the ruthleſs pillager of villages and farms, either purchaſed his impunity by dividing the ſpoil with his ſuperiors, or fell a victim to the power he abuſed, and was himſelf plundered, with as little mercy as he had ſhewn to others. The ſervants of the Company ſet out upon the plan of accumulating fortunes only by proxy; but no ſooner was it apparent that oppreſſion had nothing to fear from juſtice, than they acted without diſguiſe, and became open oſtenſible principals in violence and rapacity.

One of the moſt powerful principles to the operation of which we owe our proſperity in that unfortunate country, was, the good opinion generally entertained by the natives of the fairneſs and impartiality of our laws. They naturally contraſted the privileges of Engliſhmen, under a free conſtitution, with their own hereditary vaſſalage and dependence. They heard, with admiration and applauſe, that the Britiſh government protected every individual in all his perſonal and relative rights; that neither the prince, his nobles, or his ſoldiers of any denomination whatever, could wreſt any part of his property from him; that men in all caſes were judged by their equals; and that the rank of the aggreſſor, inſtead of entitling him to exemption, only

only raiſed him to exemplary puniſhment. Theſe impreſſions diſpoſed great numbers of the natives to favour, and in many inſtances to facilitate our territorial acquiſitions. With hopes of changing for the better, they rejoiced at our proſperity, and imagined the introduction of our laws and cuſtoms would certainly follow our power. They were ſoon, however, and fatally undeceived. The moment we got poſſeſſion of the government, orders were iſſued that leaſes and civil contracts were all to be made void on a day; that a few perſons only, known to be generals in the army, impoſed duties on neceſſaries, to one third of their value; and that their new maſters had taken things of daily uſe into their own hands, to ſell as they pleaſed.

But what reſources were adequate to the avidity of avarice. The certainty, the eaſe, and the rapidity of making fortunes, are all objects of ſeparate conſideration with adventurers. The ſervants of the Company, anxious to return in ſplendour to their native country, deemed all theſe modes of enriching themſelves tedious and unſatisfactory. The numerous monopolies eſtabliſhed in their favour were ſtill diſproportionate to their expectations. Their next expedient was therefore to collect the rice into ſtores or magazines. Aware that the Gentoos would rather die than violate the precepts of their religion by eating fleſh, they were ſure of receiving what price they pleaſed for a commodity thus eſſential to exiſtence. The inhabitants ſaw the ſituation to which they were reduced with grief and horror. Farmers finding their

crops

crops at the diſpoſal of others, cultivated their farms with indifference. This produced ſcarcity, and circumſcribed the monopoly. The people lived on roots, and food to which they had not been accuſtomed. Sickneſs and epidemical complaints of various kinds every where prevailed, and converted the whole country into one prodigious hoſpital. Proviſions increaſed in value in proportion as they diminiſhed in quantity. The laborious poor, whoſe circumſtances are always ſufficiently hard, were the firſt whoſe ſituation expoſed them to theſe accumulated diſtreſſes. Many died before any ſuſtenance could be obtained or adminiſtered. And in ſome diſtricts the living were ſo debilitated by diſeaſe and want, that the dead were even ſuffered to remain unburied.

All this, however, was but the beginning of miſery. The wretched inhabitants of Bengal ſeem only to have ſurvived the ſcourge of deſpotiſm, that the wrath of heaven might ſweep them to deſtruction in multitudes. Such is the fertility of the ſoil, and ſo genial the climate of this country, that every year is bleſſed with two crops. Their little harveſt, which conſiſts of ſmall grain, happens in April; and their great one, conſiſting ſolely of rice, happens in October. Theſe different productions are owing to the rains, which generally commence in Auguſt, and continue nearly three months. By a ſtrong drought, which exhauſted the fields of moiſture, and converted the moſt irriguous plains into ſandy deſerts, there was a failure in the great harveſt of 1769, and in the little

one

one of 1770. And ſo general and extenſive was this failure, that notwithſtanding a very conſiderable growth of rice on the higher grounds, the aggregate produce was by no means adequate to the conſumption of the natives.

Famine was no uncommon calamity in this improvident country; but the ſavage ſpirit of monopoly co-operating with the hoſtile elements, occaſioned ſuch ſcenes of exquiſite anxiety and horror as were even new to Indians. In every age and nation there are individuals atrocious enough to improve the public ruin to their own emolument. It was unfortunately not the lot of Bengal to be under the direction of men at that time diſtinguiſhed by their humanity. The ſeaſon prognoſticated an approaching dearth, and the agents of the preſidency, in their ſubordinate factories, ſuperintending the cuſtoms or managing the provincial revenues, were, in conſequence of their reſpective ſituations, as early and aſſiduous as poſſible in the purchaſe of rice. The profits in this odious and flagitious traffic were ſo enormous and immediate, that a gentleman ſtationed at the court of the nabob, who before this memorable period was known to be utterly without property, inſtantly after the famine, is ſaid to have tranſmitted about ſixty thouſand pounds to Europe.

The black merchants depoſited all the rice they could buy from the Engliſh in the granaries about Calcutta, where it was parcelled out to the inhabitants in the ſmalleſt quantities, and where, in conſequence of a dreadful fire which happened in the months

months of April and May, most of it was destroyed. This fresh calamity was a new advantage to the monopoly, as the value of what remained was by that means considerably enhanced. Complaints the most respectful, the most submissive, and at the same time the most affecting and urgent, were daily reiterated at the Durbar and the Presidency.—But the interest of the aggressors was too powerful, both in the one and the other, to be shaken by the feeble voice of suffering innocence. The nabob had no influence but what was derived from the board, and the board, wherever a contest took place between their emissaries and the natives, were biassed by a thousand considerations to give judgement without any regard to humanity or impartiality.

While many of the English beheld with admiration and sorrow the relentless sufferings of the patient Indians, the council at Calcutta were rouzed from their indolence by the critical situation into which these melancholy circumstances had plunged them. They sent into all the various districts under their government, to purchase whatever rice could be found on the Company's account, and even seized the cargoes on the river. This they publickly retailed, at the rate of between fifteen and twenty pounds for a rupee. Their principal attention, however, was to the preservation of their own workmen at the fortifications, which were then constructing. And it was not without some difficulty that the bazers or markets were furnished with a few maunds, or quantities

which

which meaſure about eighty pounds, to anſwer in part the urgent demands of the inhabitants. The nabob and ſeveral omrahs about his court, as well as other wealthy families in Moorſhedabad, diſplayed the moſt humane and princely munificence, by diſtributing rice to the needy gratis, until their reſpective granaries were exhauſted.

No ſooner were theſe liberal reſources at an end than the natives poured down upon Calcutta in prodigious and reſiſtleſs multitudes. The ſtreets were inſtantaneouſly covered and incommoded, and all the lanes and avenues which lead to the palaces of the wealthy glutted by ſwarms of famiſhed Indians, who, writhing in the agonies of want and deſpair, imputed all their miſeries to avarice, and imprecated with their laſt breath a deluge of curſes on the heads of their murderers!

In vain were the doors of the rich and powerful barricadoed and protected againſt the ſhocking unceremonious intruſion of ſtarving men, by guards of armed ſipoys. The powerful requiſitions of nature put an end, for the preſent, to all the exterior forms of decency. Every new ſpace was explored, poſſeſſed, and defended, with an anxiety proportionate to the hopes of life, or alleviation which it afforded. And wretches grappling with hunger and diſeaſe, and even calling upon death for that relief which no other power would beſtow, were not to be intimidated by the ſpear or the bayonet.

All over the city, and in the adjacent villages and plains, promiſcuous crouds bending double, with

with their ſtomachs contracted to their back-bones, were ſeen fainting and ſtruggling under a preſſure of intolerable anguiſh, quietly relinquiſhing a life thus imbittered by ſorrow, ſupplicating every paſſenger to have mercy upon them, lifting up their ſad and languiſhing eyes to Heaven in deſpondency, exerting their laſt remains of ſtrength, in ſoothing whom they were not able to ſave, or exhibiting all the various expreſſions of human paſſion, in a condition the moſt afflicting that can be conceived. The whole country ecchoed with the groans, and teemed with the ſpectres of thoſe who were ready to die. The cottages, the villages, and even many of the market and manufacturing towns, unable to ſuſtain their inhabitants, were deſerted and made deſolate. Famine drove them from their homes in ſhoals, like ſheep to the ſlaughter. The fields, the roads, and all places of public intercourſe, preſented the eye with nothing but groups of theſe forlorn creatures, pale, meagre, emaciated, and ghaſtly. Some abſolutely worn out with want and fatigue, here and there dropt down, and ſtretched themſelves at full length, in expectation of immediate diſſolution. Others ſcarce able to drag their bodies from place to place, were yet wandering up and down in a ſtate of mournful ſtupidity, regardleſs where they went or what they endured.

It is hard to ſay, whether that earneſt and painful anxiety with which the young and the active ſcrambled for the boon preſented by the hand of humanity, or that wiſtful look which accompanied the

the disappointment of the aged and the impotent, were most affecting. Multitudes flocked around every white man who approached them, and notwithstanding their timid minds and meek manners, in piteous or frantic accents implored his sympathy or urged his assistance. In these disastrous circumstances, and among the far greater number, all relative duties were for the time suspended. Individuals, chiefly engrossed by their own wants, were utterly incapable of attention to those of others. Children deserted their parents, and even mothers their infants, who were observed in great numbers expiring on the breast; while many, who survived the authors of their beings, still clung with deadly eagerness to those clay-cold bosoms which formerly afforded them warmth and nourishment.

There was not a corner in the city, or any lurking-place in the vicinity of Calcutta, where the living, the dying, and the dead, were not mingled or heaped together in melancholy confusion. It was impossible to stir abroad on business or recreation, where these offensive and mortifying associations were not in the way. The daily employment of hundreds was to remove the dead in proportion as they became a nuisance to the living. These in cart-loads, and without any funeral or religious obsequies, were promiscuously plunged into the river.

By this increasing and prodigious mortality, notwithstanding the most constant attentions to decency and cleanliness, the town and suburbs were so much infested, that, from the raging heat of the weather, the foul congregation of vapours which inceſſantly aſcended from the unburied dead, and the torid or intemperate ſtate of the atmoſphere, a peſtilential influenza was generally and ſeriouſly apprehended. Fortunately an extraordinary flock of carnivorous birds, animals, and vermin, were allured from their faſtneſſes and their ſolitudes by the putrefaction of the ſcene. The water of the Ganges become lothſome and corrupt from the loads of dead bodies which it daily received. Pork, geeſe, ducks, and every ſpecies of proviſion, fattened by ſubſtances thus groſs and abhorrent, were avoided as poiſonous. The fiſh in the river were noxious, and even ſometimes fatal to thoſe who eat them. Mutton, which could hardly be obtained at any price, became the only food which could be enjoyed with ſafety or ſatisfaction.

Diſeaſes every where broke out, and multiplied in proportion to the violence with which the famine raged. Many whom plenty exempted from the exquiſite pangs of want, natives as well as foreigners, unable to ſupport their ſpirits under the increaſing preſſure occaſioned by ſuch an awful coincidence of afflicting circumſtances, were literally the martyrs of their own apprehenſions. No language can ſufficiently exhibit the ſudden and univerſal deſtruction produced by the ravages of theſe calamities. It was as if England, in the courſe of a few weeks, ſhould loſe one half of her inhabitants. Above three millions of people are ſaid to have then periſhed for want of ſuſtenance!

This

This famine is an epoch in the history of Bengal which shall perpetuate, while the world lasts, the sinister genius of mercantile policy, and record, beyond the ravages of time, to what a shocking excess the outrages of avarice have been extended against all that is most sacred and inviolable in the rights of humanity! What must be the feelings of those monsters in whose sordid adventure this memorable catastrophe originated? Who would purchase even the Indies at the shocking expence of being thus haunted through life, by the ghosts of murdered millions!

It might have been expected that government, to alleviate the consequences of so general a misfortune, would have adopted, with a promptitude suited to the occasion, some strong and spirited measures; that those whose speculations had contributed to enhance the price or diminish the quantity of provisions, would have been called to a strict account; that an immediate stop would have been put to the prodigious and avowed exports of private dealers; that the destination of the Company's ships would have been changed, and the neighbouring seas traversed in search of sustenance; and that earnest application would have been made to all the countries in India for whatever supplies could have been procured under the pressure of so public an exigence. But instead of these laudable and urgent exertions, we are only informed of the following order for stoppages to be made out of certain stipends on account of the famine.*

* See Bengal Select Consultations of May 28, 1770.

" It appearing to the Committee highly necessary and reasonable that the tribute stipends, " and all extraordinary issues whatever, should " give place to the more urgent calls of government, *resolved*, That Mr. Becher, resident at " the Durbar, be directed to with-hold at least " thirty lacks from the tribute and other allowances, between this period and the 17th of October, so that the receipts and disbursements may " have some proportion to each other: That he be " informed, with the assistance of this reserved sum, " we expect he will continue to pay the troops, " garrison, and all other charges of his department, the civil and military charges of the presidency being the utmost which can be defrayed " from the treasury at Calcutta."

These orders were accordingly transmitted in a letter to the resident, and from such a dreadful visitation of the Almighty, it was natural to hope that the customary modes of oppression should at least for a little be suspended. In some places, indeed, the zemindars and farmers were excused a few rupees on account of the drought; but the wretched ryots, who managed at once the agriculture and manufacture of the country, were remanded to their tasks with the usual severity, and peremptorily required to accomplish the same labour, without any additional emolument; to cultivate the premises of their annual masters, while their own continued waste; to become silk-winders, spinners and weavers, and to yield their goods at an arbitrary price!

In

In other places, the cruel extortion by forfeiture was ſtill exacted with all its concomitant circumſtances of rapacious violence. Thoſe fines were even farmed as part of the rent-roll, and proved an inſuperable bar to induſtry, by occaſioning that appearance of poverty which the inhabitants of the diſtricts ſo generally affected, as ſome degree of ſecurity from the avarice of office, and thus preventing ſuch as had money from an open and liberal expenditure. The perſon who received the fine was himſelf judge of the delinquency, and the degree of the penalty to be inflicted, which was always levied, not according to the nature of the guilt, but the circumſtances of the guilty. Theft and murder were compounded at the rate of four or five rupees, while fornication and witchcraft were puniſhed by as many thouſands. Accuſations, which in other countries are uſually confined to the aged and impotent, in Bengal generally fell on the rich and ſubſtantial.

Notwithſtanding the inordinate intereſt of money, the ſyſtematic impoſition practiſed by all concerned in raiſing the duties, and every other ſpecies of oppreſſion which ſo remarkably diſtinguiſhed the various operations within the revenue department, the wrongs of the inhabitants were ſtill unredreſſed. Not all the ſufferings they had endured from the utmoſt ſeverities of nature and art, could ſoften or humanize their hard-hearted maſters. Though the Company received for the ſpace of ten years an annual revenue of a million and a half ſterling from Bengal; though over and above that enormous sum this pillaged country had afforded in the same space of time, upwards of nine millions to them and their servants; though the resources which had furnished all this treasure by wars, revolutions, and exactions of the most destructive tendency, were obviously impoverished; though the inhabitants saw no end to the demands of their conquerors, or any possibility of resisting the art and force with which these demands were made; though, in consequence of all their accumulated miseries, they were reduced to despair, and millions devoured by famine, or sacrificed at the ruthless shrine of rapacity, the Directors, in their general letter of April, 1771, coolly observe, that even this was "a time when every possible measure should be adopted for availing themselves of all the advantages which they had in prospect from the possession of the Dewannee."

Notwithstanding all the variety of calamities which their iniquitous measures had brought upon the populous and flourishing provinces of Bengal, which, in the short space of ten years, had realized to them and their numerous agents above twenty-four millions sterling, and which, in the same time, by famine and the pestilence, had also lost whatever escaped the ravages of war and oppression; from a country involved in miseries of such a magnitude and extent, a company of British merchants naturally and deliberately express the most ardent desire of deriving further emolument! Of all the tyrannies which, from time to time, have insulted the feelings, and trampled on the rights of men, those

those of a commercial government have proved the most barbarous and implacable. We may as rationally expect the most genial and delicious fruits of Asia in the coldest climates, as that a genius, equal to the liberal exercise of sovereignty, should spring from a counting-house. The great and complicated machinery of political systems depend not for the success or ultimate perfection of its multifarious operations on subtile maxims of traffic, or the rigid rules of arithmetic.

From the war with Cossim Ally Cawn, and that powerful confederacy who espoused his interest, the military on the Bengal establishment had been employed on no active service of material consequence to the general affairs of the Company. A conspiracy among the English officers in the three brigades under the command of Lord Clive, while governor and president of the council, is the only important transaction in which, for a period of several years, they were distinguished.

To render the Company's revenue efficient, an abatement in the various charges incurred by the settlement of these lucrative provinces became every day more and more indispensible. The gentlemen in the army, aware of their own consequence in the service, and deeming their share in the reform by much the heaviest, agreed among themselves to unite in a body, and assert their own interest. Immemorial usage entitled them to an extraordinary allowance called *double batta*, while on field duty. This additional pay being not thought necessary under a peace-establishment, was

 ordered

ordered to be with-held. The order announcing the retrenchment was received with a specious acquiescence, the better to disguise the sentiment and cover the design it occasioned. It was at the same time felt through the whole army with a mixture of the most serious mortification and resentment. Consultations were consequently held in every battalion, and a general correspondence established among all subordinate British officers in the Company's service. They conceived themselves insulted by a measure, which rendered them only the instruments of wealth and aggrandisement to others, and thought the profession degraded by its subjection to the little ploding manœuvres of a mercantile board. It was therefore their unanimous resolution to resign their commissions all in one day, rather than submit to an arrangement, or connive with a circumstance which every man regarded as dishonourable.

This extraordinary combination was planned with sagacity, and carried on with infinite spirit and address. It transpired, however, by one of those trivial accidents which no penetration can foresee or prevent, and which often defeats the best formed designs. A drunken quarrel divulged the plot and exposed the conspirators, only a few weeks prior to the day of general resignation. Lord Clive hastened to the cantonements where the danger was most imminent, and where he found sufficient employment for all his characteristic firmness and management. Sir Robert Barker, Colonel Richard Smith, and Sir Robert Fletcher, commanded at

that

that time the respective brigades. Their exertions in concert with those of his Lordship and General Carnac, saved the Company, by recovering the discipline of its forces, and reducing them to a state of permanent subordination to the civil power.

This had undoubtedly been one great and primary object of Lord Clive's government. And no man had a more thorough acquanitance with the ambitious views of victorious troops, the influence derived from their situation, and the enormous fortunes which those especially in command were in the habit of accumulating. The Company and the nation at large were highly incensed by the perpetration of such unexampled tragedies as had resulted from the conspiracy instigated by his Lordship, his perfidious breach of a most solemn treaty with the lawful sovereign of the country, his authenticating an imposture by forging the name of a British admiral, together with the deposition and murder of Surajah Dowlah, and a variety of other foul transactions. These were, the abuses of an army acting independent of civil authority. The precedent was awful and menacing. Few commanders in chief could carry into the field the politics, the enterprise, or the ability of Lord Clive, but the critical posture of affairs in Bengal at that period, rendered it more necessary than ever, that all military operations should, for the future, be under the controul of the Council Board.

No system could more effectually realize and substantiate the prosperity of the Company, than that which was grafted on the suppression of a mutiny

tiny which threatened the entire ſubverſion of all our acquiſitions in India. This auſpicious ſubordination has been ſteadily purſued and maintained by every ſucceeding government. From this moment the troops were ſeparated into ſmall cantonements, and diſtributed into all the country provinces and dependencies, where they have remained ever ſince almoſt ſtationary. The people in the ſeveral villages and diſtricts are conſequently kept in awe by the preſence of a force which they cannot reſiſt, the revenues are every where collected, and the inveſtments provided at the point of the bayonnet; internal regulations are introduced and preſerved, and the frontiers of our poſſeſſions ſecurely protected againſt the vigorous and artful incurſions of all our preditary neighbours. The country, it muſt be acknowledged, by this ſyſtem, was ſtill in ſome degree under military execution, as being not leſs than ever expoſed to all the outrages of a licentious ſoldiery. More temperance and moderation were however to be expected from the general deportment of the army by transferring the reſponſibility of its operations from the commanders in chief to the members of the council, as it then equally became the intereſt of both to avoid proſecuting ſchemes of rapacity, by the ſucceſs of which neither of them could be gainers.

Such was the embarraſſment of the Company's affairs towards the end of 1771, when from extreme miſmanagement both at home and abroad, it appeared upon an impartial inveſtigation, they were upwards of two millions in debt. Thus critically circum-

circumſtanced, Mr. Cartier, who was then preſident of the council, drew bills on the Company, for which he was ſeverely cenſured, and with ſeveral members of the board abruptly diſmiſſed the ſervice.

Mr. Haſtings was immediately called from the preſidency of Madras to the government of Bengal. His reputation for talents and integrity entitled him to this diſtinction. And the reader can have no objection to as much intelligence as has yet tranſpired of an individual, who, for ſo many years, has been the principal actor in ſcenes which have deeply arreſted the attention of all mankind, whoſe character and conduct have occaſioned the profoundeſt ſpeculations, in the general maxims of whoſe politics numerous factions have originated, and whoſe enemies and abettors, with an ardour and ability nearly equal, have ſo frequently arraigned and defended him.

His parentage, though not ſplendid, is reſpectable. He is ſaid to be deſcended from one of the nobleſt families in the kingdom. The education which he received at Weſtminſter School, from the attention of an able tutor*, and chiefly his own capacity and application, was eminently claſſical and polite. His faculties were manly and cultivated at the age of eighteen, when he was appointed a writer in the Company's ſervice at Bengal.—His firſt object, as ſoon as he arrived in India, was to make himſelf maſter of the Perſian and Indoſ-

* Dr. Nichols.

tan languages. And he was the first Englishman who accomplished this difficult undertaking with any degree of accuracy. It facilitated his success in every subsequent pursuit, procured him the confidence of the natives, and sensibly increased his merits in their estimation. Every office to which he was advanced, every character he sustained, and every trust for which he became responsible, were uniformly discharged with rigid and exemplary fidelity. The establishment of a factory in the interior parts of the country, was committed to his care. The project was abortive, but he acquitted himself with honour. Among all the British youth who followed the fortunes of Lord Clive, in grasping at the sovreignty of Bengal, he was the only person qualified for supporting the dignity of resident minister at the court of Meer Jaffier.—The smallest impropriety in managing the delicate and important business of this interesting station was never laid to his charge. For though he enjoyed a place for years, which, to some of his successors, has been deemed equal at least to one hundred and fifty thousand pounds annually, and at a time when Lord Clive, according to his own account, realized nearly a million of money, on Mr. Hastings's return to Europe with his friend Vansittart, while others, who had occupied very inferior stations, realized and brought home fortunes from a hundred to five hundred thousand pounds; his was said not to exceed fifteen thousand.—Happy had it been for him, perhaps for the natives of Indostan, assuredly for many of his contemporaries in England, had he never deviated

from

from this obvious rectitude, or adopted a line of conduct more obnoxious to censure or misconstruction.

He was not long in London when his philological acquirements, and an exquisite taste which he soon discovered for poetry and the fine arts, introduced him to the acquaintance of those who had most distinguished themselves as men of science and ability. He was intimate with that club of wits among whom Dr. Samuel Johnson, of classical memory, presided; and formed, in concert with that great man and others, the design of establishing a class in the university of Oxford, for teaching the Persian language. No man could be better fitted for the direction of such an institution, which however was defeated by his appointment in 1769, to be second in council at Madras, with no very remote prospect of succeeding to the chair in that presidency. He continued in this place till February 1772, when the Directors, apprised of his abilities, and confiding in his worth, named him to the government of Fort-William.

In this eminent and arduous situation, the subtilty, the versaility, and the sublimity of his mind, had the amplest range. On his accession to government, relaxation, anarchy, obliquity, every where prevailed. The distresses of the Company accumulated with enormous rapidity. Though bills were drawn on the Directors for more than a million sterling, a bond-debt to a much larger amount due to individuals in Bengal, was still undischarged. The expence and disbursement of the Company at that time actually exceeded their income.

income. The revenues were embezzled in the collection, the payments of the zimindars were retarded by a collusion with the cutcherry or rent office, the army in various parts were spreading oppression and terror over all the provinces, the courts of justice were invading the rights of the harmless and impotent, under the covert of a legal process, discontent universally assumed a gloomy and foreboding silence, monopoly suspended the natural operation of commerce, peculation more or less affected the whole system of civil arrangement, and profusion pervaded every department of the public expenditure.

The regulations which Mr. Hastings adopted under this ruinous state of things, notwithstanding the infinite prejudices which opposed his exertions, were as immediate as they seemed indispensible.—He retrenched the excessive civil charges in Calcutta, abolished all unnecessary appointments, and suppressed, both by precept and example, that profligate spirit of extravagance and dissipation which had seized and pervaded all orders of men. The face of affairs acknowledged the hand of a reformer in less than a month. Government instantly assumed a new and more decisive mode of exertion. Her resolutions were carried into effect with vigour and promptitude; and in proportion as she asserted her dignity with firmness and simplicity, her credit and respectability revived.

The Company had now determined to stand forth as dewance of the provinces, through the agency of their own servants. The Directors announced

nounced this intention in their general letter, but neither ſuggeſted any ſyſtem, nor ſuperſeded any prior orders which might defeat a new arrangement. Mr. Haſtings perceived the difficulty, but it did not prevent his endeavours to realize the wiſhes of his employers. And here a field was opened worthy of all that active and enterprizing genius which has hitherto diſtinguiſhed his conduct. Nor did he heſitate to enter with his uſual ardour into an accurate development of whatever relates to the complicated ſcenes of finance and juriſprudence.

It is impoſſible to go into the detail of ſuch a laboured variety of inſtitutions, as originated in his vigilant attention to every branch of the ſervice. A committee of circuit were inſtantly appointed to make the tour of the ſeveral provinces and out diſtricts. It conſiſted of the preſident, attended by four members of the board. They proceeded to Murſhedabad, the reſidence of the nabob, and the native officers of government, where they inveſtigated the ſtate of the revenues, reduced the expences of collecting them, and eſtabliſhed provincial courts of juſtice for preventing thoſe acts of oppreſſion and arbitrary power, which had proved ſo prejudicial both to the country and the Company.

By theſe ſubſtantial arrangements the whole fictitious apparatus of a native adminiſtration was inſtantly and effectually diſſolved. The form af authority had ſo long ſubſiſted without the ſpirit, that the plot was now univerſally diſcovered and deſpiſed. The utility and popularity of political frauds are co-existent. The nabob was known to be a cipher; and a captive in the custody of Mahommed Reza, who acted the double but natural part of being the slave of the English, and tyrant of his countrymen. He was therefore dismissed from the office of Naib Duan for the territories of Bengal and Shitabroy, from a similar situation in those of Bahar, together with every person employed by them, connected with them, or under their influence, in collecting the revenues. This material alteration in the great machinery of government, was formally proclaimed at Murshedabad and Patna.—The chief and council in both places were consequently charged with the care of finance in the several districts under their respective jurisdiction, until some regular establishment could be effected. The nabob and his subjects were delivered from the rapacity and intrigues of a tyrant, whose outrages excited the hatred and execration of the species. Muny Begum, not the mother of the nabob, though of superior rank in the Haram, but a person of plebeian extraction, of intriguing character and low manners, was immediately appointed the guardian of his minority, and to transact in his stead the political concerns of the sircar or government, and Rajah Goodrass, son of Mahah Rajah Nuncomar, became Duan of the nabob's household. Establishments obviously intended to demonstrate in the eyes of all Indostan, the absolute insignificance and degradation of the nabob's family, as contrasted with the real and assumed sovereignty of the English.

The same indefatigable perseverance in the great business of a thorough reform, discriminated the

Gover-

governor's return to the presidency, which had marked his circuit in the provinces. The odium of his countrymen was for the present at least overborne by the grateful acknowledgments of the natives, who every where hailed him as their saviour, and pictured in their fond imaginations an immediate emancipation from all their sufferings and slavery. His measures promised at least no very distant redress to the numerous wrongs they endured under former establishments, and had an aspect not less friendly to the government than the subject.—He modelled a-new the several public offices, and appointed to each its separate and independent business. The infinite swarms of collectors, and every other description of individuals retained in the multifarious department of revenue, were precluded, by positive orders, from exceeding their respective and specific powers. The general office where these matters were finally adjusted, was removed from Moorshedabad to Calcutta, and all the branches of finance brought immediately before the council. A board of inspection was at the same time instituted for the controul of the public expenditure.

The military operations could not be overlooked, under an administration thus active and enterprising. All their measures originated from the pressure of those accumulated exigencies to which the Company's affairs, both at home and abroad, were then reduced. Effectual relief was anxiously expected from the industry, the abilities, and the virtues of the new presidency, who, equally solicitous on their part to anſwer the intention of their appointment, grappled ſucceſsfully with the difficulties of their ſituation, by improving to the utmoſt all the reſources in their power.

The Marrattos, early in 1772, invaded the Rohilla country, which, after a ſhort but ineffectual ſtruggle, at Sukkertall, was abandoned to their mercy. Sujah ul Dowlah, alarmed by this formidable incurſion, on territories ſo nearly connected with his own, ſolicited aid of the Engliſh, who were then encamped at Denapore. A brigade immediately directed their march for the territories of Oude. An order of council, however, ſtopped them at Benares. It was then the Rohilla chiefs agreed to pay the vizir forty lacks of rupees, to protect them againſt the Marrattos. But the approach of the rainy ſeaſon ſoon cleared Rohilcund of the enemy. The vizir, notwithſtanding his influence on this event is eſtabliſhed by no facts on record, inſtantly put in his claim for the ſtipulated ſum. Hafez Rahmet Cawn, who managed the negociation for his countrymen, did not at firſt refuſe the validity of the debt, but evaded payment probably in the expectation of convincing the vizir, that the demand was premature, as the buſineſs on which it was founded being accompliſhed by accident, had ſuperſeded thoſe exertions for which the engagement took place. And it was not till the chiefs were provoked by the vizir's importunity, that they boldly negatived his plea. A point into which the wary and ambitious

ſubah

ſubah had, by the whole of his conduct from firſt to laſt, been anxious to enſnare or betray them.

The ſtrength and extent of the Marratto united ſtates are now pretty accurately known. They inhabit the mountaneous wilds of Indoſtan. Their territories, their armies, and their revenues are immenſe. They derive from the wiſdom of their political inſtitutions, tranquillity, and domeſtic happineſs, in time of peace; from their ſituation, their wealth, their habits, and their national genius, conduct and enterprize in war. Shaw Allum, or the great mogul, whoſe anceſtors had ſubdued the empire, was now connected with this warlike race by an aſſignment of the provinces which he derived from the Engliſh, in the treaty of Allahabad. The preſidency anticipated all the pernicious effects of this raſh connection. They conſidered ſuch an alienation of the Company's donation to his Majeſty, as a formal breach of their friendſhip on his part. They conſtrued his property in the provinces in queſtion to depend entirely on his perſonal poſſeſſion of them, but by no means to give him the right of ceding them to others. Reſponſible to the vizir in ſome meaſure for the defence of his dominions againſt every attack, the approximation of ſuch hoſtile neighbours menaced the tranquillity they expected from the pacific meaſures they wiſhed to purſue. Oude was the barrier of Bengal. It was their intereſt to protect the one for the ſake of the other. The vizir's frontiers could not be expoſed with ſafety to their own. The enemy's cavalry would be enabled,

 from

from their ſituation, to plunder and harraſs the Company's ally with impunity. Their inceſſant depradations might even diſpoſe him, from timidity, ſelfiſhneſs, impotence or policy, to leave the territories of the Company acceſſible to the enemy. For theſe reaſons, it was unanimouſly reſolved to take poſſeſſion of what his majeſty, by this meaſure, had relinquiſhed, and conſequently prevent the Marrattos availing themſelves of the grant they had obtained.

This forcible ſeizure of Corah and Kurrah was intended to operate as an effectual check to all further connection or intercourſe with the emperor of India. The Company were engaged by ſolemn treaty to pay him an yearly ſubſidy of twenty-ſix lacks of rupees for his grant of the Dewannee of Bengal, Bahar and Oriſſa. But the moment they aſſumed this important office by the agency of their own ſervants, they formally and avowedly violated the condition on which it was originally obtained. This important tranſaction was reſerved for the adminiſtration of Mr. Haſtings, and it happened not long ſubſequent to his being nominated governor of Bengal.

Dazzled by the luſtre of the imperial family, and anxious to reſume a glory thus apparently extinguiſhed, his Majeſty went to Dehli, the metropolis of the empire, where he incurred a plenitude of additional contempt, by the idle parade of a coronation. This romantic attachment to the empty pageantry of a royalty merely nominal, he abſurdly conceived might contribute to realize his

views

views or wiſhes of a more ſubſtantial aggrandizement. It was a ſcheme which had ſo abſolutely engroſſed his attention and deſires, that during his whole connection and correſpondence with the Engliſh, he conſtantly urged them to aſſiſt him in putting it in execution. Yet no ſooner was he enabled to gratify his ambition by thus viſiting the reſidence and aſcending the throne of his anceſtors, than it was eagerly interpreted a dirilection of their friendſhip.

In fact, he formed an alliance which they did not approve, their treaſury was exhauſted, and they were preſſed with difficulties which appeared inſuperable both in India and Europe. Theſe were the reaſons which induced them to with-hold the price while they retained the purchaſe. Becauſe he was unfortunate, they were determined to be unjuſt. He might have reſumed the Dewannee on the ſame principle which they urged as warranting them to detain his tribute. But it was his fortune to be weak, and theirs to be ſtrong. In that caſe, politics are ſeldom governed by equity; and perhaps it were abſurd to expect a magnanimity in Calcutta ſo rarely to be found in any other part of the world. So that it was not unnatural in a power which had already bereft his majeſty of two hundred and twenty thouſand pounds a-year, to uſurp the diſtricts in queſtion for the ſake of diſpoſing of them to more advantage.

The vizir was apprehenſive the Marrattos would endeavour to take poſſeſſion of their new territory by the route of Rohilcund. Here the Britiſh army were determined to diſpute their claim. The firſt brigade, conſiſting of one regiment of Europeans, ſix battalions of ſipoys, and twenty pieces of cannon, had therefore effected a junction with the troops of Sujah Dowlah and the Rohillas, and advanced to the banks of the Ganges by forced marches.

The Rohilla country north of the river was included within the line of operation preſcribed to the General on this expedition. In conſequence of ſuch a diſcretionary latitude, the brigade penetrated as far as Kamgent. The Marrattos, who had juſt forded the river, re-croſſed it with precipitation on their appearance, were purſued and prevented doing any other damage than merely burning a few inſignificant villages. The conduct of the Rohillas on this occaſion was undoubtedly equivocal. The vizir deemed them perfidious, and was perſuaded by their motions that they wiſhed to have aſſiſted the enemy. They did not join him until the allied army were prepared to ſtorm their camp. The Britiſh general pronounced them to be the moſt treacherous of men, and propoſed that we ſhould put the vizir in poſſeſſion of their country. The Marrattos hovered during the remainder of the campaign in the neighbourhood of the camp, without any effort to bring on another action, or once daring to approach the borders of Corah.— And the troubles which aroſe in their own proper dominions recalled them before the ſetting in of the rains.

From

From this moment Sujah Dowlah became the inveterate enemy of the Rohillas. Chagrined by their backwardneſs in literally fulfilling their engagements, he conceived them as having now added treachery to evaſion. He repeated his demand of the forty lacks, but with no better ſucceſs, though his title was no longer diſputable. He had even reaſon to ſuſpect a coluſion between Hafez Rhamet Cawn and the Marrattos. He accuſed him of ſecretly encouraging and aiding them by money. He dreaded their machinations againſt him. The Marrattos were his hereditary enemies, and would graſp with eagerneſs at any pretext for involving him in war. And this would always be in their power, while the Rohillas, by their ſituation, could ſo eaſily foment a quarrel between them. Thus circumſtanced, the only policy he had to proſecute was the conqueſt of their country. It was obvious, however, that the aſſiſtance of the Company's troops was indiſpenſible. And he repeatedly urged their compliance with his wiſhes in accompliſhing this favourite object, both to the general in perſon and the preſident by letters.

In conſequence of theſe deſigns, he earneſtly preſſed and obtained a meeting with Mr. Haſtings at Benaris, where a treaty was concluded with the vizir on theſe terms: That the provinces of Corah and Allahabad ſhould be ceded to him, on condition of his paying fifty lacks of rupees to the Company, twenty of which in ready money, and the remainder in equal payments at the expiration of one or two years. And the equivalent which the vizir was to afford for the charge of their troops when ſent to his aſſiſtance at his requiſition, was ſtipulated at two lacks and ten thouſand rupees per month.

The origin of the Rohilla war has occaſioned ſo much altercation, has been ſo violently attacked and ſo ſtrenuouſly defended, has produced indeed ſuch a deluge of ſophiſtry on both ſides, that the fact is not eaſily diſcriminated from the colouring with which it is recorded. It was, however, determined ſecretly, between the governor and the vizir, in a converſation which paſſed at Benaris.—The object, which was the extirpation of the Rohillas, ſeems from the firſt to have been equally deſireable to both. It was introduced, brought forward, and matured, in the courſe of public buſineſs, with the moſt conſummate addreſs. The orders of the Company were againſt the meaſure, and it evidently obtained, after much ſerious diſcuſſion, the approbation both of the ſelect committee and the board of council, rather in deference to the ſentiments and engagements of the preſident, than from any real conviction of its propriety, expediency, or utility. It was propoſed, in the firſt inſtance, to comply with the vizir's requiſition on terms which he was expected to deem extravagant and impracticable. The artifice ſucceeded. He rejected the propoſal with warmth. Being, however, thus formally adopted by government, he ſoon changed his mind, in the preſumption that they had gone too far to recede. He now, therefore, demanded the aſſiſtance of the brigade

gade on the terms required, in reducing that part of the country which lies between the Ganges and the mountains. To this object the operations of the troops were restricted by the presidency, who expressed the most cordial satisfaction on the requisition of Sujah Dowlah, because the absence of the Marrattos would facilitate the conquest in view, the troops would be preserved from inaction and relaxation of discipline, the barrier of the vizir's dominions, in the defence of which we were so deeply interested, would be at once strengthened and extended, the revenues of our principal ally would derive from the acquisition considerable augmentation, one third of the military charges would be saved to the Company, and a substantial obligation conferred on a friend, whose tried fidelity deserved whatever could be accomplished in his favour, and the service was finally to be rewarded by forty lacks of rupees, which the vizir engaged to liquidate whenever the object of the war was compleated.

Rohilcund, from situation, fertility, cultivation, and every other respect, was an acquisition peculiarly desireable to the vizir. His territories towards that quarter were altogether without any natural barrier, and consequently exposed to incursion, either from the impotence, inattention, or treachery of the Rohillas, whose country was calculated to afford him an absolute shelter, by the Thibet mountains on the north, and on the south and west by the Ganges. The inhabitants consisted of two different classes. Those who cultivated

the

the land, and thofe who had the management of the civil and political inftitutions. The former, confifting of farmers, mechanics, manufacturers, and dealers, were an induftrious, happy and profperous people, the defcendants of the Gentoos, innocent in their manners, united among themfelves, fedulous, contented and fuccefsful in their humble occupations. The country was one beautiful garden, in which nature and art every where fhone in the moft prolific exuberance. The government was in poffeffion of a tribe of Hagans or Pitans, who had conquered Rohilcund above feventy years ago, and had ever fince lived upon the fruits of it, without either affifting in its cultivation, or mixing with its inhabitants. They had not, however, abufed the truft they affumed. Their reign had been profperous and humane. The lands were kept in a ftate of the higheft cultivation, and all the duties, cuftoms, or revenues, yielded with readinefs and fatisfaction. The fubjects were bleffed with plenty, which they enjoyed without moleftation. And they gave no indication of wifhing on any account to change either their condition or their rulers.

In the felect committee, November 26, 1773, the fiat was given for co-operating with Sujah Dowlah, in fubjugating this rich and flourifhing country. Colonel Champion, the provifional commander in chief of the fecond brigade, was entrufted with this fervice. He arrived within the territories of Oude, by the beginning of February, 1774. The Rohilla country was actually invaded a few a few weeks after, by the whole united army.—The vizir forthwith dispatched several detachments of light infantry, to indulge the most wanton and unprovoked outrages, and infest the cottages of the poor, as well as the mansions of the wealthy, with all the horrors of war. The harmless inhabitants were instantly butchered or expelled, their property ruined, and their villages consumed by the flames. This was but an earnest of the tyrant's vengeance, which God in his wrath had destined a British army to execute.

The Rohillas, fired by the scenes of devastation which raged around them, crouded to the standard which their chiefs had raised in their defence, and regarded the approaches of the subah with resentment and defiance. On the 23d of April, the celebrated Hafez Rhamut appeared at the head of forty thousand brave men, in order of battle, who determined to sell their rights and their lives as dearly as possible. Our troops accepted the challenge with their usual fortitude. Animated by a consciousness of superiority, from reputation, from discipline, and from success, they prepared for the attack with that cool and temperate confidence, which never forsakes them in the hour of danger. The enemy fought in the presence of their fortunes and families, if not with hopes of victory, at least with those of revenge. Life was no longer valuable to men who knew they must lose whatever could render it desireable. Inflamed by all that is dear to the human heart, fury inspired them with courage, and danger taught them conduct.—

Their

Their rockets, their matchlocks, and their artillery, were discharged with unexpected rapidity and resolution, and in various places galled our lines with considerable effect. They even made several attempts to charge, but the fire of our guns and musquetry was irresistible. Unable to advance, and disdaining to retreat, they pushed with eagerness wherever the conflict was most fierce; and in proportion as they swarmed to close with our ranks, the slaughter became incredible. Their vigorous exertions, nevertheless, continued for hours equally ardent and obstinate. The British gained not a single advantage but what resulted from their superior skill in the science of war. Notwithstanding the torrent of fire which our army poured in upon them with incessant impetuosity, several of their chiefs advanced again and again with exemplary gallantry, and pitched their colours between the two armies, urging their exhausted followers to renew the attack. It was not possible for them, however, to gain the day in such an unequal contest. The interest of the vizir prevailed, and the English were victorious. Hafez Rhamut, whose enlightened mind, polished talents, beautiful poetry, and amiable morals, endeared him to his friends, and rendered him the favourite of the age and nation where he lived, was slain, rallying with great bravery the scattered remains of a broken and dispirited army. The vizir, treacherous to the commander in chief, whom he promised to meet in the field of battle, was content to sate his bloody mind with a sight of the carnage at a distance. But no

sooner

ſooner were the enemy completely routed, than his horſe were let looſe to plunder the camp, and ravage the country. Our troops, preſerving their ranks and orders inviolate, were only heard to mutter, "We have the honour of the day, and "theſe banditti the profit."

The cruelties that enſued were ſhocking and diſgraceful. The uſurper indulged the baſeſt propenſities of his nature with unbriddled ferocity. No remonſtrance of Colonel Champion could prevent the havock of the vanquiſhed territory. For three whole days after the battle, the houſes of this fertile and well inhabited ſpot were every where in a blaze. The family, the friends, and dependents of the unfortunate Hafez Rhamut, were expoſed to diſhonour, to inſult, and even to want. The commander in chief made a feeling repreſentation of their wretched ſituation to the ſelect committee, as his perſonal influence with the vizir could obtain for them no relief. He received an anſwer on the 23d of May, in which are theſe words:—"It has been an invariable maxim in the policy "of the Company's government, in the execution "of any enterprizes which they have undertaken "in behalf of their allies, to interpoſe their pro-"tection in favour of the conquered princes, for "the ſecurity of their lives and honour; and it "will unqueſtionably be the care and attention of "this adminiſtration, to adhere to this maxim, "which has ſo greatly contributed to the reputa-"tion of the Britiſh name, and to perform what "may be incumbent on them, on the preſent oc-

caſion."

" casion." Mr. Hastings, however, who likewise presided in this committee, roundly abandons this forlorn family to the rigour of their fate, in a letter to the colonel, but four days afterwards, where he observes, that " to take the family of Hafez Rhamut immediately under our protection, would " furnish him (the vizir) with a *just* plea to refuse " his compliance with the stipulation made for the " present service, as it would in effect be to conquer the country for the Company, and not for " him."

The cruelties of Sujah Dowlah was not confined to the distracted remains of this wretched house — All his prisoners experienced the same unrelenting severity. He kept them within his forts, or removed them to Fyzabad, that he might not hear the censures, or be teized by the importunities of the English on their account. He intruded on the secrecies of the women, by forcibly entering the Zenana, which is the grossest insult that can be offered to the family of a noble Moor. He divested them of their trinkets and the ornaments of their dress, provided them with no suitable accommodation, and even suffered them to want the necessaries of life. Not less than two hundred women, many of whom were persons of distinction, he ordered to be driven from Bessouleeq to his camp, almost naked, under a guard of sipoys. From Berelly, or its neighbourhood, several young women were also dragged from the arms of their agonizing relations, for the express purpose of prostitution.

The

The moſt illuſtrious of theſe captives were equally deſtitute of food and raiment, covered with vermin, and reduced to the ſevere neceſſity of ſupplicating charity, which they actually received from ſeveral Engliſh gentlemen. His treatment of Mahubulla Cawn and his brothers was, if poſſible, yet more criminal. Theſe men poſſeſſed a country worth, at leaſt, twenty lacks of rupees per annum. In conſequence of the moſt ſolemn aſſurances of protection and friendſhip, they ſhut themſelves up in Beſſoulee, the capital of their diſtricts, where they obſerved a ſtrict neutrality during the war.—He continued to applaud their conduct, by repeating the ſtrongeſt profeſſions of regard for their welfare. But the moment they were in his power, he put them under the moſt rigorous confinement, denied them acceſs to their families, robbed them of their property, and uſed themſelves and their women not only with indignity and diſhonour, but with cruelty. Theſe are the moving terms in which they deſcribe their ſituation, in their complaints to Col. Champion: " He has deprived us " of our country, of our riches, and even of our " honour; and not ſatisfied with that, he is going " to ſend us priſoners to Fyzabad. We deſire " no country, no riches, no houſes; but at Boſ- " ſualee are the tombs of our noble anceſtors!— " Near them, under ſome ſhade, we beg permiſ- " ſion to ſpend the remainder of our days as Fa- " quiers. Relying on the vizir's promiſes, we re- " mained in this country, otherwiſe we ſhould have " fled as the other chiefs did, and have preſerved " our

"our characters and honours. These he has taken away with our effects. And how he has dishonoured us is known to all."

During the perpetration of these outrages against numbers of helpless women and children, whose husbands and fathers had fallen in an abortive struggle to preserve their independence, the British army, subjected to the vizir's controul, were dragged from place to place, at his caprice. Fizulla Cawn fled at the head of his surviving countrymen, and encamped in a place of great natural strength, among the mountains at the extremity of Rohilcund. Colonel Champion had probably incurred the vizir's displeasure, by interesting himself in behalf of the army, in dividing the spoil of the vanquished, in endeavouring to restrain the depredations of the vizir's cavalry against an innocent and defenceless people, and especially in his humane attempts to procure for the prisoners some mitigation of their merciless treatment. His efforts to obtain an honourable negotiation for Fizulla Cawn, and acting as a mediator between the principals in the war, was still more offensive, though the vizir had the address for the present to conceal his resentment. The victor would allow no abatement in the terms he proposed, and Fizulla Cawn deemed them, from the temper of the chiefs connected with him, to be impracticable. The governor or president agreed in every thing with the vizir, and condemned at the same time the interference of the commander in chief. Our troops were consequently ordered, without further regard to time or place,

place, to accomplish the reduction of the enemy. The select committee who directed the war renewed their instructions to the colonel, in these words: "You are authorized and directed by us "to pursue the most vigorous measures, in conjunction with the vizir, effectually to reduce the "Rohilla army, without confining your operations "to the Rohilla dominions." The army proceeded accordingly within a few miles of Lalldong, where the Rohillas had fortified themselves in a very strong post. Here they were soon reduced to extremity for want of provision. A sickness at the same time broke out in their camp, which daily carried off great numbers. Wishing rather to starve them into a surrender, than risque the brigade in an attack which could not succeed but under peculiar disadvantages, and with a prodigious effusion of human blood, Colonel Champion suspended his operations to wait the result of these circumstances. His conduct was justified by the consequence. They redoubled their earnestness in pressing an accommodation. Fizulla Cawn presented himself before the conquerors, and the vizir, in consideration of his confidence, agreed that he should have a jaghire or district of fourteen lacks, and seventy-five thousand rupees a year; and that he should be allowed five thousand men in his service; but that in return he should deliver up one half of his treasure to the vizir, submit to him as his vassal, and pay him military tribute.

Thus ended a war, undertaken against the express prohibition of the Company, and even, in ſome meaſure, without their knowledge, in which an army of Britiſh ſoldiers acted as mercenaries under a foreign prince, for the unequivocal purpoſe of procuring their employers a ſum of money, by which a race of men were ſlaughtered or extirpated, who were at leaſt inoffenſive to their neighbours, who certainly never injured the Engliſh, and under whoſe mild and humane government the country flouriſhed, and its inhabitants were happy.

CHAPTER VI.

A Plenipotentiary from his Britannic Majesty appears on the Coast of Coromandel—The Fall of Tanjore—Lord Pigot's appointment—He restores the King of Tanjore—Is put under Military Arrest—Dies in Confinement—Three of the Majority who effected this Insurrection tried and condemned by an English Jury.

THE wreck of the Aurora frigate, which probably foundered in some of those numerous streights or shelves so common and dangerous in the eastern ocean, put a melancholy end to all expectations inspired by the commission of Supervisors in 1769. The squadron which carried out the new Commissioners was commanded by Sir John Lindsay, an officer of distinguished merit in his profession. He was at the same time appointed by the Company superintendant of their concerns in the Gulph of Persia, and commander in chief of all their ships, frigates and armed vessels in India. Government invested him with powers still higher. He carried with him credentials under the great seal to appear and act in India as plenipotentiary of his Britannic Majesty, especially to his Excellency the Nabob of Arcot, who had become an ally of the crown by the eleventh article of the treaty of Paris.

Having remained ſome months on the Malaber coaſt, Sir John arrived at Fort George in the end of July, 1770, where a tedious and intricate altercation took place, between him, as his Majeſty's plenipotentiary, and the gentlemen of the preſidency. He requeſted them to join him in paying the uſual honours in delivering his Majeſty's letters and preſents to the nabob of Arcot, and that they ſhould aſſiſt in the ceremonial cuſtomary on ſuch occaſions, by the perſonal attendance of the governor and council, the gentlemen of the ſettlement both civil and military, and by ſalutes from the forts and ſhips in the road. But all tranſactions and negociations with the princes of India having been hitherto conducted by the Company's ſervants, who were generally conſidered as charged with the intereſt and exerciſe of the Britiſh power in theſe parts, they declined a compliance with the Plenipotentiary's requiſition, leſt by their means the influence and concerns of their conſtituents might ſuffer diminution.

Notwithſtanding the obſtinacy of the preſidency, Sir John inſtantly waited on the nabob, and laid his commiſſion and inſtructions before him. He aſſured the nabob of his Majeſty's friendſhip and protection, which he was anxious and determined to continue and extend to all his allies in every part of the world, that all the credit and ability of the Engliſh adminiſtration were pledged to ſecure the Carnatic to the nabob and his poſterity; that whatever his grievances were, he might depend on receiving ſubſtantial redreſs by laying them

them at the foot of the throne; and that, as Plenipotentiary from the British court, he was empowered to demand, in his Majesty's name, a complete account of the nabob's transactions with the Company or their agents since the treaty of Paris, as upon correct information his affairs might share the advantage of his Majesty's paternal government.

The nabob replied to these gracious assurances in terms of the sincerest gratitude. Words were, indeed, inadequate to his sentiments. He was at the same time not without his fears, that claiming the attention of the crown might be attended with danger, as the individuals who now filled the presidency might still continue to possess the power which had in so many instances already oppressed him. He was aware the royal interference, however kindly intended, might have a different operation, by the passions of jealousy and chagrin it would infallibly excite. The fate of Surajah Dowlah, Meer Jaffier, and Cossim Ally, were constantly before his eyes, and made him tremble for his own. And he shuddered to give those men offence, whose resentments were implacable in proportion to their power of indulging them. The support, however proper and indispensible to his existence, was moreover distant and uncertain, while the enemy were at hand, and ready to seize every opportunity of wrecking their vengeance on the wretch who, defenceless as he was, durst appeal for protection and relief from the grasp of tyranny, or the rage of peculation.

The constant and familiar intercourse which subsisted between the nabob and the king's minister, was a source of great and habitual uneasiness to the presidency. The animosity which it produced ingrossed their whole attention. A correspondence ensued, in which their passions were not a little inflamed, as their pride was hurt and their characters at issue. The plenipotentiary urged them on topics which they thought were not within his cognizance. His powers authorized him to apply for an accurate statement of all their transactions with the nabob of Arcot since the late treaty of Paris. He announced it also to be his Majesty's pleasure, that he should enquire with the utmost care into the causes of the late war with the Subah of the Decan and Hyder Ally, and the reasons of its unfortunate consequence. These powers he stated in such a striking variety of different and important lights, and pressed them on the gentlemen of the presidency in a manner so forcible and conclusive, that they lost all temper, and had recourse to such passionate and unguarded language, as gave him a manifest advantage in the argument. They steadily persisted, however, in maintaining the ground on which they originally declined acting with him as the minister of the king. They consequently wished him to understand them as finally determined to be heartily disposed to give him their best council, whenever and upon whatever subject he should require it, so far as they deemed themselves at liberty, consistently with their oath and covenant to the Company, and that they should thankfully

accept

accept of his counsel and aid upon all such occasions as they were taught or authorised by their constituents to receive or solicit them.

These contests threw the whole presidency into parties, and the nabob's respect for their authority was evidently lessened. The great business of the Carnatic, which was always managed in concert with him, was for the present at a stand, as the nabob presumed on the friendship shewed him by the minister of the crown, and they constantly answered every requisition made to them from him, by seriously observing, that as his Majesty had sent out such extraordinary powers to India, they could do nothing. Thus, by the intrusion of a ministerial manoeuvre, the government of the Company on the Madras establishment underwent a temporary suspension. The Company's servants came at last to the resolution of putting an end to an intercourse, which produced nothing but recrimination. They consequently told the plenipotentiary, very roundly, that they had no leisure for the prosecution of such a warfare. "We desire to take our "leave of controversy with you. We have not "any time for such an employment. If the Com-"pany had thought we should have been thus har-"rassed, they would probably have engaged a "proper number of controversial writers in their "service. We leave you the field open. Advise "us to our duty. Censure us for neglecting it.—"Reproach us for ill-using the prince of the coun-"try. Continue to plead his cause against the in-"terests and rights of the country. And tell us "it is for the benefit of the nation. Affert what "you pleafe. Be as fevere as you pleafe. We "fhall be filent here, and if we reply at all, it "fhall be in another place."

It is not improbable that the intrigues of the nabob were at the bottom of this political contention. His power, from our exertions in his favour, had by this time obtained a very confiderable eftablifhment. He had fettled in Madras, with a view, it was believed, of gaining an afcendancy over the gentlemen of the fettlement, and by various means to intereft them perfonally in the profperity of his family and affairs. His army were modelled and difciplined after the European fafhion, commanded by Englifh officers, and recruited by vaft numbers of fugitive Europeans. His dignity and influence, connected with ftrong ambition, and fpecious ability, were, in confequence of thefe advantages, acknowledged in every part of India.

It was the policy of the times to embrace every object which promifed an extenfion of prerogative. The defpotic purfuits of government were fufficiently palpable in an interference with the conduct of the Company, both at home and abroad. Great unpopularity was incurred, and a very ferious controverfy occafioned by the meafure. In following up the fame fatal fyftem, it was now conceived that the crown fhould fuperintend the affairs of the Company; and, in confequence of the various oppreffions to which the princes in the country were fubjected, negociate treaties, and eftablifh connections in India, totally diftinct and feparate from that

that body. To ſubſtantiate a ſcheme thus favourable to the encroachments of power, Sir John Lindſay had been inveſted with theſe extraordinary and alarming powers, in which he now appeared on the coaſt of Oriſſa and Coromandel.

Mr. Haſtings probably never rendered the Company more eſſential ſervice, than by his ſound and ſteady advice in the detection and defeat of this contracted policy. He was ſecond in council at the time; and it is not very difficult to perceive his ſagacity, perſeverance, and diſcernment, in the manner in which the argument is taken up and proſecuted to a concluſion. Its operation, however, in ſpite of all their endeavours to keep the natives ignorant of what was going forward, was viſible and ſerious. The ſervants of the Company had not been very liberal in their deſcriptions or acknowledgments of any ſuperior authority. The Indian powers at leaſt betrayed their ignorance of that circumſtance, by the aſtoniſhment they expreſſed at the intelligence they had probably heard of the king and parliament of Great Britain. But the functions connected with theſe characters, few or none of them could poſſibly underſtand. They conſidered the Company, perhaps, as the fountain of the Britiſh power. They ſaw their ſervants enjoying a plenitude of authority which exceeded that of their greateſt potentates. They witneſſed the ſuperior proweſs of their armies, and they conſtantly heard their orders appealed to as ſovereign and inconteſtible. But when they were told that this omnipotent Company conſiſted only of a pri-

vate

vate ſociety of merchants, that none of its members had the honour to fill any important department of ſtate, and that the whole ſyſtem which they had ſeen produce ſuch effects in India, and to which they had looked up from the firſt with reverence and admiration, was ſtill under the check and controul of one every way ſuperior, they awoke as from a dream, and began to regard the individuals, who had degraded their official capacity by venality or inſolence, as occupying only a ſubordinate ſphere. They ſoon found that the powers of this mighty body were only delegated, that they were obtained and held merely for a ſpecific term of years, and that they were to look elſewhere for all future connections. And it is eaſily conceived how their pride and ſelf-importance would ſwell, when, inſtead of abject dependents on the Company or their agents, they were taught to conſider themſelves as friends, allies, ſovereigns and equals, by that ſupreme over-ruling power with whom, till then, they were in ſome degree unacquainted.

The gentlemen of the preſidency, who were on the ſame ſpot, and underſtood, from long and intimate acquaintance, the temper and ſentiments of the natives, in their general letters to the court of Directors, of July, 1771, expoſe with great energy the pernicious effects of this interference.— "It has always been our opinion, "ſay they," that "with your authority we had that of our ſovereign "and nation delegated to us through you, for ma- "naging the important concerns of our country, "under this preſidency. It is upon the preva- lence

"lence of this opinion in India, that our influ-
"ence and your intereſt are vitally founded. It
"was in the confidence of this opinion, that your
"ſervants, exerting all their vigour, acquired ſuch
"power and wealth for their country. But if this
"opinion be forfeited, they can neither act with
"ſpirit nor ſucceſs; for under the controul of a
"ſuperior commiſſion, they dare not, they can-
"not exert the powers with which they alone are
"entruſted; their weakneſs and diſgrace become
"conſpicuous, and they are held in deriſion by
"your enemies."

They continue in a chain of the moſt forcible and concluſive reaſoning to arraign the conduct of miniſters, in an attempt to enſnare and ſurpriſe them, by the introduction of a power altogether new and extraordinary in theſe parts. This was not, in their opinion, neceſſary to heighten their authority, by the ſanction of his Majeſty's name, which they had without any ſpecial interpoſition, and which, added in this manner, ſtamped all the former proceedings of the Company with illegality and uſurpation. They alledged that it was intended to terrify them into a ſurrender of their delegated authority, or to render them objects of juſt proſcription. They complained that the plenipotentiary's powers extended only to an uncandid enquiry into their paſt meaſures, an ungenerous cenſure of their conduct, a demand of their records, a partial indication of the nabob's allegations, in oppoſition to the rights of the Company, and a general deportment tending to diminiſh their conſe-

quence

quence in the eyes of their allies and enemies.— They confidered it as unconftitutional, to apply the great feal of Great Britain to the hidden purpofes of *lettres de cachet*, or to fend out fecretly the whole powers of prerogative, for the fole end of oppreffing the Company's fervants, in a fituation where they could have no poffible recourfe to the advice of law. They regarded themfelves as their predeceffors were, the only legal reprefentatives of the Britifh government in that remote part of his Majefty's dominions. Officers of the higheft commiffion from the crown had acted under them, as in other colonies of the empire. And they did not think themfelves at liberty to furrender their authority, in defiance of their duty to their fovereign, their country, or their truft. They had no fuch intimation from the Directors, their immediate fuperiors. And they concluded by obferving, that the forces they commanded fhould forthwith be configned into the hands of the crown, and transferred with the plenary powers to the abfolute direction and difpofal of his Majefty's minifter.

The fide to which the nabob leaned during the pendency of this ardent conteft, the folicitude of the Plenipotentiary to intereft himfelf in his affairs, and the ardour which appeared in his correfpondence with the prefidency to criminate the manner in which they had conducted themfelves to that prince, interrupted for a while the harmony which had formerly fubfifted between the fervants of the Company and their ally. An event, however, was now on the tapis, which in its formation, progrefs, and

and termination, ſeems to have quaſhed all differences, and united them more intimately than ever.

The Carnatic was not only infeſted by ſtraggling parties of the Marrattos, and various groupes of banditti which hovered on its frontiers, but ſeveral of its dependent Rajahs, Zemindars, and Polygars, were ſtill refractory, and declined the punctual diſcharge of their reſpective tributes. Moſt of theſe were eaſily reduced. The King of Tanjore was the moſt formidable. He was connected with ſome of the moſt reſpectable powers in India. His wealth, on ſuch a theatre of political venality, rendered his ſituation at once invidious and conſpicuous. For here, more perhaps than in any other country, the only infallible protection againſt depredation and outrage is poverty and inſignificance.

This Rajah, who owes ſo much celebrity to his ſufferings, is one of thoſe Gentoo princes whoſe anceſtors were never entirely ſubdued by the Tartars. He had been for years in the ſtricteſt alliance with the Company and the nabob, and engaged with them in the joint perils and fortunes of former wars. By the treaty of Paris, Salabatjing was recognized ſubah of the Decan, and Mahomed Ali Cawn nabob of the Carnatic. Theſe arrangements were chiefly preſcribed by the Engliſh, and the Mogul readily granted, from time to time, ſuch powers on his part as were neceſſary to give them validity and effect. Accounts were conſequently liquidated, and a convention, under the authority and guarantee of the Company, between their

their own allies, immediately took place for that purpose. Whatever arrears were due to the Mogul, as well as his future tribute, the nabob of Arcot was appointed to receive, with the allowance of a handſome premium for his trouble. The Company reſerved to themſelves the right of ſeeing this truſt properly fulfilled. The right of the Rajah to his ſeveral dominions were likewiſe eſtabliſhed. Subſequent to theſe tranſactions the nabob and Rajah were connected in a variety of undertakings. In ſettling their reſpective claims, in conſequence of theſe new engagements, the Rajah inſiſted that he ought to be allowed for certain military ſervices performed for the nabob; and the nabob, that he was entitled to the ſums ſtipulated by the late convention, withont any abatement.

The ſeveral powers in whoſe meaſures the preſidency at this time were moſt deeply intereſted, were the Marrattos, the Nabob, and the Rajah.—The former diſcovered the ſtrongeſt anxiety for engaging the Company in an offenſive alliance, not for their aſſiſtance in the field. They were themſelves more than a match for Hyder Ally.—But they very ſincerely wiſhed to inveigle us into ſuch a connection, as might determine us to take an active part in the deſtruction of his capitals, that they might have nothing further to dread from our ſubſequent attachment to the fortunes of their enemy. To this meaſure the Nabob had taught them to believe, that they had it in their power to threaten or compel us when they pleaſed. And he was the more intereſted in the accompliſhment

of

of ſuch an alliance, that he expected to have obtained in return a conſiderable ſhare of the conquered territories. The king of Tanjore had always been apprehenſive that the Nabob wiſhed to poſſeſs himſelf of his country the moment he was able, but his apprehenſions were more than ever confirmed, ſince the arrival of the Britiſh Plenipotentiary. He was conſequently deſirous of involving the Carnatic, in proportion as his own ſafety depended on the inability of the Nabob. And the Marrattos ſeemed prepared for any enterprize that would moſt effectually prevent our aſſiſting Hyder, and command our acquieſcence in the terms they propoſed.

It might have been expected, that, thus ſituated, the preſidency of Madras would have endeavoured to compromiſe the difference between the Nabob and the Rajah. They adopted, however, an oppoſite policy, and laid it down as a principle in their conſultations on the ſubject, that the Rajah was by much too powerful for his ſituation, and that his reduction was in ſome degree neceſſary to the peace of the Carnatic. Under the influence of this concluſion, an expedition againſt Tanjore was planned and executed, in concert with the Nabob, in the latter end of 1771. The king's miniſter on the coaſt was acceſſary to the meaſure, and gave it all the encouragement in his power, though the ſeaſon obliged him to leave the road before its completion.

The Company's troops were commanded by General Smith, who was enjoined to do nothing

but

but with the advice of Omdal ul Omrah Behauder, the nabob's eldest son. The army was thirty-six days before Tanjore. A breach was made in the walls, which the English, in revenge for the lives that were lost before the place, panted to storm. There was not an individual in the army who doubted the success of the enterprize, when the young nabob prevented the hazard of a repulse, by concluding a peace with the Rajah. The army were enraged from their disappointment of the plunder they expected from the capture of the town. It was an event so little foreseen, that the news of it was every where received with surprise. The terms, though adequate to the causes assigned for the war, were not satisfactory. The Nabob's son protested that he was guided by the advice of General Smith, and that matters were precipitated by the severity of the rains, the sickness which prevailed in the camp, and a strong probability that the Marrattos approached to the relief of Tanjore. The general considered the honour of the army as sacrificed in this instance, by a conspiracy between the Nabob and his son. The Nabob found it also convenient to dissemble the greatest chagrin and resentment at a transaction so unequal to his wishes. But the displeasure of the presidency was expressed in the most pointed and explicit language. They declare to General Smith, "That in the "very commencement of peace they should be "providing as if they were on the very eve of a "war." The principles, however, in which the unpopularity of the peace originated are pretty obvious.

obvious. The legal claims of the troops to the booty, which the riches of the rajah promiſed on the reduction of his capital were defeated. The creditors of the Nabob had been given to underſtand, at the ſame time, that the treaſures of Tanjore would be put in his poſſeſſion; and that then his accounts would be liquidated. The government of Madras was alſo deceived. Co-operating with the nabob, in his hoſtilities againſt their ally, put an end to their connection; and as it deſtroyed all his future expectations in the treaty of Paris, it expoſed the Carnatic to the exaſperated intrigues of a man whoſe ſituation had become deſperate.

All the hopes which the Nabob had entertained of ſupport from the crown, in oppoſition to the intereſt of the Company, as exhibited and maintained by their ſervants, were, as he had ſhrewdly ſuſpected, ultimately viſionary. The remonſtrances of Sir John Lindſay had, perhaps, not ſufficiently conſulted the perſonal conſequence of the gentlemen who managed the concerns of the Company, to produce any ſubſtantial effect. He was ſuperſeded by Sir Robert Harland in the ſame important truſt, who was inveſted by the ſame powers, and inſtructed to perſevere in accompliſhing the ſame object. His reception, notwithſtanding the orders of the Directors to treat him with all that politeneſs and reſpect due to his ſtation and character, was ſtill cold and diſtant. He avowed it as one principal end of his commiſſion, to urge the claims of the Nabob, and to obtain, if poſſible, a more ſedulous attention to his intereſts, from the

 gentle-

gentlemen of the presidency. He asserted the right which the Nabob had to rely for support and protection from the crown. He reprobated with severity the opposition given to the least appearance of substantiating these natural and well-grounded expectations. He resolved the obvious jealousy which influenced the members of the council into a narrow and mistaken policy. And he upbraided them with censuring a measure which he conceived to be the sacred privilege of Majesty. This, however, proved to be no more than the strong unmeaning phrapology of official profession. The British goverment was too wise to persist in realizing projects incompatible with the Company's prosperity. The firmness of the presidency disposed Sir Robert to relax his tone. When the passions of both parties gave way to mature reflections, mutual complaisance took place, and a cordial exchange of good offices distinguished their subsequent intercourse. They were henceforth as closely united in facilitating, as they had widely differed before in their opinions concerning the interests of the Nabob. He was himself the sole occasion of the controversy, and it afforded him those useful instructions, that all application to other resources than his own prudence for redress under the wrongs he suffered from the presidency, were vain and nugatory; that, as he was circumstanced, no system whatever would operate effectual relief, in which their station, their consequence, and their expectations, were not properly consulted; and that the most solemn assurances of European

European monarchs were not more certain or unequivocal, than those of Indian Rajahs, Nabobs, Governors and Subahs.

The only active service which the troops had undertaken, subsequent to the Tanjore expedition, was the reduction of the Marawar and Nalcooty Polligars. These countries lie by the sea side, on the frontier of Tanjore, and have always been deemed dependencies of the Carnatic. They are inhabited by a brave, industrious, and independent people, who, from their habits of life, their mode of defence, their natural situation, and their contempt of danger, have never perhaps been wholly subdued. Inaccessible hills, and impenetrable woods, afford them a secure retreat from every enemy. To these fastnesses they retire when pursued, and issue from them at pleasure, to take advantage of the invaders. They have always held their lands by a kind of military tenure, by which they attend their respective chieftains to the field. They are fierce and barbarous to none but such as visit them with hostile intentions. They have the craftiness of all rude nations beset with powerful neighbours, anxious to reduce and enslave them. The Nabob avows no other reason for invading the powerful habitations of these innocent people, but that they were backward to pay a tribute extorted from them by force of arms. And he seems to have been suspected both by the gentlemen of the council and the officers of the army, to aim rather at extirpation than conquest. The fortifications, though numerous, were only defended by a rabble, and consequently soon reduced. It was impossible to draw the enemy into any formal engagement. On the approach of the English, expecting a continuation of their ancient privileges, they remained at their ploughs, and in some measure facilitated the means of conquering their chiefs. When most of the forts had fallen into our hands, they remained for the most part neutral, until they understood that the Nabob meant to rob them of those lands which they hoped to have retained. This policy threw the whole country into a flame. The ploughman every where took arms, and the villages were instantly converted into so many camps of observation. Soldiers as well as ploughmen, they could appear in what shape they pleased, with or without arms, but were sure never to expose themselves but where they had manifestly the advantage. It was therefore represented to the Nabob, and the Presidency, in a manner that did honour to the feelings of Colonel Bonjour, who commanded in the Nalcooty province, that this mode of settling the country would require extremities of a shocking nature. Nor then would he promise, that matters should be so adjusted as to produce satisfaction. He stated, that the villages were generally abandoned by the men as the troops advanced; that whatever baggage remained behind with such straggling parties as followed the detachment, were taken by those villagers; that as the aggressors were not to be found, and reprisals were indispensible, he was under the necessity of burning the cottages of the poor, and otherwise

punishing

punifhing the innocent and helplefs, who, incapable as they were of doing them any injury, could neither efcape nor refift the refentment of an enraged foldiery.

It is obfervable in the hiftory of thefe tranfactions, how often the moft fhocking details of war, from fcenes of cruelty and horror, are replete with leffons of mercy. But thefe defcriptions, even under the fanction of official difpatches, are feldom interefting to trading politicians, whofe minds are folely engroffed by articles of lofs and gain, who fend forth their armies, as they do their fhips, on principles of calculation, and who eftimate their military operations only by the fources of profit which they lay open, or the means of peculation which they procure. Thefe humane emotions in the breaft of a foldier, inftead of exciting any fympathetic fenfations, were repreffed by the ftudied filence of the council, and he was coolly enjoined to continue his exertions, which he did until the death of Tandwaray Pilla, the chief of the country, rendered them unneceffary.

This difgraceful campaign feems no improper epitome of all the Company's wars in the vicinity of their feveral fettlements. Whatever country promifes the cheapeft conqueft, anfwers moft effectually the views of ambition, or is on the whole beft calculated to repay the expence of exterminating its inhabitants, falls within the fatal circle of their military inftructions. And whether it is fituated on the one extremity of Indoftan or the other, the Company's allies muft be affifted,

 their

their troops employed, their territories enlarged, their treasure improved. Though the people who, in these cases, never have the faculty of election, would rather embrace than oppose them, though their manners may be as unprovoking as their lives may be useful, they may unfortunately have offended some base unprincipled knave of state, who has the address to satiate his revenge on his foes by means of his friends. It was thus with Rohilcund, with Nalcooty, and with Marawar. General Smith headed the expedition against this district in person. No regular force once appeared to intercept his march. The natives only made a stand in the defence of Ramanadaporam, the capital of the province, the seat of their government, the residence of their chiefs, and the strong hold where they deposited their treasure, and to which they repaired on the appearance of danger. The British artillery soon breached the walls, and Major Braithewaite's grenadiers carried the assault sword in hand. The Coleries were animated with fury. There were in the fort about three thousand armed men. A few took refuge in the palace, and saved their lives, as the first confusion was over before our troops advanced; but far the greater number bravely died in the breach, or threw themselves over the walls. In this manner was an expedition of the Company's troops completed, about the beginning of 1773, in which the most remarkable transaction is perhaps the recrimination which took place between the young Nabob and the officers of the British army, concerning the distribution of the booty.—

When

When he was but hiſſed by the ſoldiers who fought his battles, the gentlemen of the preſidency were alarmed, reſented the inſult, and interrogated the general. The remonſtrance of thoſe who conceived their intereſt affected by his avarice, was even conſtrued into an indignity, and their cauſe abandoned by their employers, that the embarraſſments of their ally might not be ſaid to originate in council. So wonderfully delicate was their tenderneſs for the Nabob of Arcot. It was not enough to ſay, that an apparent neglect of ceremony, where an individual alone was concerned, affected them much more deeply than the maſſacre of thouſands. But there was no channel by which the misfortunes of theſe wretched mortals could poſſibly touch their hearts. It was only to the etiquette of humanity that theſe doughty arbiters of national deſtiny were callous or inattentive *.

Notwithſtanding the conſtant attention which thoſe tranſactions required, both from the Nabob and the Preſidency, they loſt no time or opportunity of watching the King of Tanjore. It was the misfortune of this prince, that he was reputed to be immenſely rich; that he poſſeſſed one of the moſt valuable diſtricts in the Carnatic, and that ſo contiguous to the preſidency, and ſurrounded by the territories of the Nabob, he preſumed to aſſert his independence. Theſe were the true cauſes of the original quarrel taken up againſt him. The termination of this had left the ally and ſervants of the Company very much diſſatisfied. Solicitous

* Rous's Appendix, page 941.

for a breach of the friendship then subsisting, his minutest actions were critically inspected. The connections which had always been cultivated between him and the neighbouring powers were imputed to intrigues with the enemies of the Carnatic. The Nabob was incensed that the Polligars, whom he had so lately expelled, should find an asylum in Tanjore; the garrison at Vellum not having been provided for in the late treaty, were not sufficiently supplied with provisions; the Collerics, who live on the frontiers of his country, had seized some cattle from the province of Trichinopoly; a trifling debt which he owed the Company for paddy had not been discharged, and he was in arrears to the Nabob. These were the mighty reasons which decided the fate of the Rajah. He saw the storm that gathered around him. He knew the Nabob to be inexorable, and that the whole strength of the Company would be exerted to substantiate his most inordinate demands. He was in the condition of a person struggling for life, where every other idea is absorbed in that of self-preservation. The only powers who could afford him adequate security from the impending danger, were Hyder Ally and the Marrattos. With both he endeavoured to procure such assistance as the exigences of his situation required. But he was certainly not chargeable with treachery, or a just object of hostility or destruction, because impelled in this manner to an equivocal conduct, adopted or avoided upon the instant, to prevent his ruin.

The

The Nabob, perfectly acquainted with the mode of securing the co-operation of the Company's forces, easily prevailed with the Presidency to appoint a second expedition against Tanjore with a large army. Without fixing any precise terms for the Company, they engaged to place the fort, when taken, in his hands, with whatever stores or effects it might contain. But in case it should be captured by storm, the plunder was to be the property of the troops. The Rajah was not to be attacked unprepared. Though neither Hyder Ally nor the Marrattos would take an active part in the conquest, he found means to muster twenty thousand men, whom he armed in his cause. These were commanded by the aged, but faithful and brave Monajee. Both Danes and Dutch are said to have secretly assisted him with men, money and stores. Our troops entered his territories in the beginning of August, 1773. On the sixth of the same month, a skirmish happened between a party of the Nabob's cavalry and the enemy, in which the former had the advantage. The detail of the siege contained nothing very important or peculiar. On the twentieth, ground was broken before the place; the twenty-seventh, our batteries were opened, but a practicable breach was not effected before the seventeenth of September, when the fort was rather surprised than stormed, at noon, under a most intense heat, and while the garrison were at victuals in their own houses. The Rajah and his family, with Monajee and his sons, were made

made priſoners; and the Nabob, having agreed to ſatisfy the army, the place was not plundered.

The news of this conqueſt were received in England with univerſal reprobation and diſguſt.—It is hard to ſay which were moſt ſeverely criminated, the intrigues of the Nabob, or the temerity of the council. The meaſure was conſidered as repugnant to the policy of the Company, and to the ſpirit of thoſe orders which their ſervants were in the habit of receiving from the Directors. The only remedy which could be applied under theſe circumſtances, was the immediate reſtoration of the Rajah. And the great difficulty to be reſolved was, how this reſolution could be executed.—Their ſervants on the ſpot, whoſe ſeals were ſet to the outrage which it was deemed ſo neceſſary to redreſs, could not be entruſted with the carrying into effect a plan ſo obviouſly intended to fix a ſtigma on their former conduct. The many eminent and important ſervices which the Company owed to Lord Pigot, while laſt governor of Madras, ſuggeſted the idea of ſending him out a-new with full powers for accompliſhing the views of this delicate and arduous commiſſion. He was in high eſtimation for his civil adminiſtration, his military exertions, and his private character. From his appearance as governor and preſident of Madras, where he had acquired the moſt general and well-grounded reſpect, very ſanguine expectations were entertained. The Nabob, however, not a little anxious to defeat the intentions of the Directors, borrowed prodigious ſums of money from the mem-

bers

bers of the presidency, and others whose influence he thought worthy of purchase. A profusion of corruption not only took place in Madras, but is said to have extended to England, where an inundation of artful apologies for his conduct, replete with the most pointed invectives against the king of Tanjore, deluged, at least for some time, the public attention. It was about the latter end of 1775, that the noble Governor arrived at Fort Saint George. He announced to the Nabob of Arcot the contents of his commission, as soon as the various formalities essential to a legal assumption of government had taken place. The Nabob was not backward to maintain the ground in which he thought himself securely entrenched. He insisted on his claim to the country, by all the laws of India, and his treaties with the Company. His representations were without effect. Lord Pigot thought it his indispensible duty to see the orders of his constituents literally fulfilled. This he effected early in the Spring of 1776. The disputes that followed were peculiarly violent, obstinate and personal. Every subsequent regulation he proposed, met, from seven members of the council, with an ardent and inveterate opposition. It is said Tanjore had been pledged to these men as a security for the property which they had trusted in the Nabob's hands. This, they apprehended, would be lost, on the restoration of the Rajah; and they were not without suspicion, that the debt itself would be found in no better predicament. And when they became intemperate, his Lordship did not

not certainly preserve his moderation. Their differing so widely from him in opinion, on grounds which struck him at least as equivocal, the consequence he derived from the confidence of his employers, the honourable manner in which the merit of his former conduct had been acknowledged, and the necessity he conceived himself under, of losing no time in realizing the arrangements prescribed by the Directors, added to the natural severity of a carriage by no means conciliating, precipitated him in measures which it is impossible to justify. He advised Messrs. Stratton and Brook, that as he had something to propose in council which concerned them personally, it would be decent for them to withdraw. They implicitly complied with his request, and were instantly suspended by his casting vote. Sir Robert Flecher, commander in chief, was at the same time, and on the same account, laid under arrest.

This arbitrary conduct in the Governor was eagerly adopted by the secluded members as a precedent for justifying the step they had meditated. They instantly determined to secure the person of the president, and effect such a revolution in the settlement, as should put the power entirely into their own hands. Colonel Stuart had of course succeeded to the command of the forces. Any violence offered to his Lordship within the precincts of the fort, would subject the actors to the penalty of the mutiny-act. From this situation, however, he was artfully inveigled, in consequence of reposing an implicit trust in the fidelity and friendship

of

of the commander in chief. This gentleman paſſed ſeveral hours in the morning with Lord Pigot, on terms of the moſt unreſerved and cordial intimacy. He prevailed on the Governor to ſleep for that night at the villa where he generally retired in the evening. The Colonel invited himſelf to a ſeat in his Lordſhip's carriage. They were ſcarce half a mile from the fort, when Colonel Edington rode up, waved his naked ſword over the horſes heads, and called out, *Sipoys!* Captain Lyſaught at the head of a party, inſtantly ruſhed to the door of the chaiſe, and preſenting a piſtol, told his Lordſhip that he was his priſoner. Colonel Stuart, having no longer occaſion for diſguiſe, tore off the maſk, and ſeizing his Lordſhip rudely by the arm, bid him *Get out.* They precipitated him into a carriage that waited for the purpoſe, hurried him to the Mount, and delivered him into the cuſtody of Major Horne, the commanding officer there, with a declaration, that, if a reſcue was attempted, his Lordſhip's life ſhould anſwer for it.

The circumſtances to which his Lordſhip was reduced by theſe violent proceedings were now perilous in the extreme. His friends were ſcattered, over-awed, and kept at a diſtance. The ſtrength of the guards placed about him, the ſtrictneſs of his confinement, and the menacing orders under which he was committed, were calculated to impreſs him with an apprehenſion of the moſt fatal conſequences. His chief reſource in this melancholy ſituation was in the firmneſs of his own mind, which, in one inſtance at leaſt was probably the

means

means of preſerving his life. One night he was ſuddenly awaked by the arrival of an officer with a party of horſe, who brought a peremptory order for his removal, without ſpecifying whether he was to be carried, or how accommodated. His Lordſhip addreſſed himſelf briefly to the ſoldiers. He deſired them to recollect who he was, the ſervices he had formerly executed, the honours he had honeſtly acquired, and the condition to which, without indictment or trial, he was now reduced. He called upon them as men, as Chriſtians, as Britons, or even as ſoldiers, whether they could bear to ſee him dragged away to be murdered in ſo baſe, ſo cowardly, ſo inhuman a manner. He declared, at the ſame time, and with a manlineſs that ſhook the moſt reſolute of the aſſaſſins, that they might now do their worſt, kill him, or tear him to pieces. Theſe were acts which he could not prevent, but they were to be done upon the ſpot, from which he was determined they ſhould not take him alive.

The majority, in conſequence of this manœuvre, aſſumed, under a courſe of legal forms, all the powers of government. They arraigned the conduct of his Lordſhip in terms of peculiar aſperity, and vindicated their own as a duty to which they had been impelled by neceſſity. They alledged that he had trampled on the moſt material of the Company's bye-laws, and, by a non-compliance with ſome ſpecific clauſes of the regulating act, had forfeited all right to preſide in council. The principal leader in the conſpiracy was conſequently appointed

appointed his successor in the government. The very measure for which they blamed him most was the first they adopted. His friends were violently expelled from their seat in the council. Both parties sent expresses to England, the one to arraign, the other to justify, what had happened.

To this outrageous and unexpected revolution, the members composing the supreme government of Bengal gave their unequivocal approbation.—However their opinions clashed in other particulars, they united in supporting the conduct of the majority. It was impossible, indeed, for these gentlemen to act otherwise. The eagerness of the governor-general to avow so decided an opinion in favour of the usurpers, it was probably expected, would operate as a pledge or guarrantee, in opposition to the apprehension, that he might be tempted to extricate himself from the embarrassments under which he laboured, by a similar expedient. It was at the same time the interest of those who constituted a majority of that board, to support a precedent which not only justified their strenuous opposition to the chair, but set them an example of acting with vigour and spirit in the last extremity.

The Major's court in Madras displayed a spirit and coolness on this emergency, which certainly did the members of it peculiar honour, and was not expected. Mr. Turing, who was then major, owes but little to his education or his parentage.—His father was a Scotsman, and lived and died in the humble occupation of a barber in London.—It was the oddity of the father that disposed Sir

Charles

Charles Raymond to procure for the ſon the appointment of a writer in the Company's ſervice. He roſe through a variety of the ſubordinate ſtages in the civil eſtabliſhment, until it was his turn to preſide in this court. He openly and ſteadily reprobated the violence of the ſucceſsful party. The far greater part of the Britiſh inhabitants were of the ſame opinion. The injury done to the intereſt of the Company, in the outrage of Lord Pigot, was in fact regarded every where with the moſt general and ſerious condemnation.

The Company at home entered on the diſcuſſion of the ſubject without loſs of time. The friends of the different parties crouded to the ſcene of altercation. The conteſt was ſupported with warmth and vigour on both ſides. After the matter, however, had been long and ably argued in the court of Directors; it was finally ſubmitted to the deciſion of the proprietors at large, who in general court, March 26, 1777, agreed upon a reſolution, which was alſo confirmed, on a ballot, by a great majority, recommending to the court of Directors to take the moſt effectual meaſures for reſtoring Lord Pigot to the full exerciſe of the powers veſted in him by the Company, as governor and preſident of the ſettlement of Madras; and for enquiring into the conduct of the principal actors in his impriſonment, and in diſpoſſeſſing him of the exerciſe of the legal powers wherewith he was inveſted.

The reſult of this important deciſion was, that the court of Directors adopted the reſolution of reſtoring his Lordſhip to the full exerciſe of the office

office and powers from which he had been thus violently degraded. His four friends, who were ejected from the council, the court also reinstated. The usurpers were at the same time suspended. A new government was nominated, in which Mr. Rumbold was appointed second in council, and of course to succeed Lord Pigot in the chair. Nor did the conduct of Lord Pigot pass without censure.

Those resolutions, though calculated to compromise the dispute, only produced new animosity.—Ministerial influence, Mahomedan intrigues, and the friends of the majority, at last carried the point so far against the friends of Lord Pigot, as under an appearance of accommodating the difference subsisting between them, to procure a ballot in favour of a motion for ordering all the parties cognizable by the laws of England home to take their trial. Such a strange and sudden revolution in the orders of the Company, was seriously astonishing to every one not thoroughly initiated in the mysteries of their politics.

Governor Johnstone, however, the avowed friend of his Lordship, forthwith brought the question before a higher tribunal. He moved the House of Commons for several resolutions, which went to a strong approbation of Lord Pigot's conduct as governor, a confirmation of all those late acts of the Company, which had either passed in his favour, or condemned the conduct of the majority who deposed him, and a formal revocation of the resolution for his recal.

The Nabob of Arcot has generally been confidered as having a principal fhare in thefe turbulent movements. A parliamentary inveftigation bared the iniquitous plot, and demonftrated, in a fatisfactory manner, that the council of Madras, his Majefty's minifters, and the whole machinery of the Britifh government, were under the fecret controul of this Tartar Prince *. The Houfe was fully in poffeffion of the fubject, by the prefence of the parties moft deeply concerned in the difcuffion, and the perfons whofe talents, fituation, and induftry, afforded the beft information. The feveral arguments for and againft the motion, which had been broached in the court of Directors, and by the proprietors at large, were confequently urged and refuted, with all the eloquence of the Britifh fenate.

The gentlemen who oppofed the motion arraigned the arbitrary government of Lord Pigot, in the moft unqualified terms. They alledged that his confinement was the unavoidable refult of a violence, which, on his part, threatened an immediate fubverfion of all legal authority; that in circumftances when accufations of fingular delinquency were made on all fides, and the leading evidences of facts depended on the prefence of the parties, it was proper and equitable, that all of them fhould be in England, where only a juft and impartial enquiry into their conduct was practicable; that reinftating the late government would

* Debret's Parliamentary Regifter, including the Debate of May 22, 1777.

operate

operate in the Company's ſettlements as an approbation of his Lordſhip's outrages, and leave all their faithful ſervants, who had riſked ſo much in promoting their ſervice at the mercy of their inveterate enemy. And with all the virtues aſcribed to his Lordſhip, while the individuals who had been moſt active in his overthrow were within his reach, and he had power to puniſh them, who would anſwer for the conſequences. The preſidency appeared to them, in its preſent ſtate of diſſenſion and diſtraction, to have altogether diſqualified itſelf for managing the Company's affairs.—Every ſpecies of evil which negligence, the blindneſs of paſſion, the obſtinacy of prejudice, or the impetuoſity of party rage, were capable of producing, might therefore be expected. To continue the council, thus circumſtanced, was to hazard every thing valuable on that eſtabliſhment; and matters of the laſt importance to the Britiſh intereſt, in theſe parts, ought not, in their opinion, to be in truſt with men ſo violently agitated by a perſonal ſtruggle for power. They treated the dangerous influence attributed to the Nabob as chimerical and abſurd. They deſcribed him as in a ſtate of the moſt abject dependence, without either force to controul, or wealth to undermine. And they boldly and vehemently declared, that all the allegations concerning his intrigues and bribery, whether in India or England, were equally unfounded, and originated only in the idle conjecture, or malicious ſuggeſtions of thoſe who wiſhed to injure his

 intereſt,

intereſt, or were utterly unacquainted with his character or circumſtances.

The reply to theſe arguments was not leſs ſpirited or explicit. The genius of a Burke, a Fox, and a Johnſtone, was never exerted, or ſtruck the houſe with greater ſplendour or more irreſiſtible energy. The whole proceedings which led to the preſent anarchy in the Preſidency of Madras were ſtated with force and preciſion, and the delegated authority under which the Company's ſervants acted, was liberally and impartially diſcuſſed. Governor Johnſtone opened the buſineſs, in a ſpeech of above two hours, in which he detailed the tranſactions of the Carnatic and Tanjore with his uſual ability, and every appearance of liberal and authentic information. He juſtified Lord Pigot, by ſuch a ſtatement of facts as could not be contradicted. His Lordſhip, he averred, had committed no violence, which, as an honeſt man who wiſhed to fulfil his engagements, he could avoid. He cenſured the motions of Sir H. Macworth in the India-houſe for the recal of his Lordſhip, as confounding the innocent with the guilty, and forming a barefaced apology for the groſſeſt uſurpation. And he thought the intrigues of the Nabob, even in this country, to be too palpable and operative, to be either overlooked or denied. The gentleman who ſeconded the motion, ſcrupled not to affirm, that the council who had aſſumed the power of the Preſidency received for their exertions from the Nabob, the enormous bribe of eight hundred thouſand pounds, in mortgages on the Tanjore country.

country. The tone of the debate was equally ſupported by the ſpeakers who followed. The reſolutions in which the argument originated were expoſed with infinite wit and ridicule to the contempt and deriſion of the houſe. They were contradictory, and impracticable. They preſcribed an equal puniſhment for thoſe who did and thoſe who did not their duty, for thoſe who had proved faithful to their truſt, and thoſe who had proved treacherous, and they involved principles of retribution which exiſted in no other part of the world. They aſſerted, that Government here had actually been bought to vindicate by its ſanction the iniquitous cauſe of a faction there. In this manner a combination among the Proprietors was formed, and influenced by motives of immediate convenience, to endanger their own intereſt in the Company. The honour of a tried and able ſervant, and the rights of a faithful ally, were, as they apprehended, groſsly and wantonly ſacrificed. To accompliſh this unworthy purpoſe, the remoteſt dock-yards had been recently ſtript of their inhabitants, and all the various departments of ſtate in every corner of the kingdom evacuated to carry a queſtion in the India-Houſe. All this, and every other miſchief that had lately happened, or might ſtill be apprehended, on the coaſt of Coromandel, they roundly attributed to the meaſure which had been adopted of ſending plenipotentiaries to negotiate treaties with the country powers, independent of the Company, and in direct violation of her chartered rights. They foreſaw the interpoſition of miniſtry in Lea-

O 3 denhall

denhall and India had hitherto been equally ruinous, and would ultimately prove fatal. What they could not do here was generally effected on the spot. The Directors were ciphers the moment they differed from his Majesty's ministers, and their orders, without the approbation of Government, only proved in India words without meaning.—The Company had no longer any authority over its own servants. Seperate interests were formed and factions established, in all its settlements and dependencies, and its former influence and respectability with the powers of the empire were no more. There was not a principle urged in behalf of this recal which might not warrant the recal of all the governors and councils, with every other description of men with whom the civil or criminal administration was lodged, in our settlements or colonies in every part of the world. The pretence of faction would always be at hand to justify every outrage. It was by the operations of this powerful and dangerous engine, a popular credulity, that tyranny became gigantic, monstrous, and detestable! The Nabob could not wish for a method better calculated to gratify the most sanguine inclination of his nature. It had no other tendency than to establish that independence, which he so anxiously desired. Whenever any of his designs were controverted, he could be at no loss how to procure a majority of the council. His treasures would operate on all future emergencies as it had done on this, and the Company would find it difficult to prevent the recal of any servant, however worthy,

worthy, popular or able, when hardy enough to undertake their orders with upright intentions.

The queſtion being at laſt put, at one o'clock in the morning, [May 22, 1777,] the motion of Governor Johnſtone was rejected, by a majority of twenty-three. All the exertions of his friends, however, had they been crowned with ſucceſs, were now too late. For, after being in confinement for a period of near nine months, harraſſed by the difficulties of a moſt critical ſituation, agitated by the workings of various paſſions excited by the extraordinary circumſtances in which he was involved, and labouring under the preſſure which he felt from the gloomy aſpect which the Company's affairs every where exhibited, he died on the 18th of May, 1777, probably of a broken heart. His brother, Admiral Pigot, moved and carried next year, ſome time in April*, in the Houſe of Commons, for an addreſs, "praying his Majeſty, "that he would be graciouſly pleaſed to give directions to his Attorney-General to proſecute "George Stratton, Henry Brooke, Charles Floyer, and George Mackay, Eſquires, for ordering their Governor and Commander in chief, "George Lord Pigot, to be arreſted and confined "under a military force, they being returned to "England, and now within the juriſdiction of his "Majeſty's courts of Weſtminſter-Hall."

It came out in evidence, before the bar of the Houſe, on this occaſion, that George Dawſon,

* Debret's Parliamentary Regiſter of this date.

Eſq;

Esq; who was a member of council during the heat of the contest, was positively offered by the Nabob's son no less a sum than forty thousand pounds, only for staying away one particular day, on which a question of consequence, relative to Tanjore, was to be agitated. It was certainly not unnatural for the friends, at least, of Lord Pigot, to presume from a fact thus specific, flagrant and authentic, that those applications could hardly be confined solely to Mr. Dawson.

In stating an impartial estimate of this important transaction, however, certain allowances ought no doubt to be made, for the joint influence of situation and emergency; the sympathy which it is so natural to feel for the weakest, who in every serious struggle must always be the suffering party; the general operation of his Lordship's high character in his favour, the obvious prepossessions under which he was invested with the government of the presidency, the prior obloquy, whether just or not, which rested on the conduct of the Company's servants, and that unavoidable crimination with which we instinctively connect the violence of the exertion with the interest and magnitude of the object.

Whatever may be said of his Lordship's abilities, great reverence and admiration are certainly due to the memory of his virtues. His former government in India was at least respectable. It exhibited both sagacity and vigour of enterprize. The situation in which he died gives the lie to all the surmises of a Benfield and others, who sought, for their

their profligate oppofition to his government, an excufe in his want of integrity. For he withftood a temptation of fix hundred thoufand pounds, to forbear only for a fhort given time carrying the orders of his conftituents into effect. And it is no contemptible proof how far he was fuperior to that general and fafhionable corruption which then predominated, that his houfes and effects in India were all fold to difcharge the debts he had there contracted. Various opinions, it is probable, may long be entertained, concerning the mode which he ought to have preferred in managing a refractory majority of council; but his error can never juftify the outrage to which his perfon and government were fubjected, by thofe who depofed and imprifoned him. And it will be remembered, when all the fophiftry by which the truth has been fo much obfcured and difguifed is forgotten, that his oppreffors were folemnly pronounced guilty by a jury of their countrymen.

CHAP-

CHAPTER VII.

The Regulating Act—Institution of the Supreme Council—Character of its Members—Posture of Affairs on the Continent of India—Government of the Majority—They censure the System of the former Administration—Condemn the Rohilla war, which Mr. Hastings defends, and withholds his Correspondence with the Resident—The Troops recalled from that Expedition—Treatment of the Great Mogul—Operations of the Army—The Governor-General charged with corrupt Practices before the Board—Death of Sujah ul Dowlah—The Story of Nuncomar—Effects of these Alterations in England.

THE politics of the East-India Company are so extensive and complicated in their operations, and so generally destructive in their effects, that Indostan perhaps is the only country in the world where they could have commanded the least prosperity. Independent of enormous charges habitually incurred by an endless series of expensive and important establishments in every department of state, the resources of this great and opulent empire are loaded with that vast and permanent commercial sustem, which is the ultimate and ostensible object of the whole arrangement. The safety, the happiness, and the prosperity of the subject, which ought to be the principal and invariable concern of of Government, are lost in a perpetual solicitude to increase the treasure of the Company, to furnish their annual investments, to supply their expenditure, and to accumulate the fortunes of individuals.

It is a fundamental maxim in the best regulated system of finance, to assess the public in proportion only to its real exigence, and to apply with a conscientious exactness whatever surplus may remain to meliorate these assessments. In the Government of the Company, however, this principle is impracticable. Those trading potentates have a personal and private interest at home, to which their possessions and dominions abroad are merely subservient. And all the ravages and merciless devastations which so invariably characterize the British conquests and authority in India, have certainly originated in a settled predilection for this interest. The resources of the country are consequently exhausted to supply a constant exportation of its wealth, for which it has no return; to enrich individuals, who reserve their expenditure for another climate; and to answer the exigences of a system from which it derives no adequate benefit. Here the prodigious deficiencies in the aggregate produce of territory and commerce, which often fall upon the Company's affairs with such a pressure as threatens their extinction, invariably arise: this accounts for all the various and frequent embarassments into which they are plunged both in India and England. A vein is thus opened, or rather a vessel burst, in the body politic, by which the

the vital fountain which feeds the current of its health and vigour is ſuddenly and ſenſibly diminiſhed. This inceſſant and increaſing drain, by which the exuberance of the eaſt has ruſhed like a flood, for above half a century, upon almoſt every nation in Europe, could not have been at any time ſupplied by ordinary means. In fact, a ſtandard of acquiſition was early eſtabliſhed in that country, on principles of violence and venality, which it has been the uniform ambition of all ſucceeding adventurers to equal, and in many inſtances to ſurpaſs.— The only ſyſtem of buying and ſelling eſtabliſhed by the ſervants of the Company, eſpecially ſince their aſſumption of ſovereignty in Bengal, has been to ſeize by force what goods they pleaſe, and at their own price, and by the ſame means to diſpoſe of them.

Theſe requiſitions, accompanied by an authority that was omnipotent, were anſwered for ſome time with punctuality. And the diſburſements of that tranſitory period did not exceed the profits of the Company. When once thoſe, however, who had lands, were wantonly deprived of them, when there remained no more money to be extorted; when the manufactures of the mechanic were torn from his loom; when the farmer, and even the Ryot, were robbed of their rice; and when the Zimindar, no longer able or willing to proſtitute the honour of his family, or the riches of his anceſtors, for the private purchaſe of protection, fell a ſacrifice to rapacity, this enormous flux of wealth obviouſly decreaſed. Britiſh adventurers, at the

head

head of armies, though ardent and indefatigable in their duty of exploring and plundering a defenceless people, were satisfied, after a series of the most shocking experiments, to admit the humiliating maxim, that the only permanent and solid resources of a commercial country do not consist in contributions raised by military coercion, but in a sedulous cultivation of the soil, in the improvement of manufacture, in the industry, the population, the general and domestic felicity of its inhabitants. Revenues, supplied by means exterior to these, must be as precarious in their nature, as they are flagitious in the acquisition. And it is not more absurd to expect life without sustenance, or strength without health, than that a government, in the common operations of which there is neither honour nor humanity, should, for any length of time, be either prosperous or lasting.

The situation of the Company, in 1772, demonstrates the truth of this observation. Their circumstances at that time were so critical and equivocal, that they were universally deemed on the very eve of bankruptcy. The general aspect of their affairs was every where alike gloomy and foreboding. Their government at home and abroad was equally without firmness and efficiency. Venality, luxury, and inattention, had pervaded, relaxed, and enervated every spring in the system.— The country was wasted and depopulated by extortion, by famine, and by emigration; the army, in various situations, were the victims of inactivity, or the instruments of outrage; the treasury was

empty,

empty, and the annual ſtipulation appropriated to government unpaid. The preſſure of theſe united difficulties was the more ſenſibly felt by the Directors, that the Bengal bills were now almoſt due.— They were impelled to make application to Miniſtry, for new pecuniary aids, who referred them to the Bank of England. Nor was it without reluctance, that the Bank conſented, after much deliberation, to advance the loan of two hundred thouſand pounds.

All theſe inconveniencies had originated, as uſual, in the flagrant miſmanagement of their ſervants. This the Company determined to correct with all poſſible expedition and efficiency, by the inſtitution of an extraordinary commiſſion for that purpoſe. This appointment, ſimilar to the plan of that which had gone out in the Aurora frigate, was confirmed in a general court of Proprietors, and even ſanctified by his Majeſty's approbation. The Company, in the mean time, was reduced to the neceſſity of applying to Parliament for a relief, in ſome degree adequate to their exigencies. They petitioned for a million and a half, at an intereſt of four per cent. with the liberty of repaying it by inſtallments of not leſs than three hundred thouſand pounds, and promiſed that their dividend ſhould not be more than ſix per cent. until the debt was reduced one-half. Much heſitation was ſhewn, and an intereſting diſcuſſion took place, when Parliament at laſt agreed, from conſiderations of neceſſary policy and expediency, to grant an immediate ſupply of one million four hundred thouſand pounds. An enquiry into the ſtate of the Company's affairs being appointed and carried

carried on by a committee of the House, it was at the same time formally stated and brought up in a report, that, notwithstanding these difficulties, a commission was actually preparing and formed, on principles of such extravagance, that the legislature would be warranted in preventing its execution.

An idea so just in itself, thus seasonably broached, was eagerly approved and adopted by the House. A bill, framed to give it effect, was therefore immediately brought in and passed, though two members in the direction earnestly pledged themselves, that the commission, which had proved so obnoxious, should not take place until such progress was made in the present enquiry, as might appear to justify the measure. But this security, however respectable in itself, or solemnly pledged to the House, was by no means deemed adequate, as the court of Directors might at any time be controuled by a majority of the proprietry at large.

Early in 1773, it was also resolved, from motives of indisputable prudence, according to some, or more probably to answer the views of ministerial intrigue, as others shrewdly conjectured, to restrain the future dividends of the Company *. By such obvious encroachments of prerogative, the public were alarmed with the idea that Government intended to seize the Company's property, and destroy their charter. The minister, however, soon put an end to these apprehensions, at least for the time, by proposing †, that the territorial

* Debret's Parliamentary Register of March 23, 1773.

† April 5—30.

acquisitions

acquiſitions ſhould remain in the poſſeſſion of the Company ſix years longer. The public clamoured and the Company inveighed, and even petitioned the Houſe in oppoſition to theſe proceedings, but without effect. The ſubject had occupied Parliament for above two months, and deeply intereſted the attention of the whole nation. Reſolutions to the following effect were at length moved for by the miniſter *, and made the foundation of a bill for eſtabliſhing certain regulations for the better management of the affairs of the Eaſt-India Company, both in India and England. That the election of Directors ſhould be put upon a new footing; that the right of voting ſhould be taken from every proprietor not poſſeſſed of a thouſand pounds ſtock; that a ſupreme court of judicature ſhould be inſtituted for India; that the judges in this eſtabliſhment ſhould be nominated by the Crown, and that a ſuperiority ſhould be given to the Preſidency of Bengal over all the other preſidencies in India.

The object of this famous regulating-act, which, after a world of altercation in both Houſes of Parliament, obtained the ſanction of the Legiſlature, was a total revolution in the whole ſyſtem of the Company's government. The Court of Directors was to derive additional force from the annihilation of thoſe factions, with the creation of which that of the proprietry was chargeable. Proviſion was made for ſecuring an impartial adminiſtration

* Debret's Parliamentary Regiſter, May 3.

of

of juſtice among the natives, under the government of the Company's ſervants in India; and thus a bar of apparent efficacy was raiſed and eſtabliſhed againſt the tyranny and oppreſſion exerciſed by British ſubjects reſident in that country, and acting under the delegated authority of their maſters. A general ſuperintending council was at the ſame time conſtituted, and inveſted with ſupreme controuling powers. The obvious view of the legiſlature in this part of the new ſyſtem, was to unite and conſolidate the ſtrength of the Company, that, on emergencies of common danger, the co-operation of all the ſettlements might be attended with that uniformity which is neceſſary to give it effect. So that, in all the Company's connection with foreign ſtates, and thoſe tranſactions eſpecially which relate to peace and war, ſhe is henceforth to be viewed as wielding the ſceptre of one vaſt and extenſive empire, the principal members of which, however remote in point of local ſituation, are all dependent on the ſame head.— Nor was it the leaſt intereſting feature in the meaſure, that the ſervants of the crown were introduced to a ſhare in the management of the Company's affairs, which were now ſo blended or involved with thoſe of the public, that it was preſumed the latter could not be properly and faithfully adminiſtered, without a ſedulous attention to the former. His Majeſty's miniſters were therefore made partakers of the Company's patronage, and in ſome degree reſponſible for the characters and capacities of the perſons employed in that ſituation.

tion. And it was ordered in the act, that every thing in the Company's correspondence from India, which related to civil or military affairs, should, within fourteen days after the receipt of it in England, be laid before the secretary of state; and matters more immediately connected with the revenue, were directed by the same authority to be inspected by the commissioners of the treasury.

Mr. Hastings was appointed governor-general; General Clavering, Colonel Manson, Mr. Barwell, and Mr. Francis, counsellors. The term of holding these important offices was limited to five years, from their arrival in Bengal, and assuming the government. Nor were they removeable, except by the King, upon a representation from the Directors. The first situation, in case of a vacancy, was to be filled by the next in rank, and the place of counsellor supplied by the Directors, with consent of his Majesty, under his sign manual, during the first five years. The establishment of a board of trade, and the regulation of such particulars as were made the specific objects of that jurisdiction, formed also a material part of this act.—It invested the governor-general, and four counsellors, with the same powers as were then, or had at any time been exercised by the president and council, or select committee in the kingdom of Bengal, Bahar or Orissa. The opinion of the majority was in all cases of difference to decide the question, and where the number present should on any account, or by any accident, be divided, the governor-general, or, in his absence, the senior member,

member, was to have a casting voice. It limited the exercise of their supremacy over the other presidencies, to the prerogative of declaring war, making peace, or negociating other treaties with Indian princes. It enjoined obedience to the orders of the Directors, and required the regular transmission of advices within a limited time. These the court of Directors was at the same time required to lay before one of his Majesty's principal secretaries of state. The governor-general and council, chief-justice or member of the supreme court of judicature, all collectors, supervisors, and any of his Majesty's subjects employed in the collection of the revenues, were prohibited from carrying on any dealings or transactions of traffic or commerce whatever. And a clause against receiving, directly or indirectly, any present, gift, donation, gratuity or reward, pecuniary or otherwise, or any promise or engagement for them, extended to every person holding either civil or military office under the crown or the Company.

Mr. Hastings was then governor, and Mr. Barwell a member of the existing council and presidency of Bengal. The three other gentlemen nominated to complete the board, left England in the month of April, [1774.] Their authority was only to take effect by the first of August, in the same year. Previous to their departure, the court of Directors agreed upon a body of instructions for their servants in their respective situations, which were approved by counsel, as legal, and consistent with the provisions and spirit of the act. These were addreſſed in the aggregate to the governor-general and council of Fort-William.

The advice which accompanied this great code of Britiſh legiſlation and juriſprudence to the banks of the Ganges, from the court of Directors to the gentlemen inveſted with this new delegation, was important and material. It inculcated the moſt perfect harmony among themſelves, as of eſſential and indiſpenſible neceſſity to the welfare of the Company, and an honourable diſcharge of the truſt repoſed in them. It preſſed the propriety and conſequence of fixing their attention on the preſervation of tranquillity, through the whole Indian empire, the protection of the Company's territories, and the improvement of their revenues. And it directed them in the exerciſe of their controul over the other preſidencies, in queſtions relating to peace and war, that they ſhould carefully ſtudy the intereſts and probable connections of the country powers with each other, with the Company, and with other European nations; that they ſhould aim at nothing by other means, which could be obtained by negociation; that the general intereſt, in all its dependencies, ſhould regulate the meaſures of their government; but that, on no conſideration, ſhould they ever be tempted to loſe ſight of the ſafety and proſperity of Bengal. A ſhort hiſtory of the ſupreme government, under the influence of a majority of the council, will abundantly juſtify the foreſight of the court, in ſuggeſting theſe ſalutary directions.

The

The new adminiſtration did not take place until the latter end of October. It was compoſed of individuals not unqualified for occupying the important ſpheres to which they were called, with a capacity, an energy, and a dignity equal to the reſponſibility connected with the duty for which they ſtood committed. The deep, ſagacious, penetrating underſtanding; the cautious, wary, perſevering temper; the daring, original, and enterpriſing genius which have uniformly diſtinguiſhed the politics of the governor-general, faſhioned him with ſingular propriety to fill the higheſt department in a government which entruſted a few foreigners with the lives and properties of millions. To a very high ſenſe of honour, General Clavering added uncommon delicacy in his diſcernment of men and things. He connected the ſpirit and liberality of a gentleman with the conſcientious diſcharge of his duty, and an inviolable predilection for the ſacred regards of right and wrong. His ſenſibilities were probably too refined, and his morality too inflexible for the obliquities of Aſiatic politics. Theſe qualities, in ſuch a ſituation, might operate as defects of character. A government, not eſtabliſhed in principle, was unlikely to proſper by the virtues of its members. Colonel Manſon poſſeſſed all the honeſty, ſimplicity, and diſintereſted complaiſance of his profeſſion. He had firmneſs without obſtinacy; and, with an affability ſingularly amiable and conciliating, a mind open to conviction, a ſound underſtanding, and a warm heart; he maintained his opinions with ſtea-

 dineſs,

dineſs, and avowed his attachments to the laſt. Mr. Barwell, from long reſidence on the ſpot, great intercourſe with the natives, a turn for obſervation, and an intimate acquaintance with the manners and peculiarities of the country, poſſeſſed ſuch a valuable ſtock of local intelligence, as could not but afford him the readieſt and cleareſt aſſiſtance in caſes of the greateſt intricacy. Mr. Francis has a cool head, and a correct judgment. His opinions are formed with no common ſhare of ſhrewdneſs and preciſion. Endowed with a liberal education, accuſtomed to exerciſes which required attention, ſelection and digeſtion, and poſſeſſing habits of the moſt indefatigable induſtry, few men were better fitted for the arrangement, the detail, and the diſpatch of buſineſs. A miniſtry combining, exerting, and directing ſuch talents as theſe to one object, was equal to the management of the greateſt empire. They wanted only ſome grand prevailing intereſt to engroſs, cement, and ſtimulate their reſpective energies, and it was impoſſible but the wiſdom of their meaſures, the harmony, the efficacy, and the promptitude of their operations, muſt enſure them ſucceſs.

The expreſs orders of the Directors to Mr. Haſtings, even while at the head of the former adminiſtration, were, that no rank, ſtation, connection, or conſideration whatever, ſhould deter him from bringing every oppreſſion to light, and every offender, native and European, to condign puniſhment. Theſe, however, he conceived to be abſolutely impracticable, and embraced the firſt opportunity of announcing

nouncing that conviction to the Directors, in very decided language. He resolved every species of delinquency into the imbecility of the established system, and asserted the incompetency of their constitution for the management of extensive dominions, under charters originally framed for the jurisdiction of trading settlements. Whether he did not choose to encounter the obloquy which a close retrospection into the conduct of other governments might have occasioned. Whether he suspected or foresaw the opposition naturally to be expected in carrying on such an invidious enquiry might overset his government. Whether the sentiments of private friendship might not operate as insuperable obstacles to the performance of public duty, or whether all these considerations might not have their weight in determining his resolution on so material a part of his office, it would be presumption to affirm. But the conduct of his colleagues in office soon afforded him full and repeated opportunities of exemplifying, in his own defence, the truth of that impracticability, which he had so firmly asserted.

The introduction of a new system was a measure which, in its own nature, implied a complete condemnation of the old. It would at least have ill become the legislature to attempt a reformation where nothing was either useless, defective, or improper. The members sent from home considered themselves as bound by this construction of the act. The spirit and tendency of former institutions had occasioned the powers with which they were invested. Their official existence, for that reason, stamped an indelible censure on the conduct of their predecessors. The character of Mr. Hastings, by the sanction of the British parliament, appeared on the face of the revolution, an honourable exception to the delinquencies in which it originated. To him was assigned the direction of the new government. He possessed the principal situation in the service of his employers. The legal prerogatives of his station were eminent and extensive. He presided in the council, he corresponded exclusively with the native princes in India. His name gave validity and authenticity to every public deed. These distinctions were by no means calculated to lessen or depreciate his personal merits in the eyes of his colleagues. They went, in fact, to India with the strongest prepossessions in his favour. If their own positive and repeated declarations are entitled to belief, they did not entertain a doubt, but that the high reputation which he bore among his friends at home, was no more than due to his exertions abroad. And notwithstanding the various surmises which they accidentally heard in their way to Bengal, and which threw some degree of shade on the flattering idea which they had previously formed of his politics, his abilities, and his virtues, they were not without hopes that he would answer the purposes of his appointment to their satisfaction, as well as that of the public.

The Governor-general, at the first meeting of the new government, [Oct. 25, 1774] embraced, with great

great propriety, that occaſion for explaining, eſpecially to the gentlemen ſo recently arrived from Europe, the preſent poſture of the Company's affairs, more particularly as connected with the preſidency, the dominions, and the dependencies of Bengal. He laid before them the whole complicated and multifarious ſyſtem of the revenne department. He directed their attention to a brief detail of the various adjuſtments and operations, by which this intricate and laborious buſineſs was managed and executed with effect. He pointed out a great number of new and nec ſſary regulations which, to anſwer the purpoſes of accuracy, expedition, and order, the late adminiſtration had introduced He ſtated, at the ſame time, in a very ſpecious manner, and with his uſual correctneſs and perſpicuity, the moſt material meaſures which the council had adopted and recorded, ſince he had the honour of ſitting in the chair. The Company's alliance with the Vizir of Oude, their treatment of the Emperor Shaw Allum, and the active and oſtenſible part which their troops had taken in reducing the Robilla tribes, he conſidered as ſo many circumſtances pregnant with the moſt ſubſtantial advantages to the Britiſh intereſt in that part of the world. Nor did he overlook, in this official narrative or ſtatement, the ſtrength, the views, or the connections of the neighbouring powers. He ſhewed what we had reaſon either to hope or fear from the friendſhip or enmity of the Marratto ſtates. He traced the diſſenſions of that powerful and warlike people through all their cauſes, progreſs, and conſequences,

quences, and diſcriminated the ſpecific aim of that competition which continued, by the domeſtic animoſities and internal convulſions it produced, to reſtrain the vigour of their government from all exterior exertion or enterprize. He exhibited the dominions of Berar as peculiarly intereſting to the Company, from their ſituation and proximity to thoſe of Bengal. Theſe too were deſcribed as involving different intereſts, from the peculiar connections, politics, and principles of the chiefs who poſſeſſed them. The movements of this mighty ſtate, eſpecially as being cloſely united by blood to that of the Marrattos, he conceived, ought to be narrowly and aſſiduouſly watched by the ſupreme government. And he concluded, with inſinuating the moſt ſanguine expectation, that by proper management on the part of the Company, no inconſiderable advantages might accrue to them and to the Britiſh nation, from the general reſult of thoſe arrangements *, which he had thus ſummarily detailed.

The

* *To elucidate this part of the ſubject, the whole of the Governor-general's minute on that occaſion ought to be inſerted. I have omitted the references to original documents in the various offices, as the former can be of no uſe except to ſuch as have acceſs to the latter.*

" All the Members of this Council being now aſſembled, I could wiſh to point out ſome general plan for carrying into execution the regulations of the new ſyſtem of government, agreeably to the inſtructions received from the Company; but upon an attentive review of the various ſubjects which occur, I find it neceſſary to ſelect ſuch particular parts of them as ſeem to claim your earlieſt notice; reſerving the reſt for future conſideration, to be taken up

in

The gentlemen from England were ſtruck with peculiar aſtoniſhment and concern by ſome parts of

in the order in which their reſpective importance or particular exigences may point out. I ſhall take the liberty to accompany every propoſition with a brief relation of ſuch circumſtances, and ſuch paſt tranſactions, as have any relation to it, and are neceſſary to be known, for the purpoſe of forming your reſolutions upon it. I mean not, gentlemen, to preclude any other Member of the Council from offering any point for preſent deliberation, which, in his judgment, may claim a preference in point of time, above thoſe which I may wiſh to introduce. I only propoſe this method as the moſt likely to facilitate the diſpatch of buſineſs, which may be retarded by undertaking too many ſubjects at the ſame inſtant. It will unavoidably take ſome time to arrange and perfect the new ſyſtem of this adminiſtration; in the mean while, the current affairs will require your daily aſſiſtance to keep them in motion; and in both, I mean both in forming the new mode of government, and conducting the daily buſineſs, you will find it neceſſary to conſult the records of the former adminiſtration, for the ſake of due connection and conſiſtency. I deſire alſo to ſhorten the time, and leſſen the trouble of ſuch a ſearch among the voluminous books of conſultations, by the mode propoſed, of laying before you a ſuccinct view of each ſubject, with references to the conſultations for the ſucceſſive orders which have been iſſued, and the advices which have been received concerning them. I think it my duty to add, and I think I may do it, without preſuming too much upon the experience which I have acquired in the affairs of this government, that I ſhall be at all times happy to aſſiſt any Member of the Council with my communications upon any point upon which he may deſire to be ſo informed.

"Profeſſions of zeal, and ſolicitude for the public good, are too commonly made uſe of to be received with implicit credit; but I feel my own honour, and my own intereſt, ſo intimately blended with the ſucceſsful iſſue of the meaſures of this government, that I may with truth, and without hazard of having my declaration ſuſpected, affirm, that I have not a wiſh, even for myſelf, which has not the good

of this intelligence. The suspicions which the rumours they had heard in their way to India, and which

good of the Company for its immediate object, and my own ultimately, as derived from it. I believe I may safely conclude the same for the other gentlemen embarked with me in this great undertaking; and I have the most thorough confidence in your disposition to unite with me in the prosecution of the Company's interests, while I, with the strictest sincerity and cordiality declare, that nothing on any part shall be wanting to render that union effectual.

"The points which I shall beg leave to submit to your consideration are, first, the mode of conducting the business of the revenue; and next, the political system of these provinces.

"The general mode which is at this time established for the management of the collections, is as follows: The provinces are formed into six divisions; each comprehending several inferior districts, under the direction of a Chief and Council; these receive their orders from the Board at large, and report to them their proceedings in a separate department, called a Council of Revenue; and for the greater facility of dispatching business with the inhabitants, and for the preservation of the ancient forms and rules of office, a Dewan or minister of the revenue is appointed to each division, who is joined to the Provincial Council, and keeps all the accounts and records of the country languages. Native superintendants are also appointed to each district of the provincial divisions, with the title of Naibs, and correspond with the Provincial Councils and Dewans. The Dewans also transmit their accounts and proceedings to an office of ancient institution, lately transferred from the city of Moorshedabad to Calcutta, named the Khalsa, which is under the charge of an officer entitled the Roy Royan, who occasionally sits at the meeting of the Councils of Revenue, and is the channel of communication between the Board and the Dewans, transmitting to the latter the counterparts of the orders of the Board, which are sent to the Provincial Councils, and receive their answers. The exceptions to this general system are, the province of Chittagong, which, from its remote situation and small revenue, has been left under the single charge of the chief of the factory; and

which a variety of circumstances inspired, on their arrival were confirmed. The great principle of govern-

and the districts of Pallamow and Ramgur, under Captain Camac; and of the Jungulterry of Curruckpoor, &c. under Captain Browne. These may be properly termed military collectorships. They are composed of the wild mountainous part of the country, which have been lately reduced to a state of submission to government, and require the continual presence of a military force to keep them in subjection. The revenue which they yield is inconsiderable; but the possession of them is a security to the peace of the cultivated and more civilized lands in their neighbourhood, which, till their reduction, were continually exposed to the ravages of wild and lawless people inhabiting them. With these military collectors, the correspondence was carried on by the Governor only; but according to the instructions now received from the Company, it seems requisite that it should in future be conducted by the Council at large.

"I must beg leave to conclude this subject with earnestly offering my advice for the continuation of this system in all its parts, with such alterations only as the late change in the government has rendered indispensably necessary. Innovations are always attended with difficulties and inconveniences; innovations in the revenue, with a suspension of the collections, and a change at this season of the year, would be particularly dangerous, as the time of the heaviest payments is now approaching. For the same reason, your speedy determination upon the future mode of managing and collecting the revenues would prove of essential service.

"The Court of Directors have been advised of the formation of this establishment, in consequence of the orders transmitted to us in their letter of the 7th of April, 1773; and we may shortly hope to be furnished with their final determination concerning it. I must likewise recommend the continuance of the separation which was originally made, of the revenue department from the other offices of the government, as the only means by which it can be regularly conducted; and as there is no branch of the Company's affairs on which their interests so essentially depend, I pro-government, to the operations of which report had attributed the moſt ſalutary and ſubſtantial amend-

ments

I propoſe that the Council do aſſemble for the conduct of it, in the ſame manner as was practiſed by the late Council of Revenue.

" It will be neceſſary to form other ſubſidiary regulations for ſeparating the revenue from the commercial department, and preventing competitions between them, and to determine what ſervants ſhall be employed in the revenue branch; that the board of trade may be enabled to make choice, from amongſt the reſt, of ſuch as will be required for conducting the commercial buſineſs.

" The next point which I have propoſed for your conſideration, is, the political ſyſtem of theſe provinces.

" The alliance with the Nabob Sujah Dowlah, the Vizir of the empire, is the only foreign connection in which the government can with propriety be ſaid to be engaged. This took place originally by the treaty formed by Lord Clive at Illahabad, in the year 1765.

" By a new treaty with the Vizir, dated Sept. 8, 1773, in conſequence of an interview I had with him at Benares, the monthly ſubſidy for the extraordinary expence of our forces employed in his aſſiſtance, was fixed at the ſum of 210,000 rupees for one brigade; and the provinces of Cora and Illahabad ceded to him for the ſum of fifty lacks of rupees, of which twenty lacks were to be immediately due, and were accordingly paid; fifteen lacks were to be paid at the expiration of a year, and the remaining fifteen at the expiration of two years.

" At the ſame time, the Vizir had ſolicited the aid of our troops to reduce the Rohilla country, lying on the north of his dominions, between the Ganges and the mountains of Tibbet. The immediate plea for theſe hoſtilities, was, the breach of faith with which the Rohilla chiefs were charged in the ſupplies of money afforded by them to the Marrattos, againſt whom they had ſolicited and obtained the Vizir's aſſiſtance, under a ſolemn engagement to pay him forty lacks of rupees on the departure of the Marrattos, and for refuſing afterwards to fulfil that engagement.

" This

ments or reform, in every part of the whole official arrangement, was materially different from what they

" This enterprize, the design of which furnished the first occasion of my meeting with the Vizir, formed an article in the original draught of our treaty; but it was afterwards omitted at his desire; and I promised that it should still take place, if it suited the affairs of the Company, at any other time when he should find himself in a condition to resume it. Accordingly, in the month of January, 1774, the Vizir made a formal requisition of the assistance of a brigade of the Company's forces, for the defence of his dominions, and for the prosecution of his former purpose of invading the country of the Rohillas. For this service he engaged to pay the Company, besides the stipulated monthly subsidy, forty lacks of rupees when it should be concluded.

" The Vizir's request was granted; the second brigade was ordered on this service, and Colonel Champion, the provisional Commander in Chief, appointed to the command. Having been joined by the Vizir and his troops, he entered the Rohilla borders on 17th April, and on the 23d of the same month, attacked and defeated the army of the Rohillas, commanded by Hafez Rahmet, their leader, who was killed in the action. This victory was decisive; no other enemy appeared in the field; and the Vizir having obtained possession of the greatest part of the country, both armies marched on the 7th of May to the city of Bisfooly, where quarters were prepared for them, and it was intended they should pass the rains there; but the remaining leaders of the Rohillas having assembled forces, under the command of Fyzoolla Cawn, at Nejeebgur, a town on the northern frontier of the country, the Vizir, apprehending their acquiring too great strength, and that the Marrattos might return to interrupt the operations before they were brought to a conclusion, prevailed upon Colonel Champion to put the brigade again in motion, about the latter end of July, and to march with him against the enemy, although the rains were then at their height. The troops enjoyed remarkable good health, and proceeded without opposition to Pottergur, the enemy flying before them to the skirts of the hills, whither the combined armies have

they expected. They ſaw the powers of the Company wantonly exerted to give ſanction and ſucceſs to

have followed them. They have lain for a conſiderable time within a ſhort diſtance of each other; Colonel Champion waiting for orders from the Select Committee, to purſue the enemy beyond the line to which he conceived himſelf limited by his inſtructions. The neceſſary orders were ſent, and we have been for ſome time paſt in daily expectations of hearing that the war was brought to a conclusion, either by the attack and defeat of the enemy, or by negociation. The laſt letters from Colonel Champion, which you, Gentlemen, have read, were dated the 2d inſtant, and adviſe, that Fyzoolla Cawn had delivered himſelf up, but that the negociation was ſtill continued.

"The advantages propoſed from this expedition were, 1ſt, an addition of territory, and, of courſe, of wealth to the Vizir, in which the Company will always participate. 2d. The completion of the defenſive line of his dominions, by freeing them from an inconvenient neighbour; and by taking into them the whole ſpace included between the Ganges and the northern mountains. 3d. The employment of a third part of our force, and a ſaving at the ſame time of its expences. And laſtly, the ſtipulation of forty lacks, to be paid on the concluſion of the undertaking. The retreat of the Marrattos to their ancient territories, and the violent diſſenſions which had ariſen in their ſtate, were arguments ſtrongly favouring the time which was choſen for beginning the war; and the juſtice of it is ſupported by the undoubted refuſal of Hafez Rahmet to fulfil the conditions of his treaty with the Vizir, of which the original, witneſſed by General Sir Robert Barker, is in our poſſeſſion.

"Many detached events, ſuch as the claim of the army to a ſhare in the plunder of the conquered country, the donation offered to them by the Vizir, a claim of the King Shah Allum to a ſhare of the conquered diſtricts, will appear in the courſe of the correſpondence between the Select Committee and Colonel Champion, and do not require further notice in this place.

"The ſecond payment of the treaty money for Corra and Illahabad ſtill remained undiſcharged by the laſt advices; but

to oppression and outrage, to prosecute and realize the wildest projects of ambition, at the expence of what-

but orders had issued for effecting it, and an English gentleman had been appointed by the Vizir to receive and take charge of it at Fyzabad, his capital.

"The monthly subsidy has been paid with sufficient exactness; at least we have had no information to the contrary. The forty lacks of rupees, stipulated for the performance of the present service, I consider as now due, though the Vizir makes some objections; but the defeat of Fyzoolla Cawn's troops, or the conclusion of the negociation with him, has, probably by this time, put the Company's right beyond dispute. There remains also a small balance of former accounts still unadjusted; these will constitute the principal part, if not the whole of our concerns with the Vizir; when the business on which we have been to this time engaged with him is concluded, I apprehend no difficulty in procuring payment.

"The bounds which I had prescribed to myself in this paper, and which I have already exceeded, will not admit of my entering into a discussion of the benefits depending on the alliance of the Company with the Vizir; these will appear at large on various parts of our records, to which I shall hereafter distinctly refer. They may be reduced to the following abridgment; a secure barrier; a constant occupation for part of our army; a reduction of our military expences; and an accumulating fund of future wealth. He cannot long subsist without our protection, and is incapable, of himself, of becoming an object of our jealousy or apprehension. For the better communication with the Vizir, and for the maintenance of that confidence which is necessary to perpetuate the alliance between the Vizir and the Company, it has been judged adviseable to appoint a resident at the Durbar, as the immediate agent of the Governor, with whom alone he officially corresponds. The gentleman employed in that station is Mr. Nathaniel Middleton, with whose discretion, integrity and ability for the discharge of this trust, I have every reason to be abundantly satisfied.

"The King remains at Delhi, the ancient capital of the empire, a mere cypher in the administration of it.

 With

whatever is moſt ſacred to juſtice and humanity, to eſtabliſh the claims, and extend the uſurpation of the

With him our connection has been a long time ſuſpended, and I wiſh never to ſee it renewed, as it has proved a fatal drain to the wealth of Bengal, and the treaſury of the Company, without yielding one advantage or poſſible ſource, even of remote benefits, in return. The tribute which he claims from the provinces hath been with-held from him ſince his deſertion of the Company, and his union with their natural enemies, the Marrattos; and a reference has been made to the Court of Directors for their orders concerning the future payments of it, with every argument urged that can induce them to forbid it.

"The Marratta ſtate, after having threatened the whole empire with ſubjection, during the active adminiſtration of their Paiſhwa, or acting Chief, Mahderow, has been for this twelve-month paſt, the ſcene of internal diſtractions, which ſtill ſubſiſts. On the death of Mahderow, his brother, Narain Row, ſucceeded him. He was treacherouſly ſlain, and his uncle, Raganot Row, releaſed from priſon, and declared Paiſhwa in his ſtead. The miniſters of the government, to whom he owed his elevation, became the objects of his jealouſy, and acting from that impreſſion, he made them his enemies; they formed a powerful combination againſt him, ſet up the new-born ſon of Narain Row in competition againſt him, and defeated him. He has ſince thrown himſelf on the protection of Takojee Hulkar, and Mahadajee Sindea, two Chiefs of conſideration, who were lately in the party of his opponents. The leaders of this oppoſition, Sookoram Bolboo, the principal miniſter; Gaujaboy, the mother of the Paiſhwas, Mahderow and Narain Row; Shubajee Bonſela, the Chief of Berar; and the Nabob Nizam Alli. The two laſt may be rather conſidered as auxiliaries; Mordajee, the brother of Shubajee, was on the ſide of Raganot Row till his defeat; both the brothers are now in Berar. The laſt letter from Mr. Moſtyn, the Reſident at Poonah, dated the 22d of Auguſt, explains the ſtate of theſe diſputes to that period; they ſeem yet likely to be of longer duration, and whenever concluded, will probably leave the prevailing party too weak to undertake any plan of remote conqueſt,

the strong, over the natural and hereditary rights of the weak and defenceless. The principles, the operations,

conquest, for some time at least to come; of course we have no cause to apprehend any disturbances from the Marrattos, during the present season.

"The province of Berar, adjoining to our own borders on the south and west side of the provinces, merits, from that consideration, and from the power and independency of its rulers, a distinct consideration. The present Chief, Shabujee Bonsela, is the brother of the late Janojee Bonsela, who for many years past enjoyed the sovereignty of the country. His brothers are Moodajee, who has been already mentioned in this narrative, and Bimbajee; the latter possesses very little consequence besides that which he derives from the credit of his family. The two other brothers have been long at variance, but by the mediation and authority of Derriaboy, the widow of Janojee, and a woman of great spirit and reputed ability, prevented from carrying their animosity to violent extremes. Their being engaged in opposite factions of the Marratto state, is not a certain proof of their mutual enmity; it being (as I understand) a policy not uncommonly practised among the Marrattos, for the same family to take different sides in civil dissensions, with a view to its aggrandizement. While I was at Benares the last year, a Vakeel from Shawbajee Bonsela arrived at that place with a letter addressed to me by that Chief, and attended me in Calcutta until the month of September last, when he received his dismission to return to his master, in consequence of orders received for that purpose. The purport of Shawbajee's letter, and the verbal propositions made to me by his Vakeel, was to solicit the friendship and alliance of this government; to which I have replied in such terms as were most likely to encourage him to nearer advances, if he has formed any designs which may make it strongly his interest to court the friendship of the Company. He is descended from the ancient Rajahs of Sittarah. The present Rajah is called Ram Rajah; he has no children. It is worthy of remark, and may serve to convey some idea of the instability of the present government of the Marrattos, that it is exercised through two subordinate gradations. The Rajah, in whose

name

operations, and the tendencies of government, appeared to them totally miſtaken or miſapplied. Inſtead of the pacific ſyſtem the Governor-general had ſo loudly profeſſed and avowed, the army was at that moment employed in the extirpation of the Rohillas, with whom he had lately been allied, againſt whom he pretended to have no reſentment, but for the maſſacre of whom a ſum of money was ſtipulated. General Clavering, Colonel Manſon, and Mr. Francis, boldly arraigned the origin, the conduct, the object of this merciless expedition. They imputed it to a colluſion between the Vizir and the Governor-general. It was unaccountable to them on any other principles than the felleſt ambition in the one, and the fouleſt corruption in the other. In theſe they unanimouſly reſolved all that petulant caprice which diſtinguiſhed the temper of Sujah Dowlah in directing the campaign, and that very exquiſite tenderneſs with which the Governor-general eſpouſed his vindication againſt the repreſentations of the commander in chief. It ſtruck them as an inſult to the repeated orders of the Company, which conſtantly enjoined and urged the obvious

name all the orders of the ſtate are iſſued, is deprived of all authority. The Paiſhwa, or prime Miniſter, an infant of nine months old, and the actual Miniſter or Regent, who exerciſes the legal powers of both; a man deriving his authority ſolely from the combination of a few wealthy individuals. From this divided ſtate of the Marratto empire, and the intereſts and pretenſions of the ſeveral competitors for power amongſt them, great political advantages may perhaps be attained to the Company, to which the preſent united ſyſtem of the Company's eſtabliſhments in India, is well calculated to contribute.

policy

policy of cultivating harmony with all the neighbouring ſtates. It ſtrengthened and extended that power which it was their intereſt to preſerve, in a ſituation of dependence. It was an encroachment on thoſe neutral rights which the Marrattos might think themſelves obliged to defend. It expoſed the dominions of the Company to depredation, and taxed their engagements with infidelity and deceit; degraded the dignity of government, by yielding to the arrogance of a barbarian; riſqued the liberty of a brigade, by reſting their departure on his option; inſulted the feelings of the troops, by forcing them on a ſervice of cruelty, and implicating their operations with a variety of ſuch horrid ſcenes as reflect the fouleſt diſgrace on the arms of an enlightened nation. They founded their reaſoning on the manner in which the war was brought on; the management which marked ſo ſtrongly its commencement and progreſs; the rapacity, perfidy, and inhumanity of the Vizier's character; the avowed object of the enterprize; and the dreadful carnage, depopulation, and general ruin in which it terminated.

To allegations illiberal or groſs, the Governor-general deigned no reply. He wiſhed to diſtinguiſh between animated declamation and diſpaſſionate enquiry. Many facts on which the majority argued were at leaſt equivocal. He denied the myſtery attributed to his perſonal conference with the Vizier; that his conduct warranted the imputations with which it had been blackened; that the Rohilcund was deſolated; or that the priſoners taken in war had been inhumanly uſed. Theſe

 were

were not the reprefentations of truth, but the exaggerations of fancy. The meafure was fuggefted by the exigencies of government. The Company's diftreffes were increafed beyond a probability of relief, from the ordinary refources of the country; and in the failure of thefe, extraordinary means became indifpenfible. The orders of the Company were in no inftance an explicit prohibition of employing their forces on fervices of fuch manifeft utility. They were dictated in a more liberal fpirit, and permitted, in circumftances not reducible to pofitive and invariable direction, a difcretional latitude for the zeal of their fervants. The Rohillas were a treacherous race. Their cataftrophe was the juft reward of their own demerits. The war was founded in the natural defire of retaliating wrongs. Our troops were not principals, but acceffories only. It was our duty, as well as intereft, to affift in accomplifhing whatever augmented the fecurity of an ally, whofe enemies were ours. The Rohillas were his aggreffors, and their reduction was, of courfe, included in our engagements to defend him. He enumerated the advantages which would redound to the Company from this difpofition of their forces. It raifed a new barrier to their dominions, by extending the frontiers of Oude, and removing the Marrattos to a greater diftance. It brought nearly half a million fterling to their treafury. It difciplined their army, and relieved them from one-third of its expence. In fhort, he fcrupled not, in the face of all the oppofition that was urged, to reft his apology on his reputation in the fervice, his conftruction of the Company's orders, the necessity of the state, and the practicability of the object.

The majority, far from acquiescing in these reasons, came to the resolution, that the correspondence of the Governor-general, with the commander in chief, and the resident at the Vizir's court, should be laid before the board. He dissented from this resolution, as equally illiberal and premature. It divested his declaration of credit, and the situation he occupied of that confidence which its utility required. Mr. Middleton was his agent. Many of his letters were confined to confidential communications, in which the public had no concern. These were made and trusted under the seal of secresy. He would not betray the unreserved opinions of a young man, which could produce no other consequence than ill-will or inconvenience to the author. They were hazarded only on the most sacred assurance, that they never should be divulged from the person to whom alone he conceived himself accountable for the part he acted in that station. Without waiting for the papers he promised to produce, or knowing whether the intelligence they conveyed was imperfect or obscure, an arbitrary demand was made for the minutiæ of a correspondence with which his personal feelings did not permit him to comply. To laying before the board Colonel Champion's official dispatches, he had no objections. Such parts of their correspondence, however, as were not altogether cordial, written with the freedom of private friends, and in a stile different from that used in transacting public business, he deemed it equally unnecessary and improper to produce.

This dissent was protested against by the majority, who finding, in consequence of the Company's engagement with Sujah Dowlah, that an enterprize had been undertaken in direct violation of that policy which they knew to be established by the highest authority, that this was not the result of any specific treaty, but of a verbal agreement only between the Vizir and the President, and that the execution of it had carried our troops to such a distance from the frontiers of Bengal, and so considerably to the north of Delhi, that the place of their encampment, in the beginning of October, was not to be found in any common map of the country, they were warranted to demand the full possession of every document which had any reference to that transaction. The connection of the late administration with the Company's ally, notwithstanding all the lights they had received, was still to them in a great measure unintelligible. All communications made by the resident at the Durbar, and the commander of the troops still in the field, to the Governor, on the subject under consideration, were, in their opinion, essential to a complete information of the board. They grounded their requisition on the express orders of the Company. The Directors, in their general letter of the 23d March, 1770, write thus:—"The Governor, singly, shall correspond with the country "powers; but all letters, before they shall be by "him sent, must be communicated to the other "mem-

"members of the select committee, and receive "their approbation; and also all letters whatever, "which may be received in answer to, or in the "course of his correspondence, shall likewise be "laid before the said select committee, for their "information and consideration." They denied that the chief of any council had a right to carry on a correspondence with the ministers or officers of government, independent of that council, much less to refuse a communication of that correspondence, when requested by them.

The recal of Mr. Middleton from the Durbar was the consequence of these debates. Colonel Champion was at the same time, though not without considerable discussion, instructed to supply his place, to wait upon the Vizir, and to require payment of his arrears to the Company, in virtue of the assistance afforded him against the Rohillas, and his other engagements. He was allowed a discretionary power to relax in part of these demands, in case it might appear to him expedient, and to accept twenty lacks, after securing installments for the remainder, at any term not exceeding twelve months for the last. His removal of the troops was to be regulated by the alternative of the Vizir's compliance or refusal. Meanwhile, advices were received, that the war, as we have before related, was finished, and, in consequence of these, some alterations took place in the Colonel's instructions.

In the course of these reiterated altercations, references were frequently and freely made to the

Gover-

Governor-general's treatment of the King Shaw Allum. His detention of the tribute, as well as his diſpoſition of Corah and Allahabad, was oftener than once obliquely imputed to principles which he had not avowed. For the non-payment of the ſubſidy he accounts, by alledging what advantage he might have derived from a colluſive acknowledgement of the treaty. The King, he ſhrewdly preſumes, would have allowed him to make his own terms, and thanked him for the remainder *. It was certainly in his power, upon the ſuppoſition of his majeſty's meanneſs to have thus preferred his own intereſt to that of his conſtituents. But to warrant oppreſſion by impotence, or to argue in favour of one ſpecies or degree of injuſtice, from the capacity of perpetrating another or greater, is reducing all claims of right to explicit principles of tyranny, and appealing directly from every mode of equity to the deciſion of force. A jury of Engliſhmen would hardly acquit the man convicted of robbery, for reſting his defence on his innocence of murder. On the ſame grounds, however, the Governor boldly juſtifies his pecuniary bargain

* The Governor-general, in his addreſs to the Court of Directors, by the ſhip Anſon, dated March 25, 1775, avows this curious reaſoning in theſe terms: "The ſtoppage of the "King's tribute was an act of mine, and I have been often "reproached with it. It was certainly in my power to have "continued the payment of it, and to have made my terms "with the King, for any part of it which I might have choſen to reſerve for my own uſe; he would have thanked me "for the remainder."

with

with Sujah Dowlah, for the territories of the prince whose tribute he had already alienated. "It was "not, says he, the want of the sunnuds of Shaw "Allum, which defeated the long concerted pro- "jects of the Duc de Choiseul; nor will the pos- "session of them quicken the designs of the Ma- "rattos against us. The sword which gave us the "dominion of Bengal, must be the instrument of "its preservation; and if it shall ever cease to be "ours, which God forbid, the next proprietor will "derive his right and possession from the same "natural charter."

The military were chiefly employed, in 1774, against various petty principalities, situated on the frontiers of the Bengal provinces, and who had hitherto acknowledged no dependence on any of the neighbouring sovereignties. In some places the Rajahs or great men were reduced and gave hostages as pledges of their future obedience; in others the peasants were every where driven from their houses, the villages consumed, and the crops utterly destroyed. Orders being issued from the council of Patna for a battalion of the Company's to seize or expel the Rajah Tuttah Shaw, Ensign Scott, who commanded the party, rigidly accurate and assiduous in the discharge of his duty, pursued the unhappy man into the dominions of Oude, and made three of the Vizir's subjects prisoners of war. Captain Crawford, under a similar direction from the chief of Burdwan, entered Patcoom the beginning of December the same year, with six companies of sipoys, took the capital, levelled it with the

the ground, and to make the poſt tenable, cleared the country. The natives, in a paroxyſm of deſpair, aſſembled to defend themſelves and families. He came up with them in a few days. They were eaſily and effectually diſperſed. The whole that ſurvived, man, woman, and child, took immediate ſhelter among the hills, and left the diſtrict without an inhabitant. This active officer coolly avows, in his diſpatches, that he endeavoured to ſow diſſenſion among the chiefs, in order to facilitate the buſineſs of reduction or extirpation. Theſe exceſſes originated in an ambition to ſubjugate a brave and warlike race of people, who, from time immemorial, had maintained their liberty in theſe mountainous and woody countries, which form ſo great a part of the weſtern diviſion of Bengal. They had no other mode of retaliating the injuries they received, than by ſudden excurſions againſt thoſe neighbouring diſtricts which lay moſt contiguous, and were moſt defenceleſs. They were conſequently proſcribed as a licentious banditti, and proceeded againſt by every means which the laws of war would allow. And in the true ſpirit of the Bengal government, in caſe no other method would bring them to terms, extirpation was deemed a meaſure perfectly conſiſtent with *juſtice and ſound policy*. The principles which have been imbibed and practiſed by all the tyrants and uſurpers, whoſe villainies have deſolated and embroiled the world, as *juſtice* and *ſound policy*, have been ſlavery, expulſion, ſlaughter, or extermination. On theſe deſpotiſm, in every corner of the globe, ſtill raiſes her

eſtabliſh-

eſtabliſhments, and ambition her trophies. It ever has been the rage of the multitude to be led, which is the fertile origin of all that power by which in all ages they have gained ſo little and ſuffered ſo much.

In the beginning of the year 1775, Sujah ul Dowlah, Vizir of Oude, whoſe health had for ſome time been on the decline, breathed his laſt. His ſon Miza Ammany, otherwiſe called Aſoph ul Dowlah, ſucceeded him in the ſubadary. He did not poſſeſs the talents of his father, whoſe ſtrength both of body and mind, was hardly equalled among his countrymen. This powerful ally of the Company had all at once been converted from a man of pleaſure to no inconſiderable adept both in buſineſs and war. His fortunes were long, various, and equivocal. He ſoon hit upon the policy of attaching himſelf to the Engliſh. Their enterprize and activity ſuited the volatility of his taſte and his genius. His exterior and addreſs were plauſible, ſpecious, and inſinuating; but the prevailing habits of his mind were bloody, treacherous, daſtardly, and vindictive. And the ſeveral treaties between him and the Company's ſervants, are a proof that however inferior to them in the field, he had greatly the advantage in almoſt every negociation. Several alterations took place in the Company's connection with the young Nabob. The ſupreme council determined that the ſpecific conditions of their former alliance with the Vizir expired with him, and that it was their duty to derive as much advantage as poſſible from a renewal of their friendſhip to his ſon. Mr. Briſtow, who had ſuc-

succeeded Mr. Middleton in the refidency of Fizyabad, fet out in the beginning of February, 1775, and in a few months agreed with the Nabob to guarantee to him the provinces of Corah and Allahabad; that the ftipulated fubfidy for the fervice of the brigade fhould be increafed; and that the Company fhould be invefted with the fovereignty and poffeffion of the diftricts under Cheit Sing in perpetuity. The majority affumed great merit from the very fubftantial benefits which it conferred on the Company. Nor would it have tarnifhed the luftre of their reign, had this been the only inftance in which even they could facrifice the claims of effential juftice to the rapacity of their conftituents. The Governor-general's only objection was, that he thought it never could be thoroughly realized. It was fully debated at the board, but ultimately carried.

Thefe diffenfions, which had feparately tranfpired before the arrival of any regular difpatches in England, very much inflamed the friends and abettors of the feveral individuals interefted in the iffue of the conteft. The Directors alarmed for the confequences of fuch violent proceedings, laid the whole fubjects in reference forthwith before the proprietary. Various courts were held, and much fubtilty and manœuvring difplayed on both fides. The object was no longer the good of the Company or community at large, but which of the parties fhould prove victorious. The fenfe of the whole may be collected from the Directors general letter, dated the 15th of December, in which they condemn

demn the principles of the Rohilla war, and justify the recal of Mr. Middleton, as dissatisfied with the policy in the one case, and in the other, giving it as their opinion that the board were fully entitled to a deliberate perusal of all the resident's letters.

The discord which prevailed in the supreme council was soon communicated to the natives. It was a species of intelligence which facilitated its own propagation, by the eager curiosity which it every where excited. The houses of the individuals who composed the majority, were suddenly surrounded with complainants, who importuned them, by an incessant repetition of their grievances, for redress. Instances of oppression in the former administration were every day exhibited, and even among that timid and diffident people, there were not wanting who had the resolution to bring personal accusations against some of the first officers of state. The black merchants in Dacca charged Mr. Richard Barwell with a series of barbarities which even shock humanity in the recital. They assert, that he extorted a considerable sum from them by menaces, by confining them in the stocks, by imprisonment, and by starving them under a military guard, into his own terms. The ignominious punishment of the stocks was inflicted on them, when the weather was exceedingly bad, and the rains insufferably heavy, and in a plain where, having no covering to their heads, or any part of their body, and nothing underneath them but the bare earth, they were equally exposed to the inclemency of the sky, and the dampness of a spot swim-

ſwimming in water. To heighten the cruelty of their ſituation, they were not unfrequently treated in this manner in the middle of the day, when the ſcorching heat of a vertical ſun is moſt intolerable. The objects of his implacable ſeverity were not young, nor accuſtomed to ſuch hardſhips as are incident to a low or laborious life, but men of a reputable profeſſion, men aged and infirm, and men who had ſerved the Company, without cenſure or complaint, for thirty years.

The retroſpection of the majority was carried with accuracy and perſeverance into every department of ſtate, and extended to all the various objects and functions of adminiſtration. It was none of the leaſt accuſations againſt Mr. Haſtings, that he had annihilated the landed property throughout the kingdom of Bengal. The ancient Zemindars, who had enjoyed their eſtates without moleſtation, by inheritance from father to ſon, for many generations, were diſinherited. Their poſſeſſions had been literally expoſed to ſale, and conſigned to thoſe who offered the higheſt terms. This ſyſtem was condemned, as peculiarly hard and oppreſſive. The greateſt men in the country were conſequently under the hard neceſſity of contending for their lands, againſt a combination of uſurers and peculators, or in lieu of their extenſive dominions, to content themſelves with their houſe, and ſuch a penſion as the ſtate thought proper to aſſign. No meaſure could more effectually alienate the minds of the natives, or deſtroy their confidence in government. The landed proprietory were at one

ſtroke

ſtroke deprived of all influence. Their power and their zemindaries were loſt together. The menial ſervants of the Engliſh, *whoſe fathers they would not have ſet with the dogs of their flock*, as an indignant Chief expreſſes it, entered into their patrimonial lands. Cantoo Baboo, the banian or native ſteward and manager to Mr. Haſtings, held two contracts in his own name, and that of his ſon, for conſiderably more than an hundred and fifty thouſand pounds per annum. With the ſame ſuſpicious appearance, the ſame favourite of power occupied farms which paid annually to the landed revenue nearly an equal ſum. The whole zemindary of Baharbund was granted to the ſon of this man, a boy not more than ten or twelve years of age, though mentioned by the Governor-general as a man of credit and property. Indeed the majority avowed it, as their ſolemn and formal opinion, that there was no ſpecies of peculation from which the late adminiſtration had thought proper to abſtain. They even thought the proofs of the Governor-general's appropriating four parts in ſeven of the ſalary with which the Company was charged for the Phouſdar or Commander of Hughly, were ſuch as, whether ſufficient to convict him in a court of juſtice, did not leave a doubt concerning his criminality in the mind of any unprejudiced perſon. The ſalary was ſeventy-two thouſand rupees, and they aſſerted that Mr. Haſtings ſhared one half, and that the late Phouſdar was turned out of office merely becauſe his terms were not ſo favourable.

In this manner the Governor-general, notwithstanding that integrity of intention, and purity of character, to which he has always been so much in the habit of appealing, was formally accused of the grossest venality and corruption. Instances were produced, in which individuals of considerable station and respectability, came forward in support of the charge. The Ranny of Burdwan impeached her duan, or treasurer, with lavishing immense sums on some of the Company's servants, in consideration of his appointment to that high and lucrative situation. When this affair came before the Board, and a motion was made for going into a serious discussion of the fact, the Governor-general, instead of daring his accusers to the proof, or confiding in that innocence which he loudly asserted, availed himself of his privilege, and would not submit to be confronted in a court where he was himself the president; but retired in disgust, with his friend Mr. Barwell. The majority, however, who thought it their duty, were willing to come at the truth; and the Ranny's agent produced accounts of fifteen thousand rupees given to Mr. Hastings, and nine thousand to other Members of the Presidency. Bridjoo Kishore, who had purchased his preferment by these pecuniary presents, objected to the authenticity of the documents thus exhibited in proof of the peculation; but his secretary swore positively that the statement, correctly as it stood, was made according to the treasurer's express order, and that he had represented the transaction precisely and literally as it happened.

The

The unfortunate Nuncomar, whofe melancholy exit can never be forgotten by his countrymen, had the temerity to produce fome heavy charges of this kind againft Mr. Haftings, and even to appear in perfon, for the purpofe of fubftantiating his allegations. When the Rajah, however, preffed to be heard, and to eftablifh the facts he had ftated, by inconteftable evidence, the Governor-general, who deemed the dignity of his fituation paramount to every confideration on earth, fuddenly diffolved the Council, and leaving it, in concert with Mr. Barwell, protefted againft whatever meafures the majority fhould adopt in his abfence. But they perfifted, notwithftanding this hardinefs and pertinacity in the exercife of a prerogative ftill undecided, to difcharge thofe obligations to the public and to juftice, which they confidered, with equal fteadinefs, as indifpenfible. Nuncomar was accordingly called in, and very clofely interrogated. He ftated with accuracy, firmnefs, and fimplicity, the feveral fums which he had himfelf paid the Governor-general, and mentioned the names of fuch individuals as had been privy to the tranfaction. He delivered, at the fame time, a letter addreffed to himfelf, under the feal and fignature of Munny Begum, in which fhe declared that the Governor-general had alfo received from her a pecuniary douceur of confiderable value. The vouchers he produced in confirmation of thefe extraordinary negociations, appeared to the Members of Council perfectly authentic and fatisfactory.

Nuncomar was in the mean time an object of machinations little suspected either by him or his friends. It seems to have been determined, that his zeal in prosecuting Mr. Hastings should, in one shape or other, be amply and speedily retaliated. While this matter pended before the Council Board, the Rajah was actually tried for a conspiracy against Mr. Hastings, in concert with Joseph Fowke, Francis Fowke, and Roy Rada Churn *. The jury, however,

* Many are the instances which might be specified to prove how cruelly the exquisite sensibility of the native Indians are sported with by our countrymen. The tragical story of Commaul O Deen will never be forgotten in India, and the dishonour it reflects on our politics, will last as long as it is remembered. This man, by the intrigues of party, while the altercation between a majority of the Council and the Governor-general was carried on with very little temper or decency on either side, was inveigled to give evidence against Joseph Fowke, Francis Fowke, Maha Rajah Nuncomar, and Roy Rada Churn, on a charge of conspiracy against Warren Hastings, Esq. His evidence was so confused and contradictory, that the verdict was given in favour of the defendants. Commaul O Deen being deep in arrears to government, these persons had interest enough, as it would seem, to instigate the officers in the revenue department against him. He was consequently imprisoned; but the Supreme Court espousing his cause, he was immediately released by Habeas Corpus. The very next day he was again imprisoned, and again released in the same manner. He then sent to Hughly for his son, to superintend his affairs, during transactions which so unavoidably engrossed and distracted his attention. In coming up the river to Calcutta, the youth was unfortunately drowned. This unexpected disaster, co-operating with his other embarrassments and sufferings, suddenly overwhelmed him with despair. He then became an object of pity and commiseration to all his friends and former acquaintance. And it was not long before he absconded, and has never been heard of since.

however, pronounced him not guilty; but an accusation, more serious and interesting, was prepared and kept in reserve against the unhappy Chief. He was soon after charged with having effected a forgery, dated several years before. For this crime he was capitally indicted, tried before the Supreme Court, condemned by an *ex post facto* statute, and hanged, though the offence of which he was arraigned was not capital, by the laws of the country in which it was committed. The multitudes of people who witnessed the execution were prodigious, and they viewed the spectacle before them with visible expressions of horror and consternation. Europeans had not heretofore menaced the inhabitants with such an awful sight, in the pacific provinces of Bengal. The privileges of Bramins are deemed, in every part of India, inviolable. They commute capital punishment, and are exempted, by what may be called the common law of the country, from every species of personal outrage. Nuncomar was at the head of this sacred cast, whom the Hindoos regard every where with an idolatrous veneration. His ignominious death was consequently much more shocking in India, than if a nobleman of the highest distinction, a prince of the blood, or even a crowned head, were in any European state sentenced to suffer by the hands of the common hangman. All the natives present, amounting to many thousands, dispersed as by common signal, the moment he was turned off, with unusual precipitation, countenances distorted by despair, and their mouths filled with exclamations of the moſt extreme agony and horror! They departed ſo inſtantly and entirely from this fatal ſpot, that the Rajah had not yet expired when no body was ſeen about the gallows, but the ſheriff and his attendants, and a few European ſpectators!

Circumſtances were implicated in this tranſaction, which rouſed and intereſted the feelings and attention of all conſiderate perſons in both countries. A man of illuſtrious rank and diſtinction, ſuffering death for a crime not capital by the laws under which he lived, and puniſhed in this manner, only in conſequence of a foreign and poſterior inſtitution; the commencement of the proſecution at the critical moment when Nuncomar ſtood forward to convict the Governor-general of the moſt abandoned proſtitution of the authority under which he filled the higheſt ſituation in the patronage of the Company; the extreme unrelenting rigour with which the proceſs was carried on, in direct violation of all thoſe regards and decencies which the remoteſt antiquity, and univerſal uſage, had rendered ſacred; the virulent eagerneſs of Mr. Haſtings, and his partizans, to expoſe, to blacken, to criminate, and even to execrate and vilify the character of an individual, thus hapleſs and degraded; and the groſs profuſion of foul intemperate language which ſtamps every apology which has yet been offered for theſe proceedings, are premiſes on which few competent and impartial judges would be apt to conclude, that in this political trial no ſpecies of ſympathy ſubſiſted between the Governor-general

general and the Supreme Court *. Justice, the stable security of property and life, when impartially

* In a minute of the Majority, whilst this important cause was pending before the Supreme Court, dated the 11th of April, 1755, it is accounted for in the manner following:

"Maha Rajah Nuncomar, whom the Governor calls "*miscreant*, we found had been, but a very little time be-"fore, his bosom friend, consulted on all occasions, and "supported by him against the united *protest* of Messrs. "Graham, Lawrel, and Dacres, who were closely connect-"ed with Mahomed Reza Cawn, although the Governor "knew him to have been, as he *now* says, guilty of a for-"gery. We have reason to suspect that the intention was "to make him Banyan to General Clavering, to surround "the General and us with the Governor's creatures, and "to keep us totally unacquainted with the real state of the "government. By this and other flimsy devices, so con-"sonant to the principles of Asiatic policy, in which the "Governor-general has been so long exercised, he pro-"bably flattered himself, that men unpractised in such arts, "might be perplexed and circumvented. Nuncomar, "finding himself deceived or disappointed by the Gover-"nor-general, soon made use of the means which his inti-"macy with the Governor had put in his power, to gratify "his resentment. Whatever might have been his mo-"tives, his discoveries have thrown a clear light upon the "Honourable Governor-general's conduct, and the means "he had taken of making the very large fortune he is said "to possess, of upwards of forty lacks of rupees, which he "must have amassed in about two years and a half."

The Governor's answer to the protest mentioned in the preceding minute, is designed, *Extract of the Proceedings of the Committee of Circuit at Cossimbuzar, dated the 28th of July*, 1772. The dispute originated in the appointment of Nuncomar's son to the office of Dewan of the household, and manager of the Nabob's finances. Messrs. Dacres, Lawrel, and Graham, objected to this nomination, because they considered it in effect the appointment of Nuncomar, whose political conduct they criminated by a great variety of evidence. The Governor vindicates his

 arrange-

tially adminiftered, was in this inftance converted into a daftardly engine of tyranny. In the riot of unbridled ambition, the beft founded claims of the innocent and obnoxious, become feeble and unavailing. The feelings of the natives were wantonly and incurably wounded, by the fufferings of Nuncomar. It was an infult to the cuftoms, the laws, the religion of all the Gentoo nations. The fact on which a criminal procefs was founded againft him, had then, and for fome time before, been under

arrangement by a minute of fome length, in which are thofe remarkable words.—"He [Mr. Haftings] thinks it "but juftice to make a diftinction between the violation "of a truft, and an offence committed againft our government, by a man who owed it no allegiance, nor was indebted for protection; but, on the contrary, was the actual fervant and minifter of a mafter whofe intereft naturally fuggefted that kind of policy which fought, by "foreign aids, and the diminution of the power of the "Company, to raife his own confequence, and re-eftablifh "his authority. He has never been charged with any infidelity to the Nabob, Meer Jaffier, the conftant tenor "of whofe politics, from his firft acceffion to the nizamut "till his death, correfpond in all points fo exactly with the "artifices which were detected in his minifter, that they "may be as fairly afcribed to the one as to the other; their "immediate object was, beyond queftion, the aggrandifement of the former, though the latter had ultimately an "equal intereft in their fuccefs. The opinion which the "Nabob himfelf entertained of the fervices, and of the "fidelity of Nuncomar, evidently appeared, in the diftinguifhed marks which he continued to fhew him of his "favour and confidence to the lateft hour of his life. His "conduct in the fucceeding adminiftration appears not "only to have been dictated by the fame principles; but "if we may be allowed to fpeak favourably of any meafures which oppofe the views of our own government, "and aimed at the fupport of an adverfe intereft, furely it "was not only *not* culpable, but even *praife-worthy*."

legal

legal inveſtigation in a civil ſuit, the event of which could only be decided by the authenticity of the deed which he was charged with having forged. In a caſe ſo perfectly new and extraordinary, why was not the execution of the ſentence ſuſpended until his Majeſty's pleaſure could be known. But the Rajah was thus denied a reſpite, at the very inſtant of arreſt under the protection of the board, in the midſt of his evidence againſt the Governor-General, on a charge of betraying the confidence of his employers, in taking money from the Company's dependents. Combining all theſe circumſtances together, it will be difficult to conſider the trial and fate of Nuncomar in any other light than a political meaſure, tending to deter the natives from accuſing, or even giving evidence of corrupt practices againſt any Britiſh ſubject in a ſituation of truſt and influence. A management thus hoſtile to the ſafety of individuals, contributed in a great meaſure to render that timid and patient people rather reſerved and diſſembling, than diſpoſed publickly to complain of abuſe, or openly to reſent injuries, not prompt to diſcover fraud, extortion, or peculation, but ſlily to take refuge from oppreſſion in the obliquities of intrigue, or the inſignificance of vaſſalage. And ſuch were the beginnings of that dark, inſidious ſyſtem of duplicity, concealment, inconſiſtency, temerity, and breach of faith, which was deſtined ſoon to colour and pervert all the departments of our Indian government, to invelop in impenetrable myſtery the moſt important and intereſting tranſactions which after-

afterwards took place between the Company's servants and the country powers, and to involve us in a series of embarrassments from which only such a combination of contingencies as could neither be foreseen nor expected could deliver.

These various and complicated transactions appeared, in the reports and accounts of them which reached England, in a shape perfectly mysterious and unintelligible. All the influence and management of the Governor-General, however, could not at that time reconcile the characteristic honesty of his countrymen to the numerous intrigues of which he stood accused. The inflexible and sturdy probity of a Clavering and his colleagues in opposition, commanded such a confidence and respect, as could only be diminished or lost by an almost total extinction of public virtue. Mr. Hastings's situation was now become desperate. His projects were not only suppressed, and his prerogatives circumscribed by a stubborn majority, but the odium raised against him by the natives, in consequence of his severities, was become personally disgusting. In proportion as the dread of his power abated, he was treated with less distinction and respect. His official duty was rendered irksome from the systematic animadversion to which all his actions were inevitably subjected, and his private hours were exhausted in digesting the materials of his public defence. It was in these circumstances that he conceived and executed an experiment in the science of politics, which is not surpassed by the most celebrated eccentricities in Machiavel, and which

which leaves all the verſatilities even of our modern ſtateſmen at the greateſt diſtance. It is fortunate where a perſon ſucceeds to a ſituation of extenſive authority, when the poſture of affairs under his management correſponds with his talents and principles; but few are the characters who can uniformly accommodate themſelves to the conſtant viciſſitudes or mutations ſo incident to every ſtate and modification of human life.

The delinquencies attributed to Mr. Haſtings's official conduct, had drawn upon him the cenſure of the Court of Directors. This ſentence was corroborated by the unanimous approbation of the Proprietors. It had even been reſolved to prepare an application for Mr. Haſtings's diſmiſſion. Another general court was however called on this proceeding, and he was openly ſupported by a conſiderable majority, who profeſſed to entertain a good opinion of his abilities and rectitude of intention, notwithſtanding the cenſure paſſed upon him. They ſeemed diſpoſed to acquieſce in what had been done, without being ſolicitous to puſh the matter farther. The offences ſpecified were of a very ſerious nature, and but recently condemned. They did not, therefore, think it politic or decent to attack directly the reſolution of the Directors, for applying to his Majeſty, but were content with ſimply voting in the ballot, "That it ſhould be re-"conſidered." The conſequence was, that the buſineſs remained in ſuſpence for ſome months.

About this time Mr. Lauchlin Macleane was delegated from India to England, as the agent both of of the Nabob of Arcot and of Mr. Haſtings. On the 10th of October, 1776, the Governor-General, by the agency of this gentleman, ſignified to the Court of Directors his deſire to reſign his office, and requeſted their nomination of a ſucceſſor to the vacancy which would by that means be occaſioned in the ſupreme council. To a requiſition thus ſerious, important, and unexpected, the Directors heſitated, until they knew by what authority Mr. Macleane acted ſo deciſive a part. He alleged, however, that the credentials with which he was intruſted, by the papers in his cuſtody being mixed with other matters of a nature extremely confidential, could not be produced in open court, but he was ready to ſubmit them to the inſpection of any three of their members they might think eligible for that purpoſe. A ſelect committee was accordingly appointed, to examine the authenticity and validity of a propoſition thus repugnant to the whole tenor of Mr. Haſtings's official conduct. The gentlemen empowered for this purpoſe were, the Chairman, Deputy Chairman, and Richard Beecher, Eſquire; who found from the purport of Mr. Haſtings's inſtructions, contained in a writing given to Mr. Macleane, and produced by him to them, Mr. Haſtings declared he would not continue in the government of Bengal, unleſs certain conditions therein ſpecified could be obtained, of which they ſaw no probability. This report was authenticated at the ſame time by Mr. George Vanſittart, who had been preſent when theſe inſtructions were given to Mr. Macleane; and Mr. Stewart likewiſe averred,

averred, that Mr. Haſtings declared to him that he had given directions to the ſame purpoſe by Mr. Macleane.

This cautious and punctilious proceeding in the Court of Directors, probably originated in their dreading the charge of becoming accomplices to an evaſion of the act, by which Mr. Haſtings, reſigning the ſervice, would eſcape the conſequence attached by law to a diſmiſſion. Hitherto he had only been ſupported by a majority in the General Court; but if on application from the Directors to his Majeſty and Council, then in contemplation, a removal ſhould have taken effect, no intereſt could have poſſibly reſtored him. A clauſe in the Regulating Act of 1773 precluded for ever his return to the Company's ſervice. Aware of a circumſtance thus critical, the part they acted was ſingularly guarded. But nothing being now wanting to their ſatisfaction, the reſignation was formally accepted. Mr. Wheeler was named to fill the vacancy, and preſented for his Majeſty's approbation, which was received. The meaſure was complete, and the ſituation thus vacated by Mr. Haſtings legally filled. The whole proceeding of courſe being notified in Bengal, General Clavering, as ſenior in council, was entitled to ſucceed to the office of Governor-General.

In no part of his official conduct has Mr. Haſtings ſubmitted to thoſe ties which have always been binding on others. On this occaſion he embraced the hardy reſolution of diſavowing his agent, denying his letter, and renouncing his friends.—

When

When General Clavering required him to surrender the keys of Fort William, and of the Company's treasures, he stoutly refused compliance, denied that his office was vacated, and declared his resolution to assert and maintain his authority by what he called every legal means. The immediate consequence of this unexpected pertinacity was an open schism in council. General Clavering asserted his right to the office, with which he conceived himself legally and formally invested by his superiors. He was strenuously supported in these pretensions by his friend Mr. Francis. Colonel Manson having died some months before, Mr. Barwell adhered to Mr. Hastings. These two parties assembled seperately. A double government of consequence took place, and every thing was running fast into confusion. All authority was for the time suspended. And so high were these dissensions carried by the various adherents of the respective claimants, that the contest might have ended in a civil war, had not the judges of the supreme court, on a reference to them, settled the controversy, by deciding "that the resignation was an invalid act, and that Mr. Hastings was still in the legal possession of his place, notwithstanding his superiors had actually dispossessed him on his own terms, and supplied it by a new appointment." It was extraordinary enough that the nullity of this resignation should not have been discovered in England, where the documents and act authorizing the resignation then were, where the agent by whom the measure had been formally executed was, where the evidences who

who substantiated these materials resided, and where there was and could be no want of legal advice, either on the part of the Company or the Crown. The judges in India, however, without any regard to the approbation of Majesty, which literally made the new appointment his, boldly superseded that appointment, by declaring that the actual assumption of the government by the member of the council next in succession to Mr. Hastings, in consequence of any deduction which could be made from the papers communicated to them, would be absolutely illegal.

This decision was seasonably interposed, and put an immediate end to the division in the meeting, though not in the minds of the Council. Mr. Hastings eagerly grasped the apparent advantage which this determination afforded, to fix a stigma on the other party in several violent resolutions, adopted for the obvious intention of menacing them with an expulsion from their former situation in the government and service of the Company.

The management in this whole affair, from first to last, appears wonderfully exquisite. To every individual whose sentiments did not perfectly coincide with those of the Governor-General, the decision of the judges, from their known politics, could not seem totally devested of partiality. The passionate and extravagant proceedings in the council-general, subsequent to such an instance of moderation in General Clavering as the relinquishment of claims thus formally established, afforded the judges an opportunity of assuming an appear-

ance

ance of that candour which so well became their character, by interposing their opinion and advice, "That all parties should be placed in the same "situation in which they stood before the receipt "of the last advices from England, reserving and "submitting to a decision in England, the respective claims that each party may conceive they "have a right to make; but not acting upon those "claims till such decision shall arrive in Bengal."

The consequences of these transactions were of a piece with the principles that produced them.—Though Mr. Hastings censured the agency of Macleane as an instance of the grossest forgery, he did not treat that gentleman as an impostor. The Directors promised to take these extraordinary measures under their most serious and earliest consideration, and with this declaration appear to have closed the account, and dismissed the subject for ever. And the members who conscientiously discharged their duty in implicitly obeying the orders of their employers, continued as usual to receive from time to time unprofitable applause and no support.

CHAPTER VIII.

The first Marratto War—Anecdotes of that People—Interference by the Bombay Presidency in their Dissensions—Treaty with Ragoba—Colonel Upton's Deputation to Poonah—The Treaty of Poorunder—Dissatisfactions produced by that Event—The Political State of India at this Period.

THE three principal intereſts, which at preſent divide and control the empire of Indoſtan, are the Hindoo, the Mahommedan, and the Britiſh. The two laſt originate and derive all their weight and eſtabliſhment from a ſeries of uſurpations on the firſt, which is native and hereditary: And it is owing to the multifarious and diſcordant parts theſe intereſts ſeparately involve, to a total want of union in their energies, and to an infinite diverſity in the objects of their reſpective politics, that they have hitherto repelled ſucceſsfully the encroachments of each other, and preſerved their mutual independence; that a balance of power, in ſome degree adequate to the regulation and adjuſtment of their ſeveral claims, ſtill operates; and that the whole continent of India is not at this moment the ſeat of one gloomy, permanent, and univerſal deſpotiſm.

The Mogul empire no longer exiſts, but in fragments. The throne of Delhi is annihilated. The later ſtages of the Mahommedan policy reſemble thoſe diſeaſes in the human frame, by which the extremities receive unnatural ſtrength, while the heart is left in a ſtate of debility. The officers of the crown every where accumulated inordinate wealth, while the general treaſury of the empire was impoveriſhed. Indolence ſucceeded to venality; and thoſe who had not courage to rebel, were at the ſame time too lazy to obey. A cruel intriguing miniſtry diſtributed the imperial preferments with a wanton extravagance. Aſſaſſination ſoon became a part of the court ſyſtem. Revolutions in the diſtant provinces were daily effected, by the murder of the reſpective governors. Thoſe who ſucceeded, warned by the fate of their predeceſſors, retained the revenues they were deputed to collect, with the notorious intention of thwarting that authority, on which they continued to laviſh the moſt ſpecious profeſſions of attachment.

The Marrattos, though not what they once were, are ſtill formidable, from the ſituation and extent of their territories, the mildneſs of their laws, their inexhauſtible reſources, their numerous armies, and their manner of making war. They inhabit the mountainous and weſtern diviſions of the Indian peninſula. By the wiſdom of their treaties, the force of their arms, and the aſylum which refractory Rajahs and zemindars have found

found in their protection, they have stretched their dominions from sea to sea, from Surat to the Bay of Bengal, and from the remotest confines of Agra, northwards, to the mouth of the river Kistna, on the coast of Coromandel, including a tract of country above a thousand British miles long, by not less than seven hundred in breadth.

This immensely extended empire is divided by several Rajahs, whose connexion with the Peishwa or chancellor is like that of the German princes with the emperor, merely nominal. In some cases, an opposition of interests produces hostilities, not only among the subordinate members, but even the Peishwa himself is not unfrequently under the necessity of standing on his own defence against a combination of his tributaries. A general confederacy of the whole indeed seldom takes place, but when mutual preservation is the object, or on such emergencies only as would unite the most discordant states. Few enterprizes of foreign conquest or plunder are of magnitude enough to collect and marshal their scattered and numerous forces in one connected army, under the general standard of the empire.

Their form of government, rather from accident than design, has of late years become purely aristocratic: It is at present in the hands of eight chiefs, who, in the Company's records and other Indian documents, are called ministers, to distinguish them from the Ram Rajah, the nominal sovereign,

vereign, in whoſe name all buſineſs is ſtill carried on, and every legal inſtrument authenticated. Though veſted with ſupreme authority, with the abſolute command of the troops, and with the ſole prerogative of making peace or war, he is bound by the Gentoo law to ſelect a council of aſſiſtance from the moſt learned among the Bramins. Theſe men, availing themſelves of their ſituation, have given new energy to their characters as politicians, by accommodating the ſanctions of their profeſſions as prieſts to all the purpoſes of civil government. Being of a caſt deemed all over India ſuperior to mortals, they are objects of the moſt ſacred and univerſal veneration; and, taking advantage of the indolence and inſignificance which diſtinguiſhed the reign of a former prince, have by degrees engroſſed the whole power of the ſtate. Superſtition, the characteriſtic foible of a rude people, extends, confirms, and ſanctifies their dominion.

In proportion as the power of the Mogul empire decreaſed, that of the Marrattos gathered ſtrength. Their annual revenues are eſtimated at ſeventeen millions ſterling; and ariſe chiefly from the tributary contributions of their various allies and dependencies; eſpecially the Rajahs of Oudepore, Joudpore, Zegnagur, Bopoul, Narva, Bundlecund, and moſt of the richeſt principalities which lie in the vicinity of the Deccan, and the upper parts of the continent; from duties on ſeveral articles of commerce, from 'plunder, from cuſtoms, and

from

from innumerable other resources. The inhabitants groan under no enormous taxes. The government, inspired by the benignant genius of the national religion, is every where lenient and humane. No blood is shed, no outrage committed against the privileges of our common nature, but in war, and against an enemy. Their armies perhaps are more numerous than those in any other part of the world. They can bring into the field at least three or four hundred thousand well-appointed cavalry. Their horses are fleet and hardy; mounted by men accustomed to war from infancy, and trained with indefatigable vigilance for all the various purposes of military execution. Their hostile excursions are generally by parties too inconsiderable to provoke formal resistance, and too rapid to be in danger from any regular attack. They pour down from the hills and forests of the Deccan, when excited to revenge the injuries of the community at large, and spread destruction in the adjacent countries, with the fury and velocity of a whirlwind.

Under the predecessor of the present Ram Rajah, the government was an absolute monarchy. It was under this simple form that it's territories had been enlarged; and that in population, finance, and martial reputation, it became so formidable to the peace of India. It was then vigorous and prosperous in all it's measures; extended it's frontiers in every quarter; and accumulated additional treasure and influence, from a constant accession of new ſubjects and territory. Sahoojei, however, was a weak effeminate prince: His predominate paſſion was indolence: His time was waſted among buffoons, and in the Haram. To the ſordid indulgence of a vulgar mind he ſacrificed his own dignity, and that of his ſucceſſor. The Peiſhwa uſurped the ſovereignty, eſtabliſhed his reſidence at Poonah, and ſhut up his maſter in Settarah (about ſixty miles diſtant), where Ram Rajah ſtill lives in the ſame torpid ſplendour, receives the ſame inſulting homage, and exerciſes the ſame unmeaning formalities of ſtate which formerly diſtinguiſhed the ſupreme magiſtrate in this mighty empire: For though he ſtill retains the name of ſovereign, and inveſts the Peiſhwa with the forms of that office, it is the only act of ſuperiority he exerts. Nor has he ſo much as an option in the nomination, as Bajirow, who firſt realized the power, had the addreſs to render it hereditary in his family. This chief left two ſons, Balajei Row and Ragoba: The one was acknowledged Peiſhwa on the death of his father; the other had the command of a diſtant province. Balajei Row died when his eldeſt ſon (Madarow) was but eighteen years of age, who, notwithſtanding, ſeized the reins of adminiſtration, and promiſed to wield them with extraordinary ſteadineſs and dexterity. Ragoba, on the news of his brother's death, haſtened to the ſcene of action, and demanded the regency, as the natural guardian of his nephew: But his claims were rejected. He next applied to the

the Subah of the Deccan, who aſſiſted him to make head againſt Madarow with a formidable army. A battle was fought, in which he had the advantage. He was then recalled to Poonah, and inveſted with the Peiſhwaſhip; where he became a ſecond time the victim of his own, or the intrigues of an intereſted junto, who, led on by the mother of the young Peiſhwa, took advantage of his inexperience to raiſe a faction againſt the uncle. Aware of the ſtorm, which threatened every moment to burſt on his head, he was more than ever anxious to make his eſcape, but was ſeized in the attempt and impriſoned. In this ſituation he remained till within a very ſhort time of his nephew's deceaſe. This young man had diſcovered, in the courſe of a few years, a peculiar capacity for government. His meaſures had proved wiſe and ſucceſsful. The career of Hyder Ally's conqueſts was effectually checked; and the Marrattos, under the politics and activity of an enterprizing leader, began to co-operate, reſumed their former prowelſs, and recaptured moſt of thoſe territories which, in the period of their debility and relaxation, had been violently wreſted from them. He was deſtined, however, to relinquiſh the proſpect of increaſing proſperity, throughout an immenſe and flouriſhing empire, in the twenty-fifth year of his age. Before he expired, he called his uncle from confinement, and, judging him by the generoſity which warmed his own breaſt, treated him with a confidence ſo perfectly cordial and

 ſincere,

ſincere, that he conſigned his brother and ſucceſſor, Narrain Row, entirely to his care; and earneſtly conjured him to take the young Peiſhwa under his protection. He ſucceeded, accordingly, to the management of affairs; but whether he conceived a diſlike to his nephew, or was duped by the politics of the Bramins, who ſtill laboured to undermine his influence; or was not ſufficiently on his guard againſt the inſidious artifices of his ſiſter-in-law, who had conceived a diſlike to his character, and uſed all her addreſs, both in public and private, to counteract and circumvent him; or, intoxicated with his recent good fortune, incurred popular odium by arts of oppreſſion; it is impoſſible to determine, from the obſcurity into which the fact has been thrown by the ſophiſtry of party diſputants. The machinations of his enemies, however, ſoon prevailed, and he was once more deprived of power, and thrown into priſon, for concerting a plan, with Hyder Ally, for uſurping the government. Gopicaboy was, at the ſame time, highly incenſed againſt him for the adoption of a near relation, by which, contrary to the cuſtom of the Eaſt, his riches and eventual title to the Pieſhwaſhip might be transferred to another family. Ragoba in the mean while conſulted his friends, or rather the enemies of Narrain Row, whoſe profligacies eſtranged from him even the miniſters of his own party; and, in concert with them, a plan was formed of effecting a revolution, which promiſed once more

to

to reinſtate him in his former ſituation. The ſcheme moſt likely to produce this important event, was the murder of the young Peiſhwa. Whether Ragoba was the author of this black action or not, it was undoubtedly perpetrated with his concurrence, as it happened in the apartment where Ragoba was confined, and where his unfortunate nephew had fled for refuge. His character became odious and deteſtable in proportion as his guilt was known and credited. His friends were unable to withſtand the general indignation excited by a charge thus marked with ingratitude and treachery. The widow of Narrain was ſoon after ſaid to be delivered of a ſon. In conſequence of theſe occurrences, Nana, Saccaram, and others of the Bramin council, acting in favour of the infant Peiſhwa, and availing themſelves of Ragoba's abſence on a remote expedition, ſtrengthened their party with infinite eagerneſs and aſſiduity, and drove him reluctantly from Poonah. Nor was it without manifeſt difficulty, that he eluded the public vengance, by abandoning his country, and taking ſanctuary in the preſidency of Bombay. The immediate conſequence of his precipitate departure from this theatre of intrigue, was the union of Sindia, Holkar, and five other Marratto chiefs, with the Bramin confederacy, who, under the denomination of *Twelve Friends*, or *Barrah Bhi*, agreed to acknowledge the title of the infant prince, for whom they obtained from the Rajah the *Sirpaw* of office, and

to

to exclude the fugitive uncle from all ſhare in the future government of the empire.

In this brief account of the Marrattos it ought not to be forgotten, that the extenſive dominions of Berar are included. Moodajee Boonſla, however, exerciſes an independent ſovereignty, throughout a populous and extenſive kingdom. Nor does he acknowledge any further connection with the Poonah government than his own immediate intereſts dictate, or than the remains of conſanguinity may incline him to cultivate. For whatever claims he may have to the ſovereignty of Poonah, from his relationſhip to the family of the Ram Rajah, he has given very ſubſtantial proof, that it is no part of his ambition to relinquiſh the reality for what is no more than the mere ſemblance of authority.

Sindia and Holkar, who trace their pedigree to Hendoo kings, of the higheſt antiquity, divide by much the largeſt parts of the rich and extenſive Subah of Malwa, which border on the Vizier's countries to the Eaſt, and thoſe of Berar to the South-weſt. The conduct of theſe politic princes was to moderate the violence of both parties, and to commit themſelves without reſerve in proſecuting the ſchemes of neither. From a regard to their own intereſts, they were naturally diſpoſed to ſupport the balance of diſſention, that no ſide might, from a conſcious ſuperiority, preſume to exact the arrears of their tribute. And they probably found themſelves upon the whole

more

more fecure, by thus participating in the general greatnefs of the ftate, and prefiding at the head of that ariftocracy, which fince the affaffination of Narrain Row guides all its councils, than by taking advantage of its temporary weaknefs, to aim at a precarious independency, under the reftrictions of a contracted influence in their own country.

Moft of the other ftates are evidently directed by circumftances and contingency, in acting under the control or co-operating in any general plan of conduct with the Poonah government. But thefe detached principalities were bound in the earlier periods of their hiftory to furnifh on emergency, and at the requifition of the fovereign, a certain quota of cavalry completely equipped for fervice. Such feverities were however exercifed for increafing their armies, as threatened the depopulation of the country. Their military force confequently no longer confifts in tributaries, but in allies, who take the field on a ftipulated fubfidy. Every cavalier, who flocks to the Imperial ftandard, knows his rifk, and is the owner both of his horfe and arms. Their mode of war, fo habitually directed to plunder, entices into their fervice, on any fudden and favourable project, every adventurer who can procure a horfe. But, as the horfe is often the whole of a Marratto's property and fortune, they folicitoufly avoid all regular conflicts with difciplined troops, and before whom, for the fame reafon, their flight

is

is no proof either of their defeat or diſperſion. They move from country to country, and change their ſituations with incredible expedition; take both their food and ſleep on horſeback; ruſh eagerly into the field at the ſummons of their ſeveral chieftains, and in their progreſs ſweep every thing before them with the rapidity of a torrent. Their principal ſtrength however conſiſts in what are called the houſehold troops or private cavalry, who are commanded by the Paha Sidars, and whoſe horſes and accoutrements are the property of the ſtate. It is their conſtant and univerſal practice to return home at the end of each campaign with their booty, except a few ſelect bodies, who are in fact the perſonal guards of their princes and great men.

The Bombay preſidency, by eſpouſing the cauſe of Ragoba, incenſed this powerful and martial people to regard the Britiſh intereſts, in every part of India, with ſentiments of deliberate and inveterate antipathy. They diſcerned the inſidious policy of the Company's ſervants, in availing themſelves of their family diſſenſions; and were eager to prevent the injuries which it indicated. Conſtruing the orders of the Directors with the ſame liberality which had uniformly been done in the other preſidencies, the Bombay council did not conceive themſelves prohibited abſolutely from hoſtilities, but immediately prepared for war, in the preſumption, at leaſt, that an addition of treaſure or territory would compenſate

with

with ſome, for what might appear to others an inſtance of delinquency. The Directors, in their general letter, ſo early as the year 1769, obſerve to their ſervants, on this ſettlement, "That Salſette and Baſſein, with their dependencies, and "the Marratto proportion of the Surat provinces, "were all that they ſought for on that ſide of "India." The reigning junto in Poonah, foreſeeing the difficulty of defeating the machinations of Ragoba, while the Engliſh perſiſted in affording him protection, was prepared for the conſequence. Nor were the preſident and council diſpoſed to omit ſo favourable an opportunity of trying their fortune in war, of gratifying their own ambition, and of realizing the wiſhes of their employers, by ſeizing the territories they were ſo anxious to poſſeſs. They conſequently invaded, under various pretexts, ſuch portions of the enemy's country as lay moſt contiguous to Bombay. The firſt ſtroke is often deciſive on the fate of a campaign. The Rajah was, in ſome degree, ſurpriſed, though he defended himſelf with unexpected vigour and addreſs. Our operations being confined, for the moſt part, to the ſea-coaſt, the promptitude of the marine and artillery was, on every occaſion, attended with the beſt effect. A demand having been made upon the Nabob of Broach, in April 1771, for a conſiderable ſum, ariſing from arrears of tribute, and an overcharge in the cuſtoms on merchants trading under the Company's protection, for years, an expedition

was,

was, at the ſame time, undertaken againſt the place, to force a compliance with that requiſition. This attempt, however, being fruſtrated, the Nabob had viſited Bombay in the interim, and compromiſed the difference. But the terms to which he agreed were ſedulouſly eluded on his part; and the council thought their honour intereſted in ſeeing them realized. This produced a ſecond enterprize; in which, though ſucceſsful, the loſs of Colonel Wedderburne, an officer of diſtinguiſhed merit, was conſidered as a misfortune which more than counterbalanced all the advantage of the capture. Baſſein, the iſland of Salſette, and a few ſmaller ones, were ſoon after reduced. Other acquiſitions were alſo made by General Gordon, who had ſuceeded Colonel Wedderburne in the command. Theſe proceedings originated in an apprehenſion, whether well or ill founded, that the Portugueze were meditating the recovery of the dominions they had formerly poſſeſſed, eſpecially Salſette and Baſſein; places of the greater conſequence to the Bombay eſtabliſhment, as the inhabitants were almoſt ſupplied with proviſions from the one, and their dockyard, the only one belonging to the Company in India, with timber from the other.

In the mean time, the preſidency of Madras entered into a freſh agreement with Ragoba, by which he ſtipulated the ceſſion of ſome valuable territories, for which they were to furniſh him with two thouſand five hundred of the Company's troops;

troops; whose service, in his behalf, was also to be entirely at his expence. These forces, under the command of Colonel Keating, were instantly embarked for Surat, and ordered to join Ragoba, who menaced Broderah, at the head of forty thousand horse. While in this position, however, the enemy, by an unexpected attack, gave him a complete defeat, obliged him to raise the siege precipitately, and to retreat with only about a thousand horse. He fled to Cambay, but was denied admittance. He next made the best of his way to Bownagar, and from thence, in a galliot, came to Surat. The confederate army lay between Ragoba and Keating, and struggled, though without success, to prevent their junction, which took place on the 19th of April, 1775. About this time great dissensions prevailed among the ministers and their associated chiefs. Moodajee Sindia openly deserted their cause, and carried with him, to his own country, twelve thousand horse; the sincerity of Holkar was doubted, and his motions were watched with suspicion; the Nizam did not fulfil his engagements; and their ally, Shabagee, who had succeeded so far in a contest with his brother, Moodajee Boonsla, as to beat him in a pitched battle, and make him prisoner, was found, next morning, dead in bed. These mortifying circumstances to the Poonah junto gave an auspicious aspect to the fortunes of Ragoba, whose want of money seemed, at this time, his only difficulty. It was not till the middle of next

month

month that an engagement took place between the two armies, when the forces under Keating and Ragoba ſuffered conſiderably, from an unfortunate order, ill repeated perhaps, and not well underſtood, to ſeize ſome of the enemy's guns. The firſt company of European grenadiers, turning rather precipately to the right, were obliged to retreat. They were followed by the Madras infantry, and theſe by ſeveral companies of ſepoys. In ſcrambling through ſome broken hedges, they were in too great a hurry to keep their ranks. At that moment a body of horſe charged them with fury and ſucceſs. They were inſtantly in confuſion, fled on all ſides, and could not be rallied and brought again to the attack, even by the commander in chief. Many officers fell; and the ſlaughter muſt have been general but for the artillery, which, being turned againſt the Marrattos, who crowded with great intrepidity wherever the battle raged moſt, ſoon diſperſed them. This was the only loſs we ſuſtained. The number of men, horſes, and elephants, which were killed of the enemy, ſo effectually damped their ſpirits, that they cautiouſly ever after avoided a regular engagement. The combined troops kept up the purſuit, but never overtook them till ſome weeks afterwards, when they cloſed in with their rear, killed many of their men, drove vaſt numbers of their horſe and camels into the ſea, and deſtroyed their cannon.

Futty Sing, who had ſided with the confederates againſt Ragoba and the Engliſh at the commencement of hoſtilities, was one of thoſe diſcontented chiefs who had deſerted the party. He was influenced by the common politics of Aſia, and of mankind, in giving that intereſt the preference, which was likely to prove the ſtrongeſt. The proſperity which began to attend the affairs of Ragoba determined him to conclude an agreement with that chief, through the agency of the Engliſh, to whom he not only confirmed thoſe grants which Ragoba had made in the country, under his government, but ceded to them, at the ſame time, an annuity of eighteen thouſand pounds. He ſubmitted to pay Ragoba the uſual tribute, to furniſh him the aid claimed by the Durbar of Poonah, and, what was of moſt material importance at this criſis, to pay him twenty-ſix lacks of rupees, within the ſpace of ſixty days. This advantageous treaty of peace and alliance was concluded in the month of July. The affairs of the Company, at the ſame time, were equally proſperous by ſea as by land. The Poonah administration had, early in the campaign, equipped a ſquadron, conſiſting of five ſhips; one of forty-ſix, two of thirty-two, and two of twenty-ſix guns; with ten gallawats or ſmall armed veſſels. Theſe were deſtined to intercept the Britiſh trade, and infeſt thoſe ſeas and coaſts where they were likely to do us moſt miſchief, and ſecure for themſelves the whole booty. But Commodore

John Moore ſoon fell in with them, and gave them a total overthrow. In this manner were the enemy's ſchemes every where defeated, and thoſe of Ragoba crowned with ſucceſs. The friends and adherents of the confederacy became unſtable, and diſperſed in proportion as the preſſure of thoſe accumulating misfortunes operated on the public. The promiſe of large ſums, which had allured the Nabobs and Rajahs who had fought their battles, to exchange domeſtic tranquillity for the perils and fatigues of war, was not punctually diſcharged. The troops were clamorous for their pay, and their leaders were naturally diſguſted with a loſing cauſe. Furkia, the general, found his ſituation peculiarly critical and hazardous. The chiefs were mutinous, and his reſources were exhauſted. Thoſe who had loſt their horſes loudly demanded their ſtipulated hire of their reſpective leaders, who preſſed in their turns the commander in chief; and the ſharffs or bankers had already refuſed to anſwer his drafts. Theſe diſtreſſes very conſiderably increaſed the diſtractions in the Durbar. Saccaram and Nana had diſpatched Vakeels, or commiſſioners, to treat of an accommodation with the preſidency. Theſe were to act ſeparately. One of them fell ſick on his arrival. Before his recovery, the preſident likewiſe became ſo ill, that he was utterly unfit for all public buſineſs. And the council were cautious of diſcovering any unneceſſary eagerneſs for peace, as ſuch a ſentiment, on ſuch a critical occaſion, occafion, would have been fufceptible of a moft improper conftruction, and might have inclined the enemy's Vakeel to demand terms infinitely more advantageous than thofe ultimately intended by the commiffion.

Thus circumftanced were the prefidency of Bombay, Ragoba, and the Marratto ftates, when pofitive orders arrived from the governor-general and council of Bengal, to withdraw the troops, and put an immediate end to all hoftilities with the Poonah adminiftraton. The majority feemed perfectly refolved to realize that pacific fyftem on which they avowedly acted, wherever their influence extended. They had left England in the expectation of finding all the Company's fettlements in a ftate of friendfhip or neutrality with every power in India: It was not without confiderable furprife and concern, that the politics of the preceding adminiftration in Bengal had undeceived them; and that, in proportion as their acquaintance with facts improved, the Company's affairs every where affumed a very different afpect. And the fame pripciples, which determined their opinion of the motives, object and confequences of the Rohilla war, were now brought forward to criminate that which the prefidency of Bombay had commenced againft the Marrattos.

From rhe moment the fupreme government had been formally announced, as directed by act of parliament, to the feveral prefidencies, that

 liberal

liberal and implicit confidence, which ought to be reciprocal and unreſerved among all the branches of the executive power, ſeems to have been wanting in the preſidency of Bombay. They did not formally diſavow their ſubordinate capacity, diſpute the ſupremacy of the governor-general and council, or ſignify in expreſs terms their diſapprobation of the new government. But, had they reſolved to ſubſtantiate every allegation againſt the Company's ſervants abroad, which had rendered them ſo odious among their countrymen at home; had they been previouſly acquainted with the rigidly inoffenſive ſyſtem, which a majority of the ſupreme council thought it their duty to maintain, and under the ſtrongeſt obligations to counteract its operations; or had they pre-concerted a ſcheme of ſatiating their ambition as effectually as ever, in a wanton defiance of the legiſlature, by taking advantage of their diſtant ſituation, to indulge their temerity before they could feel the influence of that control, under which, in the inſtance of making peace and war, they were henceforth deſtined to act; it is difficult to conceive what meaſures better calculated for anſwering theſe views could have been deviſed or adopted. Their manner of conſulting the opinion of the ſupreme government rendered their cordial acquieſcence in its authority extremely ſuſpicious. They imparted no intelligence of their proceedings but ſuch as they could not withhold. The news of their military operations generally reached

reached Bengal long before any official diſpatches were received. And theſe were drawn up with ſo little preciſion and minuteneſs, that they afforded no ſatisfactory information on the ſpecific matters they profeſſed to explain. When a battle was fought, a movement made, or a reſolution formed, they barely ſtated the fact, without any detail of thoſe circumſtances on which a proper conception of it depended. Nor were their communications more ſparing than dilatory, as if the ſupreme council had no intereſt in the knowlege of any of their ſchemes until they were finally executed. They were therefore repeatedly required to give ample and immediate information of their political ſituation, as the moſt particular account of all the events which had happened, or might occur to the intereſts of the Company in that quarter, was expected by the new adminiſtration, who were under the neceſſity of remaining inactive till they heard from Bombay.

Orders to this effect, and prohibiting in expreſs terms the ſpecific meaſures then carrying on, were ſent to Bombay, early in 1775. To theſe no anſwer was received for nearly the ſpace of three months; when their agreement and co-operation with Ragoba, with the ſole view of acquiring territory, were explicitly avowed. Mr. Haſtings on this occaſion entered a very formal and elaborate diſapprobation of the ſyſtem which predominated in the preſidency of Bombay. He condemned the hoſtilities in which they were engaged, as impolitic, unjuſt and unauthorized. In his opinion, the whole burden of the war was thrown on the Company; no injury had been received from the Marratto ſtates; and the late act of parliament had veſted the ſupreme council with the ſole authority of treating with the powers of Indoſtan. Nor did he approve of ſending the Company's troops to ſuch a diſtance from the preſidency, as an enterprizing enemy might have taken that opportunity of ſtorming the ſettlement. He owned, at the ſame time, the extreme difficulty of framing ſuch orders as the peculiarity of their ſituation might require. The original ſtate of things could not be replaced; his knowledge of circumſtances, for the moſt notorious reaſons, could not be correct; and he doubted whether the recal of the troops from Ragoba, at all events, was either ſafe or practicable. He conſequently propoſed, that the orders for the retreat of the army ſhould be limited by theſe exceptions; if the combined forces ſhould have obtained any deciſive advantages; if the ſituation of our detachment was ſuch as to make the recal dangerous; and if a negociation was actually on foot between Ragoba and his opponents. His opinion was ſuggeſted under theſe reſtrictions; becauſe, under the preſent unfortunate dilemma, he ſaw no option but that of the leaſt evil.

The majority, notwithſtanding, agreed to withdraw the troops, without regard to any conſideration but that of their ſafety; to open a negoci-

ation

ation with the ruling party at Poonah; to inform the Bombay council of their resolution; to enjoin their cordial reception of any pacific overtures which might be made to them; and to treat on these preliminaries only, that an immediate suspension of hostilities should take place, and the islands of Salsette and Bassein be confirmed to the Company. Colonel Upton was consequently appointed to execute this delicate and important business with the Poonah ministers. He was instructed to apologize, in the name of the supreme council, for the hostile conduct of the Bombay presidency in thus wantonly taking up arms in matters which did not concern them; to disavow the treaty which, without their knowledge or consent, had been entered into with Ragoba; and to express the most sincere and earnest desire, on their part, of establishing a lasting peace with the Durbar; to excuse the seizure of Salsette and Bassein, on the principle of its otherwise falling into the hands of the Portugueze; and the impossibility of restoring it without permission from the Directors; to inform them of the orders given for withdrawing our troops from Ragoba; and to include him, if possible, in the treaty. The board resolved, at the same time, to render this mission useful in other respects, and to take that opportunity of surveying the peninsula of India, and of ascertaining the geometrical distances of places through which Colonel Upton should pass; and a gentleman of science was ap-

 pointed

pointed to attend him for that purpofe. Letters were alfo written to the Poonah minifter, announcing the colonel's departure. Saccaram, who led the Poonah faction at this time, had arifen from fuch a ftate of original obfcurity and want, as prevented his receiving the very rudiments of education. Though, in fact, premier of one of the greateft ftates in the world, he could neither read nor write. Unfortunately the Bramin, who acted as his confidential fecretary, had been governor of the province in which the late captures, made by the Company's forces, were fituated. Frefh inftructions were therefore difpatched to their Vakeels at Bombay, which arrived before they had declared in form the original purport of their miffion. They now infifted on having the perfon of Ragoba delivered into their hands; the immediate reftoration of Salfette; and the complete evacuation of every other place we had wrefted from them. They promifed, in return, to make fome pecuniary compenfation for the expences we had incurred. It ought to be confidered, that hoftilities began with us; that we had received no provocation from the Marrattos; that they had a right to demand their own dominions; that thefe were not the lefs their's for our having taken forcible poffeffion of them; that their moderation was fufficiently evinced by confining their claims to a ftrict reftitution; and that the reimburfement they offered, not only proved how fincerely they were difpofed to negociate, but

was

was an article we had no title, in juſtice, to expect. Theſe are the terms, however, which the advocates for the purity of Aſiatic policy would repreſent as hard and inadmiſſible. It is thus they would decide the differences of nations, on maxims which tear up, by the roots, every barrier of property, and outrage all the feelings and principles of equity between man and man.

Under the influence of the ſame fatal ſyſtem, the proſperous ſituation of the preſidency, and of their ally's affairs, at this preciſe period, was eagerly brought forward, as an unanſwerable argument for a vigorous proſecution of the war. Thunderſtruck by the peremptory orders of the ſupreme council for the immediate recal of the detachment which co-operated with Ragoba, and the unexpected embaſſy of Colonel Upton to the court of Poonah, in their anſwer to the official diſpatches which brought the mortifying intelligence, the gentlemen of Bombay expreſs the higheſt concern at the meaſures preſcribed for effecting a general pacification; and ſignify their apprehenſions, that the intereſts of the Company would receive the moſt eſſential injury by the adoption of a plan which, at the ſame time, fixed indelible diſgrace on the preſidency. They juſtified their interference with the domeſtic quarrels of the Marratto ſtates, from the neceſſity they were under of openly vindicating their ſeizure of Salſette. They preferred the cauſe of Ragoba, notwithſtanding the atrocious treachery and mur-

der

der for which he was expelled by his countrymen; and assisted him with their troops, because he gave the Company the right of acquiring a revenue of two hundred and fifty thousand pounds per annum. They even asserted the propriety and justice of making war, in this manner, on the rebellious subjects of their ally. And they press the indignity done them in not intrusting the negociation to one of their number; alledging the facility of having accomplished it on the most honourable and advantageous terms, but for the information thus officially given to the Poonah government of the Company's eagerness to obtain peace.

Not satisfied with having remonstrated in these terms, they deputed Mr. Taylor, a member of the select committee, to state their complaints, in person, before the board. He, therefore, presented a memorial, which contains, in addition to the arguments on which the Bombay presidency ground their proceedings in their engagement with Ragoba, a variety of political reasoning against the interruption given to them by the resolution and orders of the supreme council; an introductory account of the Marratto state; the rise and establishment of the Peishwa's power; the contiguity and connection, in policy and commerce, with the Company's possessions in the West of India; the dominions or districts held by the great chiefs of the nation; in what degree dependent on the Poonah government, particularly the

Boonslas,

Boonslas, the Guicawars, and Sindia and Holkar; those various events and intrigues which occasioned the divisions in the Peishwa's family, and by that means involved the presidency of Bombay in their quarrels; the comparative situation and force of the contending parties in the war, at the time when hostilities ceased; and the probable disposition of the Nizam and Hyder Ally during these disturbances. He gives also an exact description of the situation, revenue, and other productive advantages, arising from the several cessions of territory made by Ragoba and Futty Sing. He urges, in strong and earnest terms, the dangerous and disgraceful consequences of declaring a treaty, thus beneficial, invalid and null; especially as it might impel Ragoba to throw himself, for assistance, on other powers. He concludes by strenuously insisting, that, whether it should be resolved to terminate these affairs by arms or negociation, it was absolutely expedient to revoke the orders for withdrawing the troops.

The board having considered the question, whether their former orders should be enforced, or for the present suspended, the original resolution was confirmed, except that it was agreed to leave the option with the president and council of Bombay, to withdraw their troops into such of their garrisons as they might chuse. Mr. Taylor, with no better success, after signifying the utmost concern at the determination of the board, desired, in a subsequent paper, to add a further representation of the

the very great diſhonour the Bombay council would ſuffer from intruſting the conduct of the negociation with an entire ſtranger. He put them in mind that one of their board had been appointed by the Company themſelves to reſide at Poonah, with particular inſtructions and powers for negociation with Madarow, the then Pieſhwa; and that, from their knowledge of the views, connections, and intereſts of the different perſons in the Poonah Durbar, they muſt be beſt qualified to tranſact ſuch matters; and that they ſhould all be animated by zeal for the honour and intereſt of their employers, and would pay implicit obedience to whatever directions they might receive from the ſupreme council in managing this important meaſure. Mr. Taylor was, however, given to underſtand, that the ſupreme council could not agree to repeal or change the appointment of Colonel Upton, conſiſtently with the reſolutions which they had publicly ſignified to the miniſters at Poonah; but that they by no means intended to throw any ſlight on the preſidency of Bombay, which they ſhould always endeavour to protect from every ſpecies of indignity or diſreſpect.

In the mean time, Colonel Upton proceeded acroſs the continent, and encountered, in his way, a great variety of difficulties. His correſpondence, from the different ſtages of his journey, exhibit a moſt unpleaſant account of the diſtreſs and confuſion of the countries through which he paſſed.

Notwithſtanding

Notwithstanding frequent assurances from the court of Poonah, that orders had been given to facilitate his route through the Marratto dominions, by several accounts received in Bengal, that fact appeared very doubtful. He received, as he passed through Benares, a letter from the Poonah minister, written in a stile so little flattering to the object of his embassy, that he deemed it necessary to complain of it to his superiors. He ascribed the delay of his journey to the inattention of the Durbar, from whom he had received no regular advices, and who had not even apprised the Sirdars of the different districts of the business on which he was deputed, and of his travelling through their country, which he found every where in arms; he was nearly six months on this tedious and perilous journey. By means of his route, a geographical line was first drawn across the continent of India, through the principal places or points between Agra and Poonah; and which, by establishing a great many capital and interesting geometrical positions, has become a fund of the best local intelligence, and considerably enriched the science of geography.

The colonel, who had set out on the 10th of July, did not arrive at Poonah till the 30th of December, 1775. His reception was equal to the magnitude of the objects he was deputed to address. He found the internal commotions, which agitated the Marratto states, pregnant with ruptures in almost every quarter of that mighty empire,

pire. The poſthumous ſon of Narrain Row had fruſtrated the machinations of Ragoba, who wiſhed to have extinguiſhed his brother's line. The infant being forthwith proclaimed Peiſhwa, Saccaram Pundit, and Nana Furneſe, were conſtituted the acting miniſters or regents for carrying on the affairs of ſtate in his name. Nor were the partizans of Ragoba inattentive to the various ſhapes which the aſpect of public buſineſs was accuſtomed to aſſume, under ſcenes thus fluctuating and embroiled. By artfully inflaming the proud ambitious views of the ſeveral chiefs, and exciting their perſonal jealouſies againſt each other, they kept the miniſterial party in a perpetual ferment, and rendered many of their moſt eſſential exertions in the ſervice of the public odious or abortive.

The propoſitions, which Upton laid before the Durbar, were not altogether, or at once, unexceptionable. The temerity of the preſidency in Bombay had offended the miniſters, almoſt beyond the poſſibility of forgiveneſs. The complicated ſyſtem, under which the Engliſh acted, probably ſtruck them as precarious and equivocal. They had ſeen the favourite meaſures of the Bombay gentlemen controlled by the ſupreme council of Bengal. Theſe they knew to be no more than the ſervants of a trading company, who, in common with the whole body they employed, were reſponſible for whatever they did to the Britiſh legiſlature. Involved in a variety of ſuch

em-

embarraſſing circumſtances, they regarded, at leaſt in the firſt inſtance, the overtures of the ſupreme council, with a reſerve which bordered on averſion. A debate immediately aroſe in the Durbar, from Colonel Upton being inſtructed to inſiſt on the ſignatures of all the chiefs, individually, to whatever engagements might take place between them. The miniſterial party, though obviouſly ſtrong, ſeemed yet not a little deſirous to haſten the concluſion of a peace. The conduct of the Bombay forces appeared to them, however, not without ſuſpicion. They inſiſted the more explicitly on the equivocal ſituation of ours, that they gave the moſt ſatisfying aſſurances, that the behaviour of their own was ſtrictly pacific. The preſidency of Bombay, at the ſame time, as if they intended utterly to deſtroy every ſymptom of returning friendſhip, adviſed Ragoba to accompany the Britiſh troops, with ſuch of his army as he might be able to maintain, in order to avoid the evil effects of a ſeparation. They were alſo prevailed upon, by his earneſt entreaties, to agree, that both armies ſhould remain at Corrade, a place in the neighbourhood of Surat, belonging to the Nabob, until orders ſtill more peremptory ſhould arrive from Bengal; as Ragoba might be totally deſerted when thus abandoned by them. Theſe motions of the troops were by no means calculated to facilitate the negociation, or reconcile the Marrattos to an implicit confidence in the declarations of Engliſhmen. Indeed, they had been taught to expect that Colonel Upton was empowered to treat with them on equal terms, without making any demands whatever. They were much against allowing the further possession of Salsette, or agreeing to the surrender of Bassein. They probably did not conceive it possible, that, without a better claim, our commissioner could be authorized to urge a condition, which in the estimation of common justice was absurd and ridiculous. And they asked him, as he observes, a thousand times, why we made such professions of honour, and disproved the war entered into by the Bombay government, while so desirous of availing ourselves of its advantages. They say, the governor-general and council of Calcutta have deputed you to negociate with us on terms honourable to both nations, yet all advantage and honour is confined to yourselves.

He informed the board, that he must be satisfied with a factory instead of Bassein; that he should insist on retaining Salsette, though an end to the treaty should follow their refusal of an acquiescence; that they acknowledged no grants in any part of the Guzurat to be valid but their own; that a certain stipend, and number of attendants, would be allowed to Ragoba; and that the frequent reports, of the deplorable situation to which the reigning party were reduced, were unfounded, as they still had a numerous army, no want of money, and were in alliance with the

Nizam,

Nizam, who had lately ſent a large body of horſe to join their forces.

Mr. Taylor, who was ſtill at Calcutta, repeating, both in public and private, the ſame ſtale unavailing plea againſt the majority, which had brought him from Bombay, embraced this opportunity of giving into the board a freſh remonſtrance; in which he roundly adopted the confident aſſertions of the preſidency, concerning the favourable ſituation of Ragoba's affairs; and ſupported their arguments for preferring, even on political motives, a treaty with him, to any that might be ſettled with his opponents. And that he might defeat the impreſſions of Colonel Upton's repreſentations, he adds with peculiar ſhrewdneſs, "that the colonel dated from the "fort of Poorunder, where he is ſurrounded by "the miniſters and their creatures, whoſe intereſt "it is to miſinform him with reſpect to their own "ſtrength and importance, and to ſecrete from "him every circumſtance favourable to Ragoba "and his partizans. Their patience, ſkill and "diſſimulation, in conducting political negocia"tions, are well known in India. It is almoſt uſeleſs "to inſiſt on the different credulity that is due to "the information collected under theſe diſadvan"tages, and thoſe communicated by gentlemen "in whoſe honour you have a ſecurity from in"tentional deceit, and whoſe caution is war"ranted by the danger they incur, ſhould their "ill-grounded intelligence miſlead you into mea-

" ſures that might not otherwiſe be deemed ex-
" pedient."

This tireſome negociation being procraſtinated to ſuch a length, as rendered the pacific intentions of the Poonah miniſtry ſuſpicious, even to the majority, it was at laſt unanimouſly agreed, by the governor-general and council, to direct Colonel Upton, in caſe he had not already concluded a treaty, to conform to his former inſtructions; and that, if the Poonah government did not accede to the overtures implied in theſe, he ſhould demand his diſmiſſion, and retire to Bombay within ſix days after the receipt of theſe orders. The very next day, however, a letter was received by the board from Colonel Upton, which informed them, that all hope of concluding a treaty was at an end. The ſupreme council immediately reſolved, that though the abrupt declaration of the miniſtry might be only a feint, to try what impreſſion it might make on the colonel's mind to ſupport a renewal of the war, it was neceſſary to provide the means of conducting it with the greateſt probability of ſucceſs. They were at the ſame time agreed to acquaint the ſeveral preſidencies, and their different dependencies, of the hoſtile ſituation to which the affairs of the Company were reduced. To the preſident and council of Bombay in particular, while they declared themſelves not reſponſible for the meaſures which had involved the Company in this quarrel, they releaſed that government from the

reſtrictions

restrictions which they had laid upon the operations of their army, and authorized them to give the most effectual support to Ragoba, instructing them to assign the command of the troops to General Gordon, whom alone they deemed fit to be intrusted with a charge of such consequence.

All these preparatory resolutions for war, however, by the receipt of a letter from Colonel Upton, dated the 24th of February [1776] were converted into an immediate determination to revoke them, as he informed the board, that certain articles were agreed upon between him and the ministers, which would be ready for transmission in a few days. These were dispatched from Poonah, to the supreme government, the first of the following month; when the colonel acquainted them of several particulars in regard to the difficulties he had experienced in arranging the plan, the terms, and the stile of the pacification, and of the further steps he should take in accomodating all remaining points of doubt or difference, especially the question about the cession made by Futty Sing in the Guzurat country.

The advantageous acquisitions which were secured to the Company by this treaty, were Salsette and the adjacent islands in the bay of Bombay, the city and Purgunnah of Broach, without participation or claim of any kind, and a considerable district in the neighbourhood. The whole produced above an hundred thousand pounds of clear annual revenue. It disannulled all preceding

 treaties

treaties made by the Bombay council with Ragoba or Futty Sing; revoked the ſeveral ceſſions of thoſe chiefs to the Engliſh; obliged the troops of Ragoba to diſperſe, and our's to retire within the limits of the preſidency; provided him with an aſylum in the heart of the Marratto dominions, a body guard, domeſtics, and a revenue adequate to his rank; bound up the Engliſh from affording him, or any perſon diſturbing the peace of the Marratto ſtates, the leaſt ſupport or countenance whatever; and engaged to indemnify the Company for the expences occaſioned by the war, with the ſum of twelve lacks, to be paid within two years.

This treaty, notwithſtanding the many ſolid advantages which it conferred on the Company, was deemed by the Bombay council inadequate, and highly injurious to the reputation and intereſt of the Engliſh, in that part of India. General Gordon and Colonel Upton, however, who conſidered diſintereſtedly what ought reaſonably to have been expected, from an impartial attention to the unjuſtifiable circumſtances of the riſe and progreſs of the war, the ill management of it under the command of the troops employed, the want of reſources for carrying it on, the ſtate of contending parties, and the ſentiments of the Company, thought it ſufficiently honourable and expedient. Indeed, upon the principles aſſumed in reaſoning againſt it, no political reputation can ever be valid, as it can never be equally ſatisfactory to both parties. Though the war may have left us in a ſitu-

ation

ation to inſiſt on higher terms, it was a war into which we had not been provoked by the Marrattos. The injury was given by us, and juſtice required that we ſhould have redreſſed the wrongs we inflicted.

But, from the great contrariety of opinions among the various parties concerned, it was not very likely that the peace would be laſting. In proportion as the Poonah miniſtry were ſolicitous to carry into execution the agreement ſtipulated, the Bombay council heſitated, magnified the difficulties of an immediate compliance with the mandate of the ſupreme board, and procraſtinated in every ſtep they took to fulfil their part of the engagement. Ragoba conſidered himſelf as ſold to his enemies, in whoſe cuſtody he was placed by the treaty, without any pledge or ſecurity for his ſafety. The reſidence ſtipulated for him by the Poonah miniſtry ſtruck him as a priſon, where their creatures only were to ſurround him, and where it would be impoſſible to prevent their diſpoſing of him, whenever it might ſuit their purpoſes, as they pleaſed. Theſe apprehenſions were undoubtedly heightened by a conſciouſneſs of what he deſerved, and what might be ſo eaſily perpetrated by thoſe who poſſeſſed ſimilar principles to his own. He therefore refuſed to accept of the terms in which he was included, and thought himſelf entitled to an aſylum in one of the Company's ſettlements. The preſidency of Bombay, in their diſpatches to Bengal of the 30th of

 March,

March, preſſed the requiſitions of their ally, on the ſuperior council, with great earneſtneſs. In their opinion, he ſhould have been given an option in the ation of his reſidence: Nor would the miniſters have objected to it without a ſiniſter intention. He would have proved an uſeful inſtrument for keeping the Marrattos in awe. But, circumſtanced as he was by the treaty of Poorunder, he was now determined to appeal to the juſtice of the honourable Company, and await their determination at Bombay. They lamented the dereliction of the advantages ſecured by the treaty of Surat, and predicted the loſs of the Guicawar diſtricts.

This intelligence created ſtrong debates in the ſupreme council. One party preſaged, from the obſtinacy of the Bombay preſidency, a renewal of the war, which they were ſincerely anxious to prevent. The other, by habitually apologizing for the conduct of theſe gentlemen, and partially adopting their cenſures of the treaty, ſeemed rather intent on precipitating that event. Before any direct reply could be framed to the Bombay letter, freſh information was received from Colonel Upton, of a nature ſtill more ſerious and alarming. He ſtated the peculiar uneaſineſs which the meaſures of the Bombay council produced in the Durbar, that they complained of Ragoba's being permitted to ſeek a reſidence among the Engliſh, as that circumſtance might interrupt the harmony which it was the intereſt and inclination of both nations to cultivate; that by our protracting,

ing, or rather taking part in the disputes between them and Ragoba, we occasioned the whole expence of keeping up an army, which, including the Nizam's forces, amounted to thirty lacks of rupees per month; that the stile in which Colonel Keating had proclaimed the peace, as having taken place between the honourable Company and the *Poonah ministers*, not the *Marratto states*, gave the highest offence; and that, in defiance of every delicacy due to the respective powers concerned in this solemn transaction, the commander of our troops had given the promise of protection to Ragoba, and proposed sending his elephants, horses, and other articles of equipage, into the neighbourhood of Broach, under escort of a detachment from that garrison.

It was about this time that Subada, a person of the Peishwa family, who was said to have been slain in battle, and who had been for years imprisoned in the fort of Rutnah-Geriah, had made his escape, and was joined by several chiefs, and even by the admiral of the Marratto fleet. He had pretensions also to the Peishwaship; and though these were soon effectually invalidated, his appearance afforded an apology for Ragoba not disbanding his troops, according to the terms of the late treaty. But the true reason was, that he had no money to pay them. On this little army moving to the environs of Surat, it was deemed necessary, with the troops lately under the command of Keating, to reinforce the garrisons, that no accident might

might happen from the vicinity of ſuch a force. A circumſtance which excited new jealouſies in the Poonah miniſters, who complained to Colonel Upton, that the Bombay council had not reſtored the places ceded by treaty; that they had ſupplied Ragoba with military ſtores; that, as Hyder Ally had forced the Company to fulfil their engagements, his example would juſtify their adoption of the ſame means; and that, if proper and complete ſatisfaction was not obtained in theſe ſeveral particulars, they would carry fire and ſword through all the Company's dominions. The preſidency of Bombay roundly denied theſe aſſertions, and inſiſted that they had ſent to Sûrat and Broach for delivering up the Purgunnah, but no perſons proper to receive them had appeared; that the preſent ſituation of Ragoba was owing to contingencies which they did not foreſee, and for which they were not accountable; and that they were ſo far from plotting to renew the war, as to refuſe a junction with the Nizam, or to pledge the Engliſh faith; that in reſtoring Ragoba they ſhould not oppoſe him. They recriminated with great aſperity on the Poonah government, who, notwithſtanding their ſtrong pretenſions of attachment to the intereſts of the Company, had yet permitted no communication or intercourſe with their dominions; that no perſon could come, even with vegetables or proviſions, from the neighbouring ports; that veſſels under Engliſh colours, though ſeparated from their convoy by ſtreſs of

weather,

weather, had been ſeized and carried into Gheriah; that no Vakeel had been ſent to Bombay with any explanation of theſe tranſactions; and that their connection with Futty Sing was too much involved and embarraſſed to admit of an immediate ecclairciſſement. Thus each party, from an eager anxiety, perhaps, to ſhuffle, to overreach, or to procraſtinate, excuſed themſelves from a literal compliance with the requiſitions of the treaty. A whole year was exhauſted in a fruitleſs diſcuſſion of mutual altercations and complaints, when 1777 opened, and gave riſe to a great variety of new and intereſting ſcenes.

The political ſtate of affairs, in other quarters of India, were more or leſs affected by theſe tranſactions, at this period. The diſcuſſion of many important and intricate queſtions, which then ſubſiſted between the Engliſh and Marratto governments, was, no doubt, a curious and intereſting object of attention and remark to all the different powers who occupy that great theatre of inceſſant hoſtility and intrigue. But it rarely happens, when any of the principal ſtates are engaged in war, that the other Subahs or Rajahs of the leaſt weight or conſequence, from contiguity of property, family connection, or political intereſt, can wholly, or for any conſiderable length of time, preſerve a ſtrict neutrality.

The preſidency of St. George betrayed ſtrong apprehenſions of hoſtile deſigns from Hyder Ally, in conjunction with the French, which were only allayed

allayed by the report of his preparations being chiefly deſtined againſt the Marrattos. Conſcious of having trifled with the juſt requiſitions of that prince, under emergencies of extreme neceſſity, it was not unnatural to regard his future motions with peculiar jealouſy and ſuſpicion. The return they had made to his confidence left them no room to place any in him. Ever ſince a ſhort time after the peace he concluded with them, when the board withheld thoſe ſuccours which he thought himſelf entitled to expect, and which the exigencies of his affairs impelled him to demand, he made no ſcruple of avowing a ſtedfaſt antipathy to our intereſt. The misfortunes of that war, in which he loſt his army, and a conſiderable part of his dominions, he has uniformly charged to our breach of engagement. Indeed, he had left no arguments unapplied, no meaſures unaſſayed, which could excite the Engliſh to aſſiſt him in repreſſing the formidable growth of the Marratto empire, at a time when, under the auſpices of Madarow, it menaced the independence of every power on the continent of India. But the preſidency of Madras ſeemed then equally indifferent to his intereſt and their own. Fortune had, however, interpoſed that relief, by the death of the young Marratto hero, who, by the philoſophical virtues of prudence, moderation, and military conduct, had, before he reached the twenty-fifth year of his age, reduced even Hyder Ally nearly to his original inſignificance. But that

that event, the ſubſequent diſcuſſions in the Durbar, and, moſt of all, the ſtrenuous conteſt which had ſo long ſubſiſted between the Poonah miniſtry and the Engliſh, gave Hyder time, by attending to the domeſtic regulation of his various dominions, to the improvement of his finances, and to the ſtate of his army, to recover much of his former conſequence. While our connection with Ragoba was yet in its infancy, he diſcovered no ſmall degree of diſtruſt and reſentment againſt us, by warning that unfortunate prince againſt repoſing too much confidence in his new allies, and ſeriouſly appriſing him of what he muſt expect from our ſiniſter and faithleſs conduct. He was then ſuſpected of tampering with the miniſterial party and Nizam, to the diſadvantage of Ragoba and his allies. He nevertheleſs afterwards aſſiſted that prince with money; and the reigning Peiſhwa not only threatened retaliation, but actually detached a conſiderable body of Marratto cavalry into the Myſore country, where they committed ſuch ravages and devaſtation, as impelled Hyder to ſend the flower of his army, under his ſon Tippo Saib, to oppoſe their progreſs.

During the hoſtilities which ſubſiſted between the Bombay preſidency and the Poonah Marrattos, the Nabob of Arcot had been much ſolicited by the latter to aſſiſt, by his mediation, in procuring a peace with the former. They had, however, pending the embaſſy of Colonel Upton, refuſed their acquieſcence with the articles propoſed

in

in his favour. They alledged, that the Rajah of Tanjore, a relation of the Ram Rajah, had been wantonly diſpoſſeſſed of his country, and ſtripped of whatever was valuable or dear to him; and that it was impoſſible for them to treat upon any terms of conceſſion with the Nabob, until after the reſtoration of the Marratto prince. This event had now taken place; and though the inclination of Mahommed Ally had not been much conſulted in the buſineſs, his acquieſcence, whether voluntary or not, rendered him ſo much leſs an object of reſentment to the Poonah miniſtry. Indeed, his inveterate enmity to Hyder Ally reconciled him, in a great meaſure, to the Marrattos, who, before their late troubles, had been that hero's moſt formidable opponents. It will appear, in the progreſs of theſe tranſactions, that the Nabob of Arcot was, by this time, conſidered as of but little importance to the Company, as an ally; and therefore could be regarded by other powers as no very formidable enemy.

It has been the general policy of the Subah of the Deccan to watch the viciſſitudes of fortune among the various belligerent powers in his neighbourhood; and to convert, by all the means in his power, every change or contingency to his own emolument. He had lately detached a large body of troops to join the miniſterial army; but it was well known he did not wiſh them to be engaged in action, eſpecially againſt the Britiſh forces. He was even forward in propoſing a plan of hoſtile

union

union against the very powers with whom he was apparently connected in the closest alliance.

So cautious, and perhaps equivocal, had the conduct of Moodajee Boonsla hitherto been, that, till the beginning of the year 1777, he was generally imagined to have been well disposed to the cause of Ragoba. He then, however, signified to the governor-general, in the course of their correspondence, his determination of sending Rajagee, his son, to visit the Peishwa, as a measure which their long friendship had rendered absolutely necessary. He stationed, however, a Vakeel at Calcutta, and otherwise cultivated the cordial friendship of the Company with much apparent sincerity and solicitude. But, if the insinuations of the Nizam were true, these professions were only intended to disguise his designs of suddenly urging his demand of chout, from the province of Bengal, at the head of a formidable army.

The politics of Sindia and Holkar had, in the course of these quarrels and intrigues, constantly veered with their interest. This was the great unerring standard by which all their public and private preferences and measures were uniformly regulated. Ragoba had often repeated his reliance upon their declarations in his favour; but he found himself at last the sport of their convenience and intrigue. They were now openly engaged in measures diametrically opposite to his interest. They appear, at the same time, to have proved very

very troublesome and alarming neighbours to the Vizier and territories of Oude.

The circumstances of the young Vizier, who had lately succeeded to that important and conspicuous situation by the death of his father, Suja ul Dowlah, were critical and delicate. At the head of a powerful army, possessed of immense revenues, and invested with the government of an extensive and populous territory, he found himself, notwithstanding, the splendid slave of a few merchants. His pretensions to the Vizierat had met with some interruptions; but the interest of the Company in his favour left his competitors no chance of success. On this occasion, the situation and conduct of Shaw Allum was naturally marked with doubt and irresolution. Nor did he seem at last to act with cordial or sincere attachment, when he sent an ambassador, in the month of April [1776] to invest the Nabob ul Dowlah with the Kilaat. Accounts were soon after received at Calcutta of frequent alarms from the hostile appearance of troops on the frontiers of Corah. It was apprehended, that the king, the Marrattos, the Sicks, and the Rohillas, were confederated to invade the dominions of Oude. A defensive alliance with the Nabob Nudjiff Cawn was therefore propagated, and adopted as a measure which afforded the most probable security against the sudden incursions or depradations of the enemy. This chief was then carrying on a kind of desultory warfare with various tribes of Marrattos and Jauts,

Jauts, who infested the vicinity of his and the Vizier's dominions. He was, at the same time, much distressed for money to pay his army. The confidence which the king had formerly reposed in him was sensibly diminished. Nor were the misfortunes of this degraded emperor in any degree abated. The embarrassments which he owed to the cabals of his court, and the incessant disappointments he suffered from abortive expectations of relief, visibly affected his conduct. The prospect before him was the more unpleasant that his tried friend, Nudjiff Cawn, however unable or unwilling, in the present situation of affairs, to assist him, was the only person, notwithstanding the preference given to his rivals, to whom his majesty could have any hopes of ultimately applying with success.

Such was the political posture of affairs in the continent of India, on the conclusion of the first, and the eve of the second Marratto war. But, though all the great powers had the address to feign a perfect acquiescence for the present in this apparent tranquillity, the fiend of discord was already at work, and a plot framing in the dark recesses of ambition, which, by treachery, temerity, and perseverance, was soon to involve the whole empire in one general and ruthless scene of carnage and desolation. Who, that has not an heart of stone, but must commiserate the hapless destiny of man, by which millions of innocent people are the daily victims of that caprice and

cruelty

cruelty which originate only with their leaders! Thus are the whole ſpecies doomed to ſuffer more ſerious and ſubſtantial miſery by the foul intrigues of a few urſurpers, than from all the other plagues and diſaſters that depopulate the world.

CHAP.

CHAPTER IX.

Intrigues of the Bombay Presidency—Origin and Commencement of the Second Marratto War—March of the Bengal Detachment through the interior Countries of India—Failure of the Bombay Expedition—General Goddard refuses to accede to the Treaty of Worgaum—The projected Negociation with the Rajah of Berar abortive—New Alliances with Futty Sing and the Rannah of Ghod—A general Confederacy formed against the English—The Conquest of the Guzurat—Popham's brilliant Expedition in the Province of Ghod.

TWO events had occurred before the latter end of 1777, which, by a series of rapid consequences, involved more or less, in general and promiscuous hostility, all the nations of Indostan. The power of the majority in the superior government of Bengal was annihilated by the death of Colonel Manson and General Clavering, and a commissioner from the court of Versailles had made his appearance at Poonah. The first of these contingencies had consigned, into the hands of the governor-general, that uncontrollable authority, which the ambiguity of the second tempted him to exert in reviving and carrying into effect a

 system,

ſyſtem, which now operated with the greater energy for having been ſo long ſuſpended. A ſcene of indiſcriminate animoſity and ſlaughter ſoon followed the developement of thoſe politics which this change of meaſures occaſioned. No regard, at leaſt in the firſt inſtance, was paid to contiguity of ſituation, to the merit or demerit of national character, to habits of ancient or familiar intercourſe, or even to a ſimilarity of cuſtoms, manners, laws, or religion. Europeans in almoſt every battle fought againſt Europeans! Hindoos, Mahommedans, and Chriſtans, were every where alike objects of mutual and undiſtinguiſhed maſſacre! Nor was it until the laſt ſtage of this awful conflict, that a general confederacy was formed for exterminating that party, who had thus foully embroiled the reſt.

The Bombay council continued to entertain the moſt cordial deteſtation of the late treaty. It had quaſhed all thoſe ſanguine expectations of territorial acquiſition, which filled their imaginations and prompted their ambition. Mr. Moſtyn ſucceeded Colonel Upton as reſident at the Durbar, and appriſed the preſidency that St. Lubin, the French agent, was arrived at Poonah, and received with every poſſible mark of reſpect. And though the miniſters had repeatedly proteſted that nothing was intended againſt the Company's intereſt, very ſerious conſequences were apprehended from his influence and intrigues, eſpecially in the event of a French war. Propoſals being at the ſame

time

time suggested by some discontented chiefs in favour of Ragoba, the presidency entered into the scheme with alacrity. Their agents were forthwith empowered to commence a negociation with the principal conspirators, and dispatches forwarded to the supreme council for their concurrence and support. The governor-general, no longer thwarted by an obstinate majority, not only embraced the measure, but determined to facilitate its execution by an immediate dispatch both of men and money. Previous to this intelligence, he had devised and brought forward a plan for improving the peace of Poorunder, in which the Marrattos were required to give Ragoba such security for his personal safety as he could rely on with confidence; to reimburse all those military charges which might be incurred on his behalf; to cede in perpetuity the fortress and island of Bassein, with several other specified grants and exchanges of land on the continent, to the Company; and to allow no European settlement in any part of their dominions, without the knowledge and consent of the supreme council.

The idea in which these arbitrary propositions seems to have originated was not well founded. It was evidently fabricated on false or imperfect information. And deception is perhaps the most favourable apology of which the failure will admit. But, from the moment that the presidency were possessed with the means of prosecuting the war effectually, their inclination for peace re-

 turned,

turned, at the ſame time that the ſuperior council urged and exemplified the moſt prompt and ſpirited exertions, New inſtructions were inſtantly tranſmitted to Bombay, that other and more peremptory requiſitions might be made on the ruling party in the Poonah adminiſtration. Theſe were intended to ſubſtantiate the conditions which had been formerly ſtated as the foundation of a new agreement, and a refuſal to any one of them was to be conſtrued into a formal and deliberate infraction of the peace. Such extraordinary demands announced in ſuch arrogant terms, and accompanied with ſuch menaces, would have been regarded and reſented by all independent ſtates as tantamount to a declaration of war. The preſidency of Bombay were likewiſe allowed a diſcretionary power of entering into further articles with Ragoba, according to the exigence or expediency of the ſituation and views under which he might act. But it was very cautiouſly ſurmiſed, that, notwithſtanding the favourable aſpect which theſe arrangements bore to his affairs, objects much more ſubſtantial and extenſive were ultimately in view.

It is not very eaſy to conceive by what other or more effectual meaſures the ſervants of the company could have forced the Marrattos to relinquiſh their pacific intentions. So ſtrong was their averſion to a breach with the Engliſh, that they had abſolutely given up the point of Ragoba's reſidence among them. They were ſatisfied to leave him

him under our protection, on condition that he should settle at Benares; at that time the most eligible, the most learned, and one of the most frequented cities in India, as he could not, thus remotely circumstanced, so effectually disturb the harmony of government by his projects and intrigues. In that case they promised to endow him with an annuity for life of sixty thousand pounds.

It was now that the supreme council conceived the great design of marching a strong military detachment through the interior countries of this immense continent, as a demonstration to the potentates of India, that the harmony of the British settlements, however scattered or remote from each other, would on every emergency be adequate to the general safety. This measure was strenuously opposed, as obliging an army, with no inconsiderable train of artillery, to traverse countries hitherto unknown, to encounter difficulties of the nature, number and extent of which no estimate could be formed; to invade the territories of a power with whom we affected to be on terms of amity; to risque the resentment of many populous and hostile nations, who might take that opportunity of avenging their wrongs; to increase the jealousies already subsisting between the British and Marratto interests; and to heighten that envy and odium which our ambition, rapidity, and intrigues had already excited. These objections were however overruled, and the detachment, which, including five hundred

Candahar horſe, conſiſted of nearly ſeven thouſand effective men, began to move in the neighbourhood of Corah and Allahabad, in the beginning of April, and arrived at the Marratto frontiers about the middle of May [1778]. They paſſed the Jumna, which, on the north-eaſtern extremities, waſhes ſeveral countries tributary to the Marrattos, in boats, and under the fire of their artillery, as a body of the enemy's horſe oppoſed them on the other ſide. Theſe they inſtantly diſperſed. The town and fort of Calpy were utterly abandoned on their approach. There they continued till the 3d of June, that memorable day, on which, by a fatiguing march through an extenſive country, which exhibited only one invariable ſcene of naked concker as far as the eye could reach, without a tuft of verdure, or a drop of water, between three and four hundred men, overcome by thirſt and fatigue, periſhed, raving mad! The army ſpent nearly three months in the diamond country of Bundlecund, and were expoſed to the greateſt danger by interfering with the family diſputes which took place at that time among thoſe who had pretenſions to the Rajahſhip. In theſe conteſts, thus wantonly fomented, and no doubt intereſtedly protracted, the city of Mow was ſacked with a barbarity, for which the loſs ſuſtained by the victors on that occaſion was a juſt puniſhment.

Leſlie, who had the command, died in the beginning of October, and was ſucceeded by Colonel Goddard. At this time the army was con-

confiderably reduced, no lefs than a thoufand fepoys being in the hofpital. They were now attended by an agent of Ragoba's, and in his name levied money, even while every idea of fupporting him was officially and publicly difavowed in Calcutta. The detachment had been originally configned to the management and direction of the Bombay prefidency; but, under the conftruction of having received contradictory orders, ultimately conducted themfelves by their own difcretion. Indeed, one day their march had been countermanded in confequence of the difficulties to be encountered; and another, without affigning the reafon, they were defired to proceed. Poonah, Bombay, and Surat, were alfo held out on feparate occafions as the objects of their deftination.

This management, however, was probably a part of the plan which the governor-general now brought forward in council. He propofed a treaty offenfive and defenfive with the Rajah of Berar, that this opulent and powerful prince fhould be fupported in realizing his claims on the throne of the Ram Rajah, now vacant by his late deceafe without iffue; and that the whole force of the Company fhould be exerted to effect his eftablifhment, not only as head of the Marratto empire, but likewife in his pretenfions to the Nizamut of the Deccan. Mr. Elliot was deputed to the court of Moodajee Boonfla, with full authority for accomplifhing this important negociation. The caufe of Ragoba was profeffedly abandoned. The prefidency of Fort St. George was apprifed of the project, and required to co-operate, by directing their politics to that event. And the detachment, on their march to Surat, was enjoined to regard whatever orders they might receive from the Company's Vakeel at the Durbar of Berar, with the moft facred and implicit attention.

Thefe arrangements, however, were not effected without long and ftrenuous oppofition. The abfurdity, the impolicy, the extravagance and impracticability of the meafure, were expofed and criminated in terms of unequivocal afperity and cenfure. It was arraigned as inconfiftent with the Company's orders, who had enjoined the fulleft conformity to the treaty of Poonah, and tending to a prodigal wafte of their treafure, at a time when their affairs, both at home and abroad, demanded the moft rigid œconomy in every branch of expenditure. It likewife involved a variety of inaufpicious circumftances. It was opened in a crifis when the mother country was under the immediate preffure of a war with her colonies, and one of the moft formidable confederacies that ever embroiled the powers of Europe; when the prefidency of Bombay was in no fituation to defend its own territories; when the council of Fort St. George had infulted both Hyder Ally and the Nizam beyond a poffibility of forgivenefs; and even when the news of a French war was expected every moment. It's progrefs and operations were calculated to convulfe the whole continent of India,

India, and to rouſe and unite the indignation of all the various and oppoſite powers in that extenſive country. It treated the Nizam of the Deccan, the ancient friend and ally of the Company, with a treachery which he would not fail to revenge, by exerting the whole influence of his immenſe riches and power in forming ſuch a combination againſt an ambition, thus boundleſs and inſatiable, as might ſhake the Britiſh intereſt to its baſis. Theſe arguments were reſiſted, chiefly by the advantages which were expected from the ſcheme, and the facility of accompliſhing it; the diſappointment it would give to the French views and intrigues at the Durbar; the mortification which the Poonah miniſtry would experience from a revolution, by which they muſt be diveſted of all the authority they had uſurped; the inviolable friendſhip of the Berar Rajah, whoſe dominions would be as ſtrong a barrier to Bengal on the one ſide, as thoſe of Oude were on the other. The council, which then conſiſted only of four members, were equally divided in their opinions of the queſtion, when the governor-general, boldly arrogating the reſponſibility of the whole meaſure to himſelf, carried it in the affirmative by his caſting vote.

The Poonah miniſtry, irritated by the refractory ſpirit which diſtinguiſhed the mode of realizing the late engagements of the Company, made no ſecret of their reſentment. The gentlemen of Bombay inſtantly declared the treaty of Poorunder violated,

violated, and no longer binding. They resolved at the same time to accept the offers of such chiefs as were in the interest of Ragoba, and with all possible expedition to send him to Poonah at the head of an army. The detachment from Bengal were also ordered to direct their march for the Marratto capital, instead of the route through the Guzurat to Broach or Surat. These advices were received at Calcutta about the middle of August; and though, in all important respects, diametrically opposite to the policy so recently adopted in council, met with full approbation. The negociation at the court of Berar was occasionally interrupted by the death of Mr. Elliot, on his way to Nagpour, the capital of that kingdom. It was, however, soon revived, and Colonel Goddard empowered to carry it on and bring it to an issue. He was therefore directed by the supreme council, without paying any regard to what orders might be received from Bombay, to reach the banks of the Nerbudda, which washes the Northern frontier of Berar. Indeed the presidency of Bombay, unwilling that Goddard should partake of the glory which they promised themselves from the success of their arms, seem to have plunged into a state of the most violent hostilities at random. They would not wait the approach of the detachment. Their information was essentially defective. They knew not either their allies or their enemies so perfectly or effectually, as to justify any active measures.

They

They expected the junction of the twenty thousand horse from the abettors of Ragoba. And the expedition commenced under a variety of other circumstances so very unfavourable as proved ominous of the event.

Captain Stuart succeeded in taking possession of the Bourghaut, a pass through the mountains which lead directly to Poonah. He continued in this critical situation a full month, probably in hopes of being joined by the friends of Ragoba. Not a Marratto, however, of any consequence appeared. The army from Bombay amounted to about four thousand effective men; seven hundred of these were said to be Europeans. They were supported by a fine train of artillery. Two regiments of sepoys and six hundred horse were commanded in a separate division by Ragoba. A prodigious quantity of baggage, carriages, cattle, provisions, and luxuries of all kinds, followed this little army. It was commanded by Colonel Egerton, who acted, however, under the control of a select superintending committee, an institution which, though utterly incompatible with the spirit and promptitude of the service, has uniformly disgraced our military transactions in India.

It was on the 1st of January [1779], when the Marrattos instantly appeared in prodigious swarms on all sides, that they found every inch of the ground would be vigorously disputed. The enemy hung every step we took on our rear, and our troops were obliged to proceed in the face of a severe

ſevere cannonade; at the ſame time they were inceſſantly galled by a prodigious diſcharge of rockets. The Marrattos carefully avoided every movement which led to a cloſe or a general engagement. Their object was evidently to haraſs, to fatigue, and to gradually exhauſt and diminiſh the Bombay army with as little riſk to themſelves as poſſible. Colonel Cay and Captain Stuart, two reſpectable officers, were both killed during this deſultory mode of fighting; the one on the firſt, the other on the fourth day of the march. Theſe deſperate onſets were continued with little interruption, and more or leſs ſucceſs every day, from nine in the morning till three in the afternoon. A ſcene of mercileſs devaſtation every where marked the progreſs of our army. The cottages of the poor, and the villas of the great, were, at their approach, levelled in undiſtinguiſhed ruin. The many elegant ſeats in the ſplendid village of Tullicannan could not protect it from the indiſcriminate deſolation which ſpread around. The want of taſte in its barbarous deſtroyers was ſoon and amply revenged. They were already ſo completely inveſted, that they could have no ſupply, as their intercourſe with the country was every where effectually intercepted. The enemy had increaſed to above ſixty thouſand horſe. Stung by the ſight of Tullicannan, reduced to a heap of ſmoking rubbiſh, they aſſailed our troops with a bravery, a fierceneſs, and a conduct which conſiderably damped our confidence. In a well-fought ſkirmiſh,

ſkirmiſh, which took place on this occaſion, the enemy's loſs was not much ſuperior to ours. A retreat was now (January 11th) determined on, as our laſt reſource. Not a ſingle partizan had yet joined Ragoba; and the enemy were determined to have burnt Poonah in the event of our army having forced their way to that capital. It is ſaid, this faithleſs ally of the Company meditated an inſtance of the moſt horrid perfidy on this occaſion. And who could expect leſs than the blackeſt treachery from the murderer of his nephew? It is not improbable that ſome of the army's movements originated in Colonel Cockburne's apprehenſions of Ragoba's machinations. By day-break on the 12th, the whole army was ſurrounded and furiouſly aſſaulted on all ſides. The conflict, in various ſhapes, continued for near fifteen hours, without intermiſſion, and only ceaſed at laſt through exceſſive wearineſs and want of ſtrength. The cannonade, on both ſides, was fierce and tremendous. The valour, the exertion, and evolutions of our forces were incredible. The horſe of the Marrattos returned to the charge with an intrepidity and impetuoſity which our grape-ſhot, well-timed and well-pointed, only could repel. Nothing could appear more formidable than the velocity and fierceneſs with which they repeatedly attacked our lines ſword in hand. Captain Hartly's ſituation in this engagement was peculiarly critical. The diviſion he commanded, encouraged by the ſpirit and conduct of an officer whom

whom they loved, by keeping up a constant and well-directed fire, probably saved the army from being cut to pieces. The loss, on the side of the Marrattos, was prodigious. Of Europeans and sepoys in the British army, near a thousand were left dead on the spot. All night the enemy surrounded the camp, and on the morning only preserved a kind of distant cannonade. It was now impossible we could either retreat or proceed. Our escape, on every quarter, was absolutely impracticable. A flag of truce was, therefore, our only hope of safety. It was no sooner hoisted, than all hostilities were, for the present, at an end. A convention took place. And the Marrattos gave an illustrious instance of their humanity and moderation, by the terms they imposed on the vanquished. They insisted on the English giving up Ragoba, and all their late conquest on that side of India; that the former treaty with Balajee Row should supply the place of the late one at Poorunder, and be firmly and inviolably maintained by both parties; and that the Bengal detachment should return. The committee, however, declared their incompetence to bind, by any deed of their's, the supreme council, in disposing of their forces. These conditions were agreed to by both parties; and Mr. Holmes, commissary of the army, and Mr. Farmer, secretary to the committee, remained as hostages with the Marrattos. The treaty was immediately transcribed in the English, the Persian, and the Marratto languages,

and

and ſigned by the ſeals of the contracting powers. The moment this was completed, our army, whoſe proviſions were utterly exhauſted, were liberally ſupplied by theſe humane conquerors. A body of their horſe then conducted them to the coaſt, and ſaw them embark in the veſſels which carried them back to Bombay.

Moodajee Boonſla, the Rajah of Berar, was anxious to compromiſe the diſpute. His central ſituation between Poonah and Bengal, his cloſe connection with the Marrattos, his amicable intercourſe with the Engliſh, his friendſhip for both parties, this wary, pacific and moderate temper, qualified him for mediating a reconciliation. He applied himſelf, therefore, with much aſſiduity and zeal in explaining the views and conduct of each party alternately to the other, and in reſtraining the paſſions and animoſities of both. He had the addreſs to procure the diſmiſſion of St. Lubin from the court of Poonah, as his intrigues were held out to be the oſtenſible cauſe of offence at Calcutta. He was not leſs vigilant with the Engliſh government, though leſs ſucceſsful in diſſuading them from a perſeverance in marching their troops through the territories of princes with whom they were not in a ſtate of friendſhip. He repreſented this wanton enterprize as producing univerſal diſguſt and alarm, as an audacious violation of all the rights of ſovereignty or independence, and as inſtigating every prince, through whoſe dominions the detachment was

deſtined

destined to march, to arm in his own defence, and repel the outrage. He stated the various hardships and inconveniencies to which they must be exposed; the unknown countries and wilds they were to pass; the difficuly of procuring provisions; the deceptions to which they were liable, from the improbability of obtaining faithful guides; and the numerous ambuscades which they could not but expect, from the determined hostilities which their temerity would every where provoke. His remonstrances were all in vain. He continued, notwithstanding, his good offices. Two of his principal officers were stationed on the banks of the Nerbudda, with ample supplies for the immediate relief of the army. He acquainted them with the machinations formed against them at Poonah; and, with a candour and generosity which our conduct but ill deserved, told them, after advancing so far, not only that it would be dangerous and impolitic to retreat, but even pointed out the nearest line of march for them to the Guzurat. He evidently had it in his power to have sacrificed the detachment without striking a blow, but he scorned to take the least advantage of their perilous situation. He even advanced them money upon bills from Calcutta, without which they could not have proceeded. Notwithstanding these good dispositions, he was too old and timid for effecting the revolution which the governor-general had meditated in his favour. Charmed as he might be with the intoxicating

prospects

prospects of domination and grandeur which it disclosed, the project was implicated with scenes and crimes which filled him with horror. He discovers the state of his feelings with great address and elegance in the laborious and moral correspondence which the propositions occasioned. Goddard's army had arrived on the northern frontiers of Berar, under circumstances of peculiar fatigue and embarrassment. Their carriages were broken, their draught cattle worn down, and their magazines empty. At Husnabad their wants were, however, instantly and abundantly supplied. From this place General Goddard opened his powers of treaty with the Berar Rajah. Nor was he wanting, either in address or industry. He was not permitted to advance into the interior parts of Berar. This restriction was ominous. The heart of the Hindoo revolted at purchasing an empire with the blood of the Bramins. He would conclude no alliance, or form any engagements that tended to molest or provoke either the Pieshwa or the Subah of the Deccan. He was intimately connected with the former, by blood, and with the latter by treaty. And he spurned at every temptation which implied treachery to either. He declined the proposal, at the same time, with a delicacy peculiarly amiable and conciliating. The scheme appeared to him altogether monstrous and impracticable. But he reasoned against it only from the principles of fidelity and sound policy, the improbability of success, and self-preservation, while he obviously deemed it the abortive offspring of the grossest insolence, temerity and ignorance.

Goddard certainly owed his escape to the failure of the Bombay expedition. The most distant powers in the empire crowded with all the forces they could muster to the defence of the capital. So many, so deeply buried in woods and mountains, so long, so narrow, and so peculiarly inclosed, were the defiles which he had to pass, that a very inferior force might either have stopped his progress, or reduced him, by famine, to any terms. But the adventure to Poonah created such a diversion in his favour, as left him totally unmolested. The news of this event, however, operated differently at the court of Berar. It probably disgusted the Rajah, in proportion as it facilitated the movements of our army. Soon after his removal from Husnabad, he was advised from the field committee, who attended the Bombay army, to proceed to Baroach or Surat, or otherwise to continue on the banks of the Nerbudda. The letter containing these advices had been dated before the final engagement with the Marrattos at Worgaum. But the moment this treaty was accomplished he received positive orders, from the same committee, to make good his return with as much expedition as possible for Bengal. In three days a resolution was taken of violating their engagements; and the general was then informed, that, upon mature recollection, they did not think themselves competent to issue the orders they had given. He continued

nued his march, notwithſtanding the fluctuating nature of his intelligence. On the 5th of February he arrived in the vicinity of Boorampore, the capital of Candiſh, a large populous and opulent place. Here he received diſpatches from the council of Bombay, directing him to proceed immediately to Surat. A miniſter from the Poonah Durbar arrived, at the ſame time, in the Britiſh camp, with a copy of the convention at Worgaum; in which his return to Bengal was expreſſly ſtipulated. He denied that the committee who had ſigned that convention had any authority over him; and aſſerted, that he was directed to march to Bombay, for defeating the deſigns of the French againſt the Company's poſſeſſions in that quarter, and that he was not at liberty to acquieſce with the treaty at Worgaum. He gained Surat by the end of the month.

The preſidency of Bombay were not ſlow in publicly diſavowing the treaty of Worgaum, though ratified by two members of the ſelect committee, armed with all the powers of government, and though the lives of the hoſtages might have been forfeited by their treachery. Even this check had not quaſhed that malignant ſpirit of intrigue, which ſtill predominated in their councils, and warped their politics. A ſcheme was immediately ſuggeſted of making the ſame uſe of Moodajee Sindia, which they had done of Ragoba. It was by his interpoſition that our army at Worgaum had not been diſarmed and detained as hoſtages. His power, reſources, influence and character, rendered him a much more eligible inſtrument of ambition than the flagitious Ragoba. He does not, however, appear to have been quite ſo tractable, as he ſeems to have taken no notice whatever, either of the overtures he received, or the advantages proferred to him by the revolution propoſed.

The preſidency of Bombay were ſtill as ſparing as ever in their communications to the ſupreme government. Intelligence of their defeat had arrived both from Madras and Poonah, long before it was officially announced at Calcutta, which did not happen till about the middle of March. It then occaſioned much altercation. The ſupreme council upbraided the Bombay preſidency with unſeaſonable caution and delay, when activity and expedition were required; with having, by unaccountable remiſſneſs, loſt the only opportunity which promiſed the leaſt ſucceſs; and with unpardonable temerity, in attempting the enterprize at a time when a variety of circumſtances occurred to render it abortive. To theſe accuſations it was replied, that they had not been made acquainted with the negociations at the Durbar of Berar, till it was impoſſible to derive any advantage from that fact. The diſavowal of the convention at Worgaum was however confirmed by the ſupreme council. But, on the appearance of ſome pacific diſpoſitions, General Goddard was inveſted with authority to treat once more with

with the Marrattos. His instructions were founded on this principle, that the Marrattos ought to be satisfied with the possession of Ragoba, and that they had no right to further concessions in consequence of their late success. He was restricted from relinquishing any of the new conquests or accessions, and enjoined to insist against the admission in any manner of the French, or the most distant connection with that nation.

Notwithstanding the amicable aspect which both presidencies now assumed, it was at the same time determined to revive and urge the treaty with the court of Berar with redoubled earnestness and assiduity. Moodajee Boonsla was, however, inflexibly attached to the line of politics which he had prescribed for his own conduct. His steadiness baffled all the conciliating talents and address of which Goddard was so great a master. By no artifice or argument was that cautious and intelligent prince to be tempted from the principles of a sound and moderate policy. General professions of friendship and good-will were all that could be obtained. But he continued as anxious and indefatigable as ever, to prevent any new rupture between his countrymen and the company. He even offered to become both the mediator and guarantee, and promised to settle effectually the differences, and to remove whatever jealousies or prejudices might still subsist on both sides. But these demonstrations of friendship were treated so lightly, or with such a manifest want of confi-

 dence,

dence, by the ſupreme council, that preparations for war on our part were carried on, in every quarter of the Company's poſſeſſions, with the greateſt publicity and expedition. The firſt brigade, who had been ſtationed on the banks of the Jumna, in expectation of that event, was now ſupplied with all manner of military ſtores and equipage, that on the ſhorteſt notice they might be in a capacity to carry the ſcene of war into the enemy's country. Other diviſions of troops, in the moſt advanced ſituations, were likewiſe under orders to be in conſtant readineſs for ſimilar ſervice.

General Goddard ſeems to have adopted the warlike propenſities of the preſidency, with all the characteriſtic warmth and eagerneſs of the profeſſion. And the ſtatement which he tranſmitted to Calcutta, of the politics in the weſtern diviſions of India, was peculiarly calculated to flatter thoſe moſt popular and faſhionable in Bengal. He took occaſion, as ſoon as poſſible, to acquaint the Poonah government with his powers and inſtructions for bringing matters to an amicable accommodation. But, before the Pieſhwa could make any reply, Ragoba had effected his eſcape from the cuſtody of Sindia, having fled ſo early in the beginning of June, and taken refuge in the Engliſh camp. The Bombay preſidency were rather ſhy of interfering further in the fortunes of that renegade prince. And, while a ſcheme of reconciliation was adjuſting, they ſhifted the

the reſponſibility to Goddard, though Ragoba could not conceal how much he preferred a renewal of his connection with them to a dependance on the ſupreme council. Previous to this event, the Pieſhwa, and Moodajee Sindia, had informed the Bombay council of their reſolution to retaliate the injuries received from Hyder Ally, and on that account intimated the ſinccreſt ſolicitude of coming to a final agreement with the ſervants of the Company. The aſylum which Ragoba found in our camp, in the mean while, correſponded with the wiſhes of the ſupreme council, who encouraged him to expect their protection. His politics were, however, no longer eligible, and he was conſidered only as capable of aſſiſting our army in effecting war or peace with advantage. His monthly allowance was greatly reduced; and he was given to underſtand, that our favour for the future would depend on the fidelity of his conduct, in not endeavouring by his intrigues or emiſſaries at Poonah to counteract the views of his benefactors. The Marratto government, notwithſtanding his reception in the Britiſh camp, of which they had the earlieſt intelligence, delegated commiſſioners to open a treaty with the general. But theſe commiſſioners did not arrive till the middle of Auguſt, and were in no haſte when they came to bring forward the buſineſs. Their powers were ſo limitted, that it became neceſſary to diſpatch meſſengers to Poonah on the moſt trivial difficul-

 ties

ties that arofe, and the anfwers were returned with fo little punctuality and expedition, that their pacific defires were, at leaft for the time, apparently abated.

It was about this period that the politics of the governor-general began to exhibit their natural effects on the numerous powers of India. A league was forming, which was to unite them in one general and formidable confederacy for the extinction of the Company. The principles of the Englifh government, and the various events which every where attended their operation, had produced the moft univerfal deteftation and alarm, and ultimately excited fuch a ferious apprehenhenfion of common danger from their intrigues and exploits, as combined the moft difcordant interefts and hoftile nations, to defeat their ambitious purpofes They had dethroned potentates, and ufurped their dominions. The Subah of Bengal, the Vizier of Oude, and the Nabob of the Carnatic, were reduced to a ftate of fplendid thrawldom, the contemptible inftruments of Britifh rapacity, and the miferable trophies of an ambition which threatened the dependence of every prince in the empire. The ruin of the Rohillas was an awful and inftructive picture of what each of them might expect in their turn. Their dereliction of the emperor, perfidioufly ftripping him of his tribute and the ceffion of his dominions, fo incongruous with the faith or law of nations to a creature of their own, were fo many ftrong proofs

proofs that their engagements were considered only as measures of expediency; and that they acted from no settled principles, but those of treachery and usurpation. These ideas were revived and corroborated by our very extraordinary mode of renewing hostilities with the Marrattos. The excess to which we had carried our outrages against these powerful states heightened every sense of past or more distant grievances, and rivetted that general odium which the prevailing complexion of our government had so constantly created and accumulated. A system thus natural and inveterate gathered strength from contingency, and was at last matured and rendered operative by the march of an army through the heart of the country; the utter expulsion of the French; and that violent propensity for war, which still raged in the councils of Calcutta.

This great scheme of general exertion originated with the Nizam of the Deccan, though it does not appear that he had received any intelligence of the sacrifice which it was intended to have made of him in the Berar treaty. Indeed, there wanted not enough of causes, independent of this circumstance, to stimulate him in projecting and effecting an union so necessary to the common safety. He was not without his share of apprehension from the power which menaced the whole; his connection with the Poonah administration was intimate and inviolable; he regarded Ragoba as an *invincible villain, utterly incapable of faith*; he thought

thought the Bombay expedition to Poonah ſuch a flagrant violation of treaty, that he imputed the deſtruction of their army to the immediate interference of Heaven, by which the unjuſt are often deſtined to fall in their own ſnares. Theſe facts, and the animadverſions they ſuggeſted, he had avowed ſo explicitly, that Moodajee Boonſla had early appriſed the governor-general "that the "Nabob Nizam, and others alſo, who were all "alarmed at the encroachments of the Engliſh "in the Deccan, were waiting a favourable op- "portunity to repel them." The Marrattos were, by this time, in a ſituation of peculiar embarraſſment, being under the neceſſity of either coming to a final adjuſtment with the Engliſh, on their own terms, that they might be avenged of Hyder; or of accommodating matters with the latter, that they might be able to exert their whole ſtrength in repelling the inſults of the former. Hyder made the firſt advances, by offering a large ſum of money for reimburſing their expences in the late war; a conſiderable tribute for the conquered countries; and his whole force to aſſiſt them againſt the common enemy. Their predilection, however, for an accommodation with the Engliſh, defeated, for the time, the ſucceſs of theſe overtures, when the eſcape of Ragoba, in connection with various other circumſtances, completely reverſed the face of affairs. By the Nizam's addreſs peace was immediately concluded between the Marrattos and Hyder Ally; and the ſyſtematic con-

federacy

federacy againſt the Engliſh accompliſhed. The plan of this important league directed that Hyder and the Nizam ſhould attack the Carnatic and the northern Circars; that the forces of the Marrattos ſhould be employed on the ſide of Surat and the Guzurat; and that the Rajah of Berar ſhould invade the provinces of Bengal. Nudjiff Cawn, and other chiefs on the weſtern extremities of India, were alſo invited to act their part in this great effort, and to make the confuſion and danger general, by carrying fire and ſword into Oude, Allahabad, and other provinces in that quarter. Moodajee Boonſla is the only one who ſeems to have become a partiſan to the cauſe with reluctance; and who acted a part againſt his inclination, that he might ſave his territories from the depredations of his neighbours. The enterprize intruſted to his execution was not undertaken with any degree of promptitude. His army did not reach the frontiers of Bengal until the approach of the rainy ſeaſon, which, however diſpoſed for action, muſt have ſuſpended its operations for ſeveral months. Nor did the expedition, however formidable in appearance, anſwer any other purpoſe ultimately, than that it afforded the ſupreme council an opportunity of returning the kindneſs ſhewn to the Bengal detachment on the banks of the Nerbudda, by furniſhing them ſuch a ſeaſonable ſupply of proviſion as prevented them from ſtarving.

All

All profpects of accommodation with the Poonah miniftry were now at an end. The Marratto agent in the British camp, by the decifion which the general thought neceffary at length to affume, was induced to declare, in his mafter's name, that he would accede to no overtures made by the Englifh, nor conclude a treaty with us on any other terms than an immediate furrender of Ragoba, and the reftoration of all our late captures on that fide of India. This was a crifis of the utmoft importance to the whole complicated fyftem of the Company's concerns. Our preparations for action were every where profecuted with additional energy and expedition. Bombay ftipulated with Goddard for a fhare of the conqueft, and fupplied him with all the troops not indifpenfably neceffary to their own defence. They declined, at the fame time, partaking in the refponfibility of the war, and declared their utter incapacity to defray any part of the expence. The government of Fort St. George, notwithftanding their abhorrence of a meafure fo pregnant, as they prefumed, with imminent and inevitable deftruction, were obliged, on the fame account, to part with a large portion of that force, the want of which they were foon to experience. The fuperior council concluded an alliance, offenfive and defenfive, with the Ranna of Ghod, whofe territories, from their nature and fituation, confifting partly of impenetrable woods, and partly of inacceffible mountains, and lying on the weftern banks of the Jumna, formed no inconfiderable

barrier

barrier againſt any irruptions of the enemy from that quarter. We had this ſubſtantial advantage in the outſet, that they had neither union among themſelves, nor money to ſtrengthen, inſpire, and expedite their exertions; while our moſt important enterprizes had nothing to fear, as yet, from any material defect in our pecuniary reſources.

That diviſion of the Guzurat which lies towards the Indus was held by the Marratto family of the Guicawar. In the former war, the title to the ſucceſſion being conteſted, the claims of Futty Sing Guicawar were eſpouſed, and carried into effect by our interference. On that occaſion the Company had obtained very conſiderable acceſſions of territory. The right, to ſome of theſe at leaſt, was ſubſequently maintained in the Poonah treaty, and became the principal article in reference to future inquiry, which was then left undecided. The Nabob afterwards aſſerted, that this grant was the effect of extortion, while he had not the liberty of acting as a free agent; and that, in fact, without the concurrence of the Poonah government, he had no right to make it. The co-operation of this chief was now become a deſirable object; and very advantageous offers were held out to him in a propoſed treaty of alliance. He appears, however, extremely backward to enter into any new connection with the Engliſh. Our troops paſſed the Tappee the ſecond day of 1780. It was their approach which, in all probability, brought him to acquieſce in our meaſures. The

fortreſs

fortreſs of a petty territory belonging to the Peiſhwa, which lay in the direct road to the capital of Bradera, where the Nabob reſided, was the oſtenſible object of this movement. Dubhoy, with its diſtrict, was ſoon reduced; but Futty Sing ſtill kept his diſtance. Nor was it without conſiderable management that he was induced, by the end of the month, to put his ſignature to a treaty for dividing the Guzurat between the parties, and a perpetual excluſion of the Poonah government.

It was not till the 15th of February that Goddard, reinforced by the Nabob's cavalry, inveſted the city of Ahmedabad, the capital of the province. In five days it was taken by ſtorm. The whole ſurrounding country fell at the ſame time. The Nabob, being raiſed to the government by the general, was liberal enough in paſſing grants, to his maſters, of thoſe diſtricts which they kept in their own hands. The general was anxious to delay a final partition of the capture, until the more important ends of the war ſhould be obtained. But the gentlemen of Bombay, diſſatisfied with the diviſion which had been made, adviſed the ſuperior council, from their own knowledge of Futty Sing, not haſtily to ratify the treaty, without at leaſt reſerving to themſelves the right of inſiſting on a ſubſequent adjuſtment.

A powerful army, under Sindia and Holkar, had now taken the field, and ſeemed directing their march for Surat. They were, however, intercepted

tercepted by General Goddard, who came up with them on the 8th of March, and was prevented attacking them in the night, as he intended, by a letter from Mr. Farmer, one of the gentlemen left as an hoſtage at Worgaum, and now in the enemy's camp. This informed him, that theſe two politic chiefs were only ſolicitous of obtaining his friendſhip. On the following day both hoſtages were enlarged, and preſented themſelves before their countryman. A confidential agent accompanied them, at the ſame time, from Sindia, who aſſured the general of his maſter's hatred to Nana Furneſe, the preſent Marratto regent; and deſired an explanation of what was meant with regard to Sindia and the Peiſhwa ſeparately. He likewiſe preſſed the general to make propoſals for ſuch an agreement as might equally facilitate the views of both parties. This, however, the general declined, and expected information from Sindia, who beſt knew how ſuch a revolution was to be effected as might moſt effectually repay the trouble and expence it would infallibly occaſion. It is generally conjectured, that Sindia's only view, by this manœuvre, was to obtain the poſſeſſion of Ragoba and his ſon, and by that means to aggrandize himſelf in the ſtate, without any reference to our advantage. His propoſition certainly went to that object. But his Vakeel, on delivering it, was immediately diſmiſſed, with an aſſurance that the Engliſh would, by no means, be induced to put any reſtraint upon Ragoba, nor riſk the ſafety

of

of his ſon; and, though ſincerely diſpoſed to a fair accomodation, they would not raiſe his maſter to the government, without ſome previous condition in their favour. Sindia was, at the ſame time, carrying on a ſecret correſpondence with Govindrow, a refractory brother of Futty Sing, whom he not only promiſed to aſſiſt, but had received him into his camp. This, with ſome other inexplicable inſtances in the conduct of Sindia, prompted the general to uſe all his endeavours to bring on an action between the two armies. But the wary Marratto was ſo much on his guard, that a ſurpriſe was impracticable. And it was not till Goddard, leaving every thing behind, puſhed rapidly forward with the cavalry grenadiers, and the moſt alert in the army, that he compelled the Marrattos to ſtand an engagement. Having paſſed their principal guards with dexterity, he fell in without heſitation upon their camp. The rapid diſcharge of the artillery did prodigious execution among the Marratto horſe, and the various attacks and evolutions were effected with ſo much ſpirit, and directed with ſuch ability, that the enemy were driven from their poſt and completely routed in leſs than an hour. The Britiſh officers, ſtung by the recollection of their late defeat, were anxious to wipe away that diſgrace, and retrieve the honour they had then loſt. The very ſepoys, though fighting againſt their own countrymen, were even proud to be once more found on the vanquiſhing ſide.

It

It was ſhortly after this, that Captain Campbel, returning from a foraging expedition, at ſome diſtance, with only two battalions of ſepoys, four field pieces, and a large convoy of proviſions, was intercepted by Sindia, at the head of twenty thouſand men. It is not improbable that Campbel had a choice of ground, adapted to the nature and number of his petty force. In truth, it is otherwiſe incredible that he ſhould have defended himſelf againſt ſuch an army with ſucceſs. He, notwithſtanding, repulſed the enemy with the loſs of five or ſix hundred men, and carried away his convoy unimpaired. In this action, it is ſaid, the fire of the flank companies did eminent and conſpicuous execution among the enemy's cavalry; a circumſtance which, it has been ſhrewdly enough remarked, might in a great meaſure have ariſen from ſome peculiarity in the poſition of our troops. Lieutenant Walſh experienced alſo ſimilar ſucceſs againſt an obvious diſparity of numbers. Detached, with a battalion of ſepoys and a regiment of cavalry, to ſurpriſe a camp of ſix thouſand Marrattos, and finding the infantry could not reach them before day, that the deſign might not be fruſtrated, he determined to make his attack with the horſe only. The enterprize was hazardous, but conducted with bravery and ſkill. The enemy was routed [May 3d] with great ſlaughter. Their own cannon were occupied againſt them with ſuch adroitneſs and reſolution, that many of thoſe who eſcaped were utterly at a loss how to account for so sudden a disaster. The commander, with a great number of officers and men, were left dead upon the spot; and the camp, with all it contained, fell into the hands of the English.

Soon after Major Forbes, with only two battalions of sepoys, surprised and put to flight a body of seven thousand Marrattos. The season, however, approached when both armies were obliged to repair to winter quarters, that they might avoid the pernicious effects of the rainy months. In every action with the enemy, and in spight of every advantage which numbers could bestow, our troops were uniformly victorious and triumphant. Indeed, nothing could reflect greater credit on the general, the officers, and even the privates at large, nor establish a more operative conviction of our superior prowess in the field, than the constant success which attended all our exertions during this campaign.

Nor were the atchievements of the Company's troops less splendid and material on the frontiers of the Bengal provinces. Early precautions had been taken to guard against any incursion of the enemy on this side of the country. Ghod, as had been foreseen, in consequence of its recent connection with us, was instantly attacked by a powerful body of Marrattos. But Major Popham, with only a handful of men, soon cleared the country of these marauders; drove them before him through a considerable part of their own, and com-

commanded ſuch an acceſſion of territory, as might have proved of importance, but that it could not be retained. The celebrated fortreſs of Gualier ſtood in the midſt of this petty ſtate. It was ſtill in the poſſeſſion of the Marrattos, and probably as great an eye-ſore to the natives as Gibraltar, under the command of a Britiſh garriſon, is to the Spaniards. The anxiety of Mr. Haſtings for the reduction of this place was no ſecret to the major, whoſe own ſolicitude for diſtinction, in the line of his profeſſion, powerfully excited the enterprize. The fortifications, which were of great ſtrength, incloſed the ſummit of a prodigious high hill, encircled by rocks, and equally barricaded on every ſide by the moſt tremendous precipices. The ground which lay within the works was ſo extenſive and ſo fertile as to be equal to the ſubſiſtence of any number of men which the defence of the garriſon might require. The major, perhaps, formed any hopes of ſucceſs which he might entertain, againſt a poſt which the princes of Indoſtan had always pronounced impregnable, on that confidence and ſecurity which are natural to ſuch a ſituation. Some natives, from motives which do not appear, had diſcovered a ſecret paſſage, by which they ſcrambled up the rocks, and entered with ſafety in the night. The major, informed of this important circumſtance, had the track minutely examined; and conceiving, from the report, a bare poſſibility of ſucceſs, he boldly determined to riſk all the consequences of a failure. The attempt was attended with such imminent hazard and difficulty, as rendered the success which followed uncommonly brilliant. The consternation and surprise, occasioned by a capture thus rapid and unexpected, had an immediate and powerful operation on the enemy. They instantly retreated from the whole circumjacent country; and it is said the alarm even reached Sindia in his capital, Ougein, whither he had just retired from the Guzurat.

Suspending our attention to the Company's affairs in the northern and upper parts of India for the present, it may not be improper in this place to give some account of the transactions, which, at the same time, agitated the powers and threatened our interests on the coast of Coromandel.

CHAPTER X.

French War—Pondicherry taken—Affair of the Guntoor Circar and Peſhcuſh—Hyder Ally invades the Carnatic—The Conſequences of that Event—The Preſidency and the Nabob equally unprepared—State of the Army—Sir Hector Monro takes the Field—Baillie's Situation—His Diſaſter—Sir Eyre Coote's Arrival—He beats the Enemy in four pitched Battles—The War with the Dutch—Expedition againſt their Settlements in Sumatra—The Fall of Negapatam on the Coromandel Coaſt, and of Trincomale in the Iſland of Ceylon.

AUTHENTIC intelligence of our late war with France was communicated to the governor-general of Bengal ſo early as July 1778; and his thorough conviction of this great and intereſting fact produced an immediate and ſenſible influence on all the meaſures of the ſupreme council. The deſtination of Count d'Eſtaing's fleet, which was then unknown, was not unnaturally ſuppoſed to be ſome of our capital ports on the Indian ſhore. Report, which for the moſt part magnifies where it does not fabricate, gave weight to the conjecture. The Chevalier St. Lubin was ſtill at the Durbar, and obſerved to be frequent in cloſe conference with the Peiſhwa. The ſteps which the government

ment of Calcutta took to repel the impending danger were, to bring their differences with the Marratto ſtates to a ſpeedy deciſion; to take inſtant poſſeſſion of all the French ſettlements in Bengal, and make a complete capture of all their ſhips in the river; and to recommend the ſiege of Pondicherry to the preſidency of Fort St. George, as a meaſure which ought to be adopted without delay. The papers found on Mr. Chevalier, the governor of Chandernagore, who was apprehended making his eſcape at Cuttack, confirmed the news of hoſtilities having commenced between France and England in Europe; and conſequently juſtified theſe preparatory arrangements for the ſame conflict in that part of the world.

The Engliſh had commenced hoſtilities againſt the French factories and ſettlements at Chandernagore, at Yaman, at Carical, at Maſulipatam, and other places, the moment they were authorized to conſider them as enemies with whom they were at war. Immediate depradations were at the ſame time made on their trading veſſels, both in the Ganges and on the coaſts of Coromandel. It was not, however, till the beginning of Auguſt that the preſidency of Madras were prepared for undertaking the reduction of Pondicherry. Sir Edward Vernon commanded the ſmall Britiſh naval force at that time in the Indian ſeas. The ſquadron, with which he ſailed againſt Pondicherry, conſiſted only of two frigates, a ſloop of war, and the Valentine Eaſt-Indiaman, He ſoon encountered,

tered, in a very warm engagement, which laſted laſted above two hours, a French fleet of ſuperior force, under the command of M. de Tronjolly. The Engliſh admiral, who had manifeſtly the better in this fight, expected the enemy to have met him once more, and that he would have endeavoured at leaſt to have kept the town from being inveſted by ſea, as well as by land, found it ever after impoſſible to bring on a battle. After near a month's manœuvring to no purpoſe, the French fleet abandoned the coaſt, and left the Britiſh flag triumphant. Pondicherry was immediately and cloſely blockaded. The defence was ſpirited and indefatigable. M. de Bellecombe, governor of the town, and general commandante of the French ſettlements in India, gained immortal reputation by his gallantry and perſeverance in this ſiege. The beſiegers, however, ſoon gained a viſible ſuperiority, and continued to carry on their approaches with increaſing dexterity and diſpatch, though the daring and vigorous operations of the garriſon rendered the utmoſt caution a matter of neceſſity, and, together with the violent rains which then frequently fell, conſiderably retarded their works. After a month's extreme labour, the place was deemed no longer tenable. On the day preceding that which had been fixed on for making the aſſault, the governor propoſed a capitulation, which was readily granted, in a manner which gave ample and honourable teſtimony to the bravery of the enemy. Whatever was propoſed, that did not interfere with the public ſecurity, was liberally admitted. On this account alone the European part of the garriſon were ſent to France, and the ſepoys, and other native troops in the country, diſbanded. The honours of war were allowed, and, as a particular mark of attention to M. de Bellecombe, the regiment of Pondicherry, at his requeſt, were permitted to keep their colours. Nearly three hundred pieces of artillery became the prize of the conquerors, who ſeized, at the ſame time, all public property, but ſecured whatever was private to the owners. Our loſs amounted to two hundred and twenty-four ſlain, and above ſix hundred wounded. Of the enemy, little ſhort of the ſame number were killed and wounded; a circumſtance which abundantly demonſtrates their zeal in the ſervice of their country, and the obſtinacy with which they maintained their ground to the laſt extremity.

These violences, on the part of the Engliſh, and the uniform ſucceſs which attended them, co-operated, with a variety of other cauſes, to render the extenſion of our power an object of ſerious attention and concern, eſpecially to the neighbouring princes. The fall of Pondicherry was at leaſt immediately followed by the ſettlement of the Guntoor circar. It was an acquiſition which the preſidency of Madras had, for ſome time, been very anxious to obtain, as, from its ſituation, it muſt have enabled them to exclude the French nation from

from the Deccan; to keep open a communication by land with the four northern circars; and to have preserved the continuity of their possessions, and those of their allies. Bazalet Jung, however, was in present possession of it, as a jaghire, for life, for which he was tributary to his brother, the Subah of the Deccan, and by whom he was bound not to dispose of it in any manner, or to any person, without his consent or approbation. This province, in the treaties by which the other four were conveyed and confirmed to the Company, was also ordained to become our's at the death of Bazalet Jung. We were, at the same time, restrained from all attempts by negociation or bargain, excepting by the mediation of the Nizam, to obtain the Guntoor before the time allotted. These treaties further provided, that we should assist the Nizam with our forces, in all cases of war or invasion; that we should operate as a check on the refractory disposition of Bazalet Jung, to the degree of dispossessing him of the jaghire the moment he entered on measures dangerous to his brother, or inconsistent with the tranquillity of his government; and that any alliance with the enemies of the Company, or giving them any assistance, should render him liable to a forfeiture, not only of his possessions, but of all protection, either from us or his brother.

Notwithstanding these seemingly insuperable obstacles, so eagerly desirous had the presidency been to anticipate the proprietory of this valuable territory,

tory, that overtures had been frequently submitted to the Nizam on the subject. But this prudent sovereign adopted the wise policy of not granting too much, as he found the requisitions of the Company were endless. These direct applications to him were however such unequivocal acknowledgments of his sovereignty, as ought to have been an insuperable bar to their treating with any other. But time, accident, opportunity, and ambition, dissolved the obligations which had been formerly deemed binding. Bazalet had been frequently charged with entertaining a predilection for the French. He was strongly suspected on this occasion to be solely directed by their influence. He had received a body of troops into his service, which, though composed of vagabonds from almost all the nations in Europe, were yet commanded by one Mr. Lally, a Frenchman. Strong and repeated remonstrances were made to him on this suspicious measure. His apology was not satisfactory. The friendship of the French was no longer adequate to his protection. The interest of the English predominated every where to such a degree, that it was madness to risk their resentment. Their intrigues were seconded by menaces. The approaches of Hyder Ally, who by this time had extended his conquests to the frontiers of the circar, completed the wishes of the presidency, by terrifying the timid Bazalet into compliance. He was at the same time perhaps disgusted by the licentiousness of his new auxiliaries. He had therefore, in

the end of the year 1778, thought himſelf juſtified from the difficulties to which he was reduced, and the apprehenſions he entertained for his ſafety, in applying to the Engliſh for protection and relief. He ſoon after entered into a treaty of friendſhip and alliance, and on our ſide of aſſiſtance and defence, with the council of Fort St. George. By this agreement, which took place without the knowledge or intervention of the Nizam, he diſmiſſed the French troops, and ſurrendered the Guntoor circar into the hands of the Company.

It was propoſed in council, that the gradual proceſs of this important tranſaction ſhould be tranſmitted to the Subah, and the completion of it ſuſpended till his conſent could be obtained, that ſome appearance of reſpect at leaſt might be paid to the treaties ſubſiſting between both parties. This temperate and equitable advice was however overruled by the majority. Thus did the Company's ſervants carry a compact, including new arrangements of connection, revenue, and territory, with a ſubject, without the participation or conſent of his ſovereign. Nor could the ſupreme government obtain any other information of this very extraordinary buſineſs, than that a negociation for granting the Guntoor, upon certain conditions, to the Company, was carrying on with the faireſt proſpect of ſucceſs. It was not ſo much as ſpecified either with whom it was conducted, or by whom the grant was to be made. It was even concluded, with

with every formality, full ten months before any official accounts of it reached Bengal.

The Guntoor circar was immediately farmed out, upon a leafe of ten years, to the Nabob of Arcot, who has long acted as the great farmer-general of the Company in this part of India. Whatever emoluments may accrue to the fervants, the profits of their mafters, from this extenfion of the Nabob's credit, feem rather problematical. His debts have not only reduced them to the greateft difficulty, but opened fuch a field of intrigue for a number of unprincipled individuals, as have fullied the Britifh name. Avarice feems the difeafe of his nature, and his reluctance to difcharge his pecuniary obligations is ftrengthened with his years. The Nizam had always regarded his encroachments in the Deccan with jealoufy. He knew the principles that infpired him. He faw him now under a very alarming afpect of public affairs; and the impreffion of various interefting tranfactions at once pufhed forward into a fituation, fo near, fo critical and fo unexpected, that no moderation could prevent difputes, or vigilance guard againft danger. It was expected to prove ftill more offenfive to Hyder Ally, between whom and the Nabob there fubfifted the moft inveterate and implacable animofity. Nor did that prince long difguife his fentiments of a meafure, which ftruck him as intended to obftruct his operations on the northern borders, to encourage difturbance in his new acquifitions, quisitions, or to facilitate a concerted attack upon his interest in that unsettled quarter.

Bazalet Jung soon became alarmed from the menaces he received, and the dangers which gathered round him. Not thinking the troops within reach of the Guntoors equal to his protection, he urged the presidency for an immediate and powerful reinforcement. A considerable detachment, under the command of Col. Harper, was forthwith sent on that service. He was at the same time, without leave obtained, or even requested, and perhaps without any real necessity, ordered to take his route through part of Hyder's dominions. But Hyder was too jealous and tenacious of his rights to permit the same liberties here which had been taken on the other side of India. Harper had no sooner entered the Cuddepah, than he announced to the officers of Hyder, on that station, the object and destination of his march. Their answer was, that he should be opposed, and the passes barricaded against him. He proceeded notwithstanding, but his temerity was soon checked. He found the trees cut down across the way at Atcour, other means of defence and obstruction adopted, and a large body of troops strongly posted to dispute his passage. Having no orders to commence hostilities, the dread of being inclosed by the enemy, and pressed for time, he gave up the design for the present, and fell back to Innaconda, which he reached the 14th of April [1779], after spending a week to no purpose in Cuddepah.

Aware

Aware that the treaty for the Guntoor circar was not in all reſpects conformable to the ſpirit and tenor of engagments ſubſiſting between the Nizam and the Company, it was determined immediately on the concluſion of that buſineſs to appoint a reſident at the court of Hydrabad. Mr. Hollond was therefore preferred to that ſituation, and inſtructed to declare the determination of the preſidency, to preſerve inviolably the treaty of 1776, to ſhew that their late agreement with Bazalet Jung was no infringement of it, and that they had hitherto made all their applications to the Nizam, as anſwerable for the deportment of his brother, but that their apprehenſions from the French troops had impelled them at laſt to open a negociation directly with Bazalet. He was to aſſure him at the ſame that the Peſhcuſh, or tribute, for the northern circars, which had not for ſome time paſt been punctually diſcharged, was delayed only on that account.

The account of this appointment, tranſmitted to the ſuperior government, ſtates only, that the preſidency of Fort St. George ſeriouſly dreaded the reſentment of the Nizam, from his attachment to the Poonah miniſtry, his hatred to Ragoba, and our concern in the Marratto diſſentions; that, as the northern circars were much expoſed to invaſion from the Deccan, and the Subah's friendſhip extremely doubtful, they deemed it highly expedient to have the beſt and earlieſt intelligence of his deſigns; and that for this purpoſe, and for ſet-

tling

tling whatever related to the Guntoor circar, and the diſmiſſion of the French troops, they had appointed Mr. Hollond their reſident at the Nizam's Durbar, and inſtructed him to correſpond with the ſupreme council on whatever deſerved their attention in that quarter.

Our reſident was received by the Nizam with every mark of reſpect. He ſtated a variety of inſtances, to prove with what fidelity he had uniformly maintained his engagements to the Company. He aſſumed the ſole merit of having induced his brother to part with the French troops, whom he had taken into his own ſervice, that they might not join either Hyder Ally or the Marrattos. But, when at a ſubſequent audience the affairs of the Guntoor province were opened, and he underſtood that a body of our troops had marched for the protection of the country againſt the deſigns of Hyder, in expectation that his own forces would join them for accompliſhing that purpoſe, it is ſaid that his countenance was at once exceedingly changed, and he laboured under the greateſt and moſt viſible anguiſh of mind. It appears as if he had reſolved on revenge from this moment, and that in all his ſubſequent conferences with Hollond this inſult was conſtantly uppermoſt in his mind; that he frequently urged the groſs abſurdity of affecting a friendſhip, notwithſtanding a conduct thus glaringly hoſtile; that his feelings would by no means ſuffer him to brook ſuch an interference with his family concerns; that the intentions imputed

puted to Hyder Ally, of molesting his brother's country, had no existence but in our insidious policy; that the treaty required our troops to be immediately countermanded from entering the circar; or, if the treaty was not to be regarded, he would himself oppose them; and that Hyder Ally was about to chastise the presidency for their perfidy, by suddenly falling on the Carnatic in his former mode of overrunning the country, plundering and burning every thing before him, and cautiously avoiding fixed battles.

In consequence of Hollond's favourable reception at Hydrabad, it was resolved in council to try if a remission of the tribute for the northern circars could not be obtained. These were held by a phirmaund or grant from the great Mogul, who still assumed the silly prerogative of giving away countries, into which he had not the privilege of entering. This, they presumed, established their free and unconditional right to the five circars, and their receiving them afterwards from the Nizam, on paying an annual tribute, was a surrender of the Company's property. These ideas were much laboured in a minute from the president, which was adopted. Hollond was consequently instructed to mention no compromise, nor to stipulate for any part of the Peshcush, until all his exertions to prevail with the Nizam to relinquish the whole proved unsuccessful. In that case, he was to be satisfied with an abatement from five lacks, the present standard, to two; the rate at which

which the Company had held the arrears for the first six years.

It happened rather unfortunately for the success of this proposal that it was made when the payment of the arrear was expected, and while his resentments for the injuries done to his interest, in the affair of the Guntoor province, were still warmly avowed. He now conceived the presidency to be bent on war, and openly declared himself prepared to meet them. He threatened to join Hyder Ally, and desired that his opinion might be immediately communicated to the presidency, and a speedy answer returned, lest his troops advanced on Colonel Harper, in his way to the Guntoor. Hollond, though regularly advised by the presidency to assure the Nizam that no threat was meant, but that whatever remission could be obtained should proceed entirely from his own bounty and friendship, was told, at the same time, to persist in urging the requisition, as having a solid foundation in equity, as what could not be given up, and as a measure with which the Nizam's compliance was expected. He was also authorized to add, that, though they meant to pay the whole arrears when convenient, they were not unprepared to retaliate whatever steps might be taken to embarrass or insult them. It was even insinuated, that the presidency hoped the forces under Lally would be dismissed, and directed to march towards the sea coast, that all the Europeans might without delay be sent to their respective

 countries,

countries, and that the natives ſhould in like manner be diſbanded.

Nothing could be more impolitic than the eagerneſs with which theſe invidious diſcuſſions were brought forward at preſent, and Hollond was informed, on the laſt day of Auguſt, that the Peſhcuſh would be expected, and demanded as uſual, or the payment of it enforced; that immediate war would follow the firſt refuſal, and that he might have his audience of leave in two days. Theſe declarations were ſucceeded by formal notice to prepare for his departure. The Nizam even talked publicly of taking the field whenever the rainy months were at an end. Happily, the ſupreme council totally condemned the offenſive meaſures, which for ſome time had been thus going forward with the Subah. They diſpatched a letter to that prince, as ſoon as they were made acquainted with his ſituation; in which, without arraigning the conduct of the Madras preſidency, they endeavoured to ſoothe and allay his apprehenſions, to ſatisfy him that no meaſures could be finally ſettled without their concurrence, and to conciliate his confidence, by aſſurances that they would ſuffer no infringement of the treaty between them. They told him, Hollond was directed to ſuſpend his negociation until he received further inſtructions from his immediate conſtituents, to whom they had written on the ſubject. They incloſed a copy of their letter to the Nizam in that which they directed to Madras. And, not ſe-
verely

verely condemning what had taken place, they only enjoined a ſtrict compliance with the meaſures now recommended for the reſtoration of that mutual cordiality which had formerly diſtinguiſhed their connection. The Nizam was on the eve of avenging himſelf for the wrongs done him by the Madras preſidency, when this letter arrived, which he received with the greateſt ſatisfaction: " If " what you write," ſaid he, " is from your heart, " and the government of Madras will adhere " ſtrictly to treaty, and will relinquiſh the poſ- " ſeſſion of the treaty, it is well; if not, I have " nothing of greater conſequence than defending " my country. It is from this new line of con- " duct of the Engliſh Company that the founda- " tions of enmity have been laid in the whole " country of Indoſtan."

The council of Madras were exceedingly diſguſted by this interference of the ſupreme government. They did not expect that their endeavours to relieve the Company from ſo heavy a burden ſhould be charged to a wanton violation of faith. Their conduct to the Nizam had been blameable only for the extreme forbearance they had ſhewn him. They imputed his reſentments to that temerity which ſo generally originates in a conſciouſneſs of impotence. They alledged, that whatever hoſtile intentions he might really indulge aroſe entirely from the Marratto war; and they boldly juſtified the detention of the tribute, by the example which the Bengal preſidency had ſet them of

 devest-

devesting the emperor of his. They even contended, that this was a question in which the superior board had no concern; and that the clause in the act of parliament, from which they derived their authority, could not be construed to justify their interference. They voted the recal and suspension of Hollond for obeying their instructions in corresponding with the supreme council in Calcutta, who, notwithstanding, continued his appointment as the Company's resident at the court of Hydrabad. This unhappy dispute was, after much altercation and warmth, brought to a conclusion, and satisfaction obtained for the Nizam, while the whole circumjacent country was in a state of actual invasion, by a suspension of Mr. Whitchill, who had succeeded Sir Thomas Rumbold in that government.

The failure of Harper's expedition, though owing to no misconduct on his part, brought him into disgrace with the presidency. By the spirited interference of Hyder, he had been obliged to wait for fresh orders. Nor did these arrive till he was in want both of money and provision, which prevented his march by the only way in which it ought at first, and could now be pursued. This delay disconcerted entirely the designs of the presidency. Willing to exculpate themselves at Harper's expence, they charged him with procrastination, and superseded him in the command, by appointing Colonel Baillie in his stead. The occasion of succouring the country of Bazalet Jung

Jung was the more preſſing, that Hyder Ally, in his letters to him, remonſtrated ſtrongly againſt his connection with the Engliſh, whoſe councils he treated with contempt, while he ſpoke of their politics as dangerous and profligate in the extreme. He profeſſed to know them perfectly. They were, in his opinion, the common enemies of the country, perhaps of the ſpecies. His own experience and ſucceſs in the laſt war would operate, he truſted, at the ſame time, as proofs that they were by no means ſo formidable, even in arms, as was vainly imagined by thoſe who had not courage to face them. For theſe reaſons he could not agree to putting the circar into the hands of thoſe who had been his old and inveterate enemies. Nor was the Nizam leſs importunate with his brother in diſſuading him from this ominous alliance. He aſked, whether he knew the nature of thoſe Europeans, who could never be induced to part with any thing they had once obtained. He pointed to Sujah Dowlah and his ſon, as examples of the danger and ruin which uniformly attends their friendſhip. And he threatened to puniſh his perſiſtence in this impolitic connection, by joining his troops with Hyder's, and totally diſpoſſeſſing him of all his territories.

The dilatory march of the Company's detachment gave Hyder a full opportunity of convincing both the preſidency and their new ally how much he had been in earneſt in the advice he had given. By one of thoſe rapid movements for which his military conduct has been so much distinguished, he suddenly entered the dominions of Bazalet, and, ravaging all the open country, confined him within the walls of his capital, Adoni. Thus circumstanced, he represented at Madras the absolute impossibility of now fulfilling his engagements. He therefore requested that they would withdraw their troops and civil officers from his territories, as their continuance might expose him and the whole province to still greater severities.

Differences subsisting between the presidency and Hyder Ally, which had been more or less widening ever since that disgraceful moment in which he had forced their signature to a treaty of peace and close alliance at the gates of Madras, had lately been attended with so many irritating circumstances on both sides, that sincere accommodation, however desirable, was no longer to be expected. He had, indeed, solicited our friendship with an assiduity which can only be justified by the conviction which he entertained of its utility. And every principle of just policy pointed him out as the natural ally of the Company. But their servants, by a series of ill usage; by fulfilling no promise they had given; by a breach of every treaty they had made; and by returning his kindest offices with ingratitude; converted him into one of their bitterest and most determined enemies. He was by far the most powerful neighbour they had on the coast of Coromandel. He possessed those hilly countries which bound and barricade the

the weſtern extremities of the Carnatic. His influence, from wealth, dominion, and military force, among the Nairs, Nabobs, and princes, in theſe parts, might, eſpecially in times of war, have been rendered of the moſt eſſential conſequence to our intereſt. But the politics of the preſidency had been warped, for years, with the prejudices of Mahommed Ally, who, animated by an invincible hatred to the perſon and fortunes of Hyder, employed all his artifice and intrigues to foment the difference between him and the Engliſh. This is the only probable account that has yet been given of the treatment which that great man experienced from the council of Madras. The Nabob urged them, with all his addreſs, to join the Marrattos in putting a ſtop to the progreſs of Hyder's conqueſts, and, by a well-concerted plan of co-operation, to cruſh his riſing grandeur. They might think it prudent to ſoften the abſolute rejection of his ſyſtem, by an unqualified acquieſcence in the reſentments that produced it. And perhaps it was not eaſy, under ſuch circumſtances, to preſerve the eſteem of their ally, without aſſuming a coolneſs to a power for whom he profeſſed ſo radical a diſlike.

Our expedition to Mahie, a fort ſituated on the Malabar coaſt, in the vicinity of Hyder's dominions, was, by the predilection which it diſcovered him to have for the French, the occaſion of his ſhewing an unequivocal antipathy to the preſidency of Madras. This port belonged to one of Hyder's

 tributary

tributary princes; and he considered it as within the line of that protection which he extended to all his territories. It was for this reason, and on this principle, that he remonstrated against the expedition. Here many Europeans, of all nations, had established factories, or were individually settled for the purposes of carrying on a mutual commercial intercourse with the inhabitants of his dominions, and to the reciprocal advantage of their respective countries, both in India and Europe, While these adventurers acted the part of good subjects, he thought it his duty, as well as interest, to defend them against every power who should dare to interrupt their tranquillity. He disavowed taking any share or concern in the private quarrels which might agitate the different nations in Europe; but it was his serious determination to consider the hostilities against Mahie as principally aimed at him; and that he should of course repel and revenge them to the utmost of his power. His Vakeel at Madras was authorized to denounce, in the most explicit terms, an irruption into the Carnatic, unless this mad project was laid aside.

The strength of the French, however, and their intrigues in this place, was an object of very serious attention to the welfare of the Company. It was consequently resolved to prosecute the enterprize at all hazards. The detachment was commanded by Colonel Braithwaite, whose rapid exertions and success in reducing the fort defeated the intention of Hyder, who wished to have preserved

ſerved it, and who ever after conſidered the meaſure as a perſonal inſult which he was obliged in honour to retaliate.

The Nabob of Arcot, who apprehended the moſt ſerious conſequences from the reſentments of Hyder Ally, was inceſſant in appriſing the council of the impending danger. He pointed out ſuch a diſpoſition of the forces as might beſt anſwer the exigencies of the ſervice. The ſuddenneſs, or unexpected celerity, with which the enemy would accompliſh his intention; the conſternation and diſtraction incident to an invaſion; the general moleſtation which the rapidity of the cavalry would occaſion; were circumſtances which muſt impede the collection of troops ſcattered in remote ſituations. Draught bullocks for the artillery, and coolies, or porters, for aſſiſting in the conveyance both of baggage and proviſions, in ſuch a moment of trepidation, it would be almoſt impoſſible to procure. He aſſured them, at the ſame time, that he had neither treaſure nor troops in which he could place any ſubſtantial dependence. The well-known averſion of the Nabob to Hyder Ally rendered his intelligence ſuſpicious, and defeated the natural effect of this wholeſome advice. He was the firſt, however, to announce the peace which took place between Hyder and the Marrattos; an event ſoon after but too fatally confirmed, and which ought to have been conſidered as the certain ſignal of the dreadful calamities which followed. But, though by this time hardly an an individual in the ſettlement doubted the reality of the enemy's deſigns and preparations againſt it, ſtill no meaſures were adopted for averting the conſequences. They truſted ſuch an accommodation might be effected by the ſuperior government, in other quarters of India, as would baffle, or ſuſpend at leaſt, the operations againſt the Carnatic. Theſe, however, were every where carried on with vigour, and without diſguiſe, for the avowed purpoſe of diſtreſſing the preſidency, who, notwithſtanding, perſevered in as much inattention and torpid negligence as if no ſymptoms of hoſtility had appeared.

The Nabob, at the moment when his exiſtence was threatened with inevitable deſtruction, was in debt to all the world, to the Company, to his army, and to individuals. It had been long his plan to borrow from all who would lend, and never to pay. Every article of his expenditure was loaded, and in arrears. His places of ſtrength were ill garriſoned, without ſtores, ammunition, or proviſions. His troops, deſtitute of neceſſaries, were altogether without diſcipline, and in the habit of mutiny and deſertion. His cavalry were ſeen to deſert, at noon-day, by whole regiments, with their horſes and arms. He owed the recovery of his beſt regiment from ſuch a ſituation to the generoſity of a Britiſh officer, who, to ſatisfy their demands, and reconcile them to the ſervice, advanced his whole private fortune. Even this ſum, thus ſeaſonably lent, was not repaid till the gentleman

man was in the utmoſt diſtreſs; and then only by the government of Madras on the Nabob's account.

The preſidency indeed were in poſſeſſion of a gallant and well-diſplined army of about thirty thouſand men. Lord Macleod had recently reinforced them by a new-raiſed regiment of a thouſand men from England. But this force was diſperſed into various detachments, on ſervices at the greateſt diſtance. A ſelection of the beſt troops on the eſtabliſhment were diſpatched to the aſſiſtance of Goddard in the Guzurat. Others were ſtationed in garriſons on the Malabar coaſt, and Colonel Baillie commanded no inconſiderable force in the Guntoor circar. In the Carnatic there was none of any conſideration collected. They were ſcattered in quarters and garriſons. The treaſury was without money, and the military magazine without an adequate ſtore of either amunition or proviſion. Much of this deficiency was attributed to the Nabob, who, in proportion as he predicted the approach of danger, had been urged though without effect to provide againſt the worſt. His army had formerly amounted to nearly thirty-five thouſand effective men, a number who, joined to the Company's, would have now ſufficiently protected the Carnatic. But their total want of order and ſubordination had lately rendered their number of no conſequence. It would at the ſame time have greatly altered the poſture of affairs for the better, had his forts and garriſons been in a

proper

proper ſtate of defence, his troops but tolerably diſciplined, and his large arrears to the Company conſiderably leſſened. They might then have acted with vigour and effect in his ſupport, as well as their own. And though the frequent intelligence they received had not rouſed them to ſuch a degree of activity and exertion, as the exigencies of the preſent criſis ſeemed to demand, it afforded conſtant occaſion of remonſtrating with the Nabob on the ruinous ſtate of his army and finance.

Our want of conduct and foreſight only ſtimulated the genius of the enemy, who, availing himſelf of our inſenſibility, was anxious, in his ſanguinary paroxyſm, to ſeize upon the victim of his fury by ſurpriſe. The following account of this awful event is given by a writer, whoſe maſterly powers of natural deſcription, have no equal in modern times. Hyder Ally "reſolved, in the gloomy "receſſes of a mind capacious of ſuch things, to "leave the whole Carnatic an everlaſting monu-"ent of vengeance, and to put perpetual deſola-"tion as a barrier between him and thoſe againſt "whom the faith, which holds the moral elements "of the world together, was no protection. He "became at length ſo confident of his force, ſo "collected in his might, that he made no ſe-"cret whatſoever of his dreadful reſolution. Hav-"ing terminated his diſputes with every enemy, "and every rival, who buried their mutual ani-"moſities in their common deteſtation *of the Eng-*"*liſh.* He drew from every quarter whatever

"a

" a favage ferocity could add to his new rudi-
" ments in the arts of deftruction; and, compound-
" ing all the materials of fury, havock, and de-
" folation, into one black cloud, he hung for a
" while on the declivities of the mountains. Whilft
" the authors of all thefe evils were idly and ftu-
" pidly gazing on this manacing meteor, which
" blackened all their horizon, it fuddenly burft,
" and poured down the whole of its contents upon
" the plains of the Carnatic. Then enfued a fcene
" of woe, the like of which no eye had feen,
" no heart conceived, and which no tongue can
" adequately tell. All the horrors of war, before
" known or heard of, were mercy to that new
" havock! A ftorm of univerfal fire blafted every
" field, confumed every houfe, deftroyed every
" temple! The miferable inhabitants, flying from
" their flaming villages, in part were flaugh-
" tered; others, without regard to fex, to age, to
" the refpect of rank, or facrednefs of function;
" fathers torn from children, hufbands from wives;
" enveloped in a whirlwind of cavalry, and
" amidft the goading fpears of drivers, and the
" trampling of purfuing horfes; were fwept into
" captivity in an unknown and hoftile land!

The firft accounts of this terrible difafter, which commenced in the frontiers, were fo far from being credited at Madras, that they were even treated with contempt. The burning of Conjeveram four days after the invafion, and the appearance of the enemy's horfe in the neigbourhood, were fuch pre-

fages

ſages of approaching danger, however, as could no longer be diſputed. Mr. Smith and Mr. Johnſon had indeed, with a laudable foreſight, endeavoured to make the majority ſenſible of the ſituation to which the intereſt of the Company in that quarter was expoſed. They preſſed the immediate neceſſity of aſſembling the troops, and taking ſuch other precautions as might check the arrogance of an enemy fluſhed with the expectation of finding them unprepared. The ardour, the eloquence, and the dignity of feeling, with which Mr. Sadler reprobated the remiſſneſs, which had ſo long and ſo unaccountably characteriſed the councils of Madras, are on record, and will remain an honourable teſtimony to his independent principles and patriotiſm, when the conduct that excited his manly and virtuous indignation is forgotten or execrated. The ſeverity of his ſtrictures ſerved only to irritate the delinquents, who pronounced them illiberal, inflammatory, and unfounded. They imputed them to weakneſs, envy or ſedition. Some expreſſions they conſtrued into an intention of diſturbing the public tranquillity, and others they conſidered as derogatory to the authority of the ſelect committee. On theſe charges they voted Mr. Sadler ſuſpended from his ſeat in the council, and the ſervice of the Company. Mr. Johnſon and Mr. Smith proteſted, with great propriety and earneſtneſs, againſt this violent meaſure. They avowed the moſt perfect coincidence of ſentiment with the minute on which this ſentence of ſuſpen-

ſion

ſion was founded. They inſiſted that the terror of the example was calculated to anhihilate freedom of debate. They alledged that no ſpecific charge was brought againſt Mr. Sadler, and that he had not even been heard in his own defence. And they imputed the rigour of his puniſhment rather to the angry ſuggeſtions of private pique, than the diſintereſted motives of public ſpirit.

While the preſidency of Madras were thus conſuming their time in perſonal animoſity, Hyder Ally was carrying on the ſavage buſineſs of carnage and rapine in every quarter of the Carnatic. The harmleſs inhabitants of a defenceleſs country were in this manner ſacrificed by thouſands, in revenge for a conduct which few of them knew, and none of them could prevent. The army of this fell deſtroyer conſiſted of nearly one hundred thouſand men. Thirty thouſand well-diſciplined infantry, and twenty thouſand horſe, were under his own command, every where capturing the forts, waſting the country, and rearing piles of diſhonourable triumph, amidſt heaps of laborious ruin. Wherever the grand army quartered or encamped, flying parties of various deſcriptions and magnitude extended the ſcene of deſtruction with equal rapidity and ſucceſs, in all directions far and wide. A choſen detachment, under Meer Saib, hovered on the borders of the Cuddepah, to emancipate, perhaps, the brother of the Nizam, from his dependence on the preſidency, to involve the northern circars in the general cataſtrophe, or to intercept

tercept the troops under the direction of Baillie. The terror and confusion inseparable from operations, objects and contingencies, thus fierce and tremendous, accumulated strength and consequence from the tremor and indecision of government. The council was equally without unanimity or firmness in deliberation or action. The orders they issued one day were revoked the next; and it was even agreed, that the advice and presence of the commander in chief were more necessary at Madras than at the head of the army. The temporary command of the troops was consequently delegated to Lord Macleod, who, disliking the arrangement prescribed, digested a system for himself, which he submitted to the presidency, with this declaration, that he could not adopt a responsibility in the execution of plans which did not coincide with his own judgment. Sir Hector Monro was therefore under the necessity, notwithstanding the late resolution of the select committee, to exchange the cabinet for the camp.

Mean while intelligence kept pouring in from every quarter, of the enemy's fatal progress, of his fresh devastations, and of his nearer approaches. The various representatives of towns and districts were clamorous in their complaints and requisitions to the presidency for protection against the common enemy. Accounts from all the forts and garrisons were at the same time given in, which stated their utter inability to make an effectual stand against the force who menaced them; and that nothing could

could ſave them but an immediate reinforcement of troops, and a freſh ſupply of ſtores and proviſions. Under the preſſure of ſuch various and material exigencies, the preſidency had recourſe to the Nabob for whatever money and proviſions he could procure. While he reproached them with tardineſs and inactivity, he promiſed to afford oxen, ſheep and rice, as plentifully as it was in his power, to complete four regiments of cavalry, and put them under the management of the commander in chief, during the war, and to make aſſignments of territory for whatever money might be advanced by the Company, for the pay of his troops. But the actual arrangements in the detail of his government ill accorded with theſe profeſſions. The officer to whom he intruſted the command of the ſtrong hold of Gengee, in a moment when the ſafety of the place was at ſtake, diſputed the right of a Britiſh officer, ſent with a reinforcement for his aſſiſtance, to adopt any meaſures for its defence, until ſpecific orders were received from the Nabob. Carangally was defended by a ſubaltern and only twenty miſerable ſepoys, who refuſed a ſupply of ammunition from Colonel Braithwaite, without the authority of the Durbar. And the troops which the colonel then marched from Pondicherry to join the army were reduced to the greateſt diſtreſs, by the Nabob's farmers making the want of his orders an apology for refuſing to furniſh them with proviſions. All theſe inattentions cooperated with the enemy's indefatigable activity to

 render

render the devaſtation as general and irreſiſtible as poſſible. There was ſcarcely, by this time, a place from one end of the coaſt to the other, which was not menaced or invaded. From Cape Camerin to the banks of the Kiſtna one continued ſcene of plunder, confuſion and bloodſhed, prevailed. The Company's forces, though ſtung by the ſight of theſe mercileſs marauders, becauſe incapable of aſſembling, could not act with effect, while thoſe whom the Nabob had placed in his different ſtrong holds, without diſcipline or attachment, inſtead of maintaining their poſts and defending either their maſters intereſt or their own honour, ſeemed proud of ſuch an opportunity to revenge, by mutiny and treachery, his inattention both to their ſafety and his own.

In the beginning of Auguſt a plan was committed to Colonel Coſby for collecting a conſiderable detachment from ſeveral garriſons in the neighbourhood of the army, in conjunction with two regiments of the Nabob's cavalry, for intercepting an immenſe convoy of ſtores and proviſions, which had to paſs ſome narrow defiles from Hyder's country to his camp. But no genuine information could be obtained concerning either the country or the enemy; the peaſantry, wherever found, being induſtrious only to deceive the commander, whoſe movements were, at the ſame time, exactly reported to Hyder by the ſervants and officers of the Nabob. To this obſtinacy in the inhabitants, and treaſonable conduct in the

people

people under the Durbar, the failure of an enterprize, which might have exceedingly diſtreſſed the enemy, muſt be attributed. And it was not without the greateſt danger and difficulty that Coſby, in the middle of the following month, effected his eſcape upon the retreat from Conjeveram.

Depredations by the enemy's horſe, on the villages and gardens about the mount, determined the council to adopt ſome meaſures for their own immediate defence. The intention of aſſembling the army at Conjeveram was fruſtrated for want of bullocks, which, that the enemy might not ſeize them, had been driven to a diſtant place of refuge. The mount was therefore made the place of general rendezvous, until proviſions could be collected, and the means of conveyance procured. The Nabob was, at the ſame time, repeatedly preſſed and importuned for every poſſible ſupply of bullocks and proviſions; and that he would delegate ſome perſon of conſequence to attend the army, and prevent thoſe wants and inconveniences which ſo effectually impeded their operations.

Hyder ſat down before Arcot, the metropolis of the Carnatic, on the 21ſt of Auguſt. The Nabob appeared ſenſibly intereſted in the fate of his capital. He was more than commonly earneſt in his entreaties that the army might repair immediately to the relief of Arcot, where he aſſerted they would find a plentiful ſupply of every neceſſary. Though the enemy's deſigns on this place had been artfully covered, ſuch intelligence was obtained as procured the garriſon a conſiderable reinforcement from the fortreſs of Vellore. It was a few days after Arcot was inveſted that Sir Hector Monro aſſumed the command at the head of the army.

The detachment under Colonel Baillie were, in the mean time, very critically ſituated. He had been ordered, ſince the invaſion took place, to attempt the reduction of the Cuddepah country, with, however, a latitude for the exerciſe of his own judgment in exerciſing his principal operations wherever there appeared the greateſt probability of ſucceſs. Mr. Smith and Mr. Johnſon had vigorouſly oppoſed theſe inſtructions, and aſſigned various reaſons for ordering an immediate junction of the detachment with the main body of the army. Baillie gave now ſuch a repreſentation of his circumſtances, from the proximity of Hyder's cavalry to the ſouth, and the overflowing of the Kiſtna to the northward; the difficulty, in this contracted ſituation, of providing ſubſiſtence for the troops; and the dread of not being able much longer to detain the bullocks neceſſary for a march, without which he could not move; as impelled the majority of the committee to adopt at laſt the meaſure of Smith and Johnſon, of ordering the detachment to march for the preſidency, when a variety of new circumſtances had rendered it infinitely leſs eligible and advantageous. In his return, however, it was hoped he might be able to cut off ſome of the enemy's convoys; and ſuch

a route

a route was prescribed him, with this view, as terminated in consequences peculiarly calamitous.

Sir Hector Monro found only one regiment of the Nabob's cavalry with the army when he arrived in the camp, about the latter end of August. These troops refused to continue any longer in the service, unless their arrears were immediately paid. Though the Nabob's Ameer was present, and the capital of his master in immediate danger, he declined to comply with the request. The commander in chief broke the regiment, and stript them of their horses and arms. Seventeen officers, and about sixty privates, immediately inlisted in the Company's service. The rest were ordered to to be sent, under a strong guard, as prisoners to Madras; but the Ameer next morning incorporated them with his own body guard.

The rivers had been so much swelled by the late rains, that the march of Baillie from the Guntoor was much incommoded, and his troops exceedingly distressed. A junction with this detachment was, however, eagerly desired by the general, as he then might hope to face the enemy in the field, notwithstanding their vast superiority in numbers, and other respects. He determined, in these circumstances, to move from the mount, and to wait for Baillie at Conjeveram. A whole month was wasted in collecting only eight day's rice for the army, while draught bullocks were so difficult to be obtained, that the sepoys were obliged to carry half this provision on their backs. The whole force did not exceed ſix thouſand men; but of theſe were two regiments of Europeans, two companies of European grenadiers, belonging to other regiments, and three hundred artillery. Their march was exceedingly harraſſed, both by the enemy's horſe, who hung on all ſides of them the whole way, and the violent rains, which continued without intermiſſion. In four days they reached Conjeveram, which, by this time, was wholly under war. The Nabob's officer, who attended them at this place to conduct them on their way to Arcot, on being urged to procure immediate proviſions for the army, and obtain all poſſible intelligence of the enemy, was ſatisfied with anſwering, that he had no authority for doing either the one or the other. They were conſequently obliged to put up with whatever paddy, or growing rice, could be collected from the open country, though in a great meaſure covered with water.

The ſiege of Arcot was, indeed, raiſed at the approach of our army; but the enemy endeavoured, by a judicious choice of his ground, to prevent the junction of the Company's forces, which was expected to have taken place the very next day. Baillie's march, however, had been delayed by the unforeſeen riſe of ſeveral rivers which he was obliged to croſs. The army, under ſimilar inconvenience from the inceſſant rains, were, about a week after their arrival at Conjeveram, under the neceſſity of removing their encampment

campment to higher ground. Nor was the utmoſt induſtry of the troops, in gathering paddy, more than ſufficient for their preſent ſubſiſtence. Under all theſe circumſtances, every avenue of information was ſo vigilantly watched by the enemy, that, except the accidental report of a deſerter, the general had only [on the 3d of September] heard, from one of his own officers, who was out on a detached ſervice, of Hyder's quitting his ground, croſſing the Palaar, and encamping within five miles of his front. It was known, two days afterwards, that Baillie had croſſed the river, which occaſioned him ſo much difficulty and delay. The next day the enemy made a conſiderable movement towards the north-eaſt. Sir Hector advanced, at the ſame time, to a high ground on the Trepaſſore road, where Baillie's detachment was expected. The enemy encamped about two miles to the left of the Engliſh. Hyder made this movement to cover the attack which he intended againſt Baillie. His brother-in-law, Meer Saib, began the action on the 5th, with eight thouſand of his beſt horſe, and was gallantly repulſed. Tippoo Saib, with ſix thouſand regular infantry, twelve pieces of cannon, and eighteen thouſand cavalry, renewed the conflict, next day, at Perimbancum, where they encountered Baillie's handful of heroes, who, by conduct, exertion, and perſeverance, repelled, with prodigious ſlaughter, even this vaſt ſuperiority of numbers. He loſt, however, his baggage, and a number of his men. His

 whole

whole ſorce did not exceed three or four battalions of ſepoys, and between one or two companies of European artillery. He was now within a few miles of the Engliſh camp; but the enemy's whole force intercepted their junction. Nor could he retain his preſent ſituation for want of proviſions. He therefore diſpatched a meſſenger to the general with intelligence of theſe particulars, and to urge the movement of the whole army, as that appeared the only meaſure which could effectually extricate him from his preſent difficulty. It conſequently remained with Sir Hector to determine whether he ſhould riſk a general action under circumſtances of ſuch peculiar diſadvantage as an immenſe body of cavalry would have over a few battalions of infantry, in a flat open country, for the purpoſe of ſaving the detachment; or whether this valuable object might not be obtained at leſs apparent hazard, by ſending ſuch a reinforcement to Baillie as might enable him to brave the difficulties that impeded his march. The latter part of the alternative ſeemed the moſt eligible; as, whatever the conſequences were, the army would ſtill be in poſſeſſion of their poſt, their paddy, which they had depoſited in a contiguous pagoda, and the ſtrong grounds which they occupied.

Colonel Fletcher was honoured with the command of the reinforcement, which was compoſed of the flower and moſt active part of the army, and conſiſted of the grenadier and light infantry companies from Lord Macleod's highland regiment,

two

two other companies of European grenadiers, one company of ſepoy markſmen, and ten companies of ſepoy grenadiers. Fletcher refuſed four ſix-pounders which were ordered for the ſervice, as much activity might be neceſſary on his part, to elude the ambuſhes which were probably laid for him. Hyder had the exacteſt intelligence of the whole manœuvre, the ſtrength of the party, their route, and the time they left the camp, which was at nine o'clock at night. A ſtrong body of troops were conſequently diſpatched to intercept the detatchment. They had undoubtedly ſucceeded, but that Fletcher, diſtruſting his guides, altered his courſe, and by a wide circuitous ſweep to the right defeated the ſtratagem.

The ſpirit of the enemy, by the late defeats, was ſenſibly damped, and the reinforcement of Baillie's little army alarmed the whole camp. The chiefs and foreign officers thought, by this movement, Hyder's entire force would be ſituated between two fires. Lally, whom Hyder had obtained from the Nizam, and who commanded the Europeans, in company with moſt of the native general officers, urged the Nabob to break up his camp, and repaſs the Palaar, as the only certain way of avoiding the danger that ſurrounded them. While he heſitated how to act, he received intelligence from his ſpies, that the Engliſh army was perfectly quiet in camp, nor in fact was any deſign of a movement entertained. The Europeans particularly diſcredited the information, and treated the

the idea as abſurd and impoſſible; and, in the conviction that Hyder was betrayed, and would be ruined, Lally went to his tent once more, and preſſed the neceſſity of providing for the ſafety of the artillery and infantry, by ſending them away. But Hyder, anxious to avoid the diſgrace of leaving the field to an enemy ſo exceedingly inferior, occupied and enfiladed, by ſeveral batteries of cannon, the moſt covert and difficult grounds which Baillie had to paſs. Large bodies of his beſt infantry were at the ſame time formed into an ambuſcade on every ſide, while the main body of his army, under his own command, occupied a poſt the moſt favourable for ſupporting the attack. To divert the attention of the Engliſh, on the ſide of Conjeveram, a party of irregular cavalry were employed, within ſight of the camp, in performing various movements. Ballie was perceived [Sept. 10], by day-light, directing his forces through the very defile thus fatally prepared for his reception. His devoted forces marched in columns, and knew nothing of their danger till it was announced from the mouth of a battery of twelve guns loaded with grape ſhot, which poured in upon their right flank. In half an hour fifty pieces of artillery were ſo well directed as to penetrate into every part of the Britiſh line. They were inſtantly ſurrounded, and vigorouſly aſſailed on all ſides by twenty-five thouſand cavalry, by thirty regiments of diſciplined ſepoys, by a ſtrong body of Europeans, and by a numerous artillery. This little column ſtood nothwithſtanding

firm

firm and undaunted, and repelled the repeated charges of the enemy with an incredible ſlaughter of their beſt troops. Their evolutions in the midſt of ſuch a ſtorm of rockets, cannon and muſquetry, as has ſeldom taken place in any other part of the world, were performed with a preciſion, a ſteadineſs, and directed with a promptitude and a ſkill, that filled their enemies and ſpectators with aſtoniſhment. They had only ten pieces of cannon, which were ſo well ſerved and directed as to make prodigious havock among the enemy's horſe. This dreadful conflict remained doubtful for three hours, when victory began to declare for the Engliſh. The flower of the Myſore cavalry, after many bloody repulſes, where at length completely defeated and driven back. Even the right wing, compoſed of Hyder's beſt troops, were thrown into diſorder, and every where gave way. A rapid movement, made at that inſtant by Colonel Baillie, ſeemed to decide the fortune of the day. Hyder, in deſpair prepared for a retreat, which the cavalry were ordered to cover. Lally was at the ſame time directed to draw off the artillery. It was at this critical and important moment, that the tumbrils which contained the ammunition ſuddenly blew up, with two dreadful exploſions, in the center of the Britiſh lines. This unexpected diſaſter not only overturned all their artillery, and rendered it unfit for further ſervice, but laid one whole ſide of the column bare, which expoſed every part of the army to a freſh attack. The total loſs of ammunition was ſtill more dreadful to the survivors, than even that of the troops who perished, as it left them in some degree defenceless in the face of an enraged and formidable enemy, eager to snatch the victory from those who had so nearly been their conquerors. Tippoo Saib accordingly embraced this opportunity of distinguishing himself, and fell, without waiting for orders, with infinite rapidity and fury, at the head of the Mogul and Carnatic cavalry, into the broken square which had not yet time to recover its order or form. The French corps, and the first line of infantry, immediately followed. The last efforts of these brave men, thus overpowered, however desperate, was unavailable. The carnage amidst which they fell gave full proof of their exertions. The sepoys, after exhibiting prodigies of valour, were almost to a man cut to pieces. Baillie, notwithstanding the horrors which involved him on this tremendous emergency, and almost fainting with anguish, fatigue, and loss of blood, yet rallied the Europeans, and, under the fire of the whole immense artillery of the enemy gained a little eminence; and, forming a new square, these invincible veterans, without artillery or ammunition, the officers fighting only with their swords, and the soldiers with their bayonets, and most of them desperately wounded, repulsed thirteen different charges by all the forces who could act against them. Unable longer to withstand the torrents of fresh troops, that were perpetually breaking and pouring in upon them, they were at length borne

down,

down, and individually maſſacred by multitudes, or trampled under foot by horſes and elephants. The few artillery-men who remained, when their ammunition was expended, advanced in the front of their guns, and nobly fell in their defence. Numbers, both officers and men, though cut down and miſerably wounded, diſdained to accept of quarter. While gaſping on the ground, and weltering in blood, they continued to thruſt fiercely with their bayonets to the laſt, and every other weapon they could graſp, at whoever approached them. Never, perhaps, was action ſuſtained with more obſtinacy, or ſo much execution done by ſo diminutive a force. Thus diſtreſſing the cauſe, and prepoſterous to nature, are the common effects of courage, united with ſcience, and perverted by politics, to anſwer the barbarous purpoſes of ambition!

The Engliſh loſt at leaſt near four thouſand ſepoys, and above five hundred Europeans. The gallant Fletcher was found among the number of Britiſh officers who fell on this memorable day. It is a miracle that an individual could eſcape the rage of ſuch a carnage. Baillie, however, and about two hundred Europeans, were made priſoners. He was brought before the conqueror, ſtript, wounded in three places, and covered with blood. In that moment of triumph and exultation, Hyder, forgetting the dignity and moderation which ſo eminently become the great and the brave, is ſaid to have inſulted the Britiſh veteran by an haughty and imperious demeanour. "Your high-"neſs," ſaid Baillie, indignantly, "may aſk

"your

"your ſon and the general officers what cauſe "there is for exultation on your part, and whether "the victory was not mine before that diſaſter "took place, which no human foreſight could "prevent." It was at the ſame time obſerved, by a foreigner of diſtinction on the ſpot, that "officers and men ſupported their misfortunes "with that haughty ſullen fortitude which is the "charactiſtic of their country."

This victory, complete as it appeared, was dearly purchaſed by the enemy. The ſlaughter, which was immenſe, fell only among the beſt troops. Had the main body of the Engliſh army advanced upon the rear of Hyder's troops, any time during the conflict, his whole forces had probably been cut to pieces or captured. He was mounted on an elephant, and fired at five different times by an officer of artillery. Such a panic is ſaid to have ſeized him, from the danger to which he was perſonally expoſed, that, on a mere rumour that Sir Hector Monro was advancing, he abandoned the field of battle, and fled in the greateſt terror to a place called the Round Wells, leaving all his baggage and the wounded behind him. But he grew more courageous, when informed that the Britiſh general, leaving his baggage and artillery behind him, retreated to Chingleput. A purſuit immediately took place, by a number of freſh and irregular cavalry, who ſoon returned loaded with plunder and encumbered with priſoners.

On the morning of Baillie's defeat, Monro had made ſome movements in hopes of meeting him: The

The ſmoke was ſeen and the firing heard on the left of the camp, but at too great a diſtance for affording the detachment any aſſiſtance. Indeed, no idea was entertained of attacking the enemy on that ſide; or that Baillie, in conſequence of the late reinforcement, was not perfectly able to reſiſt every obſtruction. But when ſeveral ſignal cannon were fired and no return made, and the briſk cannonade, which had been juſt heard, was ſucceeded by the profoundeſt ſilence, ſome diſaſter began to be ſeriouſly apprehended. At length, the arrival, in ſucceſſion, of two or three wounded ſepoys, gave full intelligence of the fatal event. The whole army, officers and men, natives as well as Europeans, were ſtung with anger and with grief, almoſt to madneſs, at the deſtruction of their friends. An immediate and ſevere revenge on the enemy was, independent of any regard to their ſtrength, their condition or the conſequences, the only deſire they indulged. The general thought himſelf under a neceſſity, however, of reſtraining their preſent impetuoſity. He knew the weakneſs of his force, and the critical ſituation of affairs, but was altogether uninformed of the loſs, the reſources or the movements of the enemy. He had loſt the flower of his troops, and there was not above two days proviſion in the camp: Nor had he cavalry to procure more. He might be ſurrounded by the hoſt, whom he wiſhed to ſubdue, and obliged to ſurrender without ſtriking a blow. Theſe ſuggeſtions were not likely to ſtill the clamours of an army, who only panted for an opportunity

portunity of encountering the enemy. The officers in general avowed the ſame ardour which inſpired the privates, and ſubmitted to the orders for a retreat, with that indignant reluctance which it is natural for brave men to feel, when forced by the etiquette of arms to act by the opinions of others, in defiance of their own. And to the diſorder which aroſe from this contrariety of ſentiment, all, or moſt of the inconveniences which attended the march of the troops to Chingleput, may probably be attributed. They were joined at this place by the forces under Colby, which conſiſted of ten companies of ſepoy grenadiers, an equal number of battalion and light infantry companies, with two regiments of the Nabob's cavalry.

While theſe important tranſactions diſtinguiſhed the operations of the army, the country, the preſidency, and its diſtant dependencies, were in a ſtate of the greateſt diſtraction. The danger ſeemed every where alike, immediate and inevitable. Once more Johnſon and Smith arraigned the conduct of the majority with every ſpecies and degree of miſmanagement. They conſidered them as the cauſe of all the calamities which had happened, or were likely to happen, in the Carnatic. They charged the inſtitution of the ſelect committee, as inveſting the preſident with a power independent of the council, and inimical to the conſtitution. And they objected, in very ſtrong terms, to the diſpatches now making up for Europe, which they alledged were unſupported by fact, and

calculated

calculated to miſlead their employers at home. The ſepoys, at the ſame time, on whom an attempt had been made to bring from the northern circars by ſea, revolted. Thoſe at Maſulipatam were reduced to order by the addreſs of the commanding officer on that ſtation; but at Vizigapatam they were guilty of the groſſeſt outrages: After killing many of their officers, and plundering the place, they went off in a body with their arms and booty. While Sitteram Row, who had lately become ſo much a favourite with the preſidency, kept aloof, Vizeram, notwithſtanding the injuries they had done him, collected his troops, and, with the vigorous aſſiſtance of another zemindar, the mutineers were purſued, attacked, diſarmed, and diſperſed.

Theſe circumſtances gave new vigour and diſpatch to the meaſures of the preſidency. They reſolved to recal ſuch of their forces as were on the Malabar coaſt; and that the ancient and uſeful ſettlement of Tellicherry ſhould be abandoned. It had the good fortune, however, to be exempted from this ſentence of dereliction. Sir Edward Hughes afterwards found means to ſtrengthen the garriſon from Bombay. Diſpatches were, at the ſame time, ſent to Bengal, preſſing an immediate ſupply of money and troops. The king's admiral wrote to the ſame purpoſe, and exhibited ſuch a ſtatement of facts as could not fail enforcing the urgency of the requiſition. The hourly arrival of a French fleet was now alſo expected. Misfortunes are the medicine of ſtates. The lofty pretenſions uſed but little ago at the Nizam's Durbar were for the preſent forgotten. The council was now afraid to offend whom they had thus wantonly exaſperated. Orders were inſtantly iſſued for reſtoring the Guntoor circar to Bazalet Jung, and for withdrawing the Nabob's managers. And the Nizam was addreſſed in terms as ſubmiſſive and humble as they were before imperious and inſolent.

The object of univerſal reduction was ſtill proſecuted with vigour by the enemy. Hyder renewed his deſigns on Arcot, and ſat immediately down before it. His attacks were carried on with all the regularity and ſcience of an European army. The garriſon beheld with ſurpriſe their guns diſmounted by his batteries. His horſe, every where maſters of the open country, prevented all communication between the preſidency and its dependencies. Our troops, cooped up in the vicinity of Madras, dared not to venture, even when preſſed for proviſions, above two miles beyond their entrenchments. A general diſſatisfaction prevailed in the Nabob's forts, which, from treachery, deſertion, or cowardice, ſeldom make any defence. The company's government, from its arrogance in peace, and impotence in war, became odious and contemptible, throughout the Carnatic. And Hyder, whoſe addreſs in politics was not inferior to his military conduct, was ſingularly aſſiduous and ſucceſsful in rendering his pretenſions popular, by accommodating himſelf to the genius and wiſhes of the natives

tives, in proportion as they deemed themſelves injured, betrayed, or ſlighted by the Engliſh.

No ſooner was the awful diſaſter which happened to Baillie's detachment announced to the government of Bengal, than the moſt ſpirited and probable meaſures for extricating the Carnatic were adopted and purſued. It was immediately reſolved to ſend a conſiderable reinforcement of Europeans, and fifteen lacks of rupees, by ſea; and, as ſoon as the ſeaſon and other circumſtances would permit, to diſpatch alſo a ſtrong body of ſepoys by land. It was at the ſame time ſuggeſted, that all the hopes of the ſupreme council for retrieving the company's affairs on the coaſt of Coromandel depended on the preſence of Sir Eyre Coote, who was then a member of their own body, as well as commander in chief of all the forces in India. The general, notwithſtanding the badneſs of the ſeaſon, and his precarious ſtate of health, complied with the requiſition. The treaſure was conſigned to his management, as more ſafety was apprehended from his honour in its application, than from their meaſures, in whom the preſent embarraſſment originated. Early communications were made both to the preſidency of Madras and to Sir Edward Hughes, of what had been done, and an aſſurance given of the ſincereſt diſpoſition to cultivate a peace with the Marrattos. Sir Edward was alſo requeſted to direct the operation of his ſquadron againſt Hyder's ports and navy on the Malabar coaſt.

 The

The general was only twenty-three days on his paſſage from Calcutta to Madras. Arcot was taken by aſſault on the third, and he arrived on the fifth of November. The fort, or citadel, though ſtrong, was given up without any defence. Hyder's humanity and generoſity to his priſoners having reached the garriſon, all the ſepoys, to a man, deſerted the fort in the night, and went over to Hyder, leaving their officers under an abſolute neceſſity of ſurrendering at diſcretion. This capture has been generally attributed to the treachery of the Nabob's people, by whoſe turbulence and intrigues the garriſon had been kept in diſſenſion during the whole ſiege. Hyder treated the principal officers immediately after with the greateſt confidence; and he had long before avowed the fulleſt information of the moſt ſecret tranſactions in the Nabob's Durbar.

General Sir Eyre Coote brought with him from Bengal two hundred European artillery, ſix companies of infantry, one of volunteers, and between ſix and ſeven hundred laſcars. With this reinforcement, more conſiderable indeed from the intrinſic value of the troops, than their number, all the force he could collect in two months time, at the mount where he encamped, did not exceed ſeven thouſand men. Madras was protected, and the monſoon ſeaſon covered the inaction of an army, otherwiſe totally incapable of taking the field. The general took his ſeat as ſecond in council two days after his arrival at Madras, and produced the orders

orders from the superior government for the suspension of Mr. Whitehill, the president. His obstinacy in the affair of the Guntoor circar subjected him to this sentence. He disclaimed the authority which devested him of his power. The suspension being however confirmed by a majority of the council, he assumed a merit from that moderation which induced him to prevent the evils of a civil war, by submitting. Mr. Smith, as next to the chair, succeeded. The board, thus new modelled, found the situation of affairs still worse than was expected. The passes from the mountains were unguarded; the troops belonging to the presidency were not collected; no suitable provision for even the protection of Fort St. George had been made; the carriages for field artillery were only preparing; the troops were dispirited, the sepoys deserting; the country desolated; the inhabitants treacherous; all communications cut off; their provisions consumed, and their resources exhausted. The enemy's superiority was increased in proportion as our strength diminished, which arose not only from the success of his army, but chiefly from his good policy. "Hyder," says Sir Eyre Coote, "had taken every measure, which could "occur to the most experienced general, to distress "us, and to render himself formidable; and his "conduct in his civil capacity had been supported "by a degree of political address, unequalled by "any power that had yet appeared in Indostan."

 A re-

A revolution, of the moſt favourable aſpect to the Company's intereſt, was inſtantly obſervable in the conduct of government. Unanimity was reſtored, and vigour was the immediate conſequence of deciſion. The entire management of the war was forthwith delegated to the general. Even Hyder, affected by the fame of the commander, whoſe meaſures he had now to counteract, obſerved for the future more than ordinary caution. The number of his forces was by this time much augmented. It was generally allowed to exceed conſiderably an hundred thouſand men; and, from the circumſcribed operations of our army, he was encouraged and enabled to lay ſiege at once to ſeveral of the principal towns and forts in the Carnatic.

The fate of Madras, of the Engliſh intereſt in the Carnatic, and perhaps in all India, was wrapt up in the ſmall army under the command of Sir Eyre Coote. We had not only Hyder Ally, but the whole inhabitants in the Carnatic, to combat. The Nabob's renters were every where treacherous and hoſtile. One of them, having been detected in endeavouring to betray Villore to the enemy, was put in irons by the general, that "he might "be inſtrumental to the diſcovery of thoſe dark "deſigns which Sir Eyre had long expected to exiſt "in the court of a native power, living under "the very walls of our garriſon of Fort St. George."

That the general might proceed on the ſureſt grounds, he ſubmitted his plan of operations to a council of war, compoſed of Sir Hector Monro, Lord

Lord Macleod, and Brigadier-General Stuart. Theſe officers coincided entirely with the judgement of the general for the march of the army to the relief of the beſieged places. His preſence ſeemed to inſpire the officers as well as men with freſh confidence and courage. Even Sir Hector Monro, who might have been ſuppoſed moſt chagrined by a number of the new arrangements, had the generoſity to declare that there was nothing more to be deſired than bringing the enemy to a general engagement, as he was confident the army would be ſucceſsful under its preſent leader againſt any ſuperiority of numbers. Sir Eyre Coote laid the whole proceedings of the council of war before the ſelect committee, deſiring their advice alſo in this critical and momentous buſineſs. A meaſure which effectually rivetted their confidence in his conduct, and the event was an entire acquieſcence with the opinion of the council of war.

The relief of Wandewaſh on the 17th of January [1781] was the firſt object for which the army left the mount. Hyder not only raiſed the ſiege of that place, but abandoned all the others with equal precipitation on the general's approach. Thus was the ſtorm conſiderably abated by facing it manfully. Other garriſons were alſo ſtrengthened and ſupplied with proviſions; a great extent of country recovered, and a new frontier formed. Thus a ſecurity was provided for Madras, as effectual as if the army had been encamped under its walls. The ſpirit and confidence of the troops were con-

 ſequently

ſequently reſtored, and the whole complexion of affairs began every where to put on a more favourable appearance.

The inhabitants of Pondicherry, on the commencement of the preſent war, and in direct violation of all treaty, the moment Colonel Braithwaite had evacuated the place, in return for all paſt favours, and preſent confidence, roſe in arms, plundered the ſolitary reſident, who had been left to ſuperintend their conduct, and even compelled him, with fixed bayonets at his breaſt, to ſign a written inſtrument, the contents of which he knew not. They armed a number of ſepoys, and amaſſed prodigious quantities of proviſions, which they depoſited at Carangolly a town at ſome diſtance upon the coaſt. Sir Eyre Coote had always condemned the indulgence ſhewn to the French as highly impolitic and dangerous. Their conduct on this occaſion did not therefore ſurpriſe him. But no ſooner had he relieved the beſieged places than he went againſt Pondicherry, diſarmed the inhabitants, deſtroyed their boats, and removed their ſtores. The ſquadron of M. de Orves was ſoon after obliged to leave the coaſt for want of the boats which had been thus opportunely deſtroyed. At the ſame time Sir Edward Hughes performed excellent ſervice on the Malabar coaſt, by annihilating at one ſtroke the whole of Hyder's ſhipping in his own ports of Calicut and Mangalore.

By

By Hyder's eagerneſs to reduce Trichinapoly, he was drawn into a general engagement with the Engliſh. This army was then little leſs than two hundred thouſand ſtrong. The Britiſh general was not in the leaſt diſmayed by the magnitude of the enemy. He commanded a body of veterans, on every individual of whom he placed the greateſt dependence. Such clouds of Hyder's cavalry hovered about our camp, and infeſted the whole ſurrounding country, that it was not only impracticable to ſend out a reconnoitring party, but a ſingle man could not eſcape detection. On this account, not one of the ſcouts whom the general diſpatched for intelligence ever returned, and the only knowledge he could obtain of the enemy's ſituation was from ſuch a view of them as his own advanced poſts would admit.

The army moved from the camp at Port Novo, July 1ſt [1781] early in the morning, with the ſea at no great diſtance on the right. It was neceſſary to protect the baggage from Hyder's irregular cavalry, who, upon the firſt opening, were in readineſs to pour in upon them. A detachment for that purpoſe was now therefore ordered, which conſiſted of two regiments of cavalry, and a battalion of ſepoys, with ſeven pieces of light artillery. Theſe, with the uſual guard of an hundred and fifty ſepoys, a few poligars, and a Marratto corps, were judiciouſly placed in the opening between the right of the army and the ſea.

The

The enemy's cavalry now appeared in an extensive plain, drawn up in great force. Sir Eyre Coote formed his troops in two lines, and proceeded on his march in order of battle. Hyder's principal force was seen marshalled in battle array in the rear of his works, which lay directly upon the intended line of our march, and which extended further than the eye could reach. Immense bodies of horse paraded in every direction, and great quantities of rockets were thrown, without intermission, to confound the observation, and if possible to derange the order or impede the movements of the English army. Their cannonade, which was well served, was not expended without execution, at the same time that the English general reserved his fire for an opportunity in which it would be attended with the completest effect.

Here it was proper to examine the position of the country, and the army halted; while the general, availing himself of every advantage which the ground afforded, conceived the grand movement upon which he chiefly rested his hopes of success. He was anxious to discover whether his situation would admit of his taking such a sweep on the right, as would enable him to turn the enemy's left, wishing to fall upon them rather obliquely, than to be under the necessity of making his attack on the front of their works and batteries. Fortunately, the operation was practicable, and was performed by the first line with a promptitude and celerity

celerity that aſtoniſhed and diſconcerted the enemy. The general, having by this manœuvre contracted his front, inſtantly formed a-new within reach of Hyder's artillery, but in ſome degree covered from its fire. The heights in his rear were eagerly ſeized and occupied by General Stuart, who commanded the ſecond wing, which prevented the enemy from ſeparating the two lines, and encouraged the general to advance with confidence on the enemy.

Theſe ſudden and unexpected evolutions, obliged Hyder to a freſh arrangement of his army. And his movements were formed with great expedition and exactneſs. He withdrew his guns from the batteries to the line, and received Sir Eyre Coote with a new front. He ordered a ſtrong body of diſciplined infantry, with a ſuitable artillery, a prodigious number of irregulars, and an immenſe force of cavalry, to attack the Engliſh poſted on the heights; while another detachment attempted, by getting into the interval during the conflict, to attack Sir Eyre Coote in the rear. Thus was each wing ſeparately, and almoſt equally engaged. The freſh forces, with which the enemy were inceſſantly relieved, rendered the battle long and obſtinate. It laſted above ſix hours, in which every individual in the Company's ſervice fought as if the fate of the day had depended on his ſingle prowеſs. The ſpirited, regular and unanimous exertions of ſuch a body of determined veterans, under the conduct of a brave, experienced and ſucceſsful leader, were not to be reſiſted fifted by an Indian army of any magnitude whatever. By four o'clock the firft line, triumphing over every obftacle, drove the infantry, artillery, and cavalry of the enemy, promifcuoufly before them. The fecond line, at the fame time, under the command of Brigadier-General Stuart, had not only repulfed the other divifion of the enemy, but difpoffeffed them of their poft. They likewife totally defeated the attempt made to attack the general's rear. The mafterly and well-directed exertions of the troops in this quarter prevented the enemy, notwithftanding their numbers, from making the fmalleft attempt upon the baggage.

No victory could be more complete or decifive on all fides. The tumult and confufion in the retreat of fuch numbers afforded every advantage to troops who could have purfued them with effect. The whole of Hyder's artillery and ftores might have been captured, but his cattle left the field in full trot, while our's were fcarcely able to drag the guns along. And no circumftance could be more vexatious to brave men, than their utter incapacity to feize the fruits of a victory thus dearly earned. For the behaviour of every man in the army, from the commander in chief to the meaneft fepoy, was highly meritorious. Both lines, the one commanded by Sir Hector Monro, and the other by General Stuart, did the ampleft juftice to the orders and admirable difpofitions of Sir Eyre Coote, who generoufly declared, that every individual of his little army feemed to feel

that

that all the intereſt of the nation and Company was then at ſtake. "Every nerve," ſaid he, "was exerted to the very extent of poſſibility."

Three thouſand of the enemy were killed. Meer Saib, Hyder's brother-in-law and favourite general, was mortally wounded. Among his killed and wounded were likewiſe ſeveral other of his leaders and beſt officers. The Engliſh general halted juſt beyond the enemy's ground, from inability to continue the purſuit. Here the ſecond line and baggage joined him about midnight. His loſs did not exceed four hundred, nor was there an officer of rank or diſtinction among either killed or wounded.

Hyder left the important paſs of Puravenour open as he paſſed through it in the evening. Tippoo Saib, who had ſat down before Wandewaſh with thirty thouſand men, raiſed the ſiege precipitately, and joined his father in the neighbourhood of Arcot. The Engliſh were, in a few days, ſtrengthened by a conſiderable reinforcement from Bengal, which, under the favour of Moodajee Boonſla, had marched through the territories of Oriſſa. The general, deeming himſelf able to act with vigour, laid immediate ſiege to Trepaſſore, which, after a few days, capitulated on the 23d of Auguſt. At that moment the enemy appeared in full march to its relief, and there was not then more than one day's rice in the Engliſh camp. Trepaſſore afforded ſuch a ſeaſonable ſupply as enabled Sir Eyre Coote, after obtaining ſome rice from Poonamella,

to

to march in queſt of the enemy. Hyder fell back a few miles to the very ground where he had defeated Colonel Baillie, as the Engliſh approached; where, in the determination of trying his fortune in a ſecond battle, he took a very ſtrong poſition. The country between the two armies was interſected by ſeveral very deep water-courſes, which rendered the attack, on the part of the Engliſh, peculiarly arduous. The general was under the neceſſity of forming his front under a very heavy cannonade, both from well-placed batteries and from the guns in the enemy's lines. The diſcipline and firmneſs of any troops never underwent a fiercer trial; and the general declared, that their ſteady valour could not have been ſurpaſſed by the firſt veterans of any nation in Europe. This engagement, which happened on the 27th, laſted from nine in the morning until it was near ſun-ſet. The enemy were driven ſucceſsfully from all their grounds. Our army fought as if inſpired by the manes of their countrymen and fellow-ſoldiers, whoſe memorable exertions and defeat on that very ſpot were ſtill ſo recent in their memories. Our loſs however was greater, and that of the enemy leſs, than on the former battle. The irregularity of Hyder's ground afforded more cover from our fire. General Stuart loſt a leg by a cannon ſhot, and Colonel Browne his life by the ſame means. One of the general's aid-de-camps was killed by his ſide. Theſe were the only officers of conſequence who fell.

Another

Another action, about a month subsequent to this, was fought at a place called Sholingur. Hyder's loss in these encounters, while he preserved his artillery and stores, was but trivial. It was four o'clock before this battle commenced; and the sun did not go down until the enemy were totally routed. They were now in the habit of giving way in every contest with the company's forces. On this occasion their cavalry and infantry suffered extremely, while our loss was perfectly trifling.

In the beginning of 1782, the general went to the relief of Vellore, which was now reduced to great distress for provision. Hyder watched the motions of the army; and, as they passed a deep morass, commenced a very heavy cannonade. He wished to cut off the baggage and convoy, while the troops were entangled in their march. After an action of four hours, in which the flower of Hyder's troops were severely handled, he was forced to abandon his object with disgrace. The army, which had suffered but little, having pursued its course, and accomplished the end of the expedition without further molestation, on coming up to the same morass three days after, found Hyder prepared on the other side to dispute their passage. They passed notwithstanding the fire of his cannon, about four in the afternoon, when the general having formed, and secured the baggage, advanced with his usual promptitude upon the enemy. The resistance was but feeble. A general rout ensued, and a pursuit, in which the slaughter

was

was confiderable. Thus ended a campaign, the moft ardent, the moft brilliant, the moft bloody, and attended with effects the moft general and unexpected of any, perhaps, in the hiftory of political fociety.

During thefe tranfactions, an account of the war with Holland having arrived in India, five India fhips from China, in their way home, touched at Fort Marlborough, on the coaft of Sumatra. The gentlemen of that factory inftantly conceived the practicability of capturing the Dutch fettlements on that ifland. Mr. Botham, one of the council, was intrufted with the conduct of the expedition, in concert with Captain Clements, commodore of the five fhips. Captain Mandeville, with an hundred men, were all that could be fpared from the fort. The governor of Padang, miftaking the force coming againft him, was fuddenly terrified into a furrender, not only of that place, but of all the other Dutch fettlements on the weftern extremities of the ifland.

A ftrong armament was, at the fame time, and for very obvious reafons, fent againft the Dutch fettlement in the town, port, and fortrefs of Negapatam, on the Tanjore coaft. Major-General Sir Hector Monro was appointed to conduct this enterprize in concert with Sir Edward Hughes. The land forces already in the Rajah's country were only affigned for this fervice. It proved exceedingly arduous. The garrifon was at leaft eight thoufand ftrong. The befiegers, in all, did not amount

to

to half the number. The troops were much distressed by the badness of weather, and the dampness of their situation. Most of the wounded died, and many of the seamen, from heat and fatigue, were suddenly destroyed by violent cramps and spasms. Notwithstanding these difficulties, and after the failure of two desperate sallies with their whole force, terms of capitulation took place. The town and citadel, with all the stores and contents, which belonged to the government or Company, were surrendered to the victors. Private property was secured; and the inhabitants, upon taking the oath of allegiance, were to share the protection of the English. The garrison were allowed military honours, and then made prisoners of war. The governor, council, and other civil officers, were retained on parole. Hyder's infantry, and other sepoys, threw down their arms, and made their escape on the night preceding the capture. During a service of so much hazard and action, the whole loss of the besiegers, Europeans, and natives, in killed, wounded, and missing, were little more than one hundred men. They found in the place some fine artillery, and large quantities of military stores.

The reduction of Negapatam expelled the enemy from the kingdom of Tanjore. All the forts and strong holds, which they possessed in that country and its vicinity, were evacuated without delay. The poligars of Marawar and Tinevelly, who had revolted to Hyder, were at the ſame time reclaimed, and waited only a proper opportunity of renewing their peace with the Nabob. The ſucceſs of the Company's arms againſt a force of ſuch magnitude made every where the ſtrongeſt imrepſſion in their favour. And a general faith, in the various miracles formerly attributed to the operations of their arms, began to revive.

It was early in 1782 that the expedition againſt the Dutch intereſt and monopoly, eſpecially of the ſpice trade, in the valuable iſland of Ceylon, was conceived and executed. Sir Edward Hughes was aſſiſted in carrying on this enterprize, and ſupplied by the general with five hundred volunteer ſepoys, and an officer and thirty artillery men, to garriſon the fort, in caſe it fell into their hands. After encountering a variety of impediments incident to that ſpecies of ſervice, and not a little etiquette between Sir Edward and the governor, who had been perſonally intimate, the place was at length ſtormed with ſucceſs. It contained a prodigious quantity of military ſtores. Two ſhips richly laden, with a number of ſmaller veſſels, were taken in the harbour. Four hundred European military were made priſoners, and a few Malay officers. Our loſs was very inconſiderable. The admiral was much affected by the death of Mr. Long, a young man of promiſing talents, and his own ſecond lieutenant in the Superbe, who fell as he led on his company to the aſſault. He applauded the

the conduct both of the naval and marine officers, as meriting peculiar distinction, but specified the services of Major Geils, an engineer, as instances of the most eminent and useful abilities.

CHAPTER XI.

Demands on the Rajah of Benares—He is charged with Contumacy—The Governor-General visits Benares—The Rajah is taken into Custody—The Sepoys and Officers on that Service massacred—He flies—His Relation, and Enemy, succeeds to the temporary Management of the Zemindary—The Temerity and Repulse of Captain Mayaffre—The Governor-General abandons his Quarters by Night—The Nabob Vizier's Visit—Mal-treatment of the Princesses of Oude, the Women of the Zenana, and the Royal Offspring—Disturbances in the contiguous Provinces—Military Operations—Government settled—Peace with Sindia—Booty seized by the Army.

ALL the resources of the company were unequal to the constant and extraordinary disbursements, which the hostilities now raging, in almost every part of their possessions, occasioned. They grappled with difficulties at present, which had occurred in no former period. All India was in arms. The expulsion of strangers, who aimed at universal empire, by a system of uniform rapacity and usurpation, was an object which roused, united, and sanctified their efforts. This general confederacy derived a fresh and formidable accession of strength and consequence from the declaration of a French war. The pressure of these circumstances, by touching the inmost springs, and bring-

bringing into action all the latent powers of government, produced a series of extraordinary effects. It was assumed, as an operative principle in politics, that the expenditure of a war establishment should be provided for by a revenue altogether new; that the supreme council had a right to make the state of the treasury the standard of their pecuniary requisitions, and that public exigence was a sufficient plea for private extortion.

The zemindary of Benares, which includes also the circars of Gazypour and Chunar, constituted a part of the dominions of Oude, until the year 1774, when its tribute, or quit rent of twenty-four lacks, was transferred to the English. In the year 1778, when the French war commenced, it was resolved, that Cheit Sing, the Rajah of Benares, should be required to contribute an extraordinary subsidy of five lacks, to answer the additional expence occasioned by this emergency. Great objections was raised against this demand. The Rajah, however, consented to make the payment with a very ill grace, and discharged it with a worse. Another year, the same requisition was renewed; and, though known to be extremely rich, Cheit Sing affected to dispose of his plate and jewels, as an evidence how unable he was to comply with the imposition. Two battalions of sepoys were therefore quartered in his dominions, and their pay charged to his account, until he realized the expectations of his superiors. The third year's subsidy

ſidy was not diſcharged with more promptitude, and ſimilar means of coercion were adopted. And when one lack only had been produced, the Rajah wrote to the governor-general, with his own hand, ſtating the impoveriſhed ſtate of his treaſury and reſources, and praying a remiſſion of the remainder till another year, when he promiſed to pay it with the ſtipulated revenue. No anſwer was made to this humble petition for indulgence, but a freſh order was immediately preſented for a thouſand horſe. It could hardly be expected that ſuch a ſupply could be readily obtained, where a yearly ſubſidy of ſixty thouſand pounds had been extorted with ſo much difficulty. And though the Rajah, in his remonſtrance to Mr. Haſtings, aſſerts, that five hundred horſe, and as many barkundaſſes, were ready, and at his ſervice; we are, nevertheleſs, aſſured, in an authentic narrative of that tranſaction, that no more than half that number was promiſed, and not a ſingle horſe ever ſent. Thus was the Rajah's anxiety and jealouſies of his own ſafety awakened. He was treated with a ſuſpicion that ſuppreſſed his confidence, and with a rigour that tended unavoidably to relax his attachment. The iron hand of oppreſſion was ſtretched forth, and he found himſelf without the means either of ſatisfying or reſiſting its graſp. Overwhelmed with apprehenſion, it was natural to look out for ſuch a protection as might ſupply that which he ſuppoſed to be withdrawn, to try whether the neighbouring powers would not afford him an aſylum from the

the tempeſt that impended, or what reſource he might find among his countrymen againſt the machinations of implacable foreigners. A ſtriking coincidence took place, between his own experience and the general ideas then entertained of the Britiſh character. The name of Engliſhman was now regarded, in almoſt every part of India, with execration. In the very dominions of their allies, in Oude, in the circars, and in the Carnatic, they were moſt hated, only becauſe beſt known. Weary of the yoke that galled him, and incenſed by a repetition of inſult, it is not improbable that Cheit Sing might correſpond with the princes around him on the moſt likely means of extricating himſelf from his preſent embarraſſment, ſpeculate on terms of mutual ſupport, or agree on ſuch a plan of general concert with them as promiſed the moſt effectual protection to their reſpective rights; that he might even have written to the diſcontented Begums of Oude, or caballed with the diſaffected tributaries of the Engliſh. He has certainly been charged with having exhibited unequivocal ſymptoms of this ſeditious turn of mind in his own conduct, but which were obvious in a ſtill higher degree in the behaviour of his officers and his people. Theſe facts, however, are alledged without any ſpecification of dates, names, or circumſtances; nor even included in the written complaints, which were ſtated againſt, and ſent to him on the ſpot. Indeed, the expences of the war had become ſo enormous, and the means of ſtill carrying it on had

 drained

drained the treasury to such a degree, that new sources of supply were become a matter of great and pressing importunity. The wealth and impotence of the Rajah might now, therefore, point him out as the proper and immediate object for answering the public exigence.

During this state of affairs in the zemindary of Benares, the governor-general went to visit it in person upon the 7th of Juy [1781]. He wished, at the same time, to restore harmony in the provinces of Oude, and to procure as much money as possible. Colonel Muir was then negociating a peace with Sindia, and Mr. Hastings naturally expected that his approach might expedite the business. The disappointment of aid from the Rajah, even in a crisis of the greatest public distress and danger, did not affect him so much as those instances of contumacy and disobedience, which he considered as proofs of a deliberate intention to subvert the Company's authority, and to erect his own independency on its ruins. He adopted, at the same time, the report, that the Rajah inherited immense wealth from his father Balwant Sing, which was deposited in the two strong forts of Lutteespore and Bedjeygur, and annually augmented; that his military establishment and stores were preserved on the most respectable footing; that his strong holds were numerous, in good condition, and well supplied; that he maintained an intercourse with such powers, as either were, or might become enemies to the company; and that he was prepared

prepared for open revolt, and waited only for a favourable opportunity of declaring it. By his agents and emiſſaries in Calcutta he was alſo thought to have taken an active and decided part againſt the governor-general, in thoſe conteſts which had long prevailed between him and his colleagues is office. To this ſtrenuous oppoſition to the cenſures incurred at home, by his delinquencies abroad, and to the conſtant and general expectation in India, that he muſt have been recalled from the ſervice of the Company, the governor-general roundly charged the whole of the Rajah's miſconduct. This was probably the crime which he deemed the leaſt pardonable, for which he was to be puniſhed, as an example which juſtice and policy required; which was to render his guilt the means of relief to the Company, and in conſequence of which a penalty was to be exacted from him, which he was well able to bear, and at the expence of a fund deſtined by him for purpoſes of the moſt dangerous tendency to the Britiſh intereſt in theſe parts.

The governor-general's progreſs up the Ganges laſted near ſix weeks. The Rajah was much alarmed by this unexpected journey. He ſhrewdly ſuſpected the governor was not cordially his friend. His profligate relation Ouſſaun Sing had for ſome time been much careſſed at Calcutta. And he now attended in the governor-general's train. This man, who had once been the boſom friend and chief miniſter of the Rajah, had, by mal-adminiſtation, forfeited

forfeited the esteem of his master, and squandered his substance by such an unprincipled life, that he was at length banished the country. He had soon returned, however, at the head of a most profligate banditti, who became so numerous and formidable, that he was at length only expelled by a reinforcement of the Company's forces. The Rajah could not but regard a man who had thus abused his confidence, defied his power, and outraged the tranquillity of his government, as his mortal enemy. And what could he expect from the visit of a superior who suffered his suite to be disgraced by so abandoned a character! The Rajah, however, with a great train of the principal people of his country, met the governor-general at Buxar, on the borders of Benares. The opinion, that this splendid retinue had been collected with an hostile intention, has been refuted by the event. In consequence of this meeting, a second took place next morning: A conversation occurred, which the two parties have related differently. The governor-general delivered his recollection of what happened with much caution, disclaimed all pretentions to correctness; and, because it made no part of his plan, he considered it as a contingency of no consequence. He stated, however, that Cheit Sing expressed the greatest concern for the displeasure he had incurred, and such parts of his conduct as had given offence, that he declared the zemindary, and all he possessed, was at the disposal of the Company; that the presence of Oussaun Sing filled him

him with the moſt diſtreſſing apprehenſions; and that from an uncommon agitation of mind, or to impreſs a ſtrong opinion of his ſincerity, he accompanied his words with the ſingular action of laying his turban in Mr. Haſtings' lap. In reply, the governor-general diſclaimed the idea of deſcending to become a party in the family altercation of the Rajah, but avowed the higheſt diſpleaſure, in explicit and peremptory terms. He added, that he had already been deceived by his oaths and proteſtations, and ſhould not ſuffer his purpoſe to be changed, or his duty to be overruled, by any verbal conceſſions whatever. But in the Rajah's manifeſto the governor-general's overtures are mentioned as peculiarly harſh and exorbitant. Having diſcuſſed the ſubject of the tribute, his profeſſion of attachment and fidelity to the Company, and his readineſs to comply with their deſires in every thing within his power, no leſs a ſum than a crore of rupees, or about one million two hundred thouſand pounds ſterling, was demanded as the price of forgiveneſs and future favour. The ſurrender of Bedjeygur, which he calls "his family reſidence, the depoſit of his "women and of his honour," was at the ſame time required. To the firſt of theſe demands he pleaded abſolute inability; in reply to the ſecond he ſaid, for what he had done he ſhould be puniſhed by the forfeiture of his domeſtic ſanctuary, and branded with the infamy of having relinquiſhed

the

the ſacred depoſit of his family and perſonal honour.

When they arrived at Benares, on the 14th of Auguſt, the Rajah was forbid to wait on the governor-general, as he had intended, that evening, and deſired to defer his future viſits until permiſſion was obtained, as ſome matters were previouſly to be ſettled. Next day Mr. Markham, the reſident at Benares, was diſpatched by the governor-general, with a paper, in which the ſeveral charges againſt him were ſtated, and an immediate anſwer required. Had he wiſhed to irritate the Rajah by invective, rather than to gain him to his purpoſe by conciliating language and an affable deportment, the means he purſued could not have been more properly ſelected. This extorted from the Rajah an ample vindication of his conduct. The non-payment of the extraordinary ſubſidy he attributes to circumſtances which he could not prevent or elude; that the failure of the remittance to the army was the fault of thoſe who were intruſted with the buſineſs; that the demands on him for cavalry were incapable of being literally fulfilled; that his communications on that ſubject had been neglected or diſcredited; that he had announced to the reſident his readineſs to detach, for the ſervice of the Company, five hundred horſe, and as many militia, or irregular troops; that he had written an account of theſe forces to the governor-general, who he daily expected would have ſent ſome direction for their diſpoſal; that no anſwer

ſwer was returned to this letter any more than to the former; and that Mr. Markham and he repeatedly expreſſed their mutual ſurpriſe at this ſilence. He denies that any agents or emiſſaries were ever ſent to Calcutta, or that any of his people were there, except a few whom he named, and who were openly employed on public buſineſs, with the governor himſelf. Theſe, and other imputations of a ſimilar nature, he avows to be the calumnies of his enemies, who were bent on his ruin; but he congratulated himſelf, that the governor-general would now have an opportunity of detecting the falſehood on the ſpot. That robberies and murders were committed in his country with impunity, was an allegation equally unfounded. He was careful to puniſh every ſuch crime, and no culprit ever could elude juſtice by other means than abandoning the country.

This anſwer, though couched in language the moſt humble and ſubmiſſive, was conſidered by the governor-general as an inſult of the higheſt and moſt offenſive kind, not ſo much a vindication of the Rajah, as a recrimination on himſelf; and rather a letter of defiance, than a repreſentation which betrayed any ſenſe of miſconduct, or facilitated the return of friendſhip. He admits that ſome of the Rajah's letters might not have been anſwered; but adds, in a tone of ſuperlative ſtatelineſs, that it was the Rajah's duty to obey the poſitive and repeated orders which he had received, and "not "to waſte his time with letters of excuſe, to cavil "with

" with his anſwers for evaſion, or with his ſilence " for delays." Moderation in power was not then the characteriſtic virtue of the ſupreme government. And much delicacy was not to be expected in the exerciſe of a delegated authority, by the agent of Britiſh merchants to the prince of Benares.

The governor-general deemed it impolitic, either to leave him in the full exerciſe of powers, which he had thus obviouſly abuſed, and which he apprehended might ſtill be employed to the moſt dangerous purpoſes, or to deveſt him entirely of the zemindary, though juſtifiable on the grounds he had ſtated, as this might have appeared too ſevere, and rendered the company's government obnoxious to cenſure. By laying the perſon of the Rajah under arreſt, he expected to avoid both extremes. The Rajah's palace was ſituated on the banks of the Ganges, on the ſame ſide with the city of Benares, and about two miles diſtant. Mr. Markham was inſtructed to proceed early in the morning, with only his accuſtomed guard, that it might appear no more than a common viſit, and there to put him under arreſt, and require his immediate ſubmiſſion, in the governor-general's name, and to keep him in cuſtody until he received further orders. Two company's of ſepoys from Major Popham's detachment were ordered to follow and ſupport the reſident in the execution of this delicate ſervice.

The Rajah made no reſiſtance, but reſigned himſelf to his fate, with perfect ſubmiſſion to the

reſident'

resident's authority. He was ready to obey whatever the governor-general should prescribe. His entire zemindary, his forts, and his treasure, were at his service, and even his life if demanded. But he felt the ignomy to which he was exposed by this public disgrace. He trusted his youth and inexperience would be some appology for such of his errors as had given most offence. He begged the resident would make a just representation of his obedience, and plead for him, that, in consideration of his father's name, he might obtain his freedom on proving the sincerity of his offers. These submissions he repeated in a letter to the govenor-general, which he concluded by saying, "What-" ever may be your pleasure, do it with your own" hands. I am your slave. What occasion can" there be for a guard?"

Other letters, replete with the same despondency, soon followed Mr. Markham. The governor-general's feelings, regulated as they were by the nicest policy, for the first time were so far touched by the misfortunes of the Rajah, that he thought it necessary to alleviate his apprehensions, by a short note, informing him, that all particulars should be explained in the afternoon, and desiring him to let his mind be at rest, and not to conceive any terror or dismay.

The Rajah had been early cautioned against suffering his people to behave in an unquiet or disorderly manner, as any attempt to rescue him would inevitably precipitate his ruin. The resident

dent left him in the custody of Lieutenant Stalker, who commanded his own guard, and of the Lieutenants Scot and Sims, who led the two grenadier companies of sepoys. These officers were instructed to disarm all his servants, but to allow him any eight or ten domestics whom he might prefer, for the attendance of his person. These were to be shewn to the sepoys, that no deception might be practicable. Nor was the Rajah to be refused any request consistent with the security of his person. Fortunately for Markham, the preparation of his instructions considerably delayed his return to the palace. On the opposite side of the river, and at no great distance, was situated Ramnagur, the common residence of the family. It was a pile of building which answered the double purpose of a palace and a fortress. A few additional out-works had been made to it of late years, and by degrees a very populous and compact town surrounded it. A standing garrison was kept in this place after the manner of all eastern princes. The residence of the court had produced the town and occasioned the garrison, and the inhabitants were violently attached to the prince, from the mildness of his manners, and the lenity of his government. Before Markham could set out, intelligence was received, that large bodies of armed men had crossed the river from Ramnagur, and proceeded directly to the palace where the prince was in custody. Our sepoys were in the square which surrounded the Rajah's apartments, but had, by by ſome unaccountable inadvertence, left their ammunition behind. This circumſtance was no ſooner known to Major Popham, than he diſpatched another company to reinforce the two former, and to ſupply them with ammunition. But all the avenues of the palace were ſo crowded and choked up by multitudes and armed men, determined to prevent acceſs, that the attempt was immediately relinquiſhed as impracticable. The appearance of this party probably inflamed the populace, as the attack of the grenadiers in the ſquare certainly commenced on their arrival. Theſe men, deſtitute of their uſual means of defence, were an eaſy prey to ſuperior numbers, who in an inſtant cut moſt of the party to pieces. Eighty-two were killed on the ſpot, and ninety-two ſo deſperately wounded, that the condition of the living was much leſs enviable than that of the dead. The three Britiſh officers, who were ſaid to have made a moſt vigorous reſiſtance, were found mangled in the moſt ſhocking manner, and lying near each other.

The Rajah naturally expected that his life would be made to pay for the temerity of his people. In the midſt of the tumult, and overwhelmed by the terrors of a ſcene ſo little expected, he was hurried away, however, by his attendants and friends, through a wicket on the garden ſide, which led to the river, where, from the ſteepneſs of the bank, he was let down into a boat by a number of turbans tied together, and conveyed to the other ſide. The authors of his reſcue ſeem to have acted only from impulse, without system or concert. They had no other object than his mere escape, and followed him in that tumultuous confusion which generally discriminates a mob under the direction of no superior. The additional company of sepoys, who had been prevented entering, now pushed their way as the crowds decreased. Even then so smart a scuffle ensued, that Birrel, who commanded them, had thirty of his men killed or wounded. Major Popham, who had been encamped about two miles distant, soon after arrived at the head of his detachment, and could only lament a catastrophe which it was not in his power either to alleviate or revenge.

The whole affray is attributed by Cheit Sing to the brutality of a servant belonging to the resident, who, being formerly in his service, was dismissed with disgrace, and, owing the prince a grudge, took this opportunity of treating him insolently. His people, enraged by the temerity of so contemptible a wretch, and the degradation of a chief whom they loved and adored, resented the outrage, which however seems to have originated and subsided with the feelings or paroxysm of the moment. The governor-general was lodged in a villa adjoining to the suburbs of Benares. The whole of his guard did not exceed fifty or sixty sepoys. Had the Rajah been seriously determined on resisting the Company's authority from the beginning, the governor-general might have been immediately and easily dispatched. However defective

fective these people are presumed to be in military, political, or legislative science, they are allowed to be singularly artful. And, in fact, their schemes of treachery and assassination are for the most part so well contrived as generally to succeed. The supposition, that an insurrection was seriously intended, is consequently repugnant to, what has been always understood, the well known and established character of the natives. The governor-general seems indeed to have executed this romantic expedition with a rashness which most men betray, when the immediate gratification of some strong and prevalent passion is in view. In a place so full of inhabitants, and where the native sovereign is an object of universal attachment and veneration, it was not likely all this violence should be done without popular commotion, or that his name or situation alone would carry, into a country six hundred miles from the seat of government, all its authority and effect, without such an army as might enforce his measures.

The Rajah, like all weak minds under the influence of terror and surprise, conceived no better means of safety than in distance from the scene of danger. Trusting the recovery of that fortune, which was already lost, to time and contingency, he fled from Ramnagur in the middle of the same night. Such effects as could be conveniently moved, such troops as were assembled, and such of his family as were present, he carried with him. The palace was left in the custody of its own small stationary garrison. He took immediate refuge in

 Lutteefpore,

Lutteefpore, a place of great ftrength. Mean while the governor-general appointed Ouffaun Sing to the adminiftration of the revenues, and proclaimed the appointment through the city of Benares, at the fame time that meffengers were difpatched to announce this event in every part of the country. From the obvious temper of the people, and the nature of the arrangements which now became neceffary, the troops were ordered from all their contiguous ftations, without delay, to Benares. It was fortunate fuch a precaution had been taken; for, on the fecond day after the Rajah's flight, a chofen warrior and confidential chief of the family arrived, with a body of troops, to protect Ramnagur. An emergency fo perfectly unexpected made it neceffary, by all poffible means, to expedite the arrival of the forces. Orders were immediately difpatched for that purpofe, and Captain Mayaffre, who had the command, was directed to avoid every thing like hoftility, and to halt in a fecure fituation at fome diftance, that the troops might be kept collected and ready, until Major Popham had taken his meafures and the command. The officer however, who led on the party, marched directly forward, regardlefs of the remonftrances made by thofe who acted under him, and defpifing an enemy of which he had no knowledge. Here followed a fecond maffacre, ftill more dreadful than the firft. They were foon involved in narrow ftreets and winding lanes, fired upon from all directions, and flaughtered in heaps, by a fevere

and

and invifible enemy. Captain Doxat, who led the attack, inftantly fell, with twenty-three of his men. The detachment under the conduct of Captain Blair, who followed, were not much longer in action, when fifty-feven men were killed, and nearly as many wounded. Not lefs than a hundred and feven men were loft, and nearly as many grievoufly mangled, by this temerity. Captain Mayaffre did not furvive the cataftrophe. The Rajah's people were naturally elated by thefe fucceffes. Nor was the governor-general intimidated. The refources of his genius have in general been equal to the obftacles with which he grappled. Difpatches were prepared, and fent in multiplied copies to all the military ftations within reach, for immediate fuccour to the treafury of Oude for money, and to the camp of Chunar, for all the troops that could be fpared. But the country, by this time, was every where hoftile, and in arms againft the Englifh. No communication could take place; and of the numerous meffengers occupied on this emergency, few reached their deftination.

The governor-general had taken up his refidence in Mahdoodafs's gardens, which were fituated in the heart of the fuburbs of Benares. This place confifted of many detached buildings within one large inclofure. The whole was alfo furrounded with houfes and trees, in fuch a manner as to intercept all outward profpect. Expofed by the nakednefs of the place, the want of a force adequate to its protection, the turbulence of its

 vicinity,

vicinity, and the apprehension of an assault from the proximity of an enemy, rapidly increasing; and rendered desperate, from the certainty that they could have no safety but in success; an immediate retreat was now perhaps the most eligible measure in their power. This they commenced in the evening, and accomplished without molestation by next morning, when they arrived with all their baggage and attendants at Chunar. The wounded sepoys were however left behind, in whose favour Mr. Hastings wrote to the Nabob Saadut Ally, requesting him that he would take them under his care and protection. But the humanity of the Mussulman had taught him to anticipate the governor's desire. The kindness of this generous stranger was extended to these unfortunate men the moment he knew of their condition. His feeling heart sympathized with their sufferings, at the same time that his judgment condemned the policy that produced them. He visited them in person, he supplied them with provisions, he gave them money, he ordered surgeons to attend them, and as soon as they could be removed he brought them to his own quarters. These interesting attentions were performed at a time when the Company's credit was considered, among the natives, as precarious; when the odium raised against its servants was prevalent and universal; when Hyder Ally triumphed in the Carnatic; and when the supreme government had become contemptible from gross violations of faith,

abortive

abortive ambition, and aſſumptions which it could not realize. In this good man, theſe wretched ſoldiers, though wounded, fighting againſt a cauſe in which he was much intereſted, and now in the cuſtody of their enemies, found a friend. Such are the offices of kindneſs, for which our countrymen have ſo generally ſtigmatized the Indians as barbarians!

Benaram Pundit, the Berar Vakeel, on the very evening of the retreat, had come to viſit the governor-general. All was in diſorder and confuſion when he entered the gardens. He proceeded however with the crowd, and, notwithſtanding extreme corpulence and great age, was diſcovered marching on foot, in company with his brother, and without a ſingle attendant. They continued at Chunar until the governor-general was enabled to return to Benares. He even offered, without application, all the ready money he poſſeſſed, which was a lack of rupees in ſilver, at a time when the governor-general was exceedingly diſtreſſed.

All this while the Rajah Cheit Sing was inceſſant in his application for an amicable adjuſtment of paſt differences. He complained of the extremities to which he was driven, and perſiſted in proteſting his abſolute incapacity to reſtrain the fury of his people. The very morning after the affair at Ramnagur, in which ſo many of our troops were deſtroyed, propoſals for an accommodation were offered. But Mr. Haſtings ſeems to have obſtinately adhered to one inflexible plan of unqualified ſeverity. He would not even con-

 deſcend

descendto anſwer theRajah's letters, ſome of which procured ſo little attention, that he neither recollects their dates, nor the time of their delivery. A ſupercilious conſciouſneſs of ſuperioty, a haughty diſtance, or an ominous reſerve, involved the whole of theſe violent tranſactions into ſuch perplexity and obſcurity, as are not accountable on the common principles of human conduct. His confident and treaſurer, Cantoo Bauboo, was however permitted to confer on the ſtate of affairs with Cheit Sing's Vakeel, or envoy, Mirza Abdoola Beg. It is not very eaſy to aſſign any reaſon whatever for this permiſſion, as the conference produced no effect, though the Rajah not only exculpated himſelf from the outrages which had been committed at the palace, imputing the whole to the reſident's ſervant, but made an abſolute ſurrender of all he had, and offered to depend entirely on the governor's generoſity, for every indulgence to which he might think him entitled. Cheit Sing being reduced to the neceſſity of taking up arms in his own defence, it was an obvious ſtep, in the progreſs of the tragedy, firſt to pronounce him a rebel, and then to proſcribe him as an object unworthy of all further protection, and with whom it was no longer competent for the ſtate to treat.

It was about this time that the governor-general experienced new embarraſſment from the Vizier's determination of viſiting him at Chunar. The dominions of Oude at this moment were in a ſtate of almoſt actual rebellion. The oppreſſions which they

they ſuffered from the influence of the Company's ſervants were become altogether intolerable. Indeed, the contagion had ſpread through all the neighbouring countries, but eſpecially in ſuch places as were under the immediate influence of the Begums. Theſe princeſſes, who reſided at Fyzabad, on the river Dewa, the ſecond capital of the Vizier's dominions, were ſaid openly to eſpouſe the cauſe of Cheit Sing, and even to permit their own officers to join in attacking the Engliſh. The whole provinces, ſtretching towards the mountains, were up in arms, and ready to riſk every thing for expelling the Engliſh. Colonel Hannay, with two battalions of regular ſepoys, was ſtationed in theſe parts. And ſuch was the popular indignation and reſentment againſt the Engliſh intereſt, that he was repeatedly attacked, ſurrounded, and many of his troops cut to pieces; that the zemindars inſtigated their dependents to outrage; and that it was with the greateſt difficulty Major Hannay was enabled to make his eſcape. In the midſt of theſe diſturbances, and while the neareſt and moſt diſtant diſtricts of his territories were embroiled, Aſſoph ul Dowlah came to pay his reſpects to the governor-general. It was difficult to treat a perſon of ſuch diſtinction as a friend, at the ſame time that he was ſuſpected for an enemy. And the darkeſt deſigns had been inſinuated to the governor-general as the efficient cauſe of this journey. It was even propoſed, that the perſon of the former ſhould be eſcorted, during the interview,

terview, by ſuch a guard as might operate as a ſufficient check againſt all the machinations of the latter. The preſence of the Vizier indeed would bring a freſh acceſſion of credit to the deſperate ſituation of the Company's affairs in the revolted provinces. His troops, though a rabble, might alſo tend to keep the country in awe, and divert the enemy's attention and operations. But the governor-general diſliked the advantage which the Nabob might derive from that circumſtance. Nor did he wiſh for any other aſſiſtance than the Company's troops, to ſuppreſs a rebellion immediately againſt their own authority.

It was under theſe apprehenſions that Governor Haſtings endeavoured, by letter, to diſſuade the Nabob from the viſit he intended, and that he urged his return to his own capital, promiſing to wait upon his Excellency there, as ſoon as the troubled ſtate of Benares permitted. The Nabob, however, perſiſted in his reſolution of demonſtrating his zeal and attachment. He proſecuted his journey with an expedition proportionate to the delicacy of Mr. Haſtings in diſſuading him from it. Their meeting was apparently agreeable to both, and the greateſt cordiality ſubſiſted between them during the whole time it laſted.

The ſpirit of inſurrection, which now raged ſo fiercely in the province of Benares, effected all the frontier countries under the Company's government, that were ſituated in the neighbourhood. Not only one half of the kingdom of Oude ſtruggled

gled to ſuppreſs the Engliſh influence, but various diſtricts in Bahar were alſo very ſeriouſly embroiled. Men were every where openly levied for the ſervice of the inſurgents. The Sarum circar, one of the largeſt diviſions of that province, was powerfully invaded and laid deſolate by Hutteh Shaw, a chief of conſiderable conſequence in theſe parts, and who was ſupported by Cheit Sing. Indeed, the whole functions of government were for the preſent ſuſpended. The ſcramble for property, and even exiſtence, became general. Anarchy eſtabliſhed all her horrors on a momentary annihilation of order. In ſuch a ſcene of hoſtility, all intelligence from the adjacent countries was cut off; and the governor-general, ſhut up in the fort of Chunar, knew but little either what were the effects of his orders, the ſituation of the forces, or the fate of his meſſengers.

Cheit Sing, in the mean time, delineated his ſituation to the ſurrounding princes, in a manifeſto, which for juſtneſs of conception and ſimplicity of language would not have diſgraced the page of a Livy. After narrating his father's conduct and his own; regretting, in the bittereſt terms, their unnatural partialities for ſtrangers, who had thus requited their kindneſs with ingratitude and treachery; and urging them to unite as in a common cauſe, and expel or exirpate thoſe uſurpers, whom no acquiſitions could ſatisfy or treaties bind; he gives a contraſt of the country, under his authority, and that of the Company. It is a picture which betrays

betrays the hand of a maſter, " Look" ſays, he " to " my deſtricts, look to theirs. The different aſpects " they exhibit mark the limits of them more than " the boundaries preſcribed by nature or art. " My fields are cultivated, my towns and villages " full of inhabitants, my country is a garden, and " my ſubjects are happy. The principal merchants " in India, from the ſecurity of my government, " reſort to my capital, and make it their reſi- " dence. It is the bank of India, and contains " the treaſures of the Marattos, the Jaits, the " Saiks, the native and the European nations. It is " here the orphan and the widow depoſit their all, " and find a certain aſylum from avarice and ra- " pacity. The traveller and the ſtranger, from " one end of my country to the other, lay down " their burthens and ſleep in ſecurity. In the Com- " pany's provinces, famine and miſery ſtalk hand " in hand through uncultivated fields and deſerted " villages. There you meet only the aged and " infirm, who are unable to flee, or robbers pre- " pared to ſeize or kill! When Engliſhmen paſſed " through my country, every kindneſs was ſhewn " them, and all their wants ſupplied. The very " baggage was taken from the backs of their cool- " lies, and carried for them from village to village. " My officers every where attended, to accom- " modate them with neceſſaries and carriage at " my expence, and perform all their orders as " they were my own. Aſk my people, if any " of them met with ſuch treatment in the countries

" under

" under the Company's management. Were they
" not almoſt continually robbed, and in danger of
" their lives?"

The head quarters was now at Chunar, a fort ſituated on the ſouth ſhore of the Ganges. The enemy's chief ſtrength was encamped at Pateetah, ſeven miles to the ſouthward, in the direct way to the paſs Suckroot, and the ſtrong hold of Lutteefpore. Popham's detachment was poſted about a mile from town, between the fort and the enemy.

Lieutenant Polhill, who arrived on the 27th of Auguſt, with ſix companies of ſepoys from the Nabob Vizier's body guard, encamped on the other ſide of the river, and had a ſkirmiſh with a ſtrong party of the enemy, at Seeker, a town and fort which lay within ſight of Chunar. Polhill prevailed, and a large quantity of grain, much wanted by our forces at that time, fell into their hands. Nor were the detachment under Blair, whom Popham ſent to ſurpriſe the camp at Pateetah, leſs ſucceſsful, though their victory was dearly earned. The enemy's camp was in fact abandoned, but they were drawn up, and waiting the attack a mile beyond it, in a manner moſt determined, and in an order that was not expected: The ſepoys under the command of Blair, doubly fortified as they were by the mechaniſm of diſcipline, and their confidence in European officers, met with a reception ſo vigorous and deſperate, that they were inſtantly broke and thrown into confuſion. The ſpirited attack of lieutenants Fallon and Birrel, at the head of two companies of grenadiers, upon the

the enemy's cannon, was what ſaved the detachment, and turned the fortune of the day. On our ſide, however, one fourth of the whole were killed and wounded. It was at the ſame time an advantage, and contributed to reſtore that credit and ſpirit which our army had in ſome degree loſt by the late diſaſter at Ramnagur.

About a week after this action, Major Crabbe appeared on the ſhore oppoſite to Chunar, with two regiments of ſepoys, two companies of European infantry, and thirty European artillery men, four ſix-pounders, one howitz, tumbrils, ammunition, draft and carriage cattle, and every other proviſion neceſſary for immediate ſervice. This detachment had been ſent by Colonel Morgan, to whom the governor-general had diſpatched ſeveral expreſſes for this purpoſe, but which Morgan's zeal had anticipated. For the greater expedition, they had proceeded by water down the Ganges, though much retarded on their courſe to Illahabad by ſtrong adverſe winds. Here the major diſembarked both men and ſtores, and proceeded the reſt of the way by land.

It was on the following day [the 11th of September] that Aſſoph ul Dowlah, Nabob Vizier of Oude, arrived and took his ſtation on the oppoſite ſhore. The communication between him and Mr. Haſtings was immediately opened, and ſubſiſted for ſome time with all the circumſtances of ſuperiority on the one ſide, and degradation on the other, which uſually diſtinguiſh the intercourſe of a chief a chief and his vaſſal. Unfortunately, the influence which the governor-general poſſeſſed in the councils of this puſillanimous prince was followed by a ſeries of the moſt dreadful conſequences to ſome of his neareſt relations.

Aſſoph ul Dowlah had taken and continued in his pay a certain number of our regular troops, intruſted to the Britiſh reſident at his court the entire management of all his affairs, foreign and domeſtic, and gradually become, eſpecially in the adminiſtration of his revenues, both in ſubſtance and effect, as well as in general repute and eſtimation, a mere tributary of the Company. He was, in fact, ſo materially and abſolutely under the control of their ſervants, that, in the opinion of the native powers, the honour of Great Britain ſtood pledged for every act of his government. His mother and grand-mother were left by his father, the ſon of the one and huſband of the other, in truſt of certain treaſures in money, ſome valuable moveables, and ſeveral landed eſtates, for ſupporting their own dignity, and the honourable maintenance of two thouſand perſons—his women, a numerous offspring and their dependents. The Nabob, on finding himſelf in deep arrears to his new maſters, was inſtigated by the creatures, in whoſe cuſtody they had placed him, to extort, under a variety of pretexts, ſeveral large ſums from his aged parents, amounting in all to ſix hundred and thirty thouſand pounds. They would not, however, pay the laſt of theſe ſums, but on cer-

tain

tain terms. To ſecure the ſcanty remains of what had been ſolemnly bequeathed to them by the will of the late Vizier, that his ſon, on no account whatever, ſhould moleſt them by any further claims, and well knowing whence all his former exactions and ſeverities originated, they demanded that this family compact ſhould be guaranteed by the governor and council-general. A treaty of this kind, involving theſe conditions, was accordingly executed with every poſſible formality, between the Nabob and his parents, and guaranteed by the Britiſh reſident at Oude, under the authority, and with the expreſs conſent of the ſupreme government.

Notwithſtanding a covenant thus ſolemnly ratified, the ſacred inheritance of theſe venerable perſonages was ultimately alienated to gratify the rapacity of our countrymen. It was at Chunar, and during this viſit of the Nabob to Mr. Haſtings, that a ſecret treaty took place between them, which produced all thoſe infamous tranſactions, to which the ſubſequent diſhonours of the royal family of Oude were owing. In this myſterious negociation, the Nabob was authoriſed and ſtimulated to confiſcate, for his own convenience, the patrimonial inheritance of his kindred, the very lands allotted for the ſubſiſtence of his parents. The only equivalent allowed the perſons, thus robbed of their all, was a penſion, amounting only to the net rent of their reſpective property. Nor did even this indulgence extend beyond the few for whom the

the Company were bound in the late treaty. No ſecurity was ſtipulated for the payment of the penſions, nor any compenſation provided for thoſe who had none. The miſerable pretext for this wanton violation of faith and duty was a right in the Nabob, which, according to the Mahommedan law, gave him a title, as it was alledged, to what he thus engaged to ſeize by force. A claim which, however equivocal, the governor-general eſtabliſhed, in direct defiance to the obligation to which the Nabob had ſo recently acceded and acted upon, without either ſubmitting the matter to the conſideration of the board, or appriſing the parties, thus perſonally injured, that they might have recourſe to whatever mode of redreſs their helpleſs ſituation would permit. A Britiſh magiſtrate even proſtituted the ſacred commiſſion of his Britannic Majeſty, by ſtooping at this very moment to the baſe employment of an informer, in collecting a body of hear-ſay evidence and vague report, in an exra-judicial capacity, for the purpoſe of covering the cruelties that were preparing as implements of extortion, by an attempt to convert two aged women of engaging in a plot for the depoſition of their ſon and ſovereign, and the extirpation of the Engliſh nation.

Some feeble ſtruggles of nature in the breaſt of the Vizier were the only obſtacles which oppoſed the execution of this inhuman project. But the governor-general was not to be diverted from a purſuit thus advantageous, by the ſqueamiſh remon-

 ſtrances

ſtrances of unavailing ſenſibility. The relenting heart of a ſon, againſt involving the authors of his being in immediate want, was not a conſideration to be put in competition with the gratification of revenge, the requiſitions of avarice, or the ſavage propenſities of a deſpot. The Nabob propoſed to ſeize the treaſures of his mother, rather than be acceſſary to an alienation of what he had ſo lately and ſolemnly engaged to preſerve. This alternative was readily adopted, though it did not afterwards even prevent the reſumption of thoſe lands, in lieu of which it was offered. The outrages, perpetrated in accompliſhing theſe nefarious objects, implicated ſuch an exceſs of cruelty, as never has been ſurpaſſed ſince the days of Claudius Nero. The confidential ſervants or miniſters of theſe illuſtrious females were ſeized, impriſoned, and treated like common felons. They remained in fetters for near twelve months, and owed their releaſe at laſt to the humanity of Mr. Briſtow. It fared no better with the women of the Zenana, though they had been left to Mr. Haſtings' ſpecial protection by the dying requeſt of the late Vizier. They were ſhut up in the palace of Fyzabad, and guarded by a number of regular ſepoys, under the command of an Engliſh officer. After undergoing incredible hardſhips and inſults, the ſubſidy appropropriated for their ſubſiſtence was diminiſhed. They ſoon became in want of common neceſſaries. Preſſed by hunger and deſpair, they baffled the aſſiduity of their guards, abandoned their apartments,

and

and, in a condition the most abject and degrading to the sex in that country, burst into the market place. They were however instantly remanded to the Haram, and the royal offspring of Sujah ul Dowlah, the second prince in the empire of Indostan, were actually beat with bludgeons by a relentless soldiery in the service of the East India Company. Nor will it be easy to account for the exquisite distress to which two thousand persons were thus reduced, except on the shocking supposition, that a serious design had been somewhere formed of starving them to death.

Four regiments and one battalion of sepoys, three European companies, one of grenadiers, one light infantry, one French rangers, six companies of the Nabob's body guards, and thirty artillery-men, were now assembled under the command of Major Popham. Daily reinforcements were pouring in from every quarter, and a force was immediately mustered, more than equal to any army which the enemy could bring against them. The Rajah's troops, regular and irregular, did not much exceed seven thousand effective men. A prodigious rabble, hastily assembled by various chiefs in the neighbourhood, increased the number, but added little to the strength of this unwieldy body. The Rajah himself seems to have been totally unqualified for war. His officers were equally destitute of a military education, his soldiers were without discipline, and his councils were pusillanimous and undecisive.

 He

He ſeemed ſenſible, however, that he had to contend with troops greatly ſuperior to his own, and for that reaſon was inclined to negociate rather than to fight. And, notwithſtanding all his former attempts had utterly proved abortive, he renewed his application to the governor-general, whom he importuned by variety of letters, written in a ſtile peculiarly abject. But he was ſtill repulſed with an inſolence, in proportion as he diſcovered the mortification which it was natural to feel in that ſtate of degradation to which he was reduced. Mr. Barnet and Cantoo Baboo, his priſoners, interceded for him, though without effect. Many of his letters were it ſeems loſt or deſtroyed; they were ſaid to be all ſubſtantially the ſame, and only replete with acknowledgments of ſubmiſſion, proteſtations of innocence, and ſtrong profeſſions of ſincerity for reconcilement. He declared in very ſolemn terms that he had no ſhare in the maſſacre at the palace; that he had in no inſtance been the aggreſſor; that all his ſufferings were on his part unmerited; and that he was ſtill ready to prove his allegations; to renew, to demonſtrate, and to preſerve his allegiance. He made no ſcruple at the ſame time of avowing the numerous and powerful reſources on which he placed his laſt dependence. Earneſt as he evidently was in this critical correſpondence, the governor-general perſevered in that contumelious ſilence, which ſo habitually characterizes the arrogance of the ſtrong in their intercourſe with the weak. He was ſolici-

solicitous only to make the Rajah sensible of their different situations; that he had assumed a language which in his circumstances was rather presumptuous than conciliating; and that he did not yet appear sufficiently conscious of their present inequality.

Hastings now found himself in a capacity to accomplish every object he had in view. The troops, from various success in several skirmishes which had lately happened, and the reinforcements which were incessantly increasing their number, were in high spirits. The officers were all of tried bravery and skill in their profession. The enemy were contemptible. The only impediments which seemed insuperable, were the strong places, which in general were still in the enemy's possession. Ramnagur was however suprised by a stratagem, conceived and carried into execution by the treachery and dexterity of a native. This was at one and the same time to reduce Pateetah, and secure the pass of Suckroot. The enterprize at both places was equally successful. The Rajah found himself, notwithstanding the strength of the fort of Lutteefpore, where he was, involved in circumstances of the most imminent personal danger. The pass of Suckroot was barricaded in his rear, while Popham, at the head of a powerful body of forces, closed him in front. Thus beset, his only safety depended upon flight; but in what road or passage could he escape the vigilance of an enemy who had already penetrated the inmost recesses of the mountains! Encouraged however by a few of his most faithful and intrepid adherents, he had the good fortune to elude his purſuers, and, by a circuitous ſweep over a variety of hills and ſwamps, he recovered the road ſome miles beyond Suckroot. He then made his way to Bedjeygur, with all the caution and expedition in his power. His misfortunes, brought in this manner to a criſis, extinguiſhed in one moment all that rage for inſurrection, which the commencement of his ſufferings had occaſioned and excited. The unwieldy multitude, after pillaging the defenceleſs inhabitants of Lutteefpore, diſperſed every man to his own home. The conteſt was at an end. Further exertions were deemed no longer neceſſary than other booty and more advantages were expected. To men in a ſtate of vaſſalage, and acting only from intereſt, a change of maſters can be of little importance.

In conſequence of theſe events, the country immediately reſumed its former tranquillity. The farmers, the ryots, the manufacturers, and the mechanics, returned from war and plunder to the peaceful purſuits of humble induſtry. Within a few hours the aſpect of the ſcene in the towns, the villages, and the fields, was totally changed. The peaſantry, inſtead of flocking together in groups, plotting enterprizes of revenge, or exerciſing the implements of deſtruction, were every where diſperſed, and re-engaged by their ſeveral occupations. Led on by no chief of ſyſtem or conduct, and diſappointed by his cataſtrophe, who of all others they preferred, no object ſufficiently gene-

ral,

ral, important, or interesting, remained to stimulate, combine, or direct their efforts. Thus abandoned by the destiny of the unfortunate prince, in whose behalf they abruptly flew to arms, they now as abruptly threw them down, and with one consent suddenly dissolved, just as an arch tumbles when the key-stone is removed, or a machine falls to pieces when the spring that actuates it is destroyed. To cherish these welcome symptoms of reviving loyalty and submission, the governor-general issued a proclamation, offering the most liberal indemnity to all who should tender an immediate obedience to the Company's authority. The only exceptions to the benefit of this general pardon were the Rajah, Sujan Sing his brother, and Gosse Gunge, a town in which two soldiers had been barbarously murdered during the troubles.

The Vizier Nabob having come to a final understanding, concerning what the governor-general meant his future conduct to the princesses his mother and grand-mother should be, returned to his own country, where the spirit of insurrection continued to rage with unabating violence. The natives, galled by the two-fold servitude to which they were necessarily subjected, from the double government or tyranny under which they groaned, relinquishing their characteristic patience and timidity, and provoked by an incessant repetition of fresh insult, were every where in a state of resistence and despair. The swarms of revenue officers who fastened on every district in Oude, with the

 avidity

avidity of famine, and the cruelty of our troops, who like the peſtilence ſpread havock and deſtruction wherever they were ſtationary, had by this time reduced the moſt flouriſhing provinces in India to a deſert. In every village the buſineſs of exaction, at the point of the dagger, had been daily carried on for years. It had begun with the ryot, the petty earnings of whoſe indefatigable toil were openly violated with impunity. It alienated the ſtores of the wealthy, and the heritage of the great. It reſpected not the privileges of religion, the diſtinctions of ſex, or the preſcriptions of rank. The preſent meaſures of the Durbar were even in avowed defiance to the will of a prince whoſe memory the whole kingdom of Oude ſtill regarded with the ſincereſt reverence. They ſaw the ſon and ſucceſſor of Sujah ul Dowlah, ſunk into a mere inſtrument of oppreſſion againſt his own parents and kindred, in the hands of foreigners. And their exertions were directed rather againſt that authority which overwhelmed him than his own. It was now, however, impoſſible to extricate him from the control of a power ſo greatly his ſuperior; and his dependence on the Company had become ſo abſolute, that he could no longer act for himſelf without acting at the ſame time for them. The commotions therefore, which prevailed in every part of his dominions, ſuppoſed a diſtinction, which he was not at liberty to avow, and pointed to an object, which, as he was then circumſtanced, it was at once his duty and his intereſt

tereſt to diſclaim. The policy under which he acted was on that account to haſten home, that the reviving proſperity of the Company's affairs in the adjacent countries, co-operating with his preſence, might have its full effect in facilitating the re-eſtabliſhment of tranquillity, wherever a diſpoſition to rebel had appeared.

The governor-general, having gone back to Benares, was neceſſarily occupied for ſome time in ſettling the arrangements of a new government. The next lineal heir of Bulwant Sing, Mehiparain, ſucceeded to the Rajahſhip. He was a grandſon of that popular chief, by a daughter married to Doorgbijey Sing, ſtill under age, and his parents both alive. His father, under the title of Naib, was intruſted with the ſole management of the public affairs. The tribute of the zemindary to the Company was more than doubled, two hundred thouſand a year clear gain, beſides much booty, having accrued to the treaſury of Bengal from this revolution.

The tide of ſucceſs, which has always and eminently attended our affairs in India, began now to ſwell. In two days after the flight of the Rajah, a ſtrong detachment of ſepoys, under the command of Major Crawford, arrived in the camp from Dinapore. Colonel Hannay, who had been reduced on the northern banks of the Dewa to the greateſt difficulty, had received the moſt ſeaſonable and effectual relief from the addreſs of Major Naylor. The multitude who had revolted in that country

country were difperfed, and the troubles they occafioned in a great meafure began to fubfide. Futteh Shaw was at the fame time driven out of the Sarum circar, where he had maintained for fome time a fort of independence, in defiance of all the efforts of government. News of a feparate peace and treaty of alliance and friendfhip having been concluded between Colonel Muir and Sindia, the great Marratto chief, arriving at this moment, fenfibly heightened the pleafure fo naturally produced by a fucceffion of fuch fortunate events.

Popham, confiderably ftrengthened by frefh troops, in high fpirits from the numerous advantages his forces had obtained in every encounter with the enemy, and excited by the profpect of immence booty, advanced with the army in purfuit of the Rajah to Bedjeygur. It was the envied depofitary of his father's treafures, his own, and thofe of his family. It is fituated not far from the frontiers, about fifty miles to the fouth-eaft of Chunar. The fort is on the top of a folid rock, which rifes in a perpendicular direction feven hundred and forty-five feet above the level of the adjoining countries. Next to the impregnable fort of Gualier, it was univerfally deemed the ftrongeft in India; but the ftrength of the one appeared to Cheit Sing no adequate fecurity againft the conqueror of the other. He therefore abandoned the fort with precipitation on Popham's approach. Much of his treafure was unavoidably left behind, with his women, his mother, and his wife, who ftill

remained

remained in Bedjeygur with no contemptible garrison. He took with him, however, above three hundred thousand pounds in cash, besides jewels to an immense value; being, as was alledged, all that the elephants and camels, in his immediate possession, were capable of carrying away.

In this manner, and in direct violation of all the most sacred engagements, by which nations and men are bound together or united in reciprocal obligation, did Mr. Hastings accomplish the expulsion of a prince possessing all the legal authority of his country, exercising all the rights, and performing all the duties of its internal government; who coined money, collected the revenues, administered justice, and even kept up a military force for his own defence. He was subject to the governor-general and council, only on certain stipulated terms, and on the same terms entitled to the protection of their government. And in a variety of treaties, as authentic and explicit as the ordinary forms of human transactions can render them, the public faith, at Mr. Hastings' own immediate instance, was solemnly pledged, that no future encroachments whatever should, under the Company's authority, be made on his rights. These feeble barriers, however, were soon broke down, when the wrath of a despot was to be indulged. The Rajah, from the access of his attachment to the Company, on the report of Mr. Hastings' resignation, and the accession of a new governor-general to that important situation, had prematurely

turely announced his ſatisfaction in an event, which it was conceived would have then been generally acceptable in India. This was conſtrued into an inſtance of the greateſt perſonal diſreſpect at the time, and cheriſhed with aſſiduity as a moſt heinous offence, until ſuch an opportunity might offer as it could be reſented in a manner the moſt conſpicuous and effectual. In conſequence of this petty affront, the Rajah was proſcribed, and the ſanguinary reſolution adopted of ſelling the Company's ſovereignty of Benares to the Nabob of Oude, or diſpoſſeſſing the Rajah of his territories, or ſeizing his forts, and plundering them of treaſure to the amount of five hundred thouſand pounds. And ſo determined was he in the work of deſtruction which he had thus projected, that he actually rejected the ſum of two hundred thouſand pounds, tendered by the Rajah for his redemption, rather than the extremities he meditated ſhould not be literally put in execution.

Meaſures of ſeverity, adopted without any regard to the fundamental rules of juſtice or equity, are generally extended in the accompliſhment, according to the wild and lawleſs principle in which they originate. Now that Cheit Sing had relinquiſhed all further oppoſition to the authority of the governor-general, and finally abandoned the country of Benares, and all the privileges connected with the government of it, that even his adherents began to avail themſelves of the pardon offered in the late proclamation, and the turbulence of the

inſurgents

insurgents was for the most part at an end, it was natural to expect that the passions connected with all these disturbances would have subsided, in proportion as the causes that produced them were removed. He sent, notwithstanding, a body of troops against the castle of Bedjeygur, where the mother of Cheit Sing, his wife, a person of amiable manners and singular worth, and all the other women of the Rajah's family, and that of his father, had fixed their residence. Without attempting to prove, and only pretending that whatever these innocent people possessed was the property of the Rajah, he resolved to involve them in the fate of Cheit Sing, to treat them as rebels, and without accusation or jury, or trial, to force their asylum, and confiscate their treasure. The orders issued for this purpose were cruel and barbarous, as they were peremptory and specific. "If the reports "brought to me," says he, "are true, your re-"jecting her offers, or any negociations with "her, would soon obtain you possession of the "fort upon your own terms. I apprehend that "she will contrive to defraud the captors of a con-"siderable part of the booty, by being suffered to "retire without examination. I should be very sorry "that your officers and soldiers lost any part of "the reward to which they are so well entitled."

Notwithstanding the ardour of the troops and the skill of the officers, the difficulties which attended the siege of Bedjeygur protracted it nearly to the middle of November. By that time they had

had proceeded ſo far by ſap, that a mine was ready to ſpring, which they hoped would enable them to ſtorm the place. The mother of the Rajah, who poſſeſſed the entire command, was conſequently induced to ſurrender the fort by capitulation. The only terms which in theſe circumſtances ſhe could obtain from a mercenary power, fluſhed with ſucceſs and eager after treaſure, was, to be allowed fifteen per cent. on the effects in the fort, to reſide in the country, or follow her ſon, as ſhe might incline, and in either caſe to be afforded entire protection.

Even theſe terms, hard as they were, and granted with a harſhneſs and illiberality, which even the laws of war prohibit among civilized nations, were groſſly violated. The women, who reſigned themſelves with confidence to thoſe officers whoſe faith was pledged to protect them from inſult, were yet abandoned to the ſearch of the ſoldiery, who uſed them with incivility and rudeneſs, and even ſtript them of their neceſſaries. This brutality was at leaſt obliquely authorized in a letter from Mr. Haſtings to Popham, where he hints his apprehenſion that theſe unfortunate women might be treated with an improper exceſs of delicacy from the gallantry of brave men. How deteſtable muſt that government be, in which the ſofter ties of nature have no protection; where the common victims of cruelty are the innocent, the fair, and the defenceleſs; and where all thoſe tender conſiderations

derations which have been respected in all societies, and by all the heroes in the world, are insulted, and without effect!

Thus were our forces in full possession of all those riches, which had been so long an object of the strongest solicitude to the governor-general. These however, instead of converting to the purposes of public utility, or applying to the urgent necessities of the state, he was anxious to appropriate reward for those military exertions, by which his personal resentments had been so abundantly gratified. His letter to the commander in chief, during the siege, was construed by the officers on the spot as sufficiently authenticating this disposition of the spoil. It was perhaps not unnatural to prefer on this occasion the desire of the troops to the exigence of the Company, in consequence of executing, in such a masterly manner, a plan of operations which the governor-general had so much at heart. The officers, aware however that even his authority, circumstanced as he now was, might not ultimately realize their expectations, unanimously resolved to distribute on the spot the spoil which fell into their hands. And this resolution, which put the money in their pockets beyond the possibility of a reimbursement, they literally executed the second day after the capture of the fort. The treasure in cash, which was then actually seized, amounted to twenty-five lacks. Great quantities of the richest merchandize, rubies, diamonds, emeralds, and other precious ſtones, to an immenſe value, were at the ſame time ſecured.*

The council were far from acquieſcing in this diſtribution of the Rajah's treaſure. It was repugnant to their expectations, and indeed to the orders of their ſuperiors. They conſequently arrainged it as a meaſure which might be followed by the worſt conſequences. The reſolutions which they paſſed on the ſubject ſtrongly marked their diſſatisfaction. Theſe were, that the governor-general had not either formally or by conſtruction diſclaimed, as repreſentative of the Company, their right to the booty found in the fort; that the temerity of the officers in appropriating it was a proof that they did not conſider themſelves ſufficiently ſecure by any other claim; that the acquieſcence of government in ſuch a meaſure might eſtabliſh a dangerous precedent; and that they could not relinquiſh the Company's right, but would bring the queſtion to a legal deciſion. They were, however, deſirous that the officers would ſubmit the whole to the deciſion of the board.

* The dividend which took place in the army of this booty, which in caſh amounted to three hundred and twelve thouſand pounds and upwards, was

To the commander in chief ——	£. 36750
To each of the majors —— ——	5619
To each captain an item more than ——	3000
To native officers, a very diſproportionate ſhare	
To each ſepoy	6

N. B. Two thirds of the caſh were at leaſt ſuppoſed to be diſpoſed of in this manner.

board. In that case, it was promised to put the most liberal construction on the letter of the governor-general, which they had urged in their own vindication. It was at the same time recommended that they should accommodate the treasury with a loan, upon the usual terms, of their respective shares, excepting so much as they would declare upon their honour was necessary to supply their personal wants. They were required to give in an answer to this requisition in a given time, and formally apprised that a failure would be considered by the board as a disobedience of orders, and proceeded upon accordingly.

Thus ended the memorable transactions of the governor-general at Benares, in the year 1781. These seem to have been undertaken at the instigation of his own feelings, which he conceived wounded beyond forgiveness by the conduct of this unfortunate prince, and of whose temerity or inadvertence he took this signal vengeance, as an example to all the other great landholders under the Company's government. But if the urgent necessities of the state are to be admitted as an apology for such outrages, it is an instance in point, how very abortive the severities of despotism are; for the Rajah found means to carry away the greatest part of his treasure, and the remainder was immediately converted, by the army, into booty.

CHAPTER XII.

Appearance of a French Fleet before Madras—Purſued, and ſome of the Convoy captured by Sir Edward Hughes—Partial Fight—The Enemy haul their Wind and are out of Sight in the Morning—The Sultan and Magnanime, from England, join Sir Edward—A bloody Action on the Coaſt of Ceylon—Conſequences of theſe Actions—Abingdon's Succeſs—Peace concluded with the Marrattos—Hurricane—Famine—Operations of the Army on the Coaſt of Malabar—Onore ſtormed—Hyder's Death—Canara invaded—Diſcontents in the Army—Mangalore—Panic in Cundapore—General Matthews capitulates—Fate of the General and Officers—The French Auxiliaries refuſe to fight againſt the Engliſh—Sir Eyre Coote dies at Madras—Succeſſes in the Coimbatour Country—Laſt Naval Action between the French and Engliſh Fleets—Ceſſation of Hoſtilities.

WHILE Mr. Haſtings exerted the power of the Company in cruſhing ſome of their moſt valuable dependents in the extremities of Bengal, the French meditated an utter extinction of their intereſt on the coaſt of Coromandel. When Admiral Sir Edward Hughes, after taking Trincomale, arrived in the Madras Road, he was informed by Lord Macartney, the governor, that a French fleet, amounting to thirty ſail in all, had appeared on the coaſt, captured ſeveral ſhips, and were then ſuppoſed not above twenty leagues to the northward.

ward. Our ſquadron conſiſted only of ſix ſail of the line, and had been ſo long at ſea, that the ſhips were neceſſarily much out of repair. Their crews were debilitated by ſickneſs, and they required large ſupplies of freſh proviſions. In this condition, and expoſed in the open road to the attack of an enemy ſo greatly ſuperior, the admiral's ſituation was peculiary critical. He was, however, fortunately reinforced, on the day following ſuch alarming intelligence, by the arrival of Captain Alms, in the Monmouth of 64, accompanied by the Hero of 74, and the Iſis of 50 guns.

Every diſpatch was adopted and no time loſt for rendering the fleet, in ſome meaſure, fit for actual ſervice, or in a ſtate of preparation to meet the enemy. Sir Eyre Coote, with his uſual attention and alacrity, ſupplied the ſhips with three hundred officers and men. But notwithſtanding this expedition, before the equipment was complete, the French fleet, conſiſting of twelve ſail of the line, including the Engliſh Hannibal, and another fifty-gun-ſhip, ſix frigates, eight large tranſports, and ſix captured veſſels, appeared ſuddenly in offing on the fifteenth of February. M. de Suffrein, who had ſucceeded to the command on the death of M. de Orves, not knowing till now the acceſſion of ſtrength which the Engliſh fleet had juſt received, and finding he had nine inſtead of five ſhips, which he expected to encounter, abandoned his intention of attack; and ſuddenly weighing anchor, about four in the afternoon, ſtood off to the ſouthward.

A pursuit on the part of the British instantly took place, which continued all night. It was observed, about day-break, that the enemy were now in separate directions, their twelve line of battle ships, with the frigate, bearing east of the British fleet, and about four leagues distant, while the other frigates with the transports, not more than three leagues a-head, made directly for Pondicherry. The only infallible mode of bringing on an action in these circumstances, was to throw out the signal for a general chase to the south-west, as the French admiral would undoubtedly endeavour to rescue his convoy, and no superiority of number and force could deter Sir Edward from appealing to this issue. Our fleet soon captured six vessels, five of which were English prizes, newly taken, with their crews on board. The sixth was the Lauriston, a transport of 1300 tons burthen. Its cargo consisted of a fine train of artillery, intended as a present to Hyder; a large quantity of gunpowder; a complete assortment of other military stores; a number of land officers, and three hundred soldiers, from the regiment of Lausanne. The great disadvantage under which the fleet laboured, for want of frigates, was now severely felt. A few of these must have secured the whole of this valuable convoy; most of which, on that account, were abandoned in the very moment, almost, of being captured. For the French fleet, anxious to defeat the success of so masterly a manœuvre, instantly bore down for the preservation of their convoy. This

obliged

obliged our admiral to recal his ſhips, to order the prizes which had been taken for Negapatam, and to make head with all the expedition poſſible againſt the enemy. Unequal adverſe winds and hazy weather kept the hoſtile fleets apart for ſome time, and put the nautical ſcience and acuteneſs of both commanders ſufficiently to the trial. The wind, irregular and uncertain as it ſeemed, ſtill blew in favour of the enemy; and notwithſtanding all the ſkill, experience and activity of Sir Edward, he was at laſt forced into action on very diſadvantageous terms. Wayward as theſe circumſtances were, he reſolutely threw out the ſignal to form the line of battle a-head. Eight of the enemy's beſt ſhips were conſequently enabled to direct their whole attack on five of the Engliſh, of which the Iſis of fifty guns was one. Four of our ableſt ſhips, the Eagle, Monmouth, Worceſter, and Burford, under the moſt approved commanders, were idle ſpectators in the van, without a poſſibility of affording the leaſt aſſiſtance. The Superbe of ſeventy-four guns, in which Sir Edward was, formed the central ſhip. The Hero, of the ſame force, commanded by Captain Wood; the Iſis, Lumley; the Monarca, Gill, of ſixty-eight; and Exeter of ſixty-four; the latter commanded by Commodore King and Captain Reynolds; were the four below. The Exeter being the ſternmoſt, and a bad ſailor, was conſiderably ſeparated from her ſecond a-head. Three of the enemy inſtantly bore down upon her, and commenced a furious attack.

 The

The admiral, in the Superbe, was, at the ſame time, beſet with equal vehemence and force. Theſe were the two ſhips which the enemy ſeemed chiefly intent to diſable. But after ſuſtaining theſe ſevere attacks for two hours, and not a little crippled, a ſquall of wind accidentally blowing freſh in their favour, it became their turn to make the attack. The action was conſequently returned with ſuch vigour and effect, that in twenty-five minutes, and juſt as it began to grow dark, the French ſhips within their reach, having ſuffered much damage, ſuddenly hauled their wind, and the whole ſquadron ſtood off to the north-eaſt. The two ſhips in our fleet, which ſtood the brunt of the action, were almoſt reduced to a wreck. A conſtant and prodigious fire had been poured in upon both, from all directions, during the whole action. Captain Stephens in the Superbe, and Captain Reylands in the Exeter, two officers of diſtinguiſhed merit, were killed. We loſt thirty-two men, and ninety-five were wounded. Thirty of the former, and eighty-ſeven of the latter, were in the Superbe, the Exeter, and the Hero. The ſituation of the Exeter, while the bloody conflict continued, was awful and perilous in the extreme. Every freſh broadſide was expected to decide her fate. The thunder of the enemy, from three ſhips of the line cloſing round her, and taking a ſteady aim, as at a dead mark, was inceſſant and tremendous. The cool intrepidity and compoſure of the commodore, in the midſt of a ſcene thus dreadful, was ſingularly

com-

commanding and exemplary. While the fight raged with increaſing fury, he was almoſt blinded by the blood and mangled brains of Captain Reylands, which were daſhed over him by a cannon ball. The maſter came to him ſoon after, and aſked what he ſhould do with a ſhip which already was in the moſt ſhattered condition, as two of the enemy were already bearing down upon her. "There is nothing to be done," ſaid he, coolly, "but to fight her till ſhe ſinks."

Such was the ſituation to which the Superbe and the Exeter had been reduced by this encounter, that it was deemed neceſſary to proceed to Trincomale, where only that damage could be repaired. This buſineſs, however, was effected ſo expeditiouſly, that the ſquadron appeared before Madras by the middle of March, without having either heard or ſeen the enemy. The admiral was returning to Trincomale, with a reinforcement of troops, and a ſupply of ſtores for that garriſon, when he was joined by the Sultan and Magnanime ſhips of war, of ſeventy four-guns each, from England. Though the crews inboth theſe ſhips were ſickly and ſcorbutic, anxious to receive and cover the convoy with troops and ſtores from home, he perſevered in his courſe with an intention of neither ſeeking nor ſhunning the enemy. The French, however, knowing of the convoy, and wiſhing to cut it off, or prevent the junction, appeared alſo in the north-eaſt quarter, and to leeward of the Engliſh, on the eighth of April. Both fleets continued

tinued in this relative position during that and the three following days; but Sir Edward Hughes having reached the coast of Ceylon, about fifteen leagues to windward of Trincomale, bore away directly for that place. This was unfortunate for the English fleet, as the enemy gained the wind in the night, which enabled them to bear down upon our rear in the morning. Sir Edward immediately made a signal for the line of battle a-head, on the starboard tack, two cables asunder, while the enemy were within six miles, and the wind in the same quarter, with time, place, and circumstances all in their favour. Our ships were cramped by a lee-shore, a superior enemy, and an adverse wind. Three hours were spent in manœuvring. Five sail, which composed the enemy's van, stretched forward to engage that of the English, while the admiral, with other seven ships of the line, bore down upon the Superbe, and her two seconds, the Monmouth and Monarca. Two seventy-four-gun ships rushed within pistol-shot of the Superbe, and engaged her with so much fierceness and execution, that the general opinion was, they meant to have boarded and carried her by a coup-de-main. This furious onset lasted about ten minutes, when the French admiral, having received so much damage from the deluge of fire returned by the Superbe, made room for the ships which came to supply his place, and stood on the tack of the Monmouth, which was already equally engaged. The battle raged with inconceivable fierceness,

par-

particularly in the center, where the English admiral resisted, with the characteristic firmness and intrepidity of a British seaman, superior number and force. The Monmouth at last, about three o'clock, having sustained, with unparalleled fortitude, the united fire and attack of two ships, the one of equal and the other of superior metal, besides the passing fire of a third, first lost her mizen, and then her main-mast: She accordingly fell out of the line to leeward. The enemy made a desperate effort to carry her off, but were driven back by the prodigious fire of the Monarca and the Sultan. Our admiral was disappointed in expecting the wind, as usual, to change in the afternoon; he was therefore obliged, forty minutes past three, that his ships might not be entagled by the shore, to make a signal for wearing and hauling their wind in a line of battle a-head, and fighting the enemy during the whole evolution. Both fleets seemed equally solicitous for the present to gain anchor. The French admiral had been early obliged to shift his flag; and the La Fine, of forty guns, fell so closely on board the Isis, that she struck her colours to Captain Lumley; though, from the disabled condition of that ship and the darkness of the night, she effected her escape. Indeed the condition of both fleets were so nearly the same, that similar apprehensions were entertained by each of a fresh attack in the morning. The French, however, had not lost any of their lower masts; which was of great advantage in refitting; whereas the

the Monmouth could only be repaired in a good harbour, and with new maſts.

The two admirals watched the motions of each other for ſome days. The French on the nineteenth ſtood out to ſea, and made a feint, as if they meant an immediate attack: But, perceiving the ſituation of the Britiſh line, they inſtantly ſtood eaſtward by the wind, and before evening were quite out of ſight. The admiral, having refitted the Monmouth with jury-maſts, proceeded the fourth day after to Trincomale, where the ſquadron was repaired with the utmoſt diligence, as their ſervice was become ſtill more urgent than ever. Thus ended one of the moſt fierce and bloody engagements that happened during the war. The ſlaughter of men in the Monmouth was equal to the havock of the ſhip: No leſs than forty-five were killed, and a hundred and two wounded—a full third of her whole crew! The maſterly conduct of Captain Alms, in a ſituation thus critical, was peculiarly exemplary. His recollection of this brave action was however imbittered by the loſs of his ſon, who, having been made a lieutenant in the admiral's ſhip, fell the ſame day, in a noble emulation of his father's bravery. The French fleet proceeded immediately to Batakalo, a Dutch port on the iſland of Ceylon, where they continued to repair and equip their ſhattered ſhips until the month of June. Their loſs of men was rated by themſelves at one hundred and thirty-nine killed, and three hundred and fifty-four wounded.

These

These events, with all the misfortunes that attended them, gave a most advantageous impression of our strength on the continent of India. A sufficient naval force to crush effectually that of the English, excepting some artillery and engineers, was probably all the aid expected or desired by Hyder Ally from the French: His chief solicitude was to annihilate our resources, as he knew every thing must then be at his own disposal. He must consequently have suffered inconceivable mortification to see the French, with so great an apparent superiority in the number of their ships and men, not daring to attack the English, but even pursued by them; a convoy under their protection captured; and, with every possible advantage, effecting only a drawn battle. His hopes of taking Madras, of deposing the Nabob of Arcot, and of placing Tippoo Sultan in possession of the Carnatic, were by these circumstances rendered as remote and improbable as ever.

The blockade of Tellichery, on the Malabar coast, however, still continued, and the strength and number of the enemy increased; but, unequal to a regular siege, were content with closely shutting up the place, and depending on famine or other distress to supply the want of military skill. The few works they erected were fortified by a camp at some distance. Major Abingdon, having arrived from Bombay with a considerable reinforcement of troops, determined to attempt the dislodgement of the enemy, and open a communication of the town with the country. His movements

ments deceived the enemy into ſuch a ſtate of ſecurity as conſiderably facilitated his deſigns. Having drawn ſuch part of the garriſon as could be ſpared, without notice, into his camp, he ſurpriſed and carried their ſeveral poſts before day on the morning of the eighth of January [1782]. Not allowing a moment for the enemy to recover their confuſion, he ſtormed their camp as ſoon as it was light, and completely routed them. Sados Cawn, their commander, retired with his family, and a choſen party of his friends and beſt troops, into a caſtle ſcooped on the ſide of a hill, and poſſeſſed of no other walls than ſuch as were formed of the living rock. Notwithſtanding a vigorous and manly defence, this brave man and his party were torn from their aſylum, though bomb-proof, and made priſoners. Theſe operations produced conſiderable ſpoil, conſiſting of artillery, military ſtores, and ſeveral elephants. The town was relieved, and the coaſt for ſeveral miles on both ſides entirely cleared of the enemy. Hyder's poſſeſſions on this coaſt being acquired partly by conqueſt and partly by fraud, the Nairs, native princes, and nobility, who had ſuffered ſeverely in an ineffectual ſtruggle for the preſervation of their ancient independence, were ſtill exceedingly diſaffected to his government. He was conſequently much vexed and alarmed at our ſucceſs in theſe parts, which were the dearer to him from their vicinity to the rich kingdoms of Canara and Myſore, the great ſources of his wealth and power.

This

This ſevere blow was, however, ſoon and amply retaliated on the ſouthern army. Theſe troops, under the command of Colonel Braithwaite, appear to have been deſtined for the protection of Tanjore and the neighbouring provinces. Sir Eyre Coote had, early in the year, made every effort in his power to repreſs, by the preſence of the army under his command, the deſigns of the French and Hyder Ally on the ſide of Pondicherry. But he was utterly incapable of ſuch a movement by the want of draught cattle and carriages. He was alſo detained, in ſome degree, in expecting the reſult of an application which he had made to the governor-general and council of Bengal, for reſtoring his authority over the ſouthern troops, that he might be able to direct their co-operation in ſuch a manner as would equally facilitate his own, and counteract the movements of the enemy. Braithwaite encamped on the banks of the Coleroon, which forms the northern boundary of the Tanjore kingdom. His forces conſiſted of two thouſand veteran infantry, two hundred and fifty cavalry, and thirteen field pieces. His ſituation was in an open plain, which muſt have expoſed him exceedingly to the enemy's cavalry; but ſeveral large and deep rivers which lay between him and Hyder, who was at a conſiderable diſtance, apparently ſecured him againſt any ſurpriſe. Tippoo Saib, appriſed of theſe circumſtances, determined to ſurmount them, and cut off this detachment as he had done that under Baillie. He was accompanied in this enter-

enterprize by Monſ. Lally, and four hundred French. His own forces were twenty thouſand ſtrong, one half of whom were cavalry. With this formidable army and twenty pieces of cannon, he ſuddenly ſurrounded Braithwaite's corps, which could not be ſuppoſed in any degree prepared to reſiſt a force ſo greatly ſuperior. The action, notwithſtanding, was fierce and tremendous. It commenced on the ſixteenth, and was not decided till the eighteenth of February [1782]. During twenty-ſix hours of theſe three days, an unremittted fire of cannon and ſmall arms was ſupported on both ſides. Neither ſurpriſe nor danger were attended with their uſual effects on this gallant party or their leader. Their courage and activity never once forſook them; and he, though ſeverely wounded and bleeding exceſſively, would not withdraw from the ſcene for a moment. Attacked with equal vigour from all ſides, he threw his detachment into a hollow ſquare, with his thirteen field pieces interſperſed in its faces, and his ſmall body of cavalry in the center, that he might preſent a front to every attack. Thus were they exhibited in the midſt of a large ſquare, as a mark, to which the immenſe army that ſurrounded them directed an inceſſant and univerſal fire. It was intended by a violent cannonade on all ſides to make a breach in ſome part of the line, and then, ruſhing impetuouſly with the cavalry, to complete the confuſion that circumſtance would occaſion. But all the vigour and addreſs of the enemy were incapable

pable of making any impreſſion on the Engliſh ſepoys, who withſtood ſuch exertions in the aſpect of inevitable deſtruction, as would have put the conſtancy and the diſcipline of the beſt European troops to the teſt. Not valuing the number of lives he might ſacrifice to the ſucceſs of an enterprize ſo grateful to his ambition, and expecting his cavalry to break in at ſome point or other, Tippoo led them repeatedly and with the greateſt ardour to the charge. They advanced with fury, but received ſuch powerful ſhowers of grape and muſquetry ſhot as deſtroyed them by ſhoals. The Britiſh cavalry from the ſquare, ſallying at that moment, purſued them with heavy and unreſiſted execution to a proper diſtance, and then returned to their former ſtations. On the third day, after the numbers of theſe brave men were greatly thinned, the ſurvivors worn down with wounds and fatigue, and Tippoo Saib's intention of trampling down our infantry was ſo effectually defeated, that no poſſible means could bring his cavalry to the reſolution of ever making one charge up to the lines, M. Lally, at the head of his four hundred Europeans, marched with fixed bayonets to the attack of that ſide which was moſt expoſed, or ſeemed the weakeſt. He was ſupported by ſeveral battalions of the enemy's beſt infantry, and flanked by prodigious numbers of cavalry, while their whole artillery poured in freſh columns of fire upon each of the other three faces, which at the ſame time were reſpectively menaced with dreadful bodies of

horſe,

horſe, prepared to ruſh in upon them the moment any change in their poſition took place. Our exhauſted ſepoys in that front, unable to repulſe the vigorous onſet of ſuch a body of Europeans coming freſh into action, and confident of ſucceſs from the vaſt army that ſupported them, were inſtantly broken, and the carnage that enſued by the fury and rapidity of the cavalry was exceſſive. Lally loſt not a moment in putting a ſtop to the effuſion of blood, by iſſuing orders which his own corps readily obeyed. The ferocity of the natives rendered them leſs tractable, five of whom were ſaid to have fallen by his own hand, in an attempt to reſtrain their barbarous impetuoſity. No ſooner was the dreadful ſlaughter at an end, than he prevailed upon Tippoo Saib to intruſt him with the charge of the priſoners. They were treated, eſpecially the officers and wounded, with a generoſity which is the inſeparable companion of legitimate courage; and his humanity in the field was even ſurpaſſed by his kind attentions in the camp to the men whom only his gallantry could ſubdue. The beſt ſoldiers and the braveſt men are ever the moſt merciful. In this cataſtrophe, we loſt many an excellent officer; and of the whole who were preſent, one only eſcaped without a wound. They loſt every thing but their honour, and were deſtined to ſuffer the miſeries of a long and cruel impriſonment in the capital of Myſore.

All the countries to the ſouthward were now laid open to the deſigns of the enemy, while the movements of the English general northward were not only closely watched by Hyder's main army, but exceedingly impeded for want of much necessary military apparatus. During this state of imbecility on the one side, and vigorous activity on the other, the first division of that great force, which under the Marquis de Bussy was intended for the subversion of the English power in India, were, some time in the month of March, disembarked by Suffrein at Pondicherry. These soon effecting a junction with a considerable body of Hyder's forces, the combined army marched in full confidence to besiege Cuddalore. And Captain Hughes, the commander, found himself under a necessity of capitulating on the eighth of April. Permacoil soon shared the same fate, and the whole of the enemy's forces, under the direction of Hyder in person, pointed their march towards Vandewash. It was now that Sir Eyre Coote expected to have met the enemy in the field. His movements originated in that conviction: And he possessed himself, without delay, of the strongest position he could select, for the protection of so important a fortress. Deceived in this conclusion, he determined to seek him on his own ground, not suspecting it possible that the enemy, thus strongly reinforced, could submit to the pursuit of so inferior an army. In this opinion he pushed on two days march to Hyder's camp, who was not however to be surprised from the strictest adherence to that wary system he had now adopted. He therefore secured his retreat to a post

 in

in the red hills, which he well knew could not be attacked with any probability of succefs. His magazines were at the fame time depofited in the ftrong fort of Arnee, and the general conceived a movement towards that place might tempt the enemy to relinquifh his caution for the fafety of his ftores. This fcheme, on a confultation with the officers of the army, was approved and adopted. The army marched for Arnee, and encamped within five miles of it. Hyder rufhed from the hills like a torrent, to refcue a place which contained the means of carrying on the war. This fudden irruption of the enemy commenced before our troops could reach their deftination; and it then became a queftion, whether they fhould proceed, or prefer another direction, and fight the enemy in their way. The former feemed the moft eligible mode for bringing on an action. Much as the means of information were impeded by the rapid movements of Hyder's cavalry, who in various bodies occupied all the furrounding grounds, galloping to and fro in every direction, a diftant cannonade in their rear announced the enemy's approach as the van of our army had reached Arnee. Our troops poffeffed a low fituation. The enemy feized all the high circumjacent grounds. This circumftance expofed the Englifh to great inconvenience in forming. The general however difplayed his ufual ability in making fuch difpofitions as remedied every defect in the pofition of the army, and tended to bring the enemy to a clofe and decifive cisive action. It was noon before he reduced their various attacks to such a point, as the whole of his force could bear upon them with effect. He then advanced with an ardour which routed the enemy in every quarter. The pursuit continued till night. The advantages of this victory, like those of others, were once more lost for want of cavalry. Some subsequent attempts were made to bring Hyder to meet our troops in the field, in this neighbourhood, but without effect. A body of his cavalry, however, found means to draw our main guard into an ambuscade, where they were entirely cut off, before any assistance could reach them. The general thought it necessary to fall back, that the army might be supplied with provision.

This battle, which was fought on the second of June [1782], was the last in which these two great men were destined to meet. The health of both was greatly impaired, from the fatigue to which they were exposed by the present war. The circumstances in which Hyder was involved were peculiarly gloomy and foreboding. The English interest, which he conceived to be an insuperable obstacle to all his ambitious projects, was still likely to triumph. His expectations from the French were frustrated. He foresaw his own destruction in the peace, which was nearly accomplished between the government of Bengal and the Marratto states. These powers, with whom he had alternately been in a state of hostility for so long a time, would inevitably proſcribe him, and mutually ſtipulate a participation of his dominion. Such a ſeries of mortifying reflections as theſe circumſtances muſt have ſuggeſted, to a mind goaded by ambition and accuſtomed to ſucceſs, naturally filled him with chagrin. And it was a proſpect which he had not ſufficient firmneſs to contemplate with ſerenity, that he was deſtined to become a ſacrifice at laſt to the union of two powers, who had both ſuffered ſo exceedingly from his enmity. By the ill health of Sir Eyre Coote, and the abſence of Sir Hector Monro, who had returned to Europe, the command devolved on Major-general Stuart. Both armies, from the ruinous ſtate of the country, were obliged to draw their ſupplies from other quarters. This greatly impeded the war; though Hyder felt but little inconvenience, from the contiguity of his dominions: He could not, however, be tempted any more to a general engagement. The remainder of the campaign, which conſiſted of laborious marches, and fruitleſs experiments to enſnare the enemy, was concluded without accompliſhing any enterprize of importance.

Suffrein was now returned from Batacalo to the coaſt of Coromandel, and proceeded to Cuddalore, which the French had rendered their chief magazine of arms and military ſtores, both for land and ſea ſervice. His ſhips being revictualled and recruited with freſh men, he determined to deſtroy the Engliſh before the arrival of Sir Richard Bickerton, who, with ſeveral ſhips of war, had long

ſailed

ſailed from England, and was ardently expected at Madras. The French fleet ſtill preſerved their former ſuperiority of twelve ſhips to eleven, beſides heavy frigates. All poſſible means had been uſed to prepare them in the beſt manner for immediate action. They were reinforced with four hundred French, and as many ſepoys, at Cuddalore; and, on Sir Edward Hughes' arrival in the road, they touched at Negapatam, and were further recruited by three hundred artillery-men, the moſt effective aid they could receive. Our fleet was not backward to meet the enemy, who, confiding in their ſuperiority, challenged Sir Edward before Negapatam, with eighteen ſhips. The Engliſh admiral was ſo perfectly ready, and ſo little diſpoſed to admit any delay, that by three o'clock he weighed anchor, and, putting out to ſea, ſtood ſouthward during the evening and the night, in order to gain the wind of the enemy. He ſucceeded in his evolutions for this purpoſe, and immediatly gave ſignals for every ſhip in his fleet to bear directly down upon her oppoſite in the French line. His orders were executed with promptitude. The French commenced firing before eleven. Our ſhips reſerved their fire till certain of its taking effect. By half paſt twelve the enemy's line appeared in great diſorder, and ſeveral of their ſhips extremely ſhattered. At this criſis, a a ſudden ſhift of wind ſnatched the French ſquadron from the ruin that impended. Our line was deranged by the circumſtance which preſerved

 them.

them. By this contingency, the advantage of a victory so decisive could not be prosecuted. The disabled, broken, and flying enemy were enabled to recover themselves, while their conquerors were reduced to a state of the greatest confusion. After much manœuvring, and the continuation of a partial engagement between such parts of the two fleets as came within reach of each other, the English admiral made the signal for the line of battle a-head, and was preparing, at half past one o'clock, to renew the attack; but seeing, at two, the enemy standing in shore, and collecting their ships in a close body, while his were much dispersed, and several of them ungovernable, he relinquished that design, and thought only of getting into such a condition as should prove decisive to the service next morning. Then, however, the French were observed under sail, on their way to Cuddalore, while our fleet was utterly incapable of preventing or pursuing them. They owed almost every advantage on this occasion to their frigates. It was at the same time obvious, from the event of this battle, that, had the two former been general, and all the English ships brought fairly up at once to the encounter, the result of both had been very different. Indeed the first might by that means have proved so decisive as entirely to have prevented the second. Seventy-seven men were killed, and two hundred and thirty-three wounded, in our fleet. The French had near two hundred killed, and above six hundred wounded. Among the brave officers, as well of the 98th regiment

regiment as of the naval department, who were ſlain, Captain Maclelan, of the Superbe, was ſhot through the heart, in the beginning of the action. Thus were the admiral's two immediate captains both killed within a ſhort time of each other.

While the French repaired their ſhips at Cuddalore, our fleet kept the ſea to the windward of Negapatam for near a fortnight. The ſituation of the army in all probability had at that time ſome effect on the admiral's movements, and certain ſchemes of co-operation might render it neceſſary for the ſquadron to remain ſtationary. The damage which the ſhipping had received in the late actions was great, and required immediate repair. A ſupply of ammunition and proviſion was alſo become indiſpenſable. To effect theſe purpoſes, the admiral arrived at Madras the twentieth of July, and was joined by the Sceptre of ſix-four guns, which had left England with Sir R. Bickerton: But parting with him ſoon after, ſhe had made all the expedition in her paſſage poſſible. Anxious for the preſervation of Trincomale, Sir Edward immediately diſpatched the Monmouth and the Sceptre with ſuch reinforcements, and ſupplies of men, ammunition, and proviſions, as appeared adequate to repel any deſultory attempts which the enemy ſhould think proper to make upon the place.

Mean while the Sieur d' Aymar arrived at Point de Gallis, lying on the ſouth ſide of the iſland of Ceylon, in the St. Michael of ſixty-four guns, accompanied by the Illuſtre of ſeventy-four. He had under his convoy the ſecond diviſion of the Marquis de Buſſy's troops and artillery. Suffrein, appriſed of this circumſtance, joined them at that iſland on the firſt of Auguſt. So difficult were the means of information at that time, notwithſtanding an army in the field, garriſons every where in our intereſt, and the country ſubſtantially our own, that the news of this material occurrence only reached Madras by accident. Captain Mitchel in the Coventry frigate of thirty-two guns, cruizing on the coaſt of Ceylon, encountered the Bellona of forty. The engagement continued two hours and a half, and was ſuſtained with great bravery on both ſides, till the Bellona thought proper to decline further conteſt by an endeavour to eſcape. Mitchel purſued her with ſuch eagerneſs, that he ſoon found himſelf in the midſt of a French fleet of twenty-three ſail, at the ſame time that he knew not before of any ſuch armament in theſe ſeas. He was the firſt to announce the intelligence to the admiral, who, anxious to diſappoint the deſigns of the enemy againſt Trincomale, haſtened his departure for Ceylon, with all the diſpatch in his power. But adverſe weather exceedingly retarded his progreſs. The French proceeded with alacrity to the attack of this important fortreſs. The expedition was performed with rapidity. They inſtantly landed their troops on the twenty-eighth of Auguſt. Their batteries were opened in two days, and the guns from the garriſon were ſoon ſilenced.

Next

Next morning the place was formally ſummoned to ſurrender. The terms allowed the garriſon were ſuch as proved the apprehenſions entertained by the enemy of a viſit from Sir Edward Hughes. He arrived off Trincomale on the ſecond of September, juſt as the French had ſecured their new acquiſitions. Their colours were then flying on all the forts, and above thirty ſail riding in all the bays. Of theſe there were fifteen ſhips of the line, including three fifties. Ten or eleven were frigates or fire ſhips, and the reſt tranſports. They had, therefore, beſides three fifties, twelve ſhips of ſixty-four guns and upwards, to oppoſe to the Britiſh line of the ſame number, in which the Iſis of fifty guns was deſtined to grapple with one of their ſixty-fours. The Engliſh might well have avoided an engagement under theſe circumſtances, but the whole ſquadron was fired with indignation by the unexpected fall of Trincomale. After much heſitation on the part of the enemy, and the exertion of conſummate ſkill on our's, the action commenced on the third of September. The French began to fire upon the Engliſh about half paſt two o'clock. The compliment was returned within a few minutes, and the engagement ſoon became general. The enemy's additional ſhips attacked with great ardour the extremities of our line, though the ſhips occupying theſe ſtations were already cloſely and equally engaged. The Worceſter was ſeverely preſſed, but ſhe made a gallant defence; and the Monmouth, by a dreadful and well-aimed fire, completely

pletely accomplished her rescue. The van, by the same means, was equally exposed as the rear, to the furious attack of superior numbers. Five of the enemy's ships fell down in a cluster upon the Exeter and Isis. The first of these ships seems to have been destined to fight against the greatest odds. She was so disabled in this dreadful contest as to retire from the line, while the weak and forlorn Isis was abandoned to run the gauntlet under the successive fire of several ships, before she could in any degree be supported. The center divisions on both sides were in the mean time closely engaged ship to ship, and the rival commanders in the Superbe and the Heros exhausted their rage against each other. The French admiral's second a-stern, at half past three o'clock, had her mizen-mast shot away; and, nearly about the same time, his second a-head lost both her fore and mizen-top-masts. The battle continued with equal fierceness and obstinacy, through every part of the lines, till half past five, when the wind shifted suddenly from the south-west to the east-south-east. Sir Edward Hughes then made the signal for wearing, and the evolution took place with the greatest facility and expedition. The French were either wearing or staying their ships until the English renewed the engagement on the other tack with redoubled violence. The Hero lost her main-mast at twenty minutes past six, and her mizen-mast soon after. The main-top-mast of the Worcester was shot away about the same time. It was about seven o'clock when the body of the

French

French squadron hauled their wind to the southward. They were exposed, and received a most severe fire from the rear of the English line, for twenty minutes after. They then got clear off, and the action entirely ceased.

No battle at sea was ever better fought; and it terminated a series of naval engagements, which for ardour, obstinacy and gallantry of enterprize, have not been exceeded in any part of the world. Perhaps there is no instance of the same men and the same ships meeting so often, and fighting so desperately, in so short a space of time. The darkness of the night, and the proximity of Trincomale, did not permit any pursuit of the enemy, though in fact our fleet were in no condition for such service. By day-light next morning the French were entirely out of sight. Our loss of men was so small as to be almost incredible. We had only fifty-one killed and not quite three hundred wounded. Three officers of distinguished merit, Captains Wood of the Worcester, Watt of the Sultan, and Lumley of the Isis, were among the slain. Other brave men, belonging to the 78th and 98th regiments, fell at the same time, and not a few were wounded. Colonel Fullarton, and several excellent officers, with the men under their command, deserve peculiar praise for their exertions during the whole of this very severe and trying service. The naval officers through the whole fleet were emulous only in excelling each other. They acted with a harmony, an

ardour

ardour and a promptitude, which, on every occasion, did honour to the discipline of the navy.

The French took shelter in the road of Trincomale that very night; and such was the precipitation of their flight from the scene of action, that the L'Orient of seventy-four guns, one of their best ships, was lost in the act of getting in. Four hundred and twelve of their men were killed, six hundred and seventy-six wounded. The crew of the Heros, at the beginning of the engagement, amounted to twelve hundred in number. Of these no less than one hundred and forty-seven were killed, and two hundred and forty wounded! a carnage seldom equalled, except in the cases of burning or blowing up. On this occasion, six French captains were broke and sent prisoners to the Mauritius.

During the dreadful conflict, which raged equally by sea and land in the southern extremities of *India*, the council-general of Bengal laboured, with incessant assiduity and the most consummate address, to obtain a separate peace with the Marrattos. The ruin of the Carnatic; the uncertain issue of the war with Hyder Ally; the fresh and formidable accession of strength which now co-operated with our former enemies against us, in consequence of a new scene of hostilities both with France and Holland; and the enormous and increasing expenditure, indispensable to an effective struggle for existence under all these embarrassing circumstances; controlled that turbulent spirit of ambition which had brought our interest in that country to a situation

tion of the moſt imminent hazard, and rendered the ſuperior government as anxious for the return of peace as it had formerly been for the commencement of war.

Moodajee Sindia had given early and repeated proofs of a ſtrong predilection for the Engliſh. It was at his inſtance the releaſe of the Bombay army, which had been captured at Worgaum, was ſo generouſly ordered, that the Poonah miniſters had ſhewn, all along, ſuch a ſtrong inclination to ſettle all our differences with the Durbar, rather in the cabinet than the field; and that their hoſtilities againſt us had been carried on throughout with ſo much moderation, under the moſt grievous provocations. Theſe favourable diſpoſitions were cheriſhed by the council of Calcutta, with ſuch eagerneſs and effect, that a ſeparate peace had been negociated and concluded with this chief, by Colonel Muir, about the latter end of 1781. The ſucceſs of a treaty, thus ſeaſonable and important, pointed out Moodajee as the moſt likely inſtrument of reſtoring harmony between the Engliſh and the Marratto ſtates. His immenſe territorial dominions which he held of the Marratto empire by a looſe feudal tenure; his characteriſtic reſpectability from perſonal honour; his very powerful connections in that diviſion of the empire; and eſpecially his predominant influence in the deciſions of the Durbar, qualified him, in an eminent degree, for carrying on and bringing to a concluſion this important negociation.

It

It was at a town called Salbey, where Sindia had his head quarters, that this celebrated treaty was signed, on the 17th of May [1782]. The business was transacted, on our part, by Mr. Anderson, with great address, and to whose indefatigable attention and persevering vigilance and ability, in urging and supporting our various claims, we owe the many important advantages which distinguish this peace. All places taken by the English since the treaty of Poorunder, from the Marrattos, were to be restored within two months. Salsette and the adjoining islands, with Broach and its territories, were ceded to the English for ever. A claim upon a contiguous district, formerly promised as a mark of friendship to the English, was now, at the particular request of Sindia, relinquished. The two Guiacars were to be placed exactly in the situation they occupied before the war, their territories to be subjected to all former tributes and services to the Peishwa, and no retrospection taken of their conduct, nor any demands made for the time past. Ragoba was allowed four months to determine the place of his future residence, and the English prohibited from affording him any protection or money. He had the choice of residing with Sindia; and the Peishwa was bound to allow him an annual pension of three lacks. Thus circumstanced, Ragoba was reduced to the necessity of relinquishing and revoking all territories, or grants of territories, made by him to the English. The Marrattos at the same time engaged that Hyder Ally should

surrender

ſurrender whatever he had taken from the Company and their allies during the war; and that a mutual exchange of priſoners ſhould take place. By the performance of theſe conditions, and ſo long as Hyder ſhould preſerve them inviolate, the Engliſh were bound to act in no reſpect hoſtilely againſt him. The Peiſhwa even ſtipulated, for himſelf and the whole Marratto people, that no other European nation ſhould eſtabliſh factories in any part of their dominions, or be a party in any ſyſtem of intercourſe or friendſhip whatever with the Durbar, or any individual chief or tributary of the empire. The Engliſh in return renounced all right to afford the leaſt aſſiſtance to any power in the Deccan at enmity with the Peiſhwa. In a ſubſequent article, the contracting powers mutually agreed, that neither ſhould contribute to the aid of whoever might be in a ſtate of hoſtility with the other; that the allies on both ſides ſhould be included in the benefits, and bound by the conditions of this treaty; and that the principals only ſhould be reſponſible for the conduct of all the ſubordinate members under their reſpective authority.

Sindia was the mutual guarantee of the peace, and in that reſpect pledged for the fidelity of both parties. He was thus ſpecifically and ſolemnly bound, in caſe of any violation or infraction of the terms now reciprocally adopted, to aſſiſt the injured in procuring adequate redreſs. Like all other ſtateſmen, Sindia, in the part he acted on this occaſion, was not inattentive to his own intereſt. The city of of Broach, with all its valuable territories, which yield an annual revenue of two hundred thouſand pounds, was, by private or ſeparate agreement, ceded to him and his family for ever, by the Engliſh. Such an immenſe acceſſion of dominion and treaſure facilitated his aggrandizement in the empire, and increaſed his influence to ſuch a degree, as may occaſion further revolutions in that unſettled and precarious government. And, from the length of time that elapſed before the ratification was effected, notwithſtanding the remonſtrances both of the governor-general and Sindia, it is plain the meaſure was not completed without conſiderable difficulties at the court of Poonah. Nana Furneſe and Sindia are evidently at the head of the two parties, which by their union govern, or by their diſſention may convulſe the empire. A jealouſy, originating in ſo much co-ordinate power, muſt of conſequence ſubſiſt between them. And it is not improbable that the extenſive acquiſitions, which Sindia obtained by this treaty, had already chagrined and diſguſted his powerful and wary rival.

The Engliſh fleet, after the action of the third of September, returned with all the expedition they could to Madras, where the admiral intended to ſtay no longer than while the ſhips could be haſtily repaired, and ſuch a ſtock of freſh water and proviſions procured as might ſupply them during their paſſage to Bombay. Before theſe purpoſes could be accompliſhed, the fleet was deſtined to ſuſtain one of the moſt tremendous hurricanes that ever happened

pened on that coaſt. It was fortunate that they anchored in water fifteen fathom deep, and that the tempeſt blew from the ſhore. They inſtantly parted their cables, and put out to ſea. The ſhore for ſeveral miles was a complete wreck, interſperſed with ſhocking ſpectacles of dead bodies. The howling of the tempeſt, the roaring of the ſea, and the cries of ſuch as ſtruggled hard for life, were dreadful and affecting beyond deſcription. Many Engliſh trading veſſels, of which the Earl of Hertford Indiaman was one, were either ſunk at anchor, or daſhed in pieces on the ſhore. Not leſs than a hundred coaſters periſhed in this manner. Such as had not been ſuddenly overwhelmed, but got out to ſea, for the moſt part eſcaped. A very few had even the good fortune to brave and ride out the ſtorm.

At this moment a famine raged in Madras, and every part of the Carnatic; and, by the tempeſt now deſcribed, all foreign reſources, that depended on an intercourſe by ſea, were at an end. Already had the rice ſhips, ſince their arrival on the coaſt, been ſeverely pillaged by the French; and the town of Madras was reduced to great hardſhips by the want of that article. A conſiderable ſupply had reached the harbour previous to the hurricane, but moſt of the veſſels were loſt before they could diſcharge their cargoes. Money could now procure no relief, where the neceſſaries of life did not exiſt. The roads, the outlets, and even the ſtreets, were every where choked up with

 heaps

heaps of dead, and crowds of the dying. Two hundred at leaſt of the natives periſhed every day in the city and ſuburbs: Others had ſome reſource in animal food: But the miſerable Hindoos, in this afflicting exigency, were greatly diſtinguiſhed by peculiar fortitude and reſignation; who, rather than preſerve life at the expence of their laws, religion, and cuſtoms, endured the moſt exquiſite torment without murmur or complaint. The alms of the ſettlement were certainly liberal. All was done which private charity could do. But it was a whole people in beggary; a nation who ſtretched out its hand for food. Of all the calamities which beſet and way-lay the life of man, this plague of hungar comes the neareſt to our hearts, and is that in which the proudeſt of us all feels himſelf to be nothing more than he is! Supplies were diſpatched from Bengal with more expedition than was even expected. But, notwithſtanding all the laudable diligence exerted in the godlike work of humanity and beneficence on that mournful occaſion, for eighteen months did this deſtruction rage from the gates of Madras to the gates of Tanjore! All this time theſe creatures of ſufferance, whoſe very exceſs and luxury, in their moſt plenteous days, had fallen ſhort of our ſevereſt faſts, ſilent, patient, reſigned without ſedition or diſturbance, almoſt without complaint, periſhed in ſuch multitudes, in the very granary of India, that above ten thouſand of the natives were ſup-

ſuppoſed to have been ſwept away by this ſcourge of nations !

Our fleet in the mean time had ſuffered moſt extreme diſtreſs in ſailing round for Bombay. For a whole month no two ſhips of the ſquadron had been able to ſpeak with each other. Such was the condition of the Superbe, that the admiral was obliged to ſhift his flag to the Sultan. It was not until nearly the latter end of December that our ſhattered ſhips arrived at Bombay. The crews were all ſickly, but ſoon recovered. Sir Richard Bickerton now made his appearance at Madras from Bombay, without having either experienced any ill weather or ſeen a ſingle ſhip belonging to the fleet. He had under convoy three regiments of infantry of one thouſand men each, of which one was Hanoverian, beſides Sir John Burgoyne's regiment of light horſe, amounting to three hundred and forty, and a thouſand recruits, which had been raiſed for the Company's ſervice in Ireland. The ſhips were five in the line, and in excellent condition, and both ſeamen and troops uncommonly healthy. Sir Richard inſtantly returned to Bombay, tha the might join the admiral, and, without encountering any adverſe winds whatever, arrived even ſome weeks before him.

The French, from the poſſeſſion of Trincomale, enjoyed in ſome degree the ſovereignty of theſe ſeas, and in the abſence of the Britiſh fleet conſiderably hampered and embarraſſed the coaſting

 trade,

trade, both of the Company and the natives. They afterwards proceeded to Achen, on the coaſt of Sumatra, probably for the acquiſition of ſuch ſupplies as could not be obtained in Ceylon. The mighty armament from France, containing the laſt diviſion of De Buſſy's troops, five thouſand men, ſeveral freſh ſhips of war, an ample ſupply of naval and military ſtores, and a train of artillery the moſt formidable and complete that ever was ſent to India, was at the ſame time expected. And no doubt was entertained, but, by ſuch a powerful reinforcement, the tide of war would be immediately and effectually turned againſt the Engliſh.

In conſequence, however, of our peace with the Marrattos, it was reſolved to create ſuch a diverſion on the Malabar coaſt, as would probably impel Hyder to abandon the Carnatic for the protection of his own dominions. Colonel Humberſtone, at the head of a conſiderable detachment both of the King and Company's forces, was immediately diſpatched on this ſervice, and ſoon gained poſſeſſion of the ancient and royal capital of Calicut. Quitting the ſea coaſt, he probably now bent his courſe towards the frontiers of the Coimbatour country. He encountered many difficulties, but captured in his march a great number of ſuch ſmall forts as are placed in that part of India for guarding the narrow paſſes and deep defiles which abound in theſe mountainous regions. Having taken and garriſoned Mungarry Cottah, a fort ſo ſtrongly ſituated as to afford a ſecure retreat, he advanced

to

to the ſiege of Palacatcherry, a place of more conſideration and ſtrength than any he had yet attacked. This object, however, from the appearance of the enemy, he was ſuddenly compelled to abandon. He was even purſued and attacked with ſuch fury and effect, that, beſides the number of men who fell, he loſt both his baggage and proviſions. Major Hutchinſon of the 98th regiment was mortally wounded.

The preſidency of Bombay being now liberally ſupplied with money from Bengal, for giving vigour and diſpatch to the meaſures in that quarter, and apprehenſive that Humberſtone's ſituation might be perilous, diſpatched General Matthews, with ſuch troops as could then be muſtered, to his aſſiſtance. Tippoo Saib had in the mean time, with incredible celerity and addreſs, arrived from the Carnatic, with the expreſs intention of deſtroying the Britiſh detachment at Mungarry Cottah. But the colonel, receiving intelligence of the enemy's intention, immediately razed the fortification, and retreated to Ramgarree, which Tippoo's rapid approach forced him to abandon with precipitation. In two days, and not without ſome riſk from parties of the enemy's horſe, who harraſſed our march exceedingly, he reached Panian on the twentieth of November.

Here Colonel Macleod was juſt arrived from Madras, and the command of the forces of courſe devolved on him. The detachment was ſuddenly inveſted by the enemy, conſiſting of eight thouſand regular infantry, ſome hundreds of Europeans, fix thouſand of the native militia, under the poligars, and a body of ten thouſand horſe. They were headed by Tippoo Saib and Monſ. Lally. Our troops were ſtrongly poſted, and with indefatigable induſtry and great art had improved the old by a great variety of new works. The enemy's cannonade, though kept up for ſeveral days, did little execution. The Britiſh commander attempted to ſurpriſe Tippoo's camp. The enterpriſe, however, was ſuddenly relinquiſhed, as impracticable, both from the vigilance and number of the enemy. A few days afterwards, a vigorous and well-concerted attack was made on the Britiſh lines. But the enemy, who employed their whole European force on this deſperate ſervice, were every where repulſed with the greateſt gallantry. Two hundred of their dead were abandoned to the care of the Engliſh; and the French officer, who led up one of the columns to the attack, was taken priſoner.

Tippoo's repaſſing the river Panian was a proof of the defeat. A ſtate of inaction ſucceeded on both ſides for ſome days. In the night of the eleventh of December, Tippoo ſuddenly decamped, and marched back with rapidity for the Carnatic. General Matthews, appriſed of this circumſtance, inſtantly changed his intended route down the coaſt, and directed his march to thoſe valuable territories of the enemy which appeared the moſt vulnerable and remote from ſuccour. He therefore advanced with the fleet and forces to the

river

river Mirjee, which falls into the sea eighty miles south of Goa, and five leagues north of Onore. This city lies midway between Panian and Bombay, and nearly three hundred miles distant from both. The general directed his course towards this important place. All the troops that could be spared from the defence of other posts on that extensive coast were ordered to meet him here, and assist in his intended operations. Macleod, who had been recently reinforced by some troops from Bombay, embarked as many as the transports could receive, with whom he proceeded, under convoy of the Isis and the Juno, to join the general. The two other regiments of sepoys only were left at Tellicherry, in readiness to proceed with the elephants and draught bullocks, under convoy of the African man of war, as soon as other vessels should arrive for their conveyance. Prior, however, to the junction of the troops, Onore had fallen into our hands, and the most memorable circumstance of the capture was the dreadful slaughter which took place, of all sexes, ages, and orders, as well as of the garrison. The governor, and above a thousand men, were made prisoners. The defence could not be great, as no regular troops of the enemy were within reach to lend any assistance, when the attack was made. We have no authentic accounts of the spoil, though it is conjectured to be very great, and to have occasioned that disgust among the British officers, which afterwards proved of the worst consequences to the army in general.

The time, place, and other circumſtances of Hyder Ally's death, are not aſcertained with any degree of certainty. He probably died about the end of 1782. It was, for many reaſons, a matter of the greateſt importance to keep ſo intereſting an event concealed, at the preciſe criſis when it happened. And the moment the ſecret was diſcovered, no one thought of detailing circumſtantially what had been ſo long known to all ſuch as were moſt intereſted in the conſequences. His character for enterpriſe, for ſyſtem in conduct, for firmneſs in difficulty, and for moderation in ſucceſs, was, in ſome degree, new in India. He poſſeſſed a genius, which embraced at once all the multifarious objects of government and war. The policy neceſſary to the arrangements of the one and the ſtratagem of the other he digeſted, and applied as emergencies aroſe, or contingencies took place, with equal dexterity, ſimplicity and ſucceſs. The reſumption of the ancient Mahommedan empire was among his earlieſt conceptions; and perhaps to this magnificent proſpect all his ſubſequent exertions, conqueſts, and regulations, were directed. He wiſhed, in order to the accompliſhment of this ſplendid and intereſting revolution, to reduce the Europeans in the various parts of the continent to their original ſtate of merchants and factors; to form his military on a ſyſtem of mechanical and ſcientific operation; and to create ſuch an invincible navy as ſhould protect for ever the coaſts, in every part of the continent, from all

all the invaſions and inſults of foreigners. He acted with ſo much equity and mildneſs, that no prince was ever more popular in his own dominions; he commanded ſo ably one of the moſt numerous armies that ever took the field, that no general was ever regarded with higher veneration, or obeyed with greater promptitude and zeal. He was ſeldom deceived in his politics as a ſtateſman, or cruel to his captives as a conqueror. He blended, with the authority and ſagacity of the magiſtrate, the virtues of humanity; and, in all the plenitude of power, never forgot that he was a man. He rewarded merit magnificently, but puniſhed every ſpecies of perfidy with exemplary ſeverity. He fulfilled the conditions of his friendſhips and engagements with rigid punctuality: In his enmities, as the caſe of the Company demonſtrates, he avowed the influence of every paſſion which contributed to prompt, facilitate, or accompliſh his revenge.

The preſidency of Bombay had ordered General Matthews, on ſuppoſition of Hyder's death, to uſe all his exertions in penetrating the Bednore or Canara country; and particularly to gain poſſeſſion of the capital, where the treaſures of Hyder were ſaid to be depoſited. He accordingly proceeded further down the coaſt; and, purſuing the line of conduct propoſed, ſtormed the town of Cundapore, without any material loſs or difficulty. He repreſented, at the ſame time, however, in his diſpatches, the utter impractability of executing the plan ſuggeſted to him. This deſpondency on his part

produced

produced much diſſatisfaction and chagrin on that of the preſidency, who had indulged the moſt ſanguine expectations from his ſucceſs, under circumſtances thus favourable to their inclinations. They preſerved, however, ſuch a deference for his opinion, that they relaxed their former orders, and in their new inſtruments, which they immediately diſpatched, left the proſecution of any ſuch enterpriſe, as they had formerly mentioned, utterly to his own diſcretion. But at the very time he had thus earneſtly remonſtrated againſt the orders of his employers, it ſeems to have been his determination to put them literally in execution.

It is a pity the ſubſequent part of this campaign cannot be obliterated from human remembrance. All correſpondence for the moment was ſuſpended, as all ideas of reſponſibility ſeems to have been forgotten. The ſame atrocious principles, which ſtained with indelible infamy the ſap of Onore, marked the future progreſs of the army, until the imprecations of injured innocence were ſignally realized in the deſtinies that awaited them.

Of facts which have not tranſpired no diſtinct narrative can be given; but of many cruelties not related there can be little doubt, from the nature of ſuch as are well authenticated. It was expected by the government of Bombay, that the ſubjects of Tippoo Sultan would be eager to revolt on hearing of his father's death. This idea was ſurely either not adopted or not underſtood by the army; for the ſurpriſing, ſurrounding, and maſ-

ſacreing

facreing crowds of unmilitary poligars at their posts; without pity or remorse, are among the exploits of this war, which we find retailed with the same indifference in which they probably happened. The fortress of Aumampore was taken by storm. The governor's mode of defence had not pleased the besiegers. The garrison were so entirely massacred, that only one horseman is said to have escaped, desperately wounded. In this havock might be seen four hundred beautiful women, bleeding with the wounds of the bayonet; and others expiring, while the soldiers, in brutal tumult, stript them of their jewels, and committed every outrage on their bodies. But such objects as these are of a species too horrid to be detailed or described! . . . .

By a lucky concurrence of circumstances, which sometimes connect that success with temerity which is due only to prudence and foresight, a party, consisting of the Bombay company of Europeans, and between three and four hundred sepoys, dispatched on the desperate and important service of forcing a pass or defile about eight feet wide, three miles in length, and strongly fortified, were fortunate enough to dispossess the enemy, who left five hundred of their killed and wounded behind, and the English masters of the place. Thus were the barriers of this rich and beautiful country effectually thrown down, and a free communication opened between the sea coast and the kingdom of Canara, where Hyder's favourite palace stood; where

where the principal officers of his government resided; whither all the nobility in every quarter of his dominions resorted; where his chief Haram was established; where his treasures, and every other thing on which he had set his heart, were deposited. The capital of this ancient independent kingdom, in which a long illustrious race of sovereigns, who placed their only glory in the happiness of a flourishing, faithful, free and contented people, lived and died among their subjects, like a father or patriarch in the midst of his family, was formerly called Bednore, but had of late changed its name to Hyder Nagur, or the royal city of Hyder, a name which the English did not then admit, and which they hoped to have utterly abolished. Such was the splendour, magnificence and extent of this sequestered metropolis, that some of its principal streets ran nearly in a right line six English miles in length, while its magnitude was utterly lost in the infinite variety of beauties both of nature and art, in which it abounded. The inhabitants chiefly consist of the great and the wealthy, who occupy the most sumptuous houses and spacious gardens, inclosing vast reservoirs of water and every other luxury, which the soil, the climate and the season can afford. Christianity, so congenial to the most polished state of society, had early found its way, by the pious assiduity of the Portuguese, to this elegant retreat, and still flourished so much, that above thirty thousand Christians

Chriſtians were ſaid, at this time, to be within the walls of Bednore.

Hyat Saib, a native, was intruſted with the government of this valuable town; and, from his abſolute incapacity to withſtand the efforts of ſuch a force as now appeared againſt it, he reſolved to riſk nothing but his own honour in its ſafety. The moment our army had ſtormed the gates, or ſcaled the mountains which hid and defended the country, he diſpatched agents to the camp with terms of accomodation. A private treaty then took place between him and the general, the particulars of which, in a great meaſure, are ſtill unknown. Its leading articles are ſuppoſed to have been, that the capital, the country, the fortreſs at Bednore, the public treaſures and property, were to be delivered up to the Engliſh; that the inhabitants were not to be moleſted either in their perſons or property; and that Hyat Saib was to continue in the government, with the ſame powers he enjoyed under Hyder. Theſe conditions where, however, infringed the moment the army got poſſeſſion of the place, which was early in February 1783. The governor was flung into priſon, and the inhabitants were much alarmed. Fourteen lacks were found in the Durbar, which the general ſhewed to the officers, and declared to be the property of the army. There was much more treaſure and jewels not expoſed, but the breach between Hyat Saib and the general being made up, the former claim'd the whole as his own private property, to whom, upon that

that plea, it was even reſtored by the latter. This management, which had already been practiſed at Onore, the officers reſented with indignation. Some of theſe were carried to Hyat Saib, who made the army a preſent of twenty thouſand pounds, which rather increaſed than quaſhed the ſuſpicions entertained of this myſterious tranſaction. Nor was this the only or moſt diſguſting circumſtance in the general's conduct. He had the misfortune to give a raſh deciſion in a point of etiquette between the King's officers and thoſe of the Company, which obliged Colonels Macleod and Humberſtone, with Major Shaw, to quit the army ſoon after the taking Bednore.

During the execution of theſe meaſures, no official diſpatches whatever arrived at Bombay. The preſidency received all the information which they had, concerning his operations, from the officers who refuſed to ſerve any longer under his command, and were now returned to Bombay. About a week afterwards, indeed, a letter from the general was received, but it did not mention a ſyllable of what they were moſt concerned to know. It gave a general detail of unintereſting operations, recriminated on the officers who had abandoned the ſervice, and urged the indiſpenſable neceſſity of ample and immediate reinforcements. But the ground of the diſpute, and what became of the treaſure, were points on which he vouchſafed no information. He referred indeed to ſome difference which had ſubſiſted between him and Colo-

nel

nel Macleod, concerning the manner of ſupplying the King's troops on ſervice, and to certain documents on that ſubject, which he ſuppoſed had been already laid before the board. The preſidency were therefore under a neceſſity of applying to Macleod and Humberſtone for all the verbal evidence they could afford, and whatever papers they poſſeſſed concerning the proceedings and ſtate of the army during the period of the operations in queſtion. It was conſequently declared that imputations of the moſt ſerious nature, and ſupported by the ſtrongeſt evidence, appeared againſt the general; and, ſatisfied that the ſervice could not proſper under ſuch a leader, the board thought it their duty not to continue him any longer in the command. A reſolution accordingly paſſed, of removing him from the command, and ſuſpending him from the Company's ſervice, until he ſhould clear up the charges that ſtood againſt him. Colonel Macleod was immediately appointed his ſucceſſor, and Colonel Humberſtone and Major Shaw required to join the army.

Matthews had alſo appriſed the preſidency of his apprehenſions that an enemy of great force was within thirty miles, though it was afterwards found that no ſuch enemy exiſted, or had appeared long poſterior to the date of his letter, in that country. Hyat Saib deceived the credulous general into a conviction that he would raiſe troops in defence of the Engliſh, at the ſame time that he prevented every appearance of commotion in the country, in

order

order to lull them into ſuch a ſtate of ſecurity as might render them an eaſy prey to the vengeance which was ſuddenly to overwhelm them. Their operations were at the ſame time carried on againſt ſeveral places on the coaſt, with expedition and ſucceſs. A Captain Carpenter, in that direction which lies toward Goa, invading the Soondah diſtrict, ſoon reduced the Carwar, and every other fort.

But the capital expedition was againſt Mangalore. This was Hyder's principal dock-yard, where the rudiments of a formidable navy were rapidly riſing into form; where three ſhips of the line, from fifty to ſixty guns, were nearly finiſhed; where ſeveral others of different ſizes were alſo upon the ſtocks; and where large quantities of naval ſtores were depoſited. Two battalions of ſepoys from the Bednore country were diſpatched to inveſt the place. A mine was ſoon ſprung, which it is ſaid blew up eighty ſepoys. The ſurvivors, notwithſtanding, carried the town ſword in hand. The governor, with his troops, took refuge in the fort, which, though a place of ſome ſtrength, made little reſiſtance after the general's arrival with the artillery. In thirty-ſix hours after the batteries began to play, a practicable breach was opened. The governor immediately ſurrendered. The ſecurity of perſon and private property was granted to the captured. Thus were moſt of the ſtrong holds on the Malabar coaſt in our poſſeſſion.

The

The country, however, though overrun, was not conquered. These advantages were obtained on no plan or principal that could render them secure. The Sultan, after much deliberation, and such a degree of caution, as to those not in the secret of his measures might have an appearance of hesitation, resolved on an immediate deliverance of his paternal dominions. Our expedition therefore, notwithstanding the very culpable manner in which it was executed, produced the precise effect for which it was conceived, and to which it was directed.

The general, for whose want of serious consideration in a situation so precarious it is impossible to give any satisfactory account, instead of withdrawing his troops and artillery entirely from the open Bednore country, and posting them in the gauts which were already fortified and deemed impregnable, on the first intelligence of the enemy's approach, marched at the head of little more than two thousand troops to encounter in the open field a force so numerous, that they not only filled all the adjacent plains, but covered the hills to a greater distance than the eye could reach. The attack commenced on the part of the enemy by a French detachment. Five hundred of our men are said to have fallen by this furious onset in a few minutes. The general soon felt the absence of a Baillie or a Braithwaite. And he made a precipitate retreat to the fortress, abandoning the city entirely. The Sultan took every possible precaution to shut up all communication either with the low country, or the sea coast. The garrison in the gauts, which might have preserved this important pass, made a miserable defence. The few fugitives who escaped flung the garrison of Cundapore into a panic. The precipitation and confusion, produced by an impulse thus sudden and irresistible, were so great, that numbers of men and horses were inevitably drowned in the hurry of making their escape; the magazines were set on fire, and a large train of artillery disabled or abandoned. This valuable repository of stores and provisions being at once evacuated and destroyed, the remainder of the garrison fled to Onore. Captain Torreano, who commanded in this place, had much merit in protecting his own troops from the panic which had seized their fellow soldiers, whom he had also the good fortune of restoring in some measure to their senses. He then made a spirited exertion to recover the artillery which had been left at Cundapore, but without effect, as the whole was already in possession of the enemy.

The garrison in the fortress of Bednore were in seventeen days reduced to the greatest extremities. Great numbers had been slain during the siege; their sick and wounded exceeded five hundred; they were in great want of provision; and the superiority of the enemy's fire increased prodigiously. A capitulation therefore, after some difficulties, took place. The garrison were to pile

their

their arms on the glacis, and to reſtore all public property, but allowed the honours of war; every man to have the privilege of retaining what was his own, and a ſafe paſſage to Bombay, at the enemy's expence. To the general alſo was granted a guard of four hundred of his own ſepoys, with thirty-ſix rounds of ammunition. The pecuniary article was however defeated. The fort was no ſooner ſurrendered, which happened on the twenty-eighth of April, than, that too much money might not be found on one man, the general ordered his his officers to draw on the pay-maſter for whatever they wanted. By this treachery not a ſingle rupee remained in the fort when evacuated. The Sultan's ſuſpicions being rouſed by ſeveral circumſtances which led to a diſcovery of the facts, the vengeance he inflicted was terrible and immediate. He ſent for Matthews; but, inſtead of admiting him to his preſence, he had him thrown into irons. By various pretences, all the principal officers were detached from the army. They ſuffered incredible ſeverities for the outrages they committed on the helpleſs. In company with the general, they were kept in cloſe impriſonment for ſome time in Syringpatnam. The general was put to death, it is ſaid, by pouring a certain poiſonous liquor down his throat. Twenty officers underwent the ſame fate. Captain Richardſon, who ſuffered laſt, threw himſelf on his knees, and earneſtly begged the executioners would at leaſt ſend to the Sultan for a confirmation of the ſentence. This requeſt was not granted, and he periſhed with his companions. The cataſtrophe of theſe unfortunate men can hardly be recollected, without at the ſame time thinking of the many innocent and defenceleſs women who had ſo recently ſupplicated their humanity in vain.

What were the entire amount of the treaſures found in the wealthy kingdom of Canara, *has* never been perfectly aſcertained. It is aſſerted in one private account, that the general got poſſeſſion of a ſum of thirty lacks of pagodas, beſides an infinite quantity of diamonds and precious ſtones; that all this booty was ſecreted, and ſent by his brother to Bombay; that his brother ſoon after fell into the hands of the Nabob, who beheaded him; and, that the army was ſtill uninformed whether all or any of the treaſure had ever reached the preſidency. By another account it is eſtimated at forty-eight lacks of pagodas. Both eſtimates were made ſince the releaſe of the officers from the long confinement they endured in that country.

The conduct of the ſepoys to their fellow ſufferers in this ignominious impriſonment, does honour to their feelings and attachment. They cheriſhed the Europeans, who were not ſo able to ſupport the extremities of this ſultry climate, with every humane and tender attention in their power. They reſiſted all the errors and allurements by which they were tempted to enter into the ſervice of the enemy. And when they were permitted to rejoin their officers they expreſſed the ſincereſt ſatiſ-

faction,

faction, and even presented them with such small sums of money as they had been able to save, for their immediate accommodation.

The Sultan lost no time in leading his victorious troops to the rescue of Mangalore. But here he met with resistance rather different from that which he had so easily subdued at the citadel of Bednore. Indeed the whole energy of the attack depended on his French auxiliaries. By their exertions a breach was actually made, when news arrived in the camp of a peace being concluded between England and France. This event put an immediate end to the operations of the besiegers. Not all the promises, threats, or the address of the Sultan, could prevail on the French to act in any manner against the English, or even to continue longer in his camp. The consequence was a cessation of hostilities on both sides. A mean attempt after this was made to starve our garrison into a surrender. But they were seasonably relieved by General Macleod, who, appearing on the coast with a strong reinforcement, obliged the enemy to afford them a supply. No military operation of any consequence took place after this in these parts. And in the following year a peace was concluded between the Company and the Sultan, in which the conquests on both sides were restored, and the peace of India established.

The war which continued in the Carnatic, notwithstanding the absence of the Sultan, was chiefly between the French and English. Sir Eyre Coote, who had gone to Bengal for the recovery of his

 health,

health, returned as ſoon as he found his ſtrength in ſome degree repaired, and brought with him ten lacks of rupees. The Reſolution, which carried him, was very cloſely purſued during the paſſage, by two French ſhips of the line. The general's anxiety for the conſequence, as the public were ſo deeply intereſted, kept him conſtantly on the deck during the chaſe. The ſhip and treaſure eſcaped, but the general only ſurvived his arrival two days. His loſs to the Company and his country was irreparable. Whatever might have been his imperfections in other reſpects, as a profeſſional man he had few equals. He had more military ſcience and practice perhaps, than any other general of his time. And it will be long remembered to his honour, as an eulogy to which he was well entitled, that, when our affairs on that ſide of India had become deſperate, his preſence reſtored the confidence of a diſpirited army: He was the terror of the moſt formidable adverſary we ever had in that part of the world, and literally the ſaviour of the Carnatic.

General Stuart, who had ſucceeded to the command in the abſence of Sir Eyre Coote, was, on his death, continued in that ſituation. And the action in which his abilities were moſt diſtinguiſhed happened at Cuddalore. The French, whom it was now an object to drive from the Carnatic, were ſtrongly fortified in this place. In an attempt to carry the out-poſts of this fortreſs, a moſt bloody and deſperate conflict enſued, in which the attack and defence continued to rage with equal fierceneſs

fierceness and obstinacy for some time. Our troops, however, succeeded in the enterprise. The killed, wounded, and missing, including the native troops, were not much short of a thousand men. Of the French, notwithstanding their cover, and the strength of their works, forty-two officers, and six hundred of their best troops, were killed or wounded.

This severe battle was fought on the thirteenth of June; and on the twentieth of the same month Sir Edward Hughes and Suffrein met once more, for the fifth and last time, as enemies in the Indian seas. The English, in their turn, had a superiority of force, and opposed seventeen ships to only fifteen of the enemy; but their crews had been greatly debilitated by sickness. A prodigious cannonade was kept up, from a few minutes past four till seven o'clock in the evening, without intermission. The enemy then hauled off, as they had kept a cautious distance through the whole engagement. On the morning they were wholly out of sight, and discovered the day after at anchor, in the road off Pondicherry. Here Sir Edward dared them the whole of this day, but was immediately obliged to put into Madras for fresh water. And Suffrein took that opportunity of returning to Cuddalore, where he landed two thousand and four hundred of his own men, to assist De Bussy in the defence of that valuable place.

The besieged, from this and several other circumstances, became so confident of their strength,

 that

that they determined to attempt our intrenchments. And our army was not, at that time, in the best condition for sustaining such an onset. The enforcements, which the general had ordered from Madras, had not yet arrived. Nor was Colonel Fullarton returned from an expedition on which he had been sent in the Coimbatour country. Sir Edward Hughes had departed, and the enemy's fleet were at anchor in the road. Under all these discouraging circumstances, and notwithstanding the force destined for the surprise of the English consisted of the flower of the French army, and were led to the attack by some of their most approved officers, they were received in a manner but little expected. The action commenced, on the part of the French, at three o'clock in the morning, when they endeavoured to surprise our troops. They had, on the first attack, such an advantage only as could be expected against men not regularly prepared to receive them. The assailants, however, soon found themselves on hostile ground. The English armed in a moment, and speedily revenged the insult. Not contented with maintaining their posts, they drove the enemy from the intrenchments, and pushed them so hard on every side, that a complete route instantly took place. The Chevalier de Damas, who headed the party, several officers, and about one hundred and fifty men, were taken prisoners. Our loss was inconsiderable. The sepoys who fought, and even foiled

some

ſome of the beſt troops of France, with the bayonet, ſuffered moſt.

Soon after this ſally, information was received at Cuddalore, from Lord Macartney and Sir Edward Hughes, that peace was re-eſtabliſhed between the French and Engliſh in Europe. All further hoſtilities between the two armies immediately ceaſed, and the priſoners of each were mutually exhanged.

THE END.